PIEDMONT
&
THE VALLE D'AOSTA

PAUL BLANCHARD

About the author
Paul Blanchard is a Florence-based writer, visual artist, art historian, speaker and landscape theorist. He is also the author of *Blue Guide Southern Italy*, *Blue Guide Concise Italy*, *Blue Guide Liguria* and *Blue Guide Trentino & the South Tyrol*.

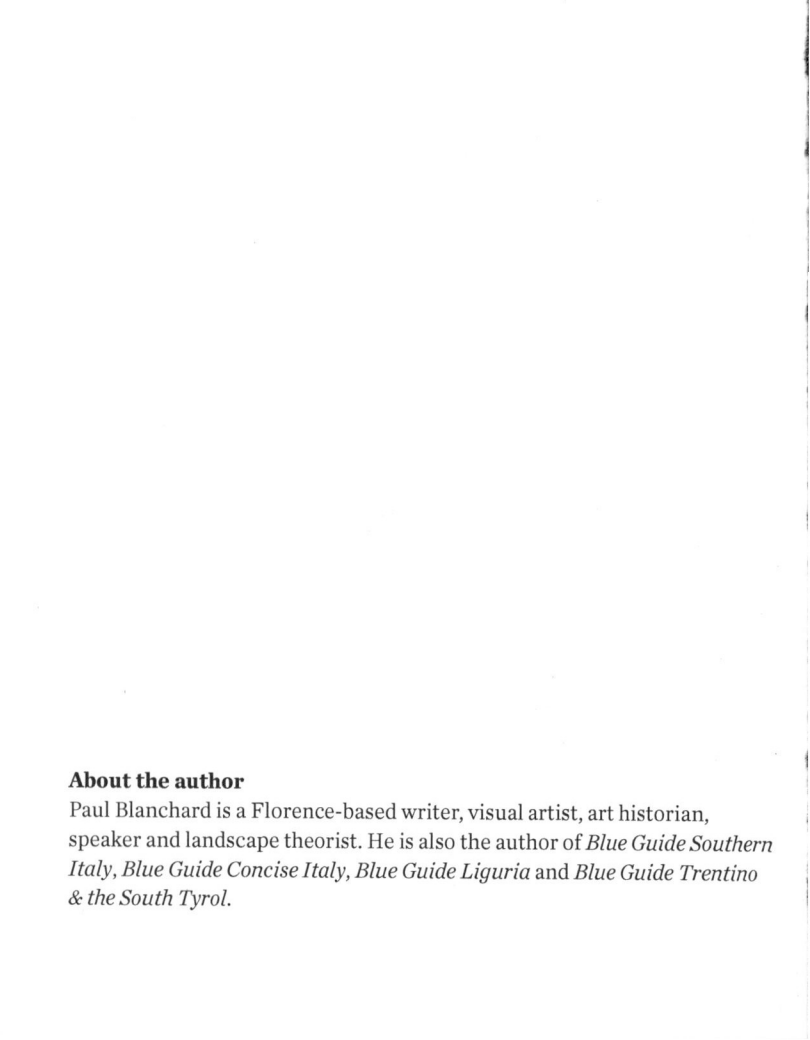

PIEDMONT & THE VALLE D'AOSTA

Published by Blue Guides Limited, a Somerset Books Company
Unit 2, Old Brewery Road, Wiveliscombe, Somerset TA4 2PW
blueguides.com
'Blue Guide' is a registered trademark.

© Blue Guides Limited 2016, revised and updated 2023

All rights reserved. No part of this publication may be reproduced or used in any form or by any means—photographic, electronic or mechanical—without permission of the publisher.

ISBN 978-1-905131-98-3

The author and publisher have made reasonable efforts to ensure the accuracy of all the information in this book; however, they can accept no responsibility for any loss, injury or inconvenience sustained by any traveller as a result of information or advice contained in the guide.

Every effort has been made to trace the copyright owners of material reproduced in this guide. We would be pleased to hear from any copyright owners we have been unable to reach.

Statement of editorial independence: Blue Guides, their authors and editors, are prohibited from accepting payment from any restaurant, hotel, gallery or other establishment for its inclusion in this guide or on www.blueguides.com, or for a more favourable mention than would otherwise have been made.

Town plans © Blue Guides; Maps: Dimap Bt. © Blue Guides
Series editor: Annabel Barber.
With thanks to Michael Partington

Front cover: View of Lago Maggiore, Piedmont
Back cover: Roman milestone at Donnas, Valle d'Aosta
Photos © Blue Guides

www.blueguides.com
We welcome reader comments, questions and feedback:
editorial@blueguides.com

CONTENTS

PIEDMONT

INTRODUCTION 6

TURIN AND ITS ENVIRONS 8
Piazza Castello: the museums and duomo 9
Along Via Roma 18
The Quadrilatero Romano 21
From Piazza Castello to the Po 22
San Salvario and the Valentino 24
Elsewhere in town 26
Around Turin: the Savoy Royal Residences 27
South and east of Turin 31
Practical tips 33

LAGO MAGGIORE 42
The lower lake 42
Stresa 46
Baveno 47
The Isole Borromee 48
Verbania 50
Ghiffa 52
Cannobio 54
The east side of the lake 54
Practical tips 56

THE LEPONTINE ALPS 60
Lago d'Orta 60
Val Grande 63
Val d'Ossola 65
Practical tips 67

THE PENNINE ALPS 69
The Valsesia 69
Biella 75
Practical tips 79

THE GRAIAN ALPS 81
The Basso Canavese 81
Ivrea 85
The Alto Canavese 87
Parco Nazionale del Gran Paradiso 91
Practical tips 92

THE COTTIAN ALPS 95
The Val di Susa 95
Pinerolo 102
The Val Chisone 105
The Valle Pellice 108
The Alta Valle del Po 109
Saluzzo and environs 112
Fossano and Savigliano 115
The Valle Varaita 117
Practical tips 119

THE MARITIME ALPS, WITH CUNEO AND MONDOVÌ AND THE ALPI LIGURI 122
Cuneo 122
The Valle Stura 126
The Valle Gesso 127
Mondovi 129
The Alpi Liguri 132
Practical tips 135

PIEDMONT ON THE PLAIN	*139*
Alessandria	*139*
Novara	*142*
Tortona	*144*
Vercelli	*146*
Practical tips	*148*
THE WINE COUNTRY	*152*
The Lange	*152*
Bra and the Roero	*164*
The Monferrato	*167*
Practical tips	*182*

VALLE D'AOSTA

HISTORY	*193*
CITY OF AOSTA	*195*
Around the cathedral and Roman Forum	*195*
Roman remains	*198*
The Sant'Orso complex	*199*
Villa della Consolata	*200*
Practical tips	*200*
EXPLORING THE MAIN VALLEY	*202*
Pont-St-Martin, Donnas and Bard	*202*
Arnad, Verrès and Issogne	*205*
Saint-Vincent	*207*
Châtillon, St-Denis and Fénis	*208*
West of Aosta	*210*
The slopes of Mont Blanc	*212*

EXPLORING THE SIDE VALLEYS	*213*
Val di Gressoney	*213*
Val d'Ayas and Valtournenche	*214*
Val di Cogne	*215*
Practical tips	*216*
THE PASSES	*217*
The Great St Bernard Pass	*217*
The Little St Bernard Pass	*219*

PRACTICAL INFORMATION

Getting there and getting around	*220*
Accommodation	*221*
Food and wine	*222*
Additional information	*224*
Index	*226*

MAPS

Turin city centre	*12–13*
Lago Maggiore	*43*
Aosta	*197*
Regional overview	*234*
Regional atlas	*235–9*

Piedmont

The ancient principality of Piedmont, the cradle of the Italian nation, occupies the upper basin of the Po river—mainly *al piè dei monti*, 'at the foot of the mountains': the Pennine, Graian, Cottian and Maritime Alps. The cultural relations between Piedmont and France have always been close and French was long spoken at the court and parliament of Turin. Its influence survives in the Piedmontese dialects. Historically Piedmont combines the territories of the old marquisates of Ivrea and Monferrato, and the county of Turin. The territory of Turin first came into the House of Savoy by marriage in 1046, though the capital remained on the French side of the mountains. In the 16th century France and Spain invaded Italy, and Piedmont was occupied by the French in 1506. In 1557 the Savoy duke Emanuele Filiberto led a Spanish counter-invasion and defeated the French at San Quintino, at the foot of the Maritime Alps. Rewarded at the Treaty of Cateau-Cambrésis with the city of Turin, he moved the seat of his duchy there in 1563. Further territory was gained in the early 18th century when Duke Vittorio Amedeo II was appointed king of Sicily. Sicily was transferred to Austria in 1713, but Vittorio Amedeo received Sardinia in exchange, and his kingdom became known as Piedmont-Sardinia. Although its existence was blotted out by the Napoleonic conquests, the Congress of Vienna reinstated the Savoy kings at Turin and also gave them suzerainty over Liguria.

The decades following the Napoleonic interlude witnessed the emergence of Piedmont as the principal agent of Italian nationhood. The Savoy king Vittorio Emanuele II—thanks to the astuteness of his prime minister, Camillo Cavour—won the goodwill of France and England by taking part in the Crimean War, then turned this privilege to his advantage by calling Napoleon III to his aid when the second War of Italian Independence broke out in 1859. The war was fought against Austria, whose empire encompassed northern Italy from Milan to Trieste. The Austrian army was crushed in a succession of defeats, most notably at Solferino in 1859. Lombardy was annexed to Piedmont, and the Piedmontese dominions west of the Alps (Savoy and Nice) were ceded to France. The remaining Italian provinces (except the areas north and east of Venice, acquired after the First and Second World Wars, respectively) were added one by one to Vittorio Emanuele's kingdom. In 1865 he transferred his capital from Turin to Florence, and the history of Piedmont became merged in the history of the fledgling nation.

Piedmont has a continental climate. Cut off from the sea, and therefore from the warm, moist breezes that make neighbouring Liguria so mild and pleasant, it has bitterly cold winters and scorching hot summers. Even in a single day, temperatures can change drastically from morning to midday, or from early afternoon to evening—a fact that should be borne in mind when setting out on a day's excursion. Thick fog tends to form in low-lying areas in autumn and winter, wrapping places like Turin and Alba in a soft mantle that smooths rough edges, absorbs sound and whets the appetite for the strong, warm flavours of truffles, chocolate and full-bodied wines—all of which are specialities here. Rainfall peaks in autumn and spring but rarely misses any season; in some Alpine and pre-Alpine areas it can exceed 3000mm per year. To understand fully what that means, think that London gets 600mm and Seattle 900mm; the wettest place in England, the Lake District, gets 2000mm.

The upside of this is that the severe climate, and a long history of protecting natural assets, have given the region some of the largest, most expertly managed forests in Italy. One finds magnificent examples of fir, larch, pine and beech in mountain areas, and immense chestnuts and oaks on lower ground. The sheer variety of plant life is sometimes stunning: around Lago Maggiore edelweiss grows in the mountain meadows, while palms and other subtropical species thrive at the lakeside. Animal life is also plentiful, especially in comparison with other areas of Italy, where much has been done—wilfully or by neglect—to demean or destroy natural assets. In addition to protected species such as the ibex and the chamois, marmots, roe deer, hare, fox, squirrel, marten and an immense variety of songbirds inhabit the steep slopes of Alpine Piedmont and the rolling hills of the Langhe, Roero and Monferrato.

All of this is in spite of the fact that, in the 19th century, Piedmont was one of the first regions of the new Kingdom of Italy to pursue industrial development. Even today its wealth is based largely on industry, which is present everywhere. Fiat, the largest Italian industrial corporation, permeates the economic life of a large part of Piedmont, to the point that economists speak of an 'industrial monoculture', with all the dangers this concept carries. But there are other important economic forces as well—for example, confectioners Ferrero and Novi, or Alstom, whose Savigliano plant makes Europe's high-speed trains—and Piedmont's farmers produce Italy's most delicious rice, hazelnuts and, according to many of those in the know, wines.

Few people beyond the borders of Italy seem to realise that Piedmont is an Alpine region. Hikers and skiers are drawn to the Valle d'Aosta as by a magnet, and visitors to the lakes rarely venture into the surrounding mountains. Yet Italians know that Piedmont holds some of the most striking Alpine landscape in Europe—and that it abounds in lovely summer and winter resorts. There are also cities at the foot of the Alps—Pinerolo, Saluzzo and Cuneo being three examples—whose artistic and architectural heritage are as striking as the peaks by which they are framed.

This part of the guide follows the International Standardised Mountain Subdivision of the Alps (ISMSA), a system for classifying the Alps. It was designed by Sergio Marazzi, an Italian researcher and author of the Orographic Atlas of the Alps, and presented with the patronage of the Italian Alpine Club in 2006. The system introduces a bipartition of the Alpine System (Western Alps and Eastern Alps) instead of the old tripartite division (Western, Central and Eastern Alps), and within that a multi-level pyramidal hierarchy based on identical scales and rules. Here we look, from east to west, at the Lepontine, Pennine, Graian, Cottian and Maritime Alps.

Turin

My arrival at Turin was the first and only moment of intoxication I have found in Italy. It is a city of palaces.
  William Hazlitt: *Notes of a Journey through France and Italy*, 1826

Turin, in Italian *Torino*, is the most important city in Piedmont. The regular Roman street plan of its ancient core, consciously developed when the city was enlarged in the 17th–18th centuries, gives it the air of a French rather than an Italian town. In its 18th-century heyday Turin must have been a very striking place indeed. The English writer Horace Walpole, who passed through on his 1739 tour of Italy, wrote of it as 'by far one of the prettiest cities [in Italy], clean and compact, very new and very regular'. His travelling companion Thomas Gray called it 'a place of many beauties', expressing particular regard for the 'streets all laid out by the line, regular uniform buildings, fine walks that surround the whole, and in general a good lively, clean appearance'. The centre of the city, with some splendid palaces and churches built in a late Baroque style by Guarino Guarini and Filippo Juvarra (*see p. 23*), is remarkably homogeneous, still retaining the orderly, rational aspect that Walpole and Gray found so appealing.

Long a centre of metalworking, Turin has been famous since 1899 as the home of the Fiat motor company. Today there is an ongoing effort to restore the city to its past splendour.

HISTORY OF TURIN
No one knows who established Turin, but it is fairly clear that the city began as a Celtic or Ligurian settlement. It was Romanised as Julia Augusta Taurinorum in the 1st century BC, and the Goths, Lombards and Franks held sway in the Middle Ages. The marriage in 1045 of Countess Adelaide, heiress of a line of French counts of Savoy, to Oddone (Otho), son of Humbert 'the White-Handed', united the Cisalpine and Transalpine possessions of the House of Savoy, with Turin as their capital. After a period of semi-independence in the 12th–13th centuries, the city consistently followed the fortunes of the princely house of Savoy. It was occupied by the French in 1506–62, but was awarded to Duke Emanuele Filiberto 'the Iron-Headed' by the Treaty of Cateau-Cambrésis (1559). It was besieged in 1639–40, and again in 1706, when it was saved from the French by the heroic action of Pietro Micca (*see p. 26*).

From 1720 Turin was capital of the kingdom of Sardinia, and after the Napoleonic occupation (1798–1814) it became a centre of Italian nationalism under the guidance of Camillo Cavour (1810–61), a native of the region and the prime mover of Italian liberty. Prince Carlo Alberto, who succeeded to the Savoy throne in 1831, had a profound influence on the appearance of the city, and most of its important art collections date from his time. In 1861–5 Turin was the first capital of a united Italy, under Vittorio Emanuele II (1820–78) as king. Allied air raids caused heavy damage during the Second World War. After the war new suburbs grew up to accommodate the huge number of immigrants from the south of Italy who came here to find work. The novelist Primo Levi (1919–87), and Carlo Levi (1902–75), writer and painter, are among the famous modern natives of Turin.

PIAZZA CASTELLO: THE MUSEUMS & DUOMO

The huge, rectangular Piazza Castello (*map Turin A, 6–7*) is the centre of historic Turin, the crossroads of the Baroque city's east–west and north–south axes. The square was laid out by Ascanio Vittozzi in 1584 around the castle, now called Palazzo Madama, and is surrounded by uniform monumental buildings with porticoes. Beneath the porticoes on the corner nearest Via Accademia delle Scienze are two elegant cafés (Mulassano and Baratti, with elaborate decorations by Edoardo Rubino), on either side of the **Galleria dell'Industria Subalpina**, a delightful shopping arcade built in 1873–4. A monument to the Duke of Aosta (d. 1931) by Eugenio Baroni (1937) and war memorials by Vincenzo Vela (1859) and Pietro Canonica (1923) stand in the centre of the square.

THE MAKING OF THE ITALIAN 'SANDWICH'
A sign in Caffé Mulassano (*Piazza Castello 15*) reads: 'Nel 1926, la signora Angela Demichelis Nebiolo, inventò il tramezzino' ('In 1926, Angela Demichelis Nebiolo invented the *tramezzino*'). Angela Nebiolo, along with her husband, Onorino, returned home from the United States in 1925, along with a toast machine and toast bread, and bought a small café in Piazza Castello. An enterprising couple, they set about introducing American bread to the *torinesi*, both toasted and untoasted, cut into small triangular shapes. It was the latter which became the Italian 'sandwich' or, as the poet Gabriele d'Annunzio later named it, the '*tramezzino*', a neologism suggestive of its 'in-between' (*tra mezzo*) and diminutive (*ino*) status. This light lunchtime snack, or accompaniment to an *aperitivo* in the evening, is now hugely popular nationwide in Italy, and can be sampled with an assortment of creative fillings: tuna and olives, egg and asparagus, lobster, and, in Piedmont, of course, truffle.

PALAZZO MADAMA
This is the most imposing of the old buildings of Turin, a four-square castle of the 15th century, one side of which has been replaced by a wing and façade of 1718–21 by Filippo Juvarra. A castle was begun here after 1276 by William VII of Monferrato on the site of the Roman Porta Praetoria, the east gate of the ancient city. The palace

takes its present name from the two regents, Maria Cristina, widow of Vittorio Amedeo I, and Giovanna Battista, widow of Carlo Emanuele II; both were entitled Madama Reale, and both resided here and remodelled the old castle. The *palazzo* was the seat of the Subalpine Senate in 1848–60 and of the Italian Senate in 1861–5.

Since 1935 the palace has housed the **Museo Civico d'Arte Antica** (*last entry 1hr before closing; palazzomadamatorino.it*), with exhibits on the palace's history (including the Roman foundations, visible through a vertiginous glass floor, and a seemingly unending suite of sumptuous rooms) and a collection of works of art. Among the exhibits are a number of valuable codices, including the illuminated 14th-century statutes of the city of Turin and the celebrated *Book of Hours of Milan* (1422), attributed to a number of hands, largely anonymous and referred to simply as 'Hands A–K'. The most interesting is Hand G, who may have been Jan van Eyck. The paintings include a *Portrait of a Man* by Antonello da Messina (whom Vasari wrongly claims to have been a pupil of Van Eyck's), signed and dated 1476, one of his best and last works. On the first floor, beyond the central hall, seat of the senate, are the royal apartments. Some of the furniture here dates from the time of Carlo Emanuele II (d. 1675), but the fittings are mainly in early 18th-century style.

THE ROYAL MUSEUMS

Map Turin B, 7. Piazza San Giovanni. Ticket office open Tues–Sun 9–6. Closed Mon. museireali.beniculturali.it.

The Royal Museums (Musei Reali) consist of the Palazzo Reale, Giardini Reali, Biblioteca Reale, Armeria Reale, Galleria Sabauda, Museo di Antichità, Palazzo Chiablese and Cappella della Sacra Sindone (Chapel of the Holy Shroud) under a single visitor-service umbrella. You can buy tickets both on-site and online. The museum cluster covers an area of three sq km, creating an extraordinary itinerary embracing 55,000 sq m of exhibits that tell a history spanning more than 2,000 years, from the first Roman settlements in Piedmont to the present day. A full morning or afternoon is sufficient to see everything, but there is a great deal to see.

PALAZZO REALE
Map Turin B, 7. Piazzetta Reale 1. Open Tues–Sun 9–7; last entry 6pm. Free entry first Sun of the month. museireali.beniculturali.it.

The centre of the Savoy state, this palace was begun in the mid-17th century for Madama Reale Maria Cristina and subsequently occupied by the dukes of Savoy, the kings of Sardinia-Piedmont, and Vittorio Emanuele II at the very outset of his reign as king of Italy. The simple, austere façade, with a rectangular central volume flanked by taller wings (by Carlo Morello, 1658) masks a lavish interior created by the most distinguished architects and artists active in the capital from the mid-17th to the mid-19th century. The State Apartments have splendid ceilings and floors, finely crafted furniture (some by the local cabinet maker and master of inlay work, Pietro Piffetti), porcelain, tapestries, and allegorical paintings (by Jan Miel and Charles Dauphin) celebrating the virtues of the Savoy sovereigns. Filippo Juvarra enlarged the palace in the 18th century, designing also the Scala degli Forbici (a double-ramped monumental staircase ingeniously inserted in a confined space) and the delightful Gabinetto Cinese, with antique lacquer fittings. Benedetto Alfieri, who succeeded Juvarra as court architect, designed the Summer and Winter Apartments and the Galleria Beaumont, on the second *piano nobile*. Carlo Alberto (1831–49) renovated much of the first and second floors to designs by his court architect, the Bolognese Pelagio Palagi. The grand staircase was added in 1862, just as the capital of the nascent Kingdom of Italy moved from Turin to Florence. Today the lavish state rooms seem frozen in time. Everything—the furniture, the paintings, the tapestries, even the great kitchen—is perfectly preserved as it was when the royal family abandoned their dynastic capital. Lacking the buzz of activity, the rooms are dark, their decoration is excessive and the atmosphere is a little spooky.

The **Giardini Reali** (*map Turin B, 7; open May–Oct daily 9–dusk*), approached through the palace, were laid out in the 17th century by André Le Nôtre, architect of the gardens of Versailles, for Carlo Emanuele II. Though there is little to be seen of Le Nôtre's original design, the gardens are nonetheless a pleasant respite from the hustle and bustle of the city centre.

The former royal chapel of **San Lorenzo**, adjoining the palace on the northwest corner of Piazza Castello (*map Turin B, 6–7*), is a superb Baroque edifice by Guarino Guarini; it has a handsome cupola and lantern and a beautiful, luminous interior filled with the curvilinear forms that are Guarini's architectural signature. The colour-scheme, all pinks, whites, creams and powder-blues, and the absolutely unsurpassed use of natural lighting to exalt colour and model form, makes this one of the most successful Baroque church designs in Europe.

BIBLIOTECA REALE

Map Turin B, 7. Piazza Castello 191. Open Mon–Fri 9–6.30, Sat 9–130. Closed Sun. museireali.beniculturali.it.

The tall wooden bookcases of the Royal Library hold more than 200,000 books, manuscripts, parchments, incunabula, maps, engravings, prints and photographs. Certainly the most celebrated holding is Leonardo da Vinci's *Codex on the Flight of Birds*; the library also holds a self-portrait by the artist and works by Dürer, Rembrandt and Raphael.

ARMERIA REALE

Map Turin B, 7. Piazza Castello 191. Open Tues–Sun 9–6; last entry 30mins before closing. museireali.beniculturali.it.

The royal armoury, one of the more important in Europe, counts more than 1,200 items, including some remarkable pieces by the great Bavarian and Austrian armourers and gunsmiths. Established by Carlo Alberto in 1837, it occupies three magnificent halls at the top of a grand staircase designed by Benedetto Alfieri. The Sala Rotonda (originally circular in plan but rebuilt to a T-plan by Pelagio Palagi) displays the collections of the last princes of the House of Savoy and arms and ensigns of the Risorgimento period. In the ceiling, *Jupiter Striking Down the Giants* by Carlo Bellosio; on the walls, scenes from the Trojan War by Francesco Gonin. The splendid

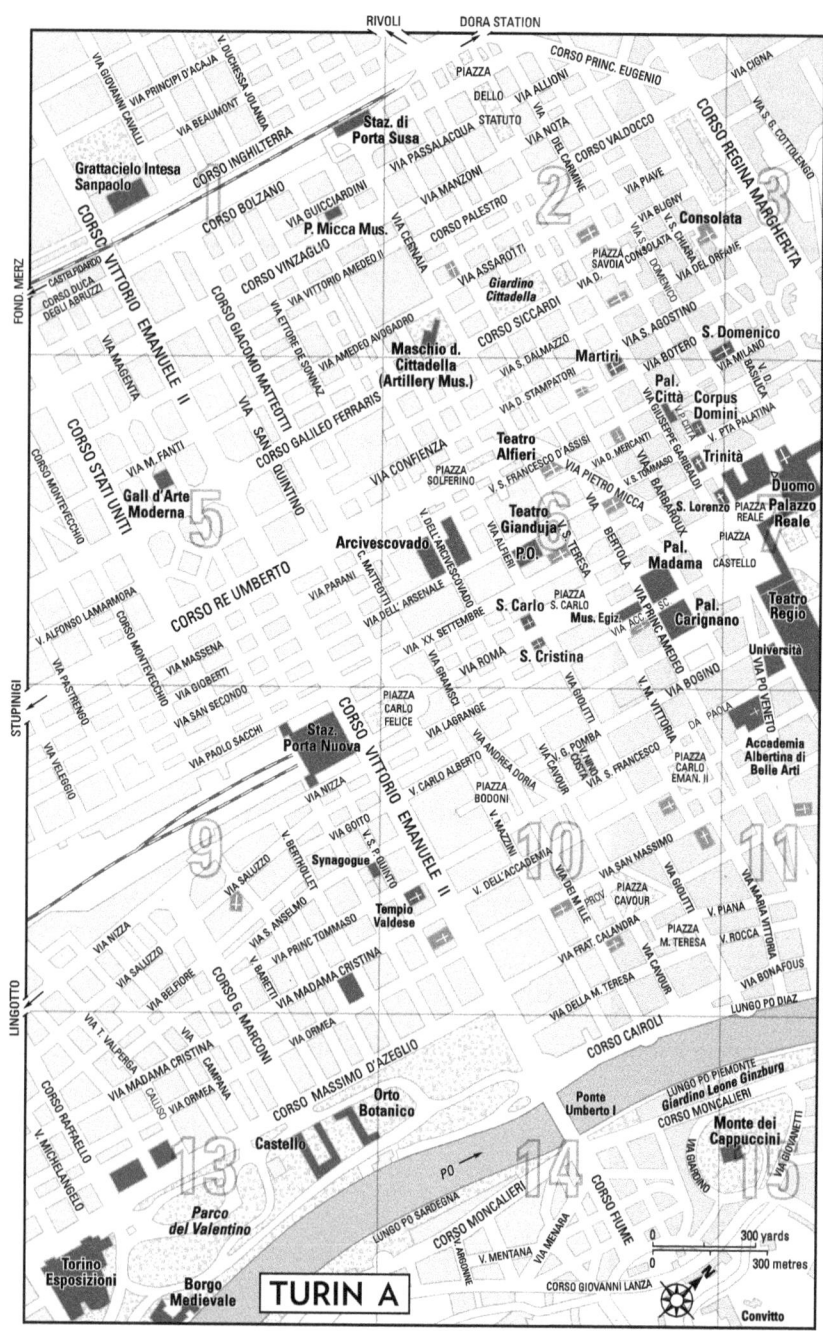

TURIN | 13

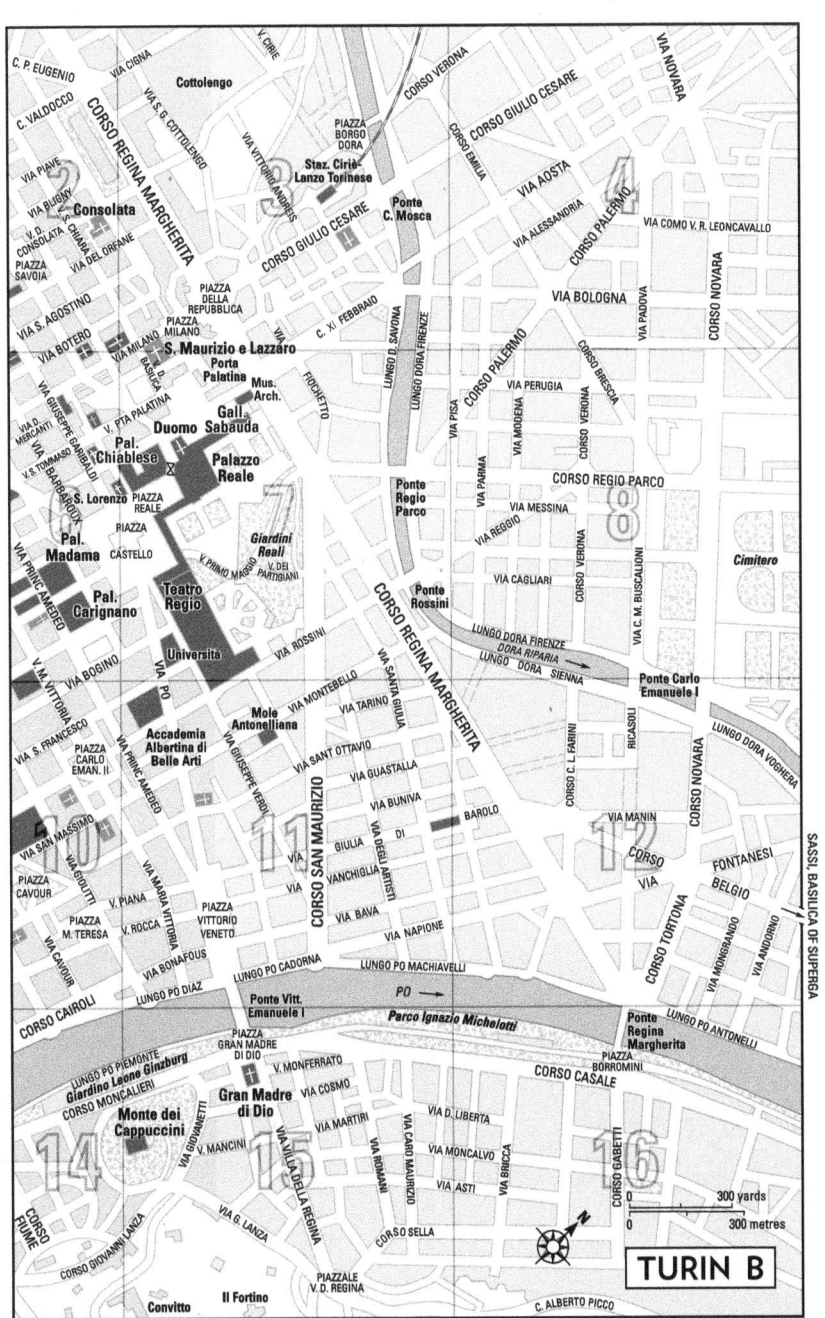

Galleria Beaumont, designed by Filippo Juvarra in 1733, is named after Claudio Francesco Beaumont, who painted the stories of Aeneas in the vault in 1738–64. It contains a superb display of about 30 complete suits of armour (12 equestrian), some of which were made for the Martinengo family of Brescia. Oriental arms are displayed in the Medagliere, designed by Pelagio Palagi for the royal collection of coins, medals and seals (Palagi also designed the beautiful Classical cabinets; not all of the 33,000 pieces are displayed). From the loggia overlooking Piazza Castello, Carlo Alberto announced the beginning of the First War of Independence, on 22nd March 1848, initiating the complex historical process that led to the birth of the Kingdom of Italy. Alfieri's staircase, the most beautiful in Turin, is an eloquent statement in stone of the Savoy delight in antiquity. Its construction dates from 1737–8 and the pale beige, ochre and grey walls and the vaulted ceilings are richly adorned with stuccos. Over the doors are four busts: classical portraits of Marcus Aurelius and Demosthenes, and modern female figures, perhaps Flora and Diana, by the French sculptor Pierre Legros. In the central niche stands a Greek *Minerva* from the collection of antiquities begun by Emanuele Filiberto.

MUSEO DI ANTICHITÀ

Map Turin B, 7. Manica Nuova di Palazzo Reale, Via XX Settembre 86. Open Tues–Sun 9–7, last entry 1hr before closing. museireali.beniculturali.it.

The common entrance for visitors to the Galleria Sabauda and the Museo di Antichità (Antiquities Museum) is via the central atrium of the Manica Nuova, where the ticket office and cloakroom for the two museums are located. From here you can go downstairs to the Museo Archeologico, in the basement, or start your visit to the Galleria Sabauda in the north (left) wing of the ground floor, continuing on the floors above.

The Museo di Antichità is home to one of the oldest collections of antiquities in Europe. Begun in the 16th century by Emanuele Filiberto of Savoy and enlarged by Carlo Emanuele I, in 1724 it was donated by Vittorio Amedeo II to the University of Turin, which placed it on public view in the Palazzo dell'Accademia delle Scienze (now home to the Egyptian Museum, originally also part of the royal collections). Today it is divided into two distinct parts: a topographical section, occupying the magnificent brick-vaulted cellars of the Manica Nuova di Palazzo Reale, and a chronological section, in a modern exhibition hall (Roberto Gabetti and Aimaro Isola) connecting with the former orangeries.

The visit begins in the Manica Nuova, where carefully studied lighting and excellent text panels and multimedia aids offer a dramatic and informative introduction to the archaeology of Piedmont and, particularly, of Turin. The highlight of the museum is the **Marengo Treasure**, a trove of silver found by chance in 1928 on a farm near Marengo, saved in part from the illegal antiquities market, restored and first exhibited in the museum in 1936. It consists of 24 pieces weighing more than 12kg, among them a portrait bust of Emperor Lucius Verus (AD 161–9) with armour adorned with a head of Medusa, a beautiful female head of Victory, a capital with gilded silver acanthus leaves, a band with representations of deities, and the lining of the headboard of a bed decorated with elegant floral patterns. Massimo Venegoni designed the installation.

In front of the museum, the **Parco Archeologico** has been designed by Aimaro Isola as part of a larger project for the renewal of the Quadrilateral, the area of Turin that stands on the ruins of the old Roman settlement, west and south of the Manica Lunga. The project is a smashing success: after a period of decline, the whole area has experienced a renaissance, with the opening fashionable shops and cafés. The concept of the park is to marry the Roman city with modern Turin: the ancient Roman road, lined with tall trees and red-brick columns and flanked by green lawns, leads to the impressive **Porta Palatina** (*map Turin B, 7*), the exceptionally well-preserved two-arched Roman gate, flanked by two 16-sided towers, that was the Porta Principalis Sinistra in the wall of the Roman colony of Augusta Taurinorum. On the north side side (facing away from the city centre) a Roman bastion demolished by Napoleon has been reconstructed. The nearby **Piazza della Repubblica** (*map Turin B, 3*), known locally as Porta Palazzo, is the scene of a popular general market (and, on Sat and the second Sun of the month, of the Balôn antiques market).

GALLERIA SABAUDA

Map Turin B, 7. Manica Nuova di Palazzo Reale, Via XX Settembre 86. Open Tues–Sun 9–6, last entry 30mins before closing. galleriasabauda.beniculturali.it.

One of the most important museums in Italy, the Galleria Sabauda presents more than 700 works by Italian and European painters produced between the 13th and the 20th centuries. Begun by Carlo Alberto of Savoy and donated to the nascent Italian State by Vittorio Emanuele II in 1860, since December 2014 it has occupied a long enfilade of magnificently restored, perfectly lit galleries on four floors of the Manica Nuova. As yet undiscovered by mass tourism, it is well worth the journey to Turin. The collections are arranged chronologically, from the ground floor to the attic.

The visit begins on the **ground floor** in the north (left) wing. The oldest works are in the rooms facing the Giardini Reali; the most recent in those facing Via XX Settembre. Here, as throughout the museum, the central corridor holds banners bearing portraits of the artists represented and commentary on their work by historic and modern writers. The artworks exhibited include paintings from the royal collections as well as works removed from locations around Piedmont for reasons of safety or conservation. There are altarpieces and polyptychs, carved dossals, wooden sculptures and stone carvings ranging in date from the late 14th to the 16th centuries and originating mainly from the Duchy of Savoy, the Marquesate of Monferrato, and the Marquesate of Saluzzo. Highlights here are Jan van Eyck's *Stigmata of San Francesco* (early 1430s, Room 1), exemplifying the artist's minute attention to detail; Fra' Angelico's *Madonna and Child* (c. 1430–50, Room 2), notable for its finely rendered architectural background, its expert use of perspective and its crystal-clear light; and The *Three Archangels*, an early work of Filippino Lippi (1477–8, Room 3) showing the influence of Botticelli, under whom he studied after the death of his father, Filippo Lippi, in 1469.

The stairs, or glass lifts, take you to the **first floor**. Here again you walk in an elongated ring, first viewing the rooms in the north wing along the gardens, then returning to the crossing via the rooms facing the street, continuing on the same side into the south wing and returning to the stairs and the lifts through the the halls on the garden side. As on the ground floor, the central corridor is conceived as a space for deepening knowledge of the artists and ideas introduced in the rooms.

The north wing is devoted to the Italian Renaissance. Rooms 8 and 9, on the garden side, hold two works by Piedmont's principal 16th-century artist, Defendente Ferrari, the imposing *Polyptych of Sant'Ivo* (Room 8) and the *Madonna and Child with Angel Musicians, St Barbara with a donor and Saint Michael* (Room 9), combining late Gothic, Flemish and German influences. The Madonna is shown nursing the Christ Child; in the predella, *St Valerianus* and *Scenes from the Life of St Catherine*. Across the corridor, in Room 12, is Paolo Veronese's *Supper in the House of Simon the Pharisee*, painted in 1556 for the refectory of the monastery of Santi Nazaro e Celso in Verona and the earliest of the artist's famous supper scenes; more large paintings by Veronese line the walls of Room 14. Works by his fellow Venetian artists Jacopo, Francesco and Leandro Bassano, three of which can be traced to Savoy commissions, grace Room 15.

A highlight of the south wing (Room 21) is Orazio Gentileschi's *Annunciation*, painted in 1623 for Carlo Emanuele I and combining the compositional clarity of the Tuscan Renaissance with the light and shadow of Caravaggio (the red curtain is a direct allusion to the latter's *Death of the Virgin*, now in the Louvre) and the vivid palette of Van Dyck. In Room 25, at the end of the south corridor, is Guido Reni's dramatic *Cain and Abel* (1617–18), in which the forces of the elements underscore the violence of the action. The return to the stairs and lifts leads through Room 29, where Rubens's languid, voluptuous *Deianeira Tempted by the Fury* and *Hercules in the Garden of the Hesperides* (both c. 1638) hang with Van Dyck's *Children of Charles I of England* and *Equestrian Portrait of Tommaso Francesco di Savoia Carignano* (both c. 1635), the latter a superb study of power partly based on Titian's *Equestrian Portrait of Charles V* (1548).

On the **second floor** the north wing focuses on the 17th century; the south on the 18th. Here are Guercino's moving *Ecce Homo* (c. 1659, Room 31) and Rembrandt's *Old Man Sleeping* (c. 1629, Room 33), identified with a painting representing the vice of Sloth commissioned by the poet Constantin Huygens as a gift for his wealthy and idle friend Jacques de Gheyn III. Room 38 holds the extraordinary series of battle scenes celebrating the successes of Prince Eugene of Savoy, painted in the early 18th century by Jan van Huchtenburg. Highlights of the south wing are Francesco Solimena's *Old Testament Scenes* painted on a commission from Vittorio Amedeo II (1720s, Room 41) and two fine *Views of Turin* by Bernardo Bellotto, painted (before 1745) for Carlo Emanuele III, the artist's first official commission. Presiding over the entire floor from Room 50 is Anton Raphael Mengs's *St Peter in Cathedra* (1774–5), an epitome of pure, sculptural Classicism.

On the **attic** level is the Gualino Collection, donated to the museum in 1928. It contains Italian paintings and sculpture (including a *Madonna* attributed to Duccio di Buoninsegna, and works by Botticelli, Veronese, and Jacopo Sansovino), German paintings, ancient sculpture, Roman and medieval ivories, goldsmiths' work, Chinese works, medieval furniture and lace. Here too is a small Modern collection with works by Italian painters between the two World Wars, particularly the Gruppo dei Sei (Jessie Boswell, Gigi Chessa, Nicola Galante, Carlo Levi, Francesco Menzio and Enrico Paulucci), who rebelled against the official art of the Fascist regime, embracing instead the Modernism of Modigliani and Fauvism.

CAPPELLA DELLA SACRA SINDONE
Part of the Duomo (map Turin B, 7) but accesssed through the Royal Museums. museireali.beniculturali.it.
The **Chapel of the Holy Shroud** was built by Guarino Guarini in the late 17th century and restored after a fire of 1997. It lies nestled at the holiest point of Turin's duomo—the extreme east end, beyond the apse—and is directly accessible from the Palazzo Reale *(for the duomo itself, see overleaf)*. The chapel is a masterpiece of Baroque theatricality, contrasting gloomy black marble on the lower walls with bright white stucco above, to create an allegory of God's love for humankind and the redemptive power of the sacrifice of Christ. The eye is drawn irresistibly upward by the light from the lantern, which rushes impetuously over the elaborate stone-basketwork geometry of the tall, tapering cupola.

The greatly revered sacred relic for which this chapel was built—the shroud or *sindone* in which the body of Christ is believed to have been wrapped after His descent from the Cross—is said to have been taken from Jerusalem to Cyprus, and from there to France in the 15th century, from where it was brought to Turin by Duke Emanuele Filiberto in 1578. In 1988 carbon dating seemed to point to a date between 1260 and 1390 for the linen wrap and its negative image of a crucified man, but discussion still continues, particularly as another, still fainter image was detected on the reverse side of the shroud in 2002. The relic has lost none of its ptency for the faithful; it is closely guarded and rarely goes on display. So far this century it was shown for the Holy Year celebrations in 2000 and went on display again in April–June 2015 *(for news and updates, see sindone.org)*.

PALAZZO CHIABLESE
Map Turin B, 7. Piazza San Giovanni 2. Open for temporary exhibitions. piemonte. beniculturali.it.
This was the office building of the Royal Court when, in 1753, King Carlo Emanuele III commissioned Benedetto Alfieri to transform it into a lavish residence for his second son, Benedetto Maria Maurizio, Duke of Chiablese. The architect redesigned the façade, built the majestic staircase that leads to the *piano nobile*, and redecorated many of the rooms.

During the Napoleonic period the palace was the seat of Governor Camillo Borghese and his wife, Pauline Bonaparte, who here posed for Canova's (scandalous) marble portrait, which shows her reclining half-nude on a *chaise longue*, ostensibly in the guise of Venus (the sculpture is in Palazzo Borghese in Rome). Returned to the Savoy with the Restoration, the palace was the birthplace in 1851 of Margherita, the first Queen of Italy. It is now a temporary exhibition space, site of the Museo Reale bookshop and information centre, and home to the offices of the Regional Directorate for the Cultural and Landscape Heritage of Piedmont.

THE DUOMO

Map Turin B, 7. Piazza San Giovanni. Usually open mornings and afternoons.

Turin's duomo, built in the late 15th century by the little-known Tuscan architect Meo del Caprino, is less splendid or obtrusive than one might expect, considering the palatial nature of its surroundings. The façade is pleasantly simple and regular, and quite unsuited to its hulking Baroque campanile, redesigned in the 18th century by Juvarra. The simple grey-and-white interior contains a superb polyptych (second south altar) in a fine Gothic frame, attributed to Giovanni Martino Spanzotti and his pupil Defendente Ferrari. It was painted c. 1498–1504 for the guild of shoemakers, and shows their patron saints Crispin and Crispinian, as well as Sts Ursus (Orso) of Aosta and scenes of mercantile life.

ALONG VIA ROMA

The main street of central Turin (*map Turin A, 6–9*) connects Piazza Castello to Piazza Carlo Felice (and Porta Nuova railway station), passing through the famous Piazza San Carlo. Oriented from north to south, it runs parallel to the grid of the ancient Roman city. The Via Nuova, as it was originally named, was designed in the late 16th century by Ascanio Vittozzi for Duke Carlo Emanuele I and immediately became the city's main traffic axis. Renamed for the capital of the new Kingdom of Italy in 1871, it received a major facelift in the early 20th century. The segment between Piazza Castello and Piazza San Carlo was rebuilt in 1931–3, largely respecting the formal canons of its Baroque predecessor (it was at this time that the imposing Torre Littoria, conceived as the regional seat of the Fascist Party but never more than a residential tower, was erected to the west). The second segment, connecting Piazza San Carlo with Piazza Carlo Felice and the station, was designed by Marcello Piacentini in a much bolder, more radically modern Rationalist style, its ill-concealed intention being to contrast the authority of the Party with that of the Crown, embodied in the venerable Baroque idiom. Today you can discern the street's commercial vocation in the almost-total absence of pedestrian or vehicular access to the buildings (the buildings' doors have been moved to the side streets), to leave maximum floor space for retail outlets. Not surprisingly, Via Roma has become Turin's main shopping street (with the parallel Via LaGrange running a close second).

In its own pretty square one block east of Via Roma stands another of the five royal palaces of the House of Savoy in the capital, **Palazzo Carignano** (*map Turin A, 6*). This remarkable brick-and-marble building refuses to stand still: everything about it speaks of movement. Built for Emanuele Filiberto di Savoia-Carignano, it is the most important palace designed in Italy in the late 17th century and the only one with a pronounced regal character. Another Guarini design, it features an ingenious interplay of concave and convex lines and an astonishing variety of interior spaces which, while revealing the architect's familiarity with the interiors of Bernini and Boromini, represent a major step forward in secular Baroque architecture. A Savoy residence until 1831, the palace has an oval vestibule with a pretty double staircase. The frescoes by the Milanese painter Leganino, completed in 1702, add light and movement to the court apartments. The exposed-brick front has a little quirk: American Indians in a frieze above the windows of the *piano nobile*, commemorating a 17th-century victory of Carignano trooops over the Iroquois, in Canada.

The palace was the birthplace of Carlo Alberto (1798) and Vittorio Emanuele II (1820). It was used for the meetings of the lower house of the Subalpine Parliament (1848–59) and of the first Italian Parliament (1861–4). The first floor hosts the **Museo Nazionale del Risorgimento** (*entered from Piazza Carlo Alberto 8; open Tues–Sun 10–6, last entry 1hr before closing; T: 011 5621147, museorisorgimentotorino.it*), possibly the most important museum in the country devoted to this crucial period in Italian history. The exhibits include paintings, sculptures, documents and mememtos, as well as the beautiful Camera dei Deputati Subalpina (Room 16), the lower house of the parliament of the Kingdom of Sardinia (the senate met in Palazzo Madama).

At the end of the piazza (*entrance on Via Accademia delle Scienze*) is the **Palazzo dell'Accademia delle Scienze**, with a fine exterior, built for the Jesuits by Guarino Guarini (1678). For nearly two centuries the building has housed one of the most important museums of antiquities in the world.

MUSEO EGIZIO (EGYPTIAN MUSEUM)

Map Turin A, 6. Via Accademia delle Scienze 6. At the time of writing, tickets had to be purchased online; museoegizio.it.

The collection

The collection here is extremely fine, comparable to those of Cairo and London. In 1824 Jean-François Champollion famously wrote, 'The road to Memphis and Thebes passes through Turin'. The first to decipher Egyptian hieroglyphics, Champollion was also the first to inventory the Savoy royal holdings.

The collection was begun in 1630 by Carlo Emanuele I, but its real founder was Carlo Felice, who in 1824 bought several thousand artefacts from Bernardo Drovetti, the Piedmont-born French Consul to the Ottoman Sublime Porte. Drovetti's friendship with Egypt's Viceroy, Mohammed Ali, enabled him to remove his collections (he sold three) to Europe; the Savoy purchase included 5,268 objects (100 statues, 170 papyri, stelae, sarcophagi, mummies, bronzes, amulets and objects of daily life), which were placed on display here, in the seat of the Academy of Sciences. Later important acquisitions came from the expeditions of Ernesto Schiaparelli (1903–20) and Giulio Farina (1930–7), notably in the Theban region, at Ghebelein (Aphroditopolis), Qaw el-Kebir (Antaeopolis, near Assyut) and Heliopolis. The museum played a leading part in the rescue digs in Nubia before the completion of the Aswan high dam and was rewarded with the rock temple of Ellesiya, which was transported by sea in sections via Genoa in 1967 and then reconstructed. Today, 6,500 objects are on display, with 26,000 more in storage.

The visit

You enter the museum through a vast basement lobby, which holds the ticket counter, information desk, cloakroom and bookshop (there is a conspicuous lack of refreshments). Ticket purchase includes a multimedia guide, which explains all of the displays in (sometimes excessive) detail. You may find this electronic aid superfluous, as throughout the museum exhibits are accompanied by excellent text panels in Italian and English.

The visit begins at the **basement** level, with exhibits dealing with the history of the collection. Here you can admire the famous *Altar of Isis*, the first piece acquired for the collection by Carlo Emanuele I (not an Egyptian original, it was made in Rome in the 1st century AD for an Isis cult outside Egypt). Here too are a statue known as the *Isis of Koptos* and the lengthy *Iuefankh Papyrus*, 18-plus metres of the *Book of the Dead*, beautifully displayed at eye level.

Escalators (or a lift) ascend directly to the **second floor**, passing on the way a wall installation by Academy Award-winning set designer Dante Ferretti, *Percorso Nilotico*.

Here begins the classic chronological itinerary, from the Predynastic Period (4000 BC) to Late Antiquity (AD 700). The highlight here is the magnificent full-scale re-creation of the Tomb of Iti and Neferu (Gebelein), a large monument cut in the rock, c. 2000 BC, with 11 rooms and a long porch that opened onto the Nile Valley. In the restrained, minimalist reconstruction, the stunning paintings that adorned the walls are placed, as in the original tomb, on the walls of the rooms and the pillars of the porch, beyond which an immense screen bearing a view of the river serves as a reminder that the tomb was open to the outside.

Descending, this time by the original staircase, you reach the **first floor**, where the chronological arrangement continues with the Late Period (c. 700–300 BC, Room 11), the Ptolemaic Period (c. 300–100 BC, Room 12), and the Roman Age and Late Antiquity (c. 100 BC–AD 700, Room 13). But there are also typological groupings: the finds discovered at Deir el-Medina (Room 6) and in the Valley of the Queens (Room 10); the Tomb of Kha (Room 7); the Galleria dei Sarcofagi (Room 8), the Papyrus Room (Room 9). Outstanding exhibits here are the wonderful *Ostrakon della Danzatrice*, painted with the figure an acrobatic dancing girl, and the sumptuously decorated Chapel of Maya (Room 6); the hundreds of objects discovered by Schiaparelli in the intact tomb of the architect Kha (director of the works at the Necropolis of Thebes) and his wife Merit (Room 7); the entire Galleria dei Sarcofagi, where the coffins have been placed standing up, creating an eerie army of the dead that greets you as you walk through; and the *Papyrus of the Kings* or *Royal Canon*, listing all the rulers of Egypt from the Predynastic Age to the end of the Second Intermediate Period (c. 4000–1500 BC, Room 9).

The visit ends on the **ground floor**, perhaps the most spectacular in the truest sense of the word. The Galleria dei Re (Rooms 14a/b) was designed by Dante Ferretti to draw crowds during the 2006 Winter Olympics and its dark walls, floor-to-ceiling mirrors and dramatic point-source lighting, which highlights only a few points of the statues, make it all too like a black-box theatre. The two large halls hold sphinxes, sarcophagi, offering tables, architectural elements, but most of all monumental statues of pharaohs and deities: Thutmose III, Amenhotep II, Tutankhamun, Horemheb, Ramesses II, Seti II (a colossal figure more than five metres high); Ptah, Amun, Hathor and Sekhmet (of whom there are 21 statues). Champollion called this collection of sculptures 'a wonderful assembly of kings and gods'. The last exhibit, on the way out, is the reconstructed rock Temple of Ellesiya (Thutmose III) in the Nubian Room (15), donated in 1966 by Egypt to thank Italy for its fundamental contribution to saving the monuments threatened by the waters of Lake Nasser.

PIAZZA SAN CARLO

The 'living room of Turin' is the magnificent, arcaded Piazza San Carlo (*map Turin A, 6*), a handsome monumental square begun in 1640. Here are the twin churches of **San Carlo** and **Santa Cristina**, the latter with a façade (1715–18) by Filippo Juvarra and 18th-century stucco decoration in the interior. The monument to Duke Emanuele Filiberto, whose equestrian figure (*El caval d'brôns*, in dialect) is shown sheathing his sword after defeating the French at San Quintino and regaining sovereignty over Piedmont (1557), is considered the masterpiece of the sculptor Carlo Marochetti (1838). The two long yellow-and-grey *palazzi* have wide porticoes, beneath which are several cafés, including, on the corner of Via Santa Teresa, the well-known **Caffè San Carlo**. On the opposite side of the piazza, **Palazzo Solaro del Borgo** (no. 183), partly reconstructed by Benedetto Alfieri in 1753, is the seat of the Accademia Filarmonica and the Circolo del Whist, an exclusive club with delightful 18th-century premises.

THE QUADRILATERO ROMANO

This term, roughly speaking, refers to the the ancient Roman *castrum*, which occupied the area bounded on the south by Via Santa Teresa (*map Turin A, 6*), on the north by Corso Regina Margherita (*map Turin A, 3 and map Turin B, 7*), on the east by Piazza Castello and the Parco Archeologico (*map Turin B, 7*), and on the west by Corso Valdocco (*map Turin A, 2*). Recently the object of a rigorous urban renewal programme, it has become one of Turin's two bohemian neighbourhoods (the other is San Salvario, along the Po south of Corso Vittorio Emanuele II and north of Corso Barmante). The main axis of the Roman city was the *decumanus*, corresponding to the present Via Garibaldi. This handsome street, closed to traffic and lined with characteristic 18th-century balconied palaces, leads west from Piazza Castello, flanked by some fine monuments.

A block west of Piazza Castello, on the north side of the street, is the church of the **Trinità** (1590–1606), by Ascanio Vittozzi, with a marble interior by Filippo Juvarra (1718). It contains fine carved confessionals.

A further block along, on Via Porta Palatina (*map Turin A, 6*), is the church of **Corpus Domini** (1607–71), also by Vittozzi, with a lavishly decorated interior by Benedetto Alfieri. Jean-Jacques Rousseau abjured the Protestant faith in this church in 1728. A few paces further on is Piazza di Palazzo di Città, laid out in 1756 by Benedetto Alfieri, with a bronze monument by Pelagio Palagi (1853) to the 'Green Count' (so named because of the colour of his ensign) Amedeo VI (d. 1383), famed for his feats of arms and for his defeat of the Turks in Greece. Here is **Palazzo di Città**, the Town Hall, begun in 1659 and modified a century later by Benedetto Alfieri. The nearby church of **San Domenico** (*map Turin A, 2–3*) dates from 1354, its belfry from 1451. It has a painting by Guercino and a chapel with 14th-century frescoes.

Back on Via Garibaldi is the church of the **Santi Martiri** (*map Turin A, 6*). Begun in 1577, probably by Pellegrino Tibaldi, it has an 18th-century cupola by Bernardino Quadri and a Baroque interior. The high altar is by Filippo Juvarra. Next-door, at no. 25, is the **Cappella dei Banchieri e Mercanti** (*open Tues, Thur and Sat 3–6, Sun 10–12; T: 011 562 7226*). A delightful Baroque chapel dating from the late 17th century, it has paintings by Andrea Pozzo, Stefano Maria Legnani, Carlo Carlone and others, in huge black frames decorated in gold. The vault is frescoed by Legnani. The high altar is by Filippo Juvarra. The benches and lanterns survive intact and the organ dates from 1748–50. In the sacristy is an ingenious mechanical calendar constructed by Antonio Plana in 1831. Northwest of here is the **Santuario della Consolata** (or Chiesa di Santa Maria della Consolazione; *map Turin A, 2*), a popular place of worship created by the joining of two churches—one oval, the other hexagonal—by Guarino Guarini (1679).

FROM PIAZZA CASTELLO TO THE PO

It is difficult to say if Via Po (*map Turin B, 7–11*) is Turin's most striking street. Via Roma (*see above*) is certainly more elegant, lined with the city's best shops, and Via Pietro Micca (*map Turin A, 6*) has some fine Eclectic-style houses. But Via Po, descending gradually from Piazza Castello towards the river, provides a splendid architectural frame for the wooded hills on the Po's south bank. This neighbourhood is also home to the building that has become the symbol of Turin, the **Mole Antonelliana** (*map Turin B, 11*). It was begun as a synagogue in 1863, just months after Vittorio Emanuele II granted freedom of worship to Jews in the new kingdom of Italy. The architect, Alessandro Antonelli, was commissioned to design a building 47m tall, but changed the plans to something more than twice that height. The delays and additional cost sparked a dispute that led to the City of Turin giving the Jewish congregation a new site, and providing Antonelli with the funds to complete his building, which rose to a final height of 167m. Recast by the municipality as a monument to Italian unity, it was the first seat of the Risorgimento Museum now in Palazzo Carignano (*see p. 19*). The granite spire was rebuilt in aluminium after it lost its upper 47m in a gale in 1953. In the 1990s the building was fitted with a glass lift (*at the time of writing open 9–7 daily except Tuesday, but see museocinema.it for updates*), which whisks you to the rooftop terrace in just under a minute. Mario Merz's *Flight of Numbers* was installed on the roof in 1998. Merz was an important exponent of the Arte Povera movement (*see p. 29*). The interior has been restored to house the **Museo Nazionale del Cinema** (*museocinema.it*), which has an absorbing collection illustrating the history of cinema (and photography) in Italy and abroad; there is also an important film library.

Close by is the Accademia Albertina di Belle Arti (*map Turin B, 11*), an academy of fine arts founded in 1678. The **Pinacoteca dell'Accademia Albertina** (*Via dell'Accademia Albertina 8; open Mon–Fri 9.30–5.30; last entry 30mins before closing; albertina.academy/biblioteca*), in the same building, is interesting mainly for its 60 drawings by Gaudenzio Ferrari (*see p. 71*), the eminent Piedmontese painter, and his workshop. There are also paintings by Filippo Lippi, Bernardino Lanino, and Piedmontese masters, in marvellously coloured (sour apple green, rust red, mauve, cornflower blue) rooms.

Via Po ends in the immense open space (c. 400m by 100m) of **Piazza Vittorio Veneto** (*map Turin B, 11*). Built during Turin's great 17th-century growth phase, it was long used as a parade ground. Now it is a centre of nightlife, attracting a young crowd to its fashionable bars beneath the arcades and along the river on the former docks known as *murazzi*.

Across the river rises the church of the **Gran Madre di Dio** (*map Turin B, 15*), its chill white façade dominating the east end of the Ponte Vittorio Emanuele I. This Neoclassical church was built in 1818–31, in imitation of the Pantheon at Rome, to celebrate the return from exile of Vittorio Emanuele I (1814). A monument to the king stands in front of the porch. On the banks of the river here are pleasant public gardens.

TWO IMPORTANT TURIN ARCHITECTS

Filippo Juvarra (1678–1736). Juvarra was an architect, draughtsman and urban planner. He was born the son of a silversmith and entered the priesthood as a young man. He trained as an architect under Carlo Fontana in Rome (1703–14) and was hired as a stage designer by a number of illustrious patrons, including the queen of Poland and the emperor Joseph I of Austria. In 1714 he was appointed architect to the King of Sicily (who resided in Piedmont) and given the commission to rebuild and enlarge Turin. Here and in the environs of the city he left many important works, including two masterpieces: the royal hunting lodge at Stupinigi (1729) and the basilica of Stuperga (1731). His style, highly decorative, light and gracious, typifies the transition between the Baroque and the Rococo.

Guarino Guarini (1624–83). As a schoolboy Guarini excelled at mathematics and chose architecture as a career. He became famous for his domes: an excellent example is that of the Sacra Sindone, the chapel to house the Holy Shroud, which plays with optical illusion. Guarini was also known for his genius at geometry, and in the Sacra Sindone he makes a repeated play on the number three, symbol of the Trinity, using equilateral triangles, and having three pendentives instead of four.

SAN SALVARIO & THE VALENTINO

The **Parco del Valentino** (*map Turin A, 13*) contains a fine botanic garden (*Viale Mattioli 25; open daily*), founded in 1729, with a museum and library. The latter contains the remarkable *Iconographia Taurinensis*, a collection of 7,500 botanical drawings dated 1752–1868. Also here are the **Castello del Valentino**, now used by the university faculty of architecture, built in 1630–60 by Maria Cristina in the style of a French château and the **Borgo e Rocca Medievali**—reproductions of a medieval Piedmontese village and of a castle in the Valle d'Aosta (*Viale Virgilio 107; open daily, Rocca closed for repairs at the time of writing; check borgomedievaletorino.it for updates*), were designed by Alfredo D'Andrade, art scholar, architect and painter, for the Turin exhibition of 1884; they are now used for events and exhibitions. Nearby is the fine equestrian monument of Prince Amedeo, the masterpiece of Davide Calandra (1902). At the southwest end of the park is an exhibition ground with various buildings erected between 1938 and 1950, notably **Palazzo Torino-Esposizioni**, whose spectacular vaulted ceiling was designed by architect and engineer Pier Luigi Nervi. It was built in 1948 for the first Turin Motor Show.

Further south (*beyond map*) is the large **Museo dell'Automobile** (*Corso Unità d'Italia 40; open Mon 10–2, Tues–Sun 10–7; ticket offices closes 1hr before closing time; museoauto.it*), with an international collection of vehicles, admirably displayed and technically documented. It was designed by Amedeo Albertini in 1958–60 and renovated by Cino Zucchi in 2006. Further on, overlooking the river, is the huge **Palazzo del Lavoro**, designed by Pier Luigi Nervi for the 1961 exhibition.

SAN SALVARIO

San Salvario (*map Turin A, 9–10*) is multi-class, bohemian-bourgeois neighbourhood today, but historically it is a working-class district, its fortunes initially following those of the royal summer residence, the Castello del Valentino, and later those of the Porta Nuova railyards and the Fiat works at Lingotto (*see below*). It is multi-denominational too—home to four Catholic churches, including the one for which it is named, as well as a Waldensian temple, Turin's magnificent synagogue (1880–4, *Piazzetta Primo Levi*), and a mosque. But most of all it is fashionable, the hip address for young entrepreneurs, professionals and intellectuals, and alive with events and activities—music festivals, film festivals, fairs, sporting events, workshops, pageants, aperitifs—so many that residents have set up a website (*sansalvario.org*) to keep track of what's going on.

PRIMO LEVI

Primo Levi was number 174517 in Auschwitz concentration camp between 1944 and 1945. He was born into a Jewish family in Turin in 1919. Apart from his time in Auschwitz, he lived his whole life in the family home at Corso Re Umberto 75 (*just beyond map Turin A, 5*). As a boy he developed a keen interest in science and determined to become a chemist.

Levi was also a keen alpinist and adored the beauty of the mountains, which fed his love of chemistry; he spoke about their relationship thus: 'the passion for the mountains went hand in hand with the passion for chemistry, in the sense of finding elements of the periodic system stuck between the rocks and encapsulated in the ice' (1984). He enrolled at the University of Turin in 1937, and despite the *numerus clausus* laws introduced by the Fascist government in 1938, Levi was able to graduate with honours in 1941. His conscience led him to join the partisans in the Valle d'Aosta, but he was soon arrested and on admitting without any reserve that he was a Jew he found himself on his way to Auschwitz.

Hell it was, as he recalls in his famous memoir *If this is a Man*, published shortly after his return to Turin in 1947. He describes how in those his eleven months in Auschwitz, he witnessed the 'demolition of a man'. Unlike the vast majority of those with whom he was interned, he had survived. This was due to his being a chemist, a skill which allowed him to work in the laboratory of a synthetic rubber factory next to the camp, and brought him certain privileges such as being allowed to wear leather shoes instead of painful wooden clogs.

Back in Turin he found employment as a research chemist and then as the manager the SIVA paint factory, for whom he worked until his retirement. In his spare time he wrote letters, poetry and books. In 1975 he published *Il Sistema Periodico* (*The Periodic Table*), which is a paean to Mendeleev's system in which he uses the elements as metaphors for life. His final book was *I Sommersi e I Salvati* (*The Drowned and the Saved*, 1986), which examines the conscience of those who stood impotently by and did nothing and the shame felt by those who survived.

Despite the horrors of his war-time imprisonment and the notoriety which followed the publication of his memoirs, Levi lived the life of an ordinary, self-effacing man, going about his daily business; a simple chemist, as he always referred to himself. His death, most probably by suicide in 1987, came as something as a shock, but it was, perhaps, the inescapable result of having to live with the knowledge that, *in extremis*, man will be inhuman to his fellow man.

The historic focus of the neighbourhood economy, the former **Lingotto Fiat factory**, is in Via Nizza (*beyond map Turin A, 9*). Fiat (Fabbrica Italiana Automobili di Torino) was founded in 1899 by the industrialist Giovanni Agnelli (1866–1945), who in effect introduced one of Italy's greatest passions to the country—the car. By 1915 the workforce of 10,000 was producing over 4,000 cars a year. This cutting-edge factory, admired by Le Corbusier, opened in 1923, drawing thousands of immigrant workers to the area, for whom housing and other amenities were specially built by the company; it was the largest car factory in the world. The production line ran from the bottom of the five-storey building to the top; raw materials entered the building on the ground floor and completed vehicles emerged onto the test track on the roof (made famous in the 1969 film *The Italian Job*). By the 1970s, global competition and advances in technology rendered the building redundant and it was closed in 1982. The question of what to do with the factory was tackled by Renzo Piano, who redesigned it as an exhibition and events centre. The complex includes the Le Méridien Lingotto hotel and the marvellously idiosyncratic **Pinacoteca Giovanni e Marella Agnelli** (*open Tues–Sun 10–7, last entry 45mins before closing; pinacoteca-agnelli.it*), on five floors. The rooftop 'jewellery box' (as it was called by Piano), holds the permanent collection: 25 masterpieces (23 paintings and two sculptures) ranging from the 18th to the mid-20th centuries. Here are works by Tiepolo, Canaletto, Bellotto, Canova, Manet, Renoir, Matisse, Balla, Severini, Modigliani and others. The lower floors host temporary exhibitions, a beautiful, luminous library, offices and classrooms.

A bold, suspended pedestrian bridge crosses the Lingotto rail yards to the **former Mercati Generali e Villaggio Olimpico**. The market, designed by Rationalist architect Umberto Cuzzi in 1932-3, is a straightforward but graceful structure in reinforced concrete that unabashedly 'quotes' the Royal Horticultural Society's Lawrence Hall in London (Easton and Robertson, 1925–8); it was restored for the 2006 Winter Olympics by Benedetto Camerana and Hugh Dutton and recast as an office complex with the aid of Albert Constantin.

Across the river, on a hillside, **Villa della Regina** (*just beyond map Turin B, 15; open Tues–Sun 10–6, last entry 1hr before closing; polomusealepiemonte.beniculturali. it*) is a Baroque residence built for Cardinal Maurizio of Savoy to a design probably by Ascanio Vittozzi, and executed by Amedeo di Castellamonte in 1620. It was altered in the 18th century by Filippo Juvarra. The villa is named after Marie-Anne d'Orléans, queen of Vittorio Amedeo II, who resided here. It has a beautiful park and garden laid out in terraces on the hillside in the style of a Roman villa and is one of the Piedmontese Residences of the Royal House of Savoy listed by UNESCO—the only one to include a working vineyard and farm.

ELSEWHERE IN TOWN

North of Corso Vittorio Emanuele II, the **Museo Civico Pietro Micca** (*map Turin A, 1; Via Guicciardini 7A; open Tues–Sun 10–6, last entry 1hr before closing; booking required, museopietromicca.it*) is dedicated to the French siege of 1706. The museum is named after the Piedmontese sapper who exploded a mine on this site and saved the city from the French at the cost of his own life. From the museum you can visit part of the remarkable underground defence works, which extend for several kilometres beneath the city.

The area around nearby Porta Susa Station is being redeveloped as an office tower district. Renzo Piano's great white **Grattacielo Intesa Sanpaolo** (*map Turin A, 1*), corporate headquarters of the important banking group, was inaugurated in April 2015. It is just 25cm shorter than the Mole Antonelliana.

South of the corso is the **Galleria Civica d'Arte Moderna e Contemporanea** (*map Turin A, 5; Via Magenta 31; open Tues–Sun 10–6, last entry 1hr before closing; gamtorino.it*). Founded in 1863 and reopened in 1993, the gallery houses one of the most important collections of 19th- and 20th-century painting in Italy. Highlights here include works by Courbet, Renoir and the Macchiaioli group of Italian post-Impressionists (Telemaco Signorini, Silvestro Lega, Giovanni Fattori), and early 20th-century works by the Futurists (Umberto Boccioni, Giacomo Balla, Gino Severini and Carlo Carrà), the Metaphysical painters (Giorgio de Chirico and his brother, Alberto Savinio), and the sublimely individual Giorgio Morandi. At the time of writing, four guest curators had arranged the collections around the themes of Infinity, Speed, Ethics and Nature.

Further south are two private foundations dedicated to contemporary art. The **Fondazione Merz** (*Via Limone 24, beyond map; closed for works at the time of writing, for updates, see fondazionemerz.org*) preserves the personal collection of Italy's most distinguished contempoary artist, Mario Merz (1925–2003), and spotlights the latest developments in the visual and performing arts, prose and poetry. The foundation occupies the former heating plant of the Lancia Automobile Works, a fabulous example of 1930s industrial architecture, and alternates exhibitions dedicated to Mario and Marisa Merz with site-specific projects by Italian and international artists. It also has strong research and education programmes.

In the same area of town is the **Fondazione Sandretto Re Rebaudengo** (*Via Modane 16, beyond map; open Thur 8–11pm, Fri, Sat, Sun 12–7; fsrr.org*). Established expressly to support and promote young artists, it combines a large temporary exhibition space in Turin with site-specific and environmental installations at other locations in the Piedmont region. The 3500 sq m building, designed by architect Claudio Silvestrin and engineer James Hardwick, hosts performing arts as well as visual arts.

The basilica of **Superga** (*map A, D2; basilicadisuperga.com*), splendidly situated on a wooded hilltop on the right bank of the Po (around 25mins' drive from the city), was built in 1717–31 by Vittorio Amedeo II in fulfilment of a thanksgiving vow for the deliverance of Turin from the French in 1706. It is considered Filippo Juvarra's finest work. It has an impressive exterior with a columned portico, a dome and two *campanili*; and a fine interior with the tombs of the kings of Sardinia, from Vittorio Amedeo II (d. 1732) to Carlo Alberto (d. 1849), in the crypt.

AROUND TURIN: THE SAVOY ROYAL RESIDENCES

When Emanuele Filiberto, Duke of Savoy, moved his capital from Chambéry to Turin in the 16th century, he began a vast series of building projects to demonstrate the power of the ruling house. The building programme was continued by his successors right up to the dawn of the modern age. It has left an outstanding complex of buildings, designed and embellished by the leading architects and artists of the time, which include not only the five royal palaces in the capital, but many country residences and hunting lodges as well. Today these royal residences are amongst the finest examples of European monumental architecture of the 17th and 18th centuries. In 1997 the Residences of the Royal House of Savoy were inscribed on the UNESCO World Heritage list in cosideration of the fact that 'the Residences of the Royal House of Savoy in and around Turin represent a comprehensive overview of European monumental architecture in the 17th and 18th centuries, using style, dimensions, and space to illustrate in an exceptional way the prevailing doctrine of absolute monarchy in material terms. The listed castles include: in Turin, Palazzo Reale, Palazzo Madama, Palazzo Carignano, Castello del Valentino and the Villa della Regina; in Piedmont, the Palazzina di Caccia di Stupinigi, the Reggia di Venaria Reale, and the castles of La Mandria, Rivoli, Moncalieri, Racconigi, Agliè, Pollenzo and Govone. All but the last three are in the immedate environs of Turin.

MONCALIERI

Also on the right bank of the Po (*map A, C3*), this town lies 8km from the centre of Turin and can be reached by train and bus. It is industrial with a pleasant historic centre. The **Castello Reale di Moncalieri** (*Piazza Baden Baden 4; open Fri–Sun and holidays for guided tours; booking online; castellodimoncalieri.it*), reconstructed in the 15th century and enlarged in the 17th–18th centuries, was the favourite residence of Vittorio Emanuele II; Vittorio Amedeo II (1732) and Vittorio Emanuele I (1824) died here. The apartment of the Savoy princess Letizia Bonaparte, and the 19th-century royal apartments, can be visited.

The large park has recently been restored. The first design, in the late-Mannerist taste, dates from 1647–52; it was commissioned by Madama Reale Christine of France and remained unchanged until 1761, when the director of the royal gardens Michel Benard redesigned it as a French garden, adapting it to the topography of the hilly site. The last transformation took place at the behest of Vittorio Emanuele II, who in 1850 had the entire property recast in the English style, with winding paths, a lily pond, and the Torre del Roccolo aviary. You can see a little of all of these today, with the formal gardens closest to the castle.

STUPINIGI

Ten kilometres southwest of Turin and surrounded by a fine park is the magnificent **Palazzina di Caccia di Stupinigi** (*map A, C3*), a hunting lodge built for Vittorio Amedeo II in 1729–30 by Filippo Juvarra. Now the property of the Mauritian Order (*open Tues–Fri 10–5.30, Sat–Sun 10–6.30, last entry 30 mins before closing; ordinemauriziano.it*), the palace has been exquisitely restored and is now a museum with paintings, furniture and decorative arts arranged in some 40 rooms. It has an ingenious plan featuring four diagonal wings, which the architect intended to recall hunting trails, meeting in an elliptical central hall. Benedetto Alfieri built more wings, and raised the height of the central pavilion's roof, after Juvarra's death. The queen's apartment has ceiling paintings by Carle van Loo and Giovanni Battista Crosato, and the splendid central hall is frescoed by Giuseppe and Domenico Valeriani (1732). The apartments of Carlo Felice and Carlo Alberto are also shown. The original 18th-century bronze stag, which used to crown the roof of the elliptical central hall, is now displayed inside the palace. A stable block is used for exhibitions.

The 1200-hectare park is divided into sectors by a geometrical composition of avenues and paths; all around are woods (with some venerable old oaks) and farmland, formerly revenue-producing components of the estate. Now they offer habitat to hares, red squirrels, dormice, foxes and weasels, as well as white storks, tree pipits and water pipits. The park can be visited on foot or on horeseback.

RIVOLI

This pretty town 13km west of Turin (*map A, C2*) was once a favourite residence of the counts of Savoy. The huge, square castle, left unfinished by Filippo Juvarra in the early 18th century, was restored and modernised in 1984 to house the splendid **Castello di Rivoli Museo d'Arte Contemporanea** (*open Weds–Fri 10–5, Sat–Sun 10–6, last entry 30mins before closing; www.castellodirivoli.org*). This is certainly one of the most impressive museums of contemporary art anywhere. The quality of the work on display and the atmosphere of the setting are exceptional. The permanent collection, on the second floor, features installations expressly created for the castle's rooms by internationally renowned contemporary artists. There is also an outstanding selection of European and American sculpture. Highlights include works by the masters of Arte Povera, whose work has made Turin one of the most vibrant art centres in Europe from the 1960s to the present.

ARTE POVERA

In November 1967, in the fifth issue of *Flash Art*, the critic Germano Celant published '*Arte Povera: appunti per una guerriglia*', stressing the parallel between a 'revolutionary' social situation and a moment of aesthetic rebellion. The artist Jannis Kounellis, in an interview published in the same issue, states, 'What is important is being free, and this freedom manifests itself concretely in aesthetic shapes'. Celant, too, speaks of freedom—from an alienating rationalistic system, from coherence, from Pop Art and Minimalism. He speaks of a 'poor' art as opposed to a complex one, of an art that does not add ideas or things to the world, but that discovers what is already there; an art interested in the present, in contingencies and events as a convergence of art and life.

Celent refers to an 'anthropological dimension of authenticity' and 'unalienated labour where man is identified with nature'. As he saw it, Arte Povera, which included a number of artists of the '60s and '70s—Giovanni Anselmo, Alighiero Boetti, Pier Luigi Calzolari, Luciano Fabro, Piero Gilardi, Paolo Icaro, Jannis Kounellis, Mario and Marisa Merz, Giulio Paolini, Pino Pascali, Giuseppe Penone, Gianni Piacentino, Michelangelo Pistoletto, Emilio Prini and Gilberto Zorio—walked a fine line between a liberation from traditional forms of art and a renewed appropriation of the world. Some critics view Arte Povera as an eccentric form of Conceptual Art; but the conceptualism of the *poveristi* always underpins an image—in the work of all, the image remains a support, an element displayed to be viewed. By retaining images, Arte Povera was able to avoid the sterile, petty radicalism typical of certain kinds of Conceptualism. Its aim is to examine the relationship between art and life, between the natural and the artificial.

VENARIA REALE

The **Reggia di Venaria Reale**, approximately 17km northwest of Turin (*map A, C2*), is a royal hunting lodge built for Carlo Emanuele II in 1660 by Amedeo di Castellamonte and destroyed by French troops in 1693. It was reconstructed by Juvarra in 1714–28 and was taken as a model for the royal palace at Versailles. Like the Palazzina di Stupinigi, the Castello della Venaria Reale has been meticulously restored, and knowledgeable guides show parts of the interior (*open Tues–Sun 9–5, lavenaria.it*). The palace is also a temporary exhibition venue; what is shown depends on what exhibitions are underway at the time of your visit. The Grand Gallery, with its soft white stuccoes and brilliantly reflective black-and-white chessboard floor, and the tall, domed Cappella di Sant'Uberto, are the most spectacular of the interior rooms; the formal gardens, with their carefully tended parterres and cobblestone pathways shaped to imitate interlaced hunting horns, are exquisite. There are also a couple of well-balanced contemporary touches: a Giardino delle Sculture Fluide by the Piedmontese artist Giuseppe Penone, known for his sculptures involving natural phenomena, develops along the reflecting pool or *pescheria*, and a spectacular neo-Baroque play of lights and water jets (*giochi d'aqua*) is staged at the historic Fontana del Cervo, in the *cour d'honneur*, on Saturday and Sunday evenings at 7pm.

A long avenue of plane trees leads to the **Castello della Mandria** (*closed Jan–mid-March; for details, see lavenaria.it*) built for Vittorio Amedeo II in 1713 by Filippo Juvarra, in a large park that was once a hunting reserve (*open daily; bicycles for hire*).

RACCONIGI

This town bordering the Langhe (*map C, C1*) is the site of one of the most famous castles of Piedmont, which is also the summer home of Turin's symphony orchestra. The **Palazzo Reale di Racconigi** (*closed Mon–Tues; residenzerealisabaude.com*) belonged to the Carignano branch of the Savoy family, who entrusted its renovation to Guarino Guarini (garden façade, 1676) and Giovanni Battista Borra (main façade, 1755). It was the favourite summer residence of Carlo Alberto, who had Pelagio Palagi redesign the interior.

Racconigi was a genuine pleasure palace, a place where the king could escape from the pressures of the capital while entertaining state visitors in an atmosphere at once regal and relaxed. Palagi's interiors reflect that character. Visits take in most of the royal apartments, plus the impressive kitchens; each of the rooms is fascinating in its own way, thanks to Guarini's magic touch. The most interesting are the Appartamenti di Rappresentanza, designed to convey the power and wealth of the royal family to official visitors; the exotic Sale Cinesi, intended for more intimate occasions, and the Gabinetti di Apollo and degli Etruschi, dedicated to artistic creation and contemplation.

The immense park was designed in the late 17th century by the French architect André Le Nôtre as an orderly ensemble of flowerbeds and walkways—echoing his celebrated design for Versailles. A century later Josephine de Lorraine, Princess of Carignano, had her court designer Giacomo Pregliasco replant part of the park as an English garden. Carlo Alberto continued the transformation, engaging the German landscape architect Xavier Kürten (*see p. 89*; he also designed the Savoy gardens at Govone, Agliè and Pollenzo) to replace Le Nôtre's rational geometric patterns with emotion-laden meadows and woodlands, curving trails and a sinuous lake complete with a grotto and architectural follies. The park was abandoned in the early 20th century and Kürten's design for Carlo Alberto has only recently been restored. Although the park is understaffed, hence a bit overgrown, it is a wonderful place for a walk: to amble leisurely from the entrance (along the left flank of the palace) to the *limonaia* at its far end (where concerts take place in summer) will take the better part of an hour. It is particularly pleasant in spring when rivers of flowers flow through the woods and meadows. Racconigi also hosts a centre for the protection of birds, and storks nest in the tree-tops and on the chimney-pots.

SOUTH & EAST OF TURIN

South of Turin near the Po, is **Carignano** (*map A, C3*) an ancient lordship long associated with the royal house of Savoy. The cathedral (1757–67) is the masterpiece of Juvarra's successor as court architect Benedetto Alfieri.

To the east of Turin is the pleasant little industrial town of **Chieri** (*map A, D2–3*). The cathedral has a 13th-century baptistery and a small crypt incorporating Roman work. The 14th-century church of San Domenico and remains of the Commandery of the Templars are also worth seeing.

From Chieri a road leads eastwards to the hill-village of **Castelnuovo Don Bosco** (*map A, D2*), birthplace of the saint and founder of the Salesian Order. The little town has some fine monuments, from the Romanesque church of Sant'Eusebio to the 18th-century church of Sant'Andrea, which holds a painting by Moncalvo. Most people, however, come to Castelnuovo Don Bosco to visit the imposing shrine dedicated to St John Bosco—popularly Don Bosco—who was born and worked here. The town is also the birthplace of St Joseph Cafasso and the Blessed Giuseppe Allamano; and St Dominic Savio died here.

DON BOSCO AND THE SALESIANS
Giovanni Melchior Bosco was born in 1815, in a mountain hut at Becchi, near Castelnuovo. He worked as a shepherd before training for the priesthood. Shocked by what he saw of the brutal and loveless existence endured by child prisoners in the gaols of Turin, he set up a seminary in 1841 to care for street urchins and teach them the Bible. In 1859 he founded the Salesian Society, aimed at caring for boys from poor backgrounds, and training them for a trade or for the priesthood. The society took its name from St Francis de Sales (1567–1622), by whose example Don Bosco was inspired. After only a few years the original 17 members has swelled to 400. Don Bosco would take them on Sunday excursions in the hills outside Turin, where he would celebrate Mass in the open air, light a camp fire, and treat the boys to a picnic lunch. Don Bosco died in 1888 and was canonised in 1934.

The Salesian Charter describes the society's mission as 'the Christian perfection of its associates obtained by the exercise of spiritual and corporal works of charity towards the young, especially the poor, and the education of boys to the priesthood'. The Salesian teaching method was based on love and understanding rather than on punishment and retribution. By the time of Don Bosco's death, the original group of 17 members had grown to more than 1,000 and had 57 foundations in Italy, Spain, France, England, Uruguay and Brazil. The congregation continued to spread so rapidly that it soon became the third largest among men's orders. Its works have expanded to include agricultural, trade and academic schools; seminaries; recreational centres and youth clubs in large cities; summer camps; and parishes.

The Salesian Sisters are now also one of the largest Roman Catholic religious congregations of women, founded in 1872 at Mornese (near Alessandria), by St John Bosco and St Mary Mazzarello. Like their male counterparts, the sisters followed Don Bosco's norms for education: reason, religion and amiability, and the employment of all that is humanly useful in character formation—academic studies, manual skills, work, clubs and athletic games.

It was in honour of the bicentenary of Don Bosco's birth that the Turin Shroud went on display in 2015.

Don Bosco's birthplace, in the hamlet of **Becchi**, is a favourite destination of tourists and pilgrims. The **Museo Etnologico Missionario Salesiano** (*for details of opening times, see colledonbosco.it*) is part of the immense Salesian complex that includes the church of Santa Maria Ausiliatrice and the modest farmhouse where Don Bosco was born. The museum displays material produced and used by the indigenous peoples of South America, Asia, Africa and Oceania, collected by the Salesian missionaries—over 10,000 items. The items from the Rio Negro (Brazil) and from Patagonia and Tierra del Fuego can be considered unique, as they are artefacts of extinct populations. The African collection (about 900 pieces) reflects the relatively recent history of the Salesian missions on the continent. The Chinese collection consists of watercolours on rice paper, votive statuettes, clothes and traditional ornaments and various other objects expressing local culture and religiosity. The Japanese collection includes dolls in paper, fabric, plaster and straw originally intended for domestic ceremonies and Shinto festivals dedicated to girls and children. The collections from Southeast Asia and India have various objects for ritual and household use, such as utensils in vegetable fibre (baskets, sieves and rain covers), ornaments made of composite animal materials (boar, tiger and elephant tusks, goat wool, shells and insects), clothing and accessories that reflect the aesthetic and socio-economic structure of native ethnic groups.

ALBUGNANO

Situated high on a hill, Albugnano (*map A, D2*) enjoys magnificent views of the Alps, the Po Valley and the Monferrato hills. Its countryside is a classic Mediterranean patchwork, partly wooded and partly cultivated, with vineyards that produce excellent wine thanks to the iron-rich soil. At the top of the town is the Piazzale della Torre, taking its name from a tower that of the ancient castle, conquered in 1401 by Gascon mercenaries in the service of the Prince of Acaja, who tore it down. The rest of the town's history is tied to its abbey.

Set in a little vale amid hills blanketed with vineyards, the **Abbazia di Vezzolano** (*Via Vezzolano 34; summer and winter opening times differ; check on vezzolano.it*) is one of the most important Romanesque monuments in Piedmont. According to an undocumented legend, the abbey was founded at the behest of Charlemagne in 773: after recovering from an epileptic seizure during a hunting trip near Albugnano, the king of the Franks is said to have ordered an abbey to be built in honour of the Virgin Mary. Certainly, in the Middle Ages Vezzolano was both powerful and wealthy. Approaching it by a path that leads through fields and woods, the abbey appears suddenly. The bell tower, placed according to the Romanesque tradition on the north side of the church, is low and squat; the façade, adorned with columns and statues and constructed of alternating bands of brick and sandstone, is pierced by with a beautiful doorway with low reliefs.

The church was built in 1095, but was fully overhauled in later centuries. The interior, in a transitional Romanesque–Gothic style, is split into two distinct areas by a rood screen added in the late 12th century and decorated with low reliefs depicting Mary's *35 Ancestors*, her *Deposition* and her *Assumption and Triumph in Heaven*, accompanied by symbols of the Evangelists. A small door admits to the cloister, where elements from different periods again coexist, including some beautifully preserved frescoes of the 13th and 15th centuries.

TURIN PRACTICAL TIPS

GETTING AROUND

• **By rail:** The main train station in Turin is Porta Nuova (*map Turin A, 9*) which connects to Rome, Milan, Florence, Venice, Genoa and Paris; Milan- and Paris- bound trains also stop at Porta Susa (*map Turin A, 1*) and Genoa-bound trains at the intermediate station Lingotto. There is a direct link in 20mins from Turin International Airport Sandro Pertini (Caselle) to Porta Dora, but it is not in the city centre (take the DoraFly bus service from Porta Dora for which train tickets are also valid, about 10–15mins).

From Turin Porta Susa there are direct services to Moncalieri (c. 10mins) and Chieri (27mins). There are also local connections to places throughout Piedmont. Information from Trenitalia (*trenitalia.it*).

• **By car:** The old city centre is a Restricted Traffic Zone (ZTL, *Zona Traffico Limitato*); however there are underground car parks at Porta Nuova and Piazza Castello (Roma San Carlo Castello) and Piazza Vittorio Veneto (Vittorio Park).

For most purposes, you do not need a car in Turin; you can walk across the centre of the city from Stazione Porta Nuova to Porta Palatina in about 30mins.

• **By bus:** The principal bus station is at Corso Vittorio Emanuele II 131 (near Porta Susa; *map Turin A, 1*), with extensive regional, national and international links, *autostazionetorino.it*. For Chieri, take GTT suburban line 30 from Corso San Maurizio (Turin) to Via Gozzano (Chieri; c. 35mins); VIGOBUS (*vigobus.it*) also runs a service from Corso San Maurizo (25mins).

• **By bicycle:** Bicycles can be hired from numerous bike-share stations around the city. For details, see the city bike website (*comune.torino.it/bici*).

• **By taxi:** Taxi Torino (*T: 011 5737, T: 011 5730; taxitorino.it*).

PUBLIC TRANSPORT IN TURIN

The metro, trams and buses run by GTT (*www.gtt.to.it*) are well run, efficient and a good way to get around if you need to travel any distance. Turin's beautiful driverless Metro is helpful for visiting Lingotto, Racconigi and Castello di Rivoli.

Public transport can also be used to reach the Basilica of Superga and the Savoy Royal Residences on the outskirts of Turin. For Superga, take Bus 15 (from Piazza Castello) or 61/68 (from Piazza Vittorio) to the suburb of Sassi, then cog railway to the basilica. For the Palazzina di Caccia di Stupinigi take Bus 41 from Stazione FS Lingotto; travel time is 20mins. The Castello di Rivoli is located 13km west of the city centre. Take the Metro from Porta Susa to STPAR-Paradiso Station (Corso Francia/Via Podgora), then Bus 36 to stop no. 2794, Martiri della Libertà; journey time is 61mins. For the Reggia di Venaria Reale there is the Venaria Express shuttle, operated by GTT. For further information on public transport, see GTT (Transport Group Turin; *www.gtt.to.it*).

VISITOR CARDS

The Torino + Piemonte Card, available in various permutations, gives free access and/or discounts to sights and monuments in Turin and the wider region. For details, see turismotorino.org/en/your-trip/torinopiemonte-card.

WHERE TO STAY IN TURIN

€€€€ **Sitea**. A luxurious hotel, with a lovely small garden, in the centre of town, this is historically the best address in Turin. The architecture is Liberty, the décor is refined and you'll find every comfort—plus excellent concierge service. *Via Carlo Alberto 35. grandhotelsitea.it. Map Turin A, 10.*

€€€ **Torino Piazza Carlina**. A refined modern hotel in a historic building in what may well be Turin's most beautiful neighbourhood, between Piazza San Carlo and the Po. (The Egyptian Museum is three minutes to the west, on foot; the nightlife of Piazza Vittorio and the Murazzi, three minutes to the east.) The architecture is 'glocal' (geothermal heating, hardwood floors and furniture made by local artisans), as is the food. *Piazza Carlo Emanuele II 15. T: 011 8601611,* *nh-hotels.it/hotel/nh-collection-torino-piazza-carlina. Map Turin A, 10.*

€€ **Boston**. Art hotel in the heart of a residential area west of Porta Nuova station. The difference with other art hotels is that the works are by internationally acknowledged contemporary artists, with a strong bias towards those from Turin. *Via Massena 70. hotelbostontorino.it. Map Turin A, 9.*

€€ **Dei Pittori**. Occupying the Liberty villa built in 1897 for chocolatier Carlo Stratta (whose family shop is described below), this small hôtel de charme is situated in the historic Borgo Vanchiglia district, a five-minute walk from the Mole Antonelliana and the Giardini Reali. There are 12 quiet, comfortable, individually decorated rooms, each dedicated to a painter of the period, 1890–1914, and an in-house restaurant. *Corso Regina Margherita 57. hoteldeipittori.it. Map Turin B, 11–12.*

€€ **La Luna e i Falò**. This lovely, large flat in a quiet residential neighbourhood west of Porta Nuova Station was Cesare Pavese's home in Turin between 1930 and 1950. Here the great 20th-century novelist wrote his most celebrated works: the B&B in fact takes its name from the best known of all, *The Moon and the Bonfires*. The three spacious, refined rooms are furnished with genuine antiques, and breakfast is served with silver cutlery. *Via Alfonso Lamarmora 34. lalunaeifalo-torino.it. Map Turin A, 5.*

€€ **Victoria**. An elegant, family-run boutique hotel in an unassuming building in the heart of town. Lovely, individually decorated rooms, a spa and indoor pool, and private parking. Guests borrow bicycles to get around, and the breakfast buffet is second to none. *Via Nino Costa 4. T: 011 561 1909, hotelvictoria-torino.com. Map Turin A, 10.*

WHERE TO EAT IN TURIN

€€€ **Del Cambio**. Established in 1757, this is indisputably the restaurant of Turin's high society: the décor was the same when Cavour dined here a century and a half ago, and the cuisine has maintained the same exquisite standards. Lunch Tues–Sun, dinner Tues–Sat. *Piazza Carignano 2. T: 011 546690, delcambio.it. Map Turin A, 6.*

€€€ **Dolce Stil Nuovo**. On the top floor of the Reggia, above the Gallery of Diana, this gourmet restaurant enjoys breathtaking views of the gardens, the Corte d'Onore and the Fontana del Cervo. Chef Alfredo Russo uses the Piedmontese tradition as a springboard for delicious leaps into creative fantasy. He also offers cooking lessons. Closed Sun evening and all day Mon. *Reggia di Venaria Reale, Piazza della Repubblica 4, Venaria Reale. T: 39 346 269 0588, dolcestilnovo.com. Map A, C2.*

€€ **Casa Vicina**. Eataly, Italy's gourmet supermarket chain created by Piedmont entepreneur Oscar Farinetti (Alba, 1954–) has become a world-renowned success since it was established in 2004. In Turin the group occupies the former Carpano vermouth plant, across Via Nizza from Lingotto. Inside the wine-red building is the country's most prestigious privately owned market, as well as innumberable places to eat—the best being this family-run establishment now in the hands of the children of the founders. Creative interpretations of

traditional recipes in a contemporary ambience. Closed Sun evening and Mon. *At Eataly, Via Nizza 230 (n Green Pea). T: 011 664 0140, casavicina.com. Beyond map Turin A, 9.*
€€ **Magorabin**. Founded in the winter of 2003 by chef Marcello Trentini and sommellier Simona Beltrami, this is one of Italy's most innovative gourmet restaurants (Trentini has a Fine Arts degree). It is also nicely priced: there is a four-course tasting menu for €50 and a €30 lunch menu—all in a building designed by Alessandro Antonelli, not far from the Mole. Lunch Tues–Sat, dinner Mon–Sat. *Corso San Maurizio 61b. T: 39 392 289 6148, magorabin. com. Map Turin B, 11.*
€ **Porto di Savona**. This popular restaurant, once the departure point of the stage coach to Liguria, boasts a warm friendly setting as well as honest, wholesome Piedmontese cuisine, including ratatouille. It was the favourite of writer and director Mario Soldati. Crowded in the evening. Lunch and dinner daily. *Piazza Vittorio Veneto 2. T: 011 817 3500, foodandcompany. com/ristorante-portodisavona. Map Turin B, 11.*
€€€ **Vintage 1997**. A good year in Piedmont: there are eleven categories of wine on the wine list— how many bottles, no one knows—at this fine (Michelin-starred) restaurant 10 minutes west of Piazza Castello on foot. The dominant colour of the interior décor is red, coupled with rich, dark boiserie. The cuisine, in contrast, is light and colourful, the presentation delightfully witty. Closed midday Sat and all day Sun. *Piazza Solferino 16h. T: 011 513 6722, T: 011 535948, vintage1997.com. Map Turin A, 6.*

CAFÉS AND CONFECTIONERS

From the 18th onwards, café society has been woven into the wider social fabric of the city of Turin, a society which has produced *bicerin*, vermouth and the *tramezzino*, all of which can be sampled in the refined splendour of the places in which they were first served.

The home of café society today is undoubtedly Piazza San Carlo, which boasts three stand-out bars with notable histories and interiors: **Caffè San Carlo** (*Piazza San Carlo 156*), which since 1822 has seen an illustrious array of artists and intellectuals sit at its tables, for example, Dumas, who drank his first glass of bicerin here; **Caffè Torino** (*Piazza San Carlo 204*), opened in 1903, has a splendid Liberty style interior featuring a gliding staircase, and sells a fine collection of chocolates and pastries; and **Stratta** (*Piazza San Carlo 191*), known as '*il salotto di Torino*', dating from 1836, is housed in the 18th century Palazzo Solaro del Borgo.

At, and around, Piazza Castello one finds **Mulassano** (*Piazza Castello 15, caffemulassano.com*), with its tasteful Liberty café (a coffered ceiling in wood and leather, mirrored walls and a countertop with onyx backsplash), staff in period attire, the place where the *tramezzino* was invented; and **Baratti & Milano** (*Piazza Castello 29–Galleria Subalpina, barattiemilano. it*), where Nietzsche regularly sought refreshment, another *Belle Époque* interior of decorative richness with bronze bas-reliefs and inlaid marble, opened in 1858 in Via Garibaldi and moved to the Galleria Subalpina in 1875; there are also the two royal retreats of

Caffè Madama (*Piazza Castello 51*), where one can enjoy refreshments within the ambience of Juvarrian Baroque; and **Caffè Reale** (*Piazzetta Reale*), which has converted rooms which once housed a royal library of esoteric books and collections of porcelain and silver. (Both these cafes can be visited independently of the museums). Five minutes on foot from Piazza Castello is **Caffè Norman** (*Via Pietro Micca, 22, normantorino.it*), in existence since 1918.

Towards Piazza Vittorio Veneto, there is **Caffè Fiorio** (*Via Po 8*), founded in 1780 and for generations the haunt of the ruling political classes; **Pasticceria Ghigo** (*Via Po 52/b, pasticceriaghigo.it*), established in 1870 as a confectioner's and dairy, this *pasticceria* is still famed for its light whipped cream known as '*fiocca*' ('snow') and hot chocolate in the winter; and **Caffè Vittorio Veneto** (*Piazza Vittorio Veneto 2*), opened its doors in 1878, and has an excellent view on to one of the largest squares in Europe, the church of Gran Madre di Dio and the hills beyond Turin

In the now newly fashionable Quadrilatero Romano, situated in front of the city's favourite church, Santuario della Consolata, there is the famous **Al Bicerin** (*Piazza della Consolata 5, bicerin.it*), which dates from 1763, and is most famous for (purportedly) inventing the three-layered chocolate drink *bicerin* (Piedmontese for 'little glass'), one part hot chocolate, one part coffee and one part cream, not to be mixed.

Along Corso Vittorio Emanuele there is **Caffè Platti** (*Corso Vittorio Emanuele II 72, platti1875.com*), which prides itself on its year of opening, 1870, the year of Italian unification, and is sometimes called the 'Principe Umberto'; it sports a wonderfully eclectic interior, at heart Liberty but with some Art Deco motifs in the 'Sala degli Specchi', a Louis XIV-style pastry shop (from which excellent pastries are served), and neo-Baroque stucco work in the 'Sala del Caffè'. It is still frequented by the Agnelli family, founders of FIAT and owners of Juventus football club.

SPECIALITY FOOD SHOPS

Turin is most famous for chocolate, wine and breads (especially breadsticks, *grissini*).

The most characteristic form of **chocolate** is the *giandujotto*; first produced in 1865, this chocolate made with paste from toasted hazelnuts (*Tonde Gentile Trilobata* from the Langhe hills) is presented in the shape of an upturned boat in an individually wrapped silver or gold paper.

This and other fine chocolates are to be found at **Baratti & Milano** at Piazza Castello 29; **Confetteria Giordano** (*Piazza Carlo Felice 69, giordanocioccolato.it*); **Peyrano Pfatisch**, Corso Vittorio Emanuele II 76 (*peyrano.com*), and **Pfatisch**, Via Sacchi 42 (*pfatisch.com*), both founded by the German Gustavo Pfatisch; the chocolate laboratory and shop **La Fabbrica del Cioccolato**, Via Cagliari 19/b, and its sister *bottega* **Guido Gobino**, Via Giuseppe Luigi Lagrande 1/a (*guidogobino.it*) are prize-winningly famous for their hazelnut chocolates and hot chocolate; **Peyrano**, Corso Moncalieri 47 (*peyrano.com*); **Stratta**, Piazza San Carlo 191 (*stratta1836.it*); and **Confetteria Avvignano**, Carlo

Felice 50 (*confetteria-avvignano. it*). And for lovers of ice cream try the experimental *gelateria* **Alberto Marchetti**, Corso Vittorio Emanuele II 24 and Via Po 35/b (*albertomarchetti. it*), which sells a granduja-flavoured creation.

For *grissini*, **breads and cakes**, try **Panificio Guala** (*Piazza Statuto 13; map Turin A,2*) and **Perino Vesco** (*Via Cavour 10; perinovesco.it*), which does a wonderful *torta langarola* (a cake made with hazelnuts, a speciality of the Langhe region).

THE ORIGIN OF GRISSINI

No plate of pasta or glass of wine is ever complete without those very moreish, long, dry, crispy breadsticks, *grissini*. Few realise, however, that they were officially invented for medicinal purposes at the Savoy court in the late 17th century.

In 1675, the court physician, Don Teobaldo Pecchio, was called by the newly-widowed Maria Giovanna Battista of Savoia-Nemours (the second 'Madama Reale'), to tend to her little son, Vittorio Amedeo, the future Vittorio Amedeo II, King of Sardinia, who had fallen ill with stomach pains due to a weak constitution and most probably due to eating only partially cooked bread (a common complaint at the time). Don Teobaldo requested that the court baker, Antonio Brunero, produce such a bread so well cooked that no bacteria could survive to trouble the boy's digestive system. Brunero's solution was to roll out the thick dough used for making the Turinese bread known as *ghersa* into very long, thin pieces, and cook them twice over: the result, *grissini*.

Napoleon dubbed the breadsticks '*les petits bâtons de Turin*' and was so fond of them that he ensured that they arrived at his dining table on a daily basis, wherever he was soldiering.

There are many varieties of *grissini*, however the two basic types are *grissino rubatà*, which is rolled, and is the type young Amedeo and Napoleon would have eaten, and the crispier *grissino stirato*, which is stretched.

For fresh pasta, there is **Pastificio Renato** (*Corso Renata Margherita 17, pastificiorenato.it; map Turin B, 12*) and **Pastificio Giustetto** (*Via Santa Teresa 19, pastificiogiustetto.it; map Turin A, 6*), and, in business since 1956, **Gallo Gastronomia & Enoteca** (*Corso Sebastopoli 161; www.gallogastronomia. com*) offers a huge range of fresh pastas (*agnolotti* a speciality), meats, cheeses and desserts.

The best **wines** come from the region of the Langhe hills: from the Nebbiolo grape. Barolo, a structured and robust wine, which goes especially well with aged cheeses, as well as red meats, and Barbaresco, a little more refined than Barolo, also sits well with red meats, around Alba and Cuneo; Dolcetto, a dry and soft wine, a well-matched accompaniment to *polenta*, from vineyards around Dogliani, Alba, Asti, Acqui and Ovada, and the more full-bodied Barbera, the object of an historic rivalry between Alba and Asti, is excellent with rustic dishes. **Enoteca Rabezzana** (*Via San Francesco Assisi 23/c; enotecarabezzana.it*), has been in business since 1911. The Rabezzana family has been producing wines near

Monferrato since 1884; **Enoteca Il Vinaio** (*Via Cibrario 38*) has over 1000 wine labels (mostly Italian and French) and a cellar full of collector's wines, especially Barolo. There is also **Il Bottigliere** (*Via San Francesco da Paola 43; map Turin A, 10*), a young-crowd wine and whisky bar, which serves plenty of appetisers; and **La Petite Cave** (*Via De Gasperi 2; map Turin A, 5*), which maintains a wide selection of Italian, French, and New World wines.

CINEMA

As befitting the first home of Italian cinema, the city of Turin is replete with art-house cinemas offering retrospectives and modern-day multiplexes showing the latest releases. Though since re-modelled as a three-screen theatre, **Cinema Lux** in the glorious Galleria San Federico (just north of Piazza San Carlo (*map Turin A, 6*) still bears the hallmarks of its Art Deco design (1934), not least the façade with its stylised scroll and foliage motifs (relatively rare in Fascist Italy when state-sponsored architectural Rationalism ruled).

The other notable cinema in the centre of town is **Massimo** (*Via Giuseppe Verdi 18, T: 011 813 8574, cinemamassimotorino.it*), which stages some of the events of the Museo Nazionale del Cinema.

SHOPPING AND MARKETS

Note: many shops are closed on Mon mornings and Sun.

Designer and high street shopping
The main shopping streets in central Turin are Via Roma, Via Lagrange, Via Carlo Alberto, Via Mazzini, Via Cavour, Via Maria Vittoria, Via Santa Teresa, Via Pietro Micca, Via Monte di Pietà, Via Garibaldi and Via Santí Agostino. The arcaded Via Roma leading to Piazza San Carlo is the natural home of high-end designer fashion, accessory and jewellery stores, while the 1km plus pedestrianised (one of the longest in Europe) Via Garibaldi (*map Turin A, 6*), leading from Piazza Castello to Piazza Statuto, offers more affordable high-street options, along with plenty of newsagents, banks, ice-cream parlours, cafés and market stalls. There is also an excellent little bookstore devoted to all things Turin, Libreria Dora Grossa, at no. 11/b.

Bookshops Along the left-hand side of Via Po (*map Turin B, 11*), from Piazza Castello leading to Piazza Vittorio Veneto, there is a run of *bancarelle* (book 'stalls') under the porticoes which sell new titles, second-hand books and out-of-print publications; plus the well-stocked bookshop Mercurio (no. 6), and La Bussola (no. 9), which specialises in remainders. The largest bookstore in the city is the three-floor La Feltrinelli (Piazza Comitato Liberazine Nazionale, just behind Piazza San Carlo; *map Turin A, 6*) and for foreign-language titles, there is Libreria Internazionale Luxemburg (*Via Cesare Battisti 7; map Turin A, 6*).

Artisanal and craft shops In the quarter of the city known as *Contrada dei Guardinfanti* (meaning 'farthingales', hoops worn under skirts by women), which encompasses Via Giuseppe Barbaroux, Via dei Mercanti and Via San Tommaso (*map Turin A, 6*), one can purchase high quality hand-made items, such as jewellery and hats, leather goods and dresses. On Via Giuseppe Barbaroux, there is, for example, the delightful Restaurant Bistrot Liù (no. 12), which mixes French and Piedmontese cuisine and doubles as a women's dressmaker's, and an art and design shop with an Indonesian flavour, Sayang Ku (no.14), which sells costume jewellery and accessories; at Via dei Mercanti no. 11/e there is the book-binder's and restorer's Bottega Fagnola (*bottegafagnola.it*).

Markets The market at Porta Palazzo (Piazza della Repubblica, *map Turin B, 3*) is the largest open-air fruit and vegetable market in Europe (*open Mon–Fri 7–1, and Sat 6.30–7.30*); there is an outdoor farmer's market (*open Mon–Fri 7–1 and Sat 7–7*) as well as various indoor markets selling meat produce (suckling pig, wild boar sausages) cheese (*toma, castelmagno*), pastries and bread (including *grissini*), fresh pasta (*agnolotti*), clothing and footwear. There is also Il Balôn and Il Gran Balôn in Borgo Dora, a regular antiques and flea market (every Sat and each second Sun of the month, *balon.it*), where one can buy craft goods, vintage clothes, old toys, second-hand books, trinkets and ornaments, furniture, etc. (There is also a Christmas market held at Borgo Dora in Dec.) Piazza della Città (*map Turin A, 2*) holds the Oltremercato (organic food products) on the fourth Sat of every month (*7–7, not July, Aug and Dec*).

FESTIVALS AND EVENTS: CITY OF TURIN

Patronal feast day
The *Festa Patronale di San Giovanni Battista* is celebrated with a 2000-strong street parade in historical costumes from Piazza Carlo Felice to Piazza Castello and culminates in a firework display (23–24 June).

Music and dance
The annual contemporary music festival *Colonia Sonora* is held in Parco della Certosa Reale, Collegno (Torino) during the summertime; Torino Jazz Festival in April/May (*torinojazzfestival. it*); Turin also hosts, alongside Milan, the *MITOSettembreMusica*, orchestral and chamber music series, Sept (*mitosettembremusica. it*); and *Torinodanza Festival* is the contemporary dance festival (Sept–Nov; *torinodanzafestival.it*).

Film and theatre The Turin Film Festival takes place at La Mole Antonelliana and Cinema Massimo (Via Giuseppe Verdi) in Nov (*www. torinofilmfest.org*).

The International Festival of Street Theatre, at sites across the city, Sept; and *Incanti,* International Figure Theatre Festival, based at Casa del Teatro, Corso Galileo Ferraris 266, Oct (*festivalincanti.it*).

The *Festival delle Colline Torinesi* (*festivaldellecolline.it*) is a summer theatre festival in town and in castles, villas, churches and villages in the hills around Turin.

Art and literature
Held at Lingotto Fiere, *Artissima* displays international contemporary art to a world audience, Nov (*artissima. it*); *Luci d'Artista*, sees the city's main squares (Piazza Castello, Piazza San Carlo, etc) and streets (Via Roma, Via Po, Via Garibaldi, etc.) illuminated by the light installations of contemporary

artists, Nov–Jan; Turin hosts the most important book fair in Italy, the annual *Salone Internazionale del Libro*, Lingotto Fiere, May (*salonelibro.it*).

Food and wine
The *Salone Internazionale del Gusto*, and its sister event *Terra Madre*, showcases the market and ethos of the Slow Food movement and its adherents, Lingotto Fiere, biennial, Oct, *salonedelgusto.it*; *CioccolaTó* celebrates the city's abiding love of chocolate, Piazza San Carlo, Nov, *cioccola-to.it*; the small one-day Moscato Wine Festival is organised by Go Wine, June.

Carnival
The main festivities take place in Parco della Pellerina (about 40mins on public transport from Piazza Castello), which is turned into a 'Luna Park' for the duration of the celebration. Here there are parades and floats, rides and games, food and drink (wine) stalls. One can sample, for instance, *bugie*, fried dough biscuits covered in icing sugar. The main attraction at the park, however, is the Street Parade, which sees the Torinesi don their *Commedia dell'arte* masks and costumes in the guises of the likes of Gianduja (a stout Piemontese farmer in a tricorn hat) and his partner Giacometta. There are chocolates named Giandujotto and Giacometta after both of these characters, who began life as puppets at the end of the 18th century.

FESTIVALS AND EVENTS: PROVINCE OF TURIN

Chieri *Nel Borgo di Landolfo*, pageant in 14th-century costume, late May; *Sagra della bagna caôda*, dedicated to the famous hot sauce of anchovies, garlic, butter and olive oil in which one dips raw vegetables, second Sunday in Nov. Chieri has its own local carnival characters, la Bela [sic] Tessiòira and Il Mangiagrop, whose investiture at the end of the first day is the highlight of the festival; allegorical floats and parades aplenty.

Moncalieri *Festa Patronale di Beato Bernardo Baden* (patron saint, Margrave of Baden, died at Moncalieri 1458), pageant in medieval costume and religious procession with reliquaries of the saint, July; Moncalieri Folk Festival, June, and the Moncalieri Jazz Festival (*www.moncalierijazz.com*), Nov; *Fera dij Subièt*, whistle and flute fair, begun by Amedeo V of Savoy in 1286 (there is also the Museo dij Subièt); *Bue Grasso* festival sees bulls, cows and calves from the region in competition for their beauty and weight, food stalls, too, second Sunday in December.

Rivoli *C'era una Volta un Re*. Historic re-enactment and celebration of the late-Baroque age of Vittorio Amedeo II, who abdicated in favour of his son Carlo Emanuele III (at Rivoli, 1730), biennial event, second week in Sept Rivoli celebrates carnival too, with a pageant rich in courtly splendour. As well as the typical processions of allegorical floats and historical parades, and its own *Palio*, there is the ceremony of the investiture of Amedeo VI of Savoy, known as *Conte Verde* due to the habit dressing himself, his knights, his horses, his pages, and all the rooms in his palaces, and his furnishings, in a (very regal) green; there is also a masquerade ball, and, to close, the *Cena dei Conti* (the 'Banquet of the Counts').

Lago Maggiore

Surrounded by picturesque snow-capped mountains, Lago Maggiore (*map B, C3*) is the second largest lake in Italy after Lake Garda. Its 121 square kilometres divide Piedmont to the west from Lombardy to the east. The north end (about one-fifth of its area), including Locarno, is in Swiss territory.

Lake Maggiore became well known at the beginning of the 19th century as a European resort, visited for its romantic scenery and good climate. The lake is often called Verbano, from the Latin *Lacus Verbanus*, a name derived from the vervain (*verbena*) that grows abundantly on its shores. The central part of the lake, around Stresa, is particularly lovely. Since the 15th century the Italian family of Borromeo have held important possessions on the lake, notably the Isole Borromée and the castle of Angera.

THE LOWER LAKE

The Simplon road from Geneva to Milan, constructed by Napoleon in 1800–5, skirts the lake's southwest shore from Sesto Calende at the southern tip. The lower reaches of the lake are largely built up and semi-industrial. There is a protected area, however, on the lakefront at **Dormelletto**, the Riserva Naturale Speciale dei Canneti, which preserves the last remaining example of lacustrine vegetation on Lake Maggiore's west shore. The reeds of Dormelletto (*Phragmites australis*) purify the water by absorbing harmful substances and, with the surrounding woodlands, offer an ideal nesting and wintering environment for well over a hundred bird species. The Villa Tesio estate, within the reserve, is famous for its thoroughbreds, particularly the Dormello-Oliata breed.

Between Dormelletto and Arona is the **Parco Naturale dei Lagoni di Mercurago**, created to protect the six moraine circles formed around Lake Maggiore during the last ice age. The great forests that characterise this protected area consist mainly of oak, birch, pine and alder, chestnut and black locust. The wetlands are home to a precious water and marsh flora that includes the tiny, carnivorous *Utricularia vulgaris*, the white water lily and the sundew, another carnivorous plant. The wetlands of the park offer habitat for the many bird species that breed, winter or migrate through the area. Four self-guided trails—blue (wetlands), red (woods), purple (archaeology) and orange (trades)—offer educational insights into the park, and there is a 10km-long bicycle trail.

LAGO MAGGIORE

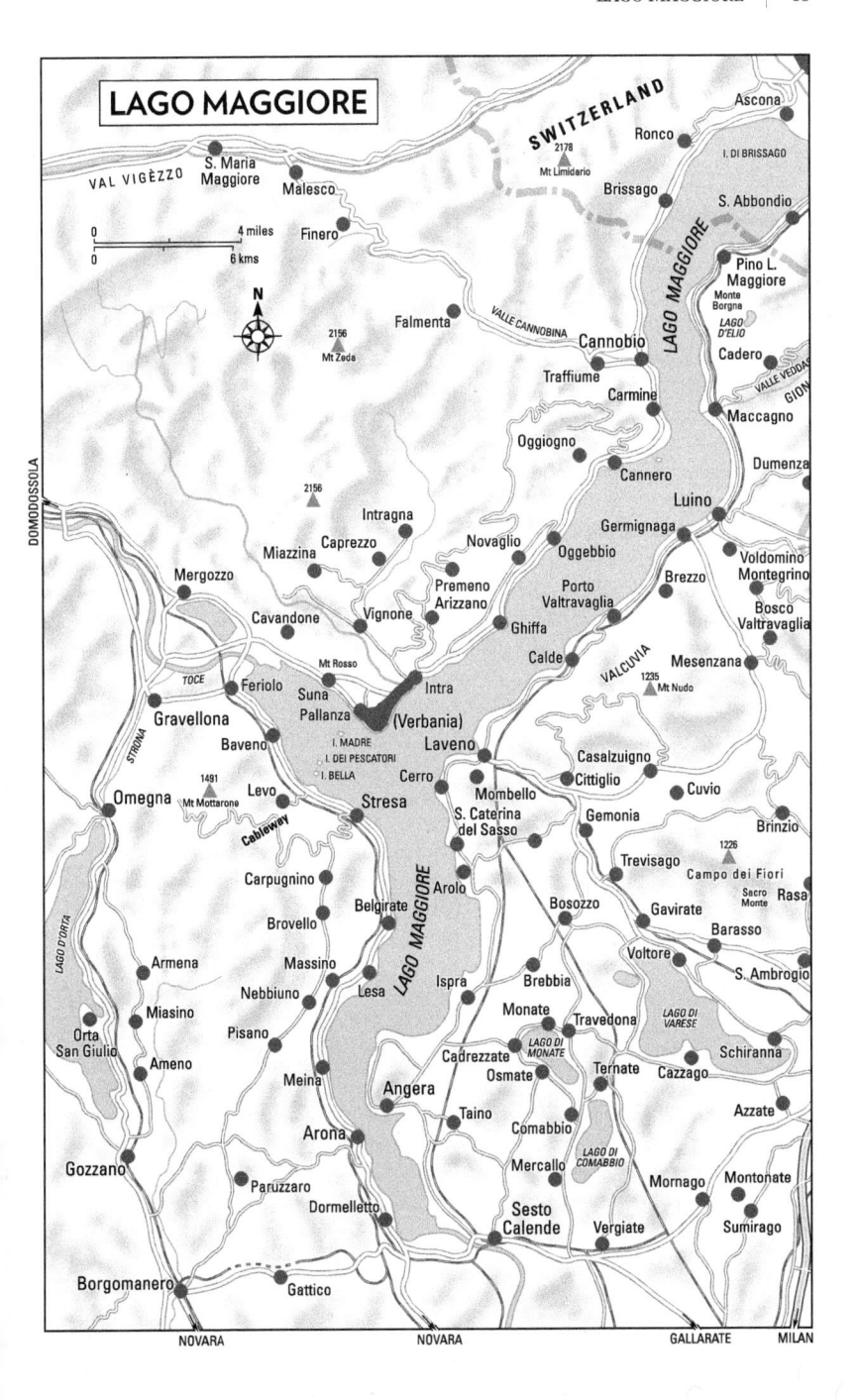

ARONA

Arona is an ancient town looking across the lake to Angera; in the past it was an important market centre handling trade between the Po River Valley and the Canton Ticino in Switzerland. It came under Visconti rule in 1277, and was a fief of the Borromeo from 1439 to 1797.

The town centre

From the little park on the waterfront, near the ferry landing, there are excellent views of Angera on the Lombard side of the lake. Parallel to the waterfront is Via Cavour, the shopping street, and above that (access along narrow lanes) opens the cobbled Piazza San Graziano. Here, in a wing of the former covered market hall, is **Archeo Museo**, a small archaeology museum (*Piazza San Graziano 34; open Tues 10–12, Sat–Sun 3.30–6.30; archeomuseo.it*). Its collection covers the lower part of Lake Maggiore, with finds from the Bronze Age Lagoni di Mercurago site (*described above*) and from a Gallic necropolis recently discovered at Dormelletto, together with Roman glass from the Tomba Gentilizia at Gravellona Toce and material from the Golasecca culture. Known for their burial sites in this area of Italy, the people used an alphabet known as Lepontic and buried their dead in black pottery vessels with incised decoration. Their civilisation spanned the Bronze and Iron ages and numerous metal artefacts (tools, weapons and ornaments) have been found.

From Piazza San Graziano a stepped street leads up past the yellow and white church of the **Santi Martiri** (*often closed*), which has an altarpiece by Bergognone. It was here that St Charles Borromeo celebrated his last Mass. Above it, in Piazza de Filippi (turn right) is the **Collegiata**, the main church of Arona, dedicated to the Virgin of the Nativity (Santa Maria Nascente). The lunette over the main door has a charming 15th-century relief of the Holy Family. At the head of the north aisle is a beautiful early polyptych (1511) by Gaudenzio Ferrari (*see p. 71*), showing the influence of Perugino. The central scene shows the *Nativity* (with a particularly beautiful lute-playing angel). In the panel above is God the Father and in the predella, Christ and the Apostles. The kneeling figure on the right is thought to be Veronica Borromeo, grandmother of St Charles Borromeo. Six canvases by Morazzone showing scenes from the life of the Virgin are displayed in three of the side chapels (dark and difficult to see): *Visitation* and *Nativity* in the first chapel on the left; *Marriage of the Virgin* and *Annunciation* in the second; and the *Adoration of the Magi* and *Adoration of the Shepherds* in the second right. St Charles Borromeo was baptised here in 1538.

Via Cavour leads into the attractive, arcaded **Piazza del Popolo**, with restaurants and cafés and more splendid views of Angera, where the church of Santa Maria di Loreto (1592), with a fine façade approached by a double stairway, is attributed to Pellegrino Tibaldi (although this has been disputed). The interior contains a replica of the Holy House of Loreto. The former Palazzo di Giustizia on the piazza (also known as the Broletto) dates from the 15th century. It has brick arcades borne on stone pillars and (damaged) terracotta busts of members of the Visconti family, under whom it was built.

Parco della Rocca

At the north end of town is the Parco della Rocca, which can be accessed on foot. A Borromeo fortress once stood on the high cliff here, the companion to the surviving fortress of Angera. Between them they controlled access to the lake. It was in the Arona fortress that St Charles Borromeo was born in 1538. It was destroyed by Napoleonic troops in 1800 and the 18th-century **Villa Ponti** on Via San Carlo, built for a Flemish merchant, now occupies part of its grounds. It can be hired for events and it also hosts exhibitions and concerts during the Settimane Musicali di Stresa international music festival. The lovely garden follows a classical design featuring beech and silver cedar trees, and magnolias, azaleas and rhododendron.

The Colosso di San Carlo Borromeo

To the north of Arona, on Via Verbano above the main lakeside road, stands the **Colosso di San Carlo Borromeo**, a colossal copper statue of Arona's most famous son (*open March–Dec at differing times, closed Jan–Feb; for up-to-date opening hours, see statuasancarlo.it*). Standing 23m high, on a pedestal 12m tall, it was commissioned from Giovanni Battista Crespi (Il Cerano) by a relative of the saint and completed in 1697. Popularly called *San Carlone*, it is second in size only to the Statue of Liberty in New York. It can be climbed by steps and an internal stair; there are lookout holes in his ears, eyes, nose and shoulders.

ST CHARLES BORROMEO

Charles Borromeo (1538–84) was born in the castle of Arona and from an early age was destined for the Church. He studied Law and Theology at the University of Pavia and after that was summoned to Rome by his uncle Pius IV, who sped him on in his career, creating him Cardinal in 1560 and Archbishop of Milan in 1564. Charles Borromeo was one of the leading lights of the Counter-Reformation, in 1562 spurring on his uncle to re-convoke the Council of Trent, which had broken up in disarray a decade previously. Many reforms to religious orders, the clergy and the liturgy were introduced by Borromeo. He also inaugurated a sweeping programme of rebuilding and extending churches, employing a coterie of favourite architects (notably Pellegrino Tibaldi) and painters. He was ruthless in his persecution of Protestants, notably in the Valtellina. However, during an outbreak of plague in 1576 he did much for the poor and destitute, selling goods and property and turning his money over to charitable causes, an action which made him greatly loved. Miracles were attributed to him and he was beatified in 1602, just 18 years after his death. Canonisation followed in 1610. His body lies, magnificently robed, in the crypt of the Duomo of Milan.

MEINA AND BELGIRATE

The splendid neo-Neoclassical **Villa Faraggiana**, overlooking the lake just before the centre of Meina (*Strada Statale Sempione 23*), its gateway guarded by lions, stands in the midst of a seven-hectare park. It was built in 1855 and gives a vivid idea of the lives that were being led in the early heyday of the resort.

Pretty **Belgirate** is said to derive its name ('Lovely Curves') from its location at the tip of the promontory that separates the lower basin of Lake Maggiore from the Borromeo Gulf. The Romanesque church of Santa Maria with its tall, slender bell tower is a landmark on the lake. In the 19th century the villas of Belgirate were frequented by poets, patriots, and statesmen; the town crops up in an unusual number of literary works, beginning with Stendhal's *Charterhouse of Parma*.

STRESA

The most important place on the west side of the lake is Stresa, nestled in a charming position on the south shore of the Gulf of Pallanza. Mentioned in the Middle Ages as Strixia ('small strip of land'), in the 15th century it was transformed from a small fishing village to a seat of the powerful Visconti and, later, Borromeo families. It became fashionable as a European resort in the mid-19th century (Stendhal, Charles Dickens and Lord Byron stayed here).

The Stresa waterfront

South of the ferry landing is **Villa Pallavicino**, built in 1855 for Queen Margherita and King Umberto I, with a small formal garden at the front of the house. It is surrounded by a fine wooded park (*open mid-March–early Nov daily from 10am; isoleborromee.it/parco-pallavicino*) planted with palms, magnolias and cedars and with a zoological garden.

Further along the lakefront, past the Town Hall and Pasticceria Bolongaro (*see p. 59*) is the pale-peach-and-grey former **Villa Ducale**, an 18th-century edifice that once belonged to the philosopher Antonio Rosmini (1797–1855). It is now a study centre and museum devoted to Rosmini, who founded an order of charity in 1852 (the Rosminian College is above the town). Beyond the grand Regina Palace Hotel, which opened in 1908, is the huge monumental **Hotel des Iles Borromées**, which has had many famous guests since it opened in 1863. Frederick Henry in Hemingway's *Farewell to Arms* also stayed here.

ABOVE STRESA: MOTTARONE

Above Stresa is **Monte Mottarone** (1491m). At present it can be reached by road, while the Funivia Stresa-Mottarone cableway is being rebuilt. In May 2021 one of the cables snapped and a cablecar plummeted to the ground, resulting in the deaths of 14 of the 15 passengers, an appalling tragedy which shocked the community deeply. The cableway replaces a funicular inaugurated in 1911.

Halfway up the mountain is Alpino (803m), from where you can walk to the Giardino Alpinia (605m), a botanical garden founded in 1933, with some 544 species of Alpine plants (*open April–mid-Oct Tues–Sun 9–6*). Here a private toll road, owned by the Borromeo since 1623 (9km; always open), continues through the meadows, woods and summer pastures of the Parco del Mottarone.

At the summit (1385m), beyond the little chapel of the Madonna of the Snow, there is the Alpyland bobsleigh piste. The Albergo Eden offers refreshments (there is an outdoor terrace where you can sit overlooking the lake far below). The summit of Mt Mottarone commands truly breathtaking views of the whole chain of the Alps from Monte Viso in the west to the Ortles and Adamello in the east, and the Monte Rosa group especially conspicuous to the northwest. Below, on a clear day you can make out seven lakes and the wide Po Valley. Even on hazy days the prospect is majestic, with layer upon layer of peaks and arêtes revealed to your view.

In the village of **Gignese**, the local industry of umbrella-making is recorded in the Museo dell'Ombrello (*www.gignese.it/museo*), founded in 1939, which has a collection of umbrellas and parasols going back many centuries. It also explores the history of the boy apprentices who were sent from home to learn their trade from the ages of just seven or eight.

HILAIRE BELLOC ON LAKE MAGGIORE

The English author Hilaire Belloc, who visited Lago Maggiore in 1902, left this impression of a beauty so intense as to seem almost immoral: 'The Italian lakes have that in them and their air which removes them from common living. Their beauty is not the beauty which each of us sees for himself in the world; it is rather the beauty of a special creation; the expression of some mind. To eyes innocent, and freshly noting our great temporal inheritance—I mean to the eyes of a boy and girl just entered upon the estate of this glorious earth, and thinking themselves immortal, this shrine of Europe might remain for ever in the memory; an enchanted experience, in which the single sense of sight had almost touched the boundary of music. They would remember these lakes as the central emotion of their youth. To mean men also, who, in spite of years and of a full foreknowlege of death, yet attempt nothing but the satisfaction of sense, and pride themselves upon the taste and fineness with which they achieve this satisfaction, the Italian lakes would seem a place for habitation, and there such a man might build his house contentedly. But to ordinary Christians I am sure there is something unnatural in this beauty of theirs, and they find it in either a paradise only to be won by a much longer road or a bait and veil of sorcery, behind which lies great peril. Now, for all we know, beauty beyond the world may not wear this double aspect; but to us on earth—if we are ordinary men—beauty of this kind has something evil. Have you not read in books how men when they see even divine visions are terrified? So as I looked at Lake Major in its halo I also was afraid, and I was glad to cross the ridge and crest of the hill and to shut out that picture framed all round with glory.'

BAVENO

Baveno, a short way further up the lake from Stresa, is in a fine position on the south shore of the Gulf of Pallanza, opposite the Isole Borromee and with fine views of the

Isola dei Pescatori. The landing stage has attractive Art Nouveau wrought ironwork. The shore road from Stresa is flanked by villas and hotels built in the 19th century when the town was well known as a resort. Among these is the red-brick, turreted **Villa Branca** (or Villa Maria), built in 1872, where Queen Victoria spent the spring of 1879. Partially destroyed by fire in 2007, it has now been restored.

Above the waterfront is a pretty little cobbled square, **Piazza della Chiesa**, on which are grouped the church and its baptistery, and an arcade with painted Stations of the Cross. The church, dedicated to Sts Gervase and Protase, has a fine Romanesque portal and bell-tower. The **baptistery** is entered under a Renaissance porch, though its internal structure is much older. The interior is frescoed with scenes from the life of St John the Baptist, with God the Father, the Evangelists and Doctors of the Church in the dome. Also on the square (*Piazza della Chiesa 8*) is an exhibition room entitled **Granum**, a small museum of the pink granite which is quarried here. Behind Baveno to the northwest rises Monte Camoscio (890m), with large quarries, a defining aspect of Baveno from a distance. As you return from the church square to the waterfront, note the **sculpture of a quarryman**, shown seated and chipping at a lump of rock.

THE ISOLE BORROMEE

This group of beautiful little islands is named after the Italian Borromeo family, who still own the Isola Madre, Isola Bella and Isola San Giovanni. There are regular daily boat services for Isola Bella, Isola dei Pescatori and Isola Madre from Stresa, Baveno, Pallanza and Intra.

ISOLA BELLA
This is the most famous of the islands. It was just a barren rock with a small church and a few cottages before it was almost totally occupied by a huge palace with terraced gardens built in 1631–71 by Angelo Crivelli for Count Carlo III Borromeo, in honour of his wife, Isabella d'Adda, from whom it takes its name. The island measures just 320m by 180m, and there is a tiny hamlet by the pier outside the garden gates: no longer a true hamlet, its winding narrow streets are now filled with restaurants, cafés and gift shops (the Borromeo have their own line of products). A combined ticket gives admission to the palace and gardens (*open late March–late Oct daily 9–5.30; isoleborromee.it*).

The palace
To the left of the pier is the vast grey **palace**, entered from an open courtyard with four palm trees and tiny cobbles. On the right of the courtyard is the chapel, which contains three family tombs (seen through a grille) with elaborate carvings by sculptors including Benedetto Briosco and Bambaia, brought from demolished churches in Milan. On the left of the courtyard is the entrance to the palace. Twenty-five rooms on the *piano nobile*, decorated with Murano chandeliers and Venetian

mosaic floors, can be visited (the three floors above are the private apartments of the Borromeo family). The English historian Edward Gibbon stayed here as a guest of the Borromeo in 1764.

The octagonal blue-and-white **Sala dei Concerti** was built in 1948–51 in Baroque style following the original plans. There is a view of the Isola dei Pescatori and (*right*) the Isola Madre. The **Sala di Musica** has musical instruments, two Florentine cabinets in ebony and semi-precious stones (17th–18th centuries), and paintings by Jacopo Bassano and Tempesta. In 1935 a conference took place here between Mussolini and the French and British governments in an attempt to guarantee the peace of Europe. Napoleon and Josephine stayed in the next room in 1797. The **library** preserves, besides its books, some paintings by Carlevalis. Another room has paintings by Luca Giordano, and beyond a room with views of the Borromeo properties, by Zuccarelli, is the ballroom.

Stairs lead down to the **grottoes** built on the lake in the 18th century. Beyond a room with 18th–20th-century puppets (once used in puppet shows held in the 'amphitheatre' in the garden) are six grottoes encrusted with shells, pebbles, marble, etc. Displayed here are statues by Gaetano Matteo Monti and the remains of an ancient boat found in the lake off Angera. A spiral staircase in an old tower that predates the palace leads up to a short corridor of mirrors and from there to the **anticamera**, with a ceiling tondo attributed to Giovanni Battista Tiepolo and two paintings by Daniele Crespi. Beyond the chapel of St Charles Borromeo is the **gallery of tapestries**, with a splendid collection of 16th-century Flemish tapestries commissioned by St Charles Borromeo. The painting of *St Jerome* is by Moretto.

The gardens

The famous gardens, inhabited by white peacocks, are composed of terraces built out into the lake (an extraordinary sight from the water). Soil for the plants had to be brought from the mainland. A double staircase leads up onto a terrace with a huge camphor tree, camellias, bamboos, breadfruit, sugar cane, tapioca and tea and coffee plants. Beyond is the 'amphitheatre', an elaborate Baroque construction with statues, niches, pinnacles and stairs, crowned by a unicorn (the family emblem). The terrace at the top looks straight to Stresa, and below is the Italianate garden with box hedges and yew, and ten terraces planted with roses, oleanders and pomegranates descending to the lake. Other parts of the garden are laid out in the English style, with beds of tulips and forget-me-nots in spring and geraniums in summer. Below the terraces are rhododendrons and orange trees (protected in winter). The azaleas are at their best during April and May. The second exit leads out of the gardens through the delightful old-fashioned greenhouse.

ISOLA DEI PESCATORI

The Isola dei Pescatori, also known as Isola Superiore, is not owned by the Borromeo. Between it and Isola Bella is a tiny islet, Isolotto della Malghera, inhabited by cormorants in winter. Isola dei Pescatori is on regular ferry routes all year round. Once home to a pretty little fishing village, this has now been given over almost exclusively to tourism. Nevertheless, with its church tower and cluster of houses, it is an extremely picturesque sight, especially when seen from the water, or from Baveno, with snow-capped mountains behind. There are souvenir shops here, as well as restaurants and places to stay. The island makes a good place for a boat trip, stopping for lunch before catching the ferry back—or on, to the next destination.

ISOLA MADRE

The Isola Madre is nearer to Pallanza than to Stresa. It is entirely occupied by a Borromeo villa and **botanical garden** (*open late March–end Oct daily 9–5.30; isoleborromee.it*) and inhabited only by a custodian. It has one restaurant. The landscaped gardens, at their best in April, are laid out in the English manner and were replanted in the 1950s by the botanist Henry Cocker. The particularly mild climate allows a great number of exotic and tropical plants to flourish here. Viale Africa, with the warmest exposure, is lined with a variety of plants, including citrus fruits. The camellia terrace has numerous species of camellia and mimosa. Beyond a wisteria-covered arboured walk is the Mediterranean garden and a rock garden. The cylindrical tower was once used as an ice house; beyond it are ferns. From the little port with its boathouse (and an 18th-century boat suspended from the roof) is a view of Pallanza. Nearby is the oldest camellia on the island (thought to be some 150 years old). On a lawn is a group of taxodium trees, with their roots sticking up above ground—an odd sight; there are more of them on the tip of Isola Bella, facing Isola dei Pescatori—and beyond are banks of azaleas, rhododendrons, camphor trees and ancient magnolias. Beside steps up to the villa, by a remarkable Kashmir cypress— said to be 200 years old—is an aviary with parrots that nest in the cedar of Lebanon here. Near the villa are ornamental banana trees and the Art Nouveau family chapel. The terrace by the villa is planted with tall palm trees, including a majestic Chilean palm, planted in 1858, which bears miniature edible coconuts. The steps nearby are covered with a trellis of kiwi fruit.

The 18th-century **villa** is also open to the public. It contains 17th- and 18th-century furnishings from Borromeo properties and servants' livery, as well as a collection of porcelain, puppets and dolls (19th-century French and German) and paintings by Pitocchetto. The little theatre dates from 1778.

VERBANIA

Sprawling Verbania, across the lake from Baveno and Stresa, is the largest town on Lago Maggiore. It takes its name from the alternative name of the lake, Verbano, and is in fact an amalgamation of two settlements, Pallanza and Intra. It can be reached by boat from Stresa and Baveno and has boat connections to the islands. The road to Verbania from Baveno follows the curve of the lake across the Toce river and its nature reserve.

PALLANZA

Pallanza occupies the promontory of the Punta della Castagnola, on the slopes of

Monte Rosso (697m). The western part of it is known as Suna. Pallanza's waterfront is in a charming position in full view of the Isole Borromee, facing west, which makes it a particularly good place to sit with a drink in the evening. It has a mild climate which makes the flora particularly luxuriant; the lakefront is planted with magnolias.

The main waterfront square is **Piazza Garibaldi**. In the park here is a WWI monument of a widow holding her child and offering a rose in memory of her fallen husband. It is the work of Paolo Troubetzkoy (*see below*). Beyond it, right on the water, is Marcello Piacentini's mausoleum of Marshal Cadorna (1850–1928), Italian Chief of Staff during the first 30 months of the First World War and a native of Pallanza.

Next to the Town Hall, Via Ruga leads inland (and uphill) to the **Museo del Paesaggio** in the Baroque Palazzo Viani-Dugnani (*Via Ruga 44; museodelpaesaggio. it*), founded in 1914 and containing a beautifully displayed collection of sculptures and plaster models by Paolo Troubetzkoy. The model for his WWI monument here in Pallanza is here, as well as for the monument to Cadorna (different from the mausoleum) that also stands on the main waterfront square. Troubetzkoy was born in Intra and spent his summers here in Pallanza, on the bay of Suna. There is also a room with sculptures by Arturo Martini. Upstairs is the collection of paintings, including some by Sophie Browne (*see below*) and by Mario Tozzi, whose frescoes can be seen in the church of Santa Lucia in Suna.

At the end of Piazza Garibaldi, where the street becomes Corso Zanitello, a street and steps lead up to the church of **San Leonardo** (16th century; modernised in the 19th century), the tall tower of which was completed by Pellegrino Tibaldi in 1589.

On the Punta della Castagnola headland

From the Pallanza waterfront a road curves round the Punta della Castagnola. It is one-way for cars coming in the other direction, but there is a pedestrian and bicycle lane (bikes can be hired outside the ferry landing stage). There are views from here of the **Isolino di San Giovanni** (*no public access*). The villa on the island was once the summer home of Toscanini. The **Villa Giulia** (1882; signed) or Kursaal, built in 1847 by Bernardino Branca (who invented the Fernet Branca liqueur) has fine gardens, open to the public.

The **Hotel Majestic** opened in 1870. Around the headland is the **Villa San Remigio**, built in 1903 and still privately owned (but available for rent; *villasanremigio.it*). The formal gardens, when they were laid out in 1905 by Sophie Browne, an Irish painter, and her husband, the marquess Silvio della Valle di Casanova, were among the best in northern Italy, with topiary terraces, fountains, and statues by Orazio Marinali, who produced much of the statuary for the Palladian villas near Vicenza.

Next to Villa San Remigio is the 19th-century **Villa Taranto**, with famous botanical gardens (*open mid-March–end Oct; villataranto.it*)—the villa has a landing stage served by regular boat services. The huge estate was bought in 1930 by the Scotsman Captain Neil McEacharn (1884–1964), ex-army officer, botanist and heir to a considerable fortune, which he poured into creating these gardens. Together with head gardener Henry Cocker, he created a garden with an outstanding collection of exotic plants from all over the world, which he later donated to the Italian state. The plants include magnolias (at their best at the beginning of April), superb camellias (which flower in April), rhododendrons (which flower May–June), azaleas and paulownias (best in May). The herbaceous borders and dahlias (over 300 varieties) are at their best in July and August. Birches, maples and conifers distinguish the woodlands. There is a very pleasant café and bar beside a shallow pool. Here too is McEacharn's mausoleum, where his tomb-chest is surrounded by beautiful stained-glass windows of flowers of all seasons. There is no access to the villa itself, which has been much altered and now houses local government offices.

Off the main road across the promontory between Pallanza and Intra, on Viale Giuseppe Azari, is the fine church of the **Madonna di Campagna**, consecrated in 1547. Its exterior is remarkable for the fine octagonal arcaded lantern drum. Inside are 16th-century decorations (notably works attributed to Carlo Urbini, Aurelio Luini and Gerolamo Lanino).

Where the main road meets the water again, this time facing the Lombard side of the lake, is a public park and sandy beach with the attractive **Villa Maioni**, now the public library. Next to it is the **Il Maggiore** concert hall and events space (Salvador Pérez Arroyo, 2016), with its billowing zinc roofs. The café here has lovely views across the lake to the cable car going vertically up the Sasso del Ferro.

Above Verbania is the **Parco Nazionale della Val Grande** (*see p. 64*), a protected mountainous area with fine walks.

INTRA

Intra occupies a valley floor created by the San Bernardino and San Giovanni torrents. It has an attractive old centre. From here a car ferry (every 20mins) crosses the lake to Laveno on the opposite shore. The **Casa del Lago** (*Via Felice Cavallotti 16; lacasadellago.it*) is an interactive museum exploring the history of the lake and its traditional industries. To the north, close to the lake, are the beautiful private gardens of the Villa Poss and Villa Ada. Roads lead up to Miazzina (719m) at the foot of Monte Zeda (2188m), and Premeno (802m), a winter and summer resort.

GHIFFA

The road skirts the lake to Ghiffa. The lake reaches its greatest depth (372m) just off this point. From the waterfront in the centre of Ghiffa, between the Town Hall (Municipio) and the ferry landing, Via Marconi leads to a series of winding lanes which turn into a cobbled track through chestnut woods up to the Sacro Monte della Santissima Trinità di Ghiffa (30mins). The journey can also be accomplished by car up Via Santissima Trinità.

The Sacro Monte

The Sacro Monte complex consists of the main sanctuary chapel, three further chapels and a portico with the Via Crucis. The **Sanctuary** stands on the site of the original Romanesque oratory. Work began on enlarging it in 1605. Its portico faces the **Chapel of the Coronation of the Virgin** (1647), an octagon with a rectangular apse. The interior is whitewashed, with a terracotta group of the *Coronation of the Virgin* and terracotta prophets and saints.

Behind the Sanctuary is the **Chapel of St John the Baptist** (1659), octagonal in three tiers. You can process around it and, through a barred window, see the dramatic statue group of St John baptising Christ in the River Jordan. Symbolically, the chapel is built above a water cistern.

The chapel of the Coronation and of the Baptism are linked by the **Porticato della Via Crucis**, made up of 14 arches on stone columns, with scenes from Christ's Passion in moulded and painted terracotta with frescoed backgrounds. It was added in 1752.

The third chapel, the **Chapel of Abraham**, is a bit further away from the others (signed). It takes the form of a Greek Cross with a small rectangular portico (1701–3). Within, a sculptural group represents three angels appearing to Abraham, a scene which is interpreted as foreshadowing the Holy Trinity.

The Sacro Monte enjoys spectacular views of the lake and the Lombard Alps. A trail leads into the adjacent forest preserve, deciduous woodland with a prevalence of chestnut accompanied by maple, ash, alder and birch, as well as exotic species such as white pine. The fauna includes deer, badgers, foxes, squirrels, martens, weasels and black woodpeckers. Adjacent to the Porticato is an attractive restaurant.

THE SACRI MONTI

The *Sacri Monti* ('Holy Mountains') of northern Italy, groupings of 16th–17th-century chapels and shrines, were conceived as bastions of the Counter-Reformation strategically located at the border between the Roman Catholic Mediterranean and the lands of Calvin and Zwingli beyond the Alps. In 2003 UNESCO added the Sacri Monti of Piedmont and Lombardy to its World Heritage List, because 'in addition to their symbolic spiritual meaning, they are of great beauty by virtue of the skill with which they have been integrated into the surrounding natural landscape of hills, forests and lakes. They also house much important artistic material in the form of wall paintings and statuary.' The settings of the seven major *Sacri Monti* of Piedmont (Belmonte, Crea, Domodossola, Ghiffa, Oropa, Orta and Varallo) have been designated nature reserves in an effort to ensure the historical and artistic preservation of the monuments and to safeguard the surrounding environment.

BEYOND GHIFFA

The little 13th-century church of **Novaglio**, above the road north of Ghiffa, is built in a mixture of Lombard and Gothic styles; it offers lovely views of the lake from its lovely green knoll. Above **Oggebbio** in chestnut groves is the little oratory of Cadessino, with 15th–16th-century frescoes. Ahead, across the lake, Luino comes into view, as, beneath Oggiogno high up on its rock, the road passes the villa of the statesman Massimo d'Azeglio (1798–1866), who effectively launched Camillo Cavour on his career, but fell out with him shortly afterwards. He retired from public office as a result, and spent his latter years writing his memoirs here. **Cannero Riviera** is a resort lying in a sheltered and sunny position at the foot of Monte Carza (1118m). Off the coast are two rocky islets on which stood the castles of Malpaga, demolished by the Visconti in 1414. One island is now occupied by the picturesque ruins of a castle built by Ludovico Borromeo in 1519–21. On the hill above the town is the 14th–15th-century church of Carmine Superiore, built on the summit of a precipice. It has some ceiling paintings and a triptych of the 14th-century Lombard school.

CANNOBIO

Cannobio, at the windy top end of the lake, has ancient origins and preserves some medieval buildings. Its stone-paved waterfront promenade (Via Magistris), lined with attractive colourful houses, their ground floors occupied by shops and restaurants, is extremely pleasant. In high season a boat leaves from here for the Wednesday market at Luino. At the end of Via Magistris, just behind the waterfront, is the **Santuario della Pietà** (reconstructed in 1583–1601), with a fine altarpiece of the *Way to Calvary* by Gaudenzio Ferrari (*see p. 71*). The church also has paintings on the wall of the nave, by Francesco Antonio Petrolino, showing the miraculous shedding of blood and the dropping of a rib by the venerated icon here, which once hung on the wall of a tavern but, since the miracle, has been housed in the high altar of this sanctuary, built on the site where the tavern stood.

The old kernel of town further inland, around Via Giovanola, has the high belltower and stout stone building of the old Palazzo della Ragione, known as **Il Parasio**, a 13th-century building with 17th-century alterations.

ORRIDO DI SANT'ANNA
Inland from Cannobio is the Val Cannobina. To get there, follow signs to Traffiume and then to Orrido. The road leads past waterfalls to a car park beside a miniature hump-backed bridge and the oratory of the Madonna di Loreto and St Anne, with a roof tiled in large *piode*. This beautiful spot is the Orrido di Sant'Anna, a romantic gorge with a stream at the bottom. At this point the stream passes through a wide cavern to form a pool and cataracts. There is a very pleasant restaurant here.

Just beyond Cannobio is the frontier with Switzerland. The road goes on via Brissago to Ascona and Locarno, which are famous for their climate and views.

THE EAST (LOMBARD) SIDE OF THE LAKE

LUINO AND LAVENO
Luino is the most important centre on the Lombard side of the lake. A small industrial town, it lies a little north of the junction of the Tresa and Margorabbia,

which unite to flow into the lake at Germignaga. Near the landing stage is a statue of Garibaldi, commemorating his attempt, on 14th August 1848, to renew the struggle against Austria with only 1,500 men, after the armistice that followed the defeat of Custozza. The Town Hall occupies an 18th-century *palazzo* by Felice Soave. An *Adoration of the Magi*, attributed to Bernardino Luini, who was probably born here, decorates the cemetery church of San Pietro, and the Madonna del Carmine has frescoes by his pupils (1540). The little Museo Civico Archeologico Paleontologico (*Via Dante 6; T: 033 253 2057*) has local antiquities, minerals and fossils, and a small painting collection. A market has been held in the town on Wednesdays since 1541. On the landward side of the town is the railway station where the Swiss line from Bellinzona meets the Italian line from Novara and Milan. This was an important frontier station (with custom-house) on the St Gotthard line.

Between Luino and Laveno is **Caldè**, interesting when seen from the water for its row of disused lime kilns, now decorated with colourful murals by street artists.

Laveno, now part of the municipality of Mombello, is in a fine position on the lake, with good views of the Punta della Castagnola and the Isola Madre in the distance. Its small port serves the car ferry to Intra. The old-fashioned railway station of the Milano-Nord line for Varese and Milan (one of two stations in Laveno) adjoins the ferry station. A monument in the piazza by the waterside commemorates the *garibaldini* who fell in an attempt to capture the town from the Austrians in 1859 (the Austrian fort was on the Punta di San Michele). The town was once noted for its ceramics and there is a ceramics museum, MIDeC (Museo Internazionale Design Ceramico) in the adjacent village of **Cerro** (*Lungolago Perabò 5; midec.org*).

LEGGIUNO AND SANTA CATERINA DEL SASSO

The road follows the shore of the lake past the ceramics museum at Cerro (*see above*) and **Leggiuno**, where the Oratory of Santi Primo e Feliciano (9th century) has Roman foundations. The solitary convent of **Santa Caterina del Sasso** (reached in 10mins by a steep path that descends from the main road, or by boat from Laveno or Stresa in high season) was founded in the 13th century and reinhabited by Dominicans in 1986 (*opening times vary according to the time of year; for up-to-date hours, see santacaterinadelsasso.com*). It is spectacularly built into a sheer rockface directly above the lake (there is an 18m drop to the water). The picturesque Romanesque buildings, particularly attractive when seen from the water, were restored in 1624 and have a good view of the Gulf of Pallanza and the Isole Borromee. They contain 15th- and 16th-century frescoes and a 17th-century *Last Supper*.

ISPRA, ANGERA AND SESTO CALENDE

Ispra is the seat of Euratom, the first centre in Italy for nuclear studies. **Angera** has a pleasant spacious waterfront planted with horse chestnuts. A road (signposted) leads up to the Rocca Borromeo (*isoleborromee.it/en/rocca-di-angera*). Formerly a castle of the Visconti, it passed to the Borromeo in 1449 and is still owned by them. It was extensively restored in the 16th–17th centuries. The fine gateway leads into a charming courtyard with a pergola open to the south end of the lake. Off the second courtyard is a wine press dating from 1745. The Sala di Giustizia has interesting

14th-century Gothic frescoes commissioned by Giovanni Visconti, Bishop of Milan, with signs of the zodiac and episodes from the battles of Archbishop Ottone Visconti. In other rooms are displayed paintings, Roman altars, and detached frescoes from Palazzo Borromeo in Milan. It also has a doll and toy museum, and you can climb the 13th-century Torre Castellana. In Via Mazzini, for grappa lovers, is a distillery dating from 1850.

Sesto Calende is the southernmost town on the east bank of the lake. It is said to derive its name from its market day in Roman times—the sixth day before the Calends. A small Museo Civico (*irregular opening times; T: 033 192 8160, www.comune.sesto-calende.va.it*) houses archaeological finds from tombs of the local Golasecca culture (800–450 BC).

LAGO MAGGIORE PRACTICAL TIPS

GETTING AROUND

- **By bus:** The Piedmont side of the lake is served by buses operated by VCO TRASPORTI (*vcotrasporti.it*) See the website for routes and details. Other services are operated by SAF (*safduemila.com*), who also run a shuttle service between Lake Maggiore and Milan's Malpensa airport, in April–Oct.
- **By rail:** The EuroCity train service from Milan (Stazione Centrale) to Geneva, Bern and Basel passes through Stresa (55mins). There is also a direct regional service from Milan (Stazione Centrale) to Stresa (1hr 8mins) and Verbania-Pallanza (1hr 15mins). For timetables, see trenitalia.it.
- **By boat:** For information about **ferry routes** and timetables on the lake, visit the Navigazione Laghi (*www.navigazionelaghi.it*). Routes tend to be organised in three separate clusters: Arona and Angera; the central lake (Stresa, Baveno and the islands); and Cannobio and the north. A number of other companies also run ferry services. Their booking offices are by the waterside in all the main ports. These can be particularly useful out of season, when the Navigazione Laghi ferries (known as 'ferries of the line') are running to sparser timetables. The local custom is to dock the boats by nudging the prows right up onto the hard. **Private boats** can be hired from a number of companies. A reliable one, in Verbania (very close to the Il Maggiore events space), is Rent Boat Lago Maggiore (Nautica Bego; *Via dalla Chiesa 6, rentboatlagomaggiore.com*).

WHERE TO STAY

ARONA
€€ **Giardino Segreto**. Nicely appointed apartment in a pleasant little house with a secluded garden and tennis court. *Piazza del Popolo 17ilgiardinosegretoarona.com*.

CANNOBIO
€€ **Pironi**. Twelve individually furnished rooms in a 15th-century building in the heart of the old town,

and an 18th-century fresco in the breakfast room, are the distinguishing features of this tiny hotel. The building is medieval, so the rooms tend to be small. 12 rooms. *Via Marconi 35, pironihotel.it.*

€€ **Villa Belvedere**. Colourful, comfortable, folksy décor in a pretty yellow villa, set back from the water in a quiet position against a backdrop of green hills. Gardens and pool. *Via Casali Cuserina 2, villabelvederehotel.it.*

€ **Lago Maggiore**. This B&B in a quiet garden, 5mins by foot from the centre of Cannobio, was opened in 2014. It occupies a former stable, restored (over five long years) to create a zero-emission building. It burns woodchips from the surrounding forest for heat and uses thermal solar panels to make hot water; it has LED lighting and a hi-tech chilled-ceiling system for efficient cooling and heating of the rooms. It is also attractive and comfortable, with stunning lake views. Most of the six rooms are colour-themed; the Black Room may be a bit dark on grey days. *Via Casali Amore 9, bnblagomaggiore.com.*

DAGNENTE

€€ **White Lilac B&B**. Beautiful rooms in a lovingly renovated villa of 1920, with a swimming pool. Just north of Arona. *Via Verbano 79, en.whitelilac.it.*

LESA

€ **Casabella**. *Casabella* is one of the oldest and most widely respected journals of architecture in the world (it was founded in 1928 by Italian Modernist Giuseppe Pagano), and you can leaf through 50 years of the venerable magazine in the library of this delightful B&B in a villa constructed in roughly the same epoch. The name hints at what can be expected of this charming property, carefully restored by an architect and his family in 2004–6. They have transformed the interior to make a truly beautiful home (literally a *casa bella*), and furnished it with icons of 20th-century design, together with older pieces and a seemingly infinite number of books, paintings, records (vinyl!) and magazines. There is a garden shielded from view by laurel and box hedges, for lazy summer afternoons. *Via Rosmini 35, BBCasabella.com.*

STRESA

€€€ **Grand Hotel Des Iles Borromées & Spa**. Created at the same time as the Kingdom of Italy, this fairy-tale grand hotel was a favourite haunt of the European nobility. In 1870, Alexandra, Grand Duchess of All Russia, etched her name on a window with a diamond. In 1884, the agreement to build the Simplon Tunnel was signed here. During the Stresa Conference of 1935, which tried to bridle Hitler's Germany, it was the hotel of the heads of state and their ministers. For the Aga Khan, Gabriele D'Annunzio, the Rockefellers and Sacha Guitry, it was a home away from home. Hemingway writes of it in *A Farewell to Arms*. It still meets the highest standards of luxury accommodation. *Lungolago Umberto I 67, borromees.com.*

€€ **Verbano**. A romantic place a few minutes by boat from Stresa and Baveno, this small restaurant-cum-hotel on the picturesque Isola dei Pescatori has long been a favourite of artists and writers. Among those who have stayed here are Arturo Toscanini,

Ernest Hemingway, George Bernard Shaw, the Emperor of Japan, the royals of England, Risorgimento patriot Alessandro Manzoni, philosopher Antonio Rosmini, and poet Gabriele d'Annunzio. Rooms are warm and comfortable and dinner on the lakeside terrace, as the sun sets on a balmy summer evening, is unforgettable. 12 rooms. *Isola dei Pescatori, Via Ugo Ara 2, ilverbano.com.*

VERBANIA

€€€ **Grand Hotel Majestic**. Large luxury hotel with its own restaurant in newly renovated *Belle Époque* building. *Via Vittorio Veneto 32, grandhotelmajestic.it.*

€€ **Il Chiostro**. Hotel based in a beautiful 16th-century monastery. It is a popular conference venue but it is also possible to book individually. Set in fine grounds. *Via Fratelli Cervi 14, chiostrovb.it.*

WHERE TO EAT

ARONA

€€€ **Taverna del Pittore**. Pleasant fish restaurant with an open veranda on the lake, now also with a *bistrot prêt à manger*, offering a limited gourmet menu, and a *carpacceria*, both inexpensive (€). Closed Thur. *Piazza del Popolo 39, ristorantetavernadelpittore.it.*

CANNOBIO

€€ **Grotto Sant'Anna**. At the Orrido di Sant'Anna, just behind the church. Excellent restaurant with good food and wine and an idyllic atmosphere. In fine weather you can eat outside at stone tables placed overlooking the gorge and its stream far below. Closed Mon. *Via Sant'Anna 30. T: 0323 70682.*

GHIFFA

€–€€ **La Trinità**. The restaurant at the Sacro Monte is very pleasant, with stone tables and benches outside under the trees in fine weather and cosy seating indoors. Sometimes closed on weekdays in low season (phone to check). *Via Santissima Trinita, ristorantelatrinita.it.*

ISOLA DEI PESCATORI

€–€€ **Trattoria Imbarcadero**. There are plenty of places to eat on the island but this is perhaps the best, in business since 1899, right beside the landing stage. There are tables right out on the water in fine weather. Excellent unfussy food, good wine and friendly service. *imbarcaderoisolapescatori.it.*

€€ **Verbano**. See *Where to Stay, Stresa, above*.

RANCO

€€€ **Il Sole di Ranco**. Michelin-starred restaurant famous for its lake fish and seafood. It merits a side-trip to Ranco, on the eastern shore. Closed midday Mon and all day Tues. *Piazza Venezia 5, ilsolediranco.it.*

STRESA

€€ **Il Ristorante Piemontese**. Restaurant in a 17th-century townhouse with private garden. It is known for its fine regional cuisine—Piedmontese, as the name suggests. There is a lovely little courtyard with a pergola for summer dining. Closed Mon. *Via Mazzini 25, ristorantepiemontese.com.*

€–€€ **Il Vicoletto**. Cosy, friendly and popular. Refined food and a wide selection of wines. A gourmet choice.

Closed Thur. *Vicolo Del Poncivo. 3, ristorantevicoletto.com.*
€ **Caffè Torino**. On the main square, just inland from the waterfront. Bustling, busy and friendly, serving very simple food and pizza. Stays open year-round. *Piazza Cadorna 23. T: 0323 30652.*
€ **Paulon diVino Caffè**. Popular and friendly wine bar, just in from the waterfront, ideal for early evening drinks. They have a good range of wines on offer and serve good nibbles. You can also eat a snack meal here. *Via Principe Tomaso 1, T: 0323 31921.*

VERBANIA (PALLANZA)
€€ **Antica Osteria Il Monte Rosso**. In business since 1854; fushion food and Mediterranean fish specialities. In the bay of Suna, where the sculptor Troubetzkoy spent his summers. *Via Paolo Troubetzkoy 128, osteriamonterosso.com.*
€€ **Dei Cigni**. Modern *trattoria* specialising in fish and seafood. *Vicolo dell'Arco 1, corner of Viale delle Magnolie. T: 0323 558 842.*
€€ **Il Portale**. Serves delicious seafood; lakeside terrace (in Pallanza). *Via Sassello 3, ristoranteilportale.it.*
€€ **Caffè delle Rose**. Stylish restaurant on the main pedestrian street of Pallanza. Restored in Bell Époque style, recalling a refined and elegant era. A place to treat yourself to lunch after visiting Villa Taranto. *Via Ruga 36, caffedellerosebistrot.it.*

EVENTS AND FESTIVALS

Stresa *Stresa Festival*. Renowned international festival of classical music. July–Sept. *stresafestival.eu.*
Verbania *Festival LetterAltura*. Festival centred around mountain literature, travel and adventure, talks, readings and workshops, last week of June. *associazioneletteraltura.com.*

LOCAL SPECIALITIES

In **Stresa** they sell small round crumbly biscuits called *margheritine*, which claim to have been invented in 1868 by the pastry chef **Pietro Antonio Bolongaro**, in the shop (and now café) that bears his name on Piazza Matteotti, facing the waterfront. It shares its premises with the Town Hall. The biscuits are said to have been a particular favourite of Queen Margherita, hence their name, in her honour. You can buy them from the elegant little Chocolaterie des Iles, just behind the Pasticceria Bolongaro at Via Cavour 3.

The Lepontine Alps

The Lepontine Alps (Italian *Alpi Lepontine*, French *Alpes Lépontiennes*, German *Lepontische Alpen*), the section of the Western Alps along the Italian–Swiss border, are bounded by the Pennine Alps on the west-southwest, the Upper Rhône and Vorderrhein river valleys on the north, the Rhaetian Alps on the east-northeast, and the Italian lake district on the south. They take their name from the ancient Leponti, whose capital the Romans called *Oscela lepontorum* and we call Domodossola. The Lepontine Alps have a granite core surrounded by crystalline schist, limestone and clay. The highest peak, Monte Leone (3552 m), rises at the western end of the range, and deep glacial valleys—as well as beautiful glacial lakes—characterise the southern slope. There are several important passes—the Simplon, St Gotthard, Lukmanier, San Bernardino and Splügen—all of whose roads led to Milan.

LAGO D'ORTA

Lago d'Orta (*map B, B3*) is a beautiful little lake 13km long and about 1km wide, surrounded by steep mountains almost sheer to the water, and lying just west of the much more famous Lago Maggiore. Also called Cusio (from the Roman Cusius), the lake has been admired by numerous travellers over the centuries, including Balzac and Nietzsche. Its only outlet is the little River Nigoglia, which flows northwards from Omegna (all the other subalpine Italian lakes have southern outflows).

ORTA SAN GIULIO

Orta San Giulio is the best known and most visited place on the lake. Its main square is right on the waterfront, from where there is a splendid view of the Isola San Giulio just offshore. The wrought-iron balconies that adorn many houses reflect a craft tradition that flourished here until quite recently.

On the main road at the neck of the peninsula, from where the Via Panoramica leads around the headland, stands **Villa Crespi** (now a hotel), a remarkable building in the Moorish style. From here it is possible to walk to the centre on foot. Follow the brown sign to 'Centro Storico', to the right off Via Panoramica. At the cobbled path signed 'Ortello' go left down to the water. From the little harbour a path between houses leads to the lakefront promenade, which takes you into the main square.

Piazza Motta, the main town square opening onto the lake, is lined with restaurants and cafés. In the centre is the little Palazzo della Comunità, the former Town Hall, built in 1582, with a small bell-tower and a roof in piode slabs. It features the coat of arms of Orta San Giulio, a solitary cypress tree within a walled garden, a hortus conclusus. From here a wide thoroughfare with steps, Via Corinna Caire Albertoletti, leads up past a number of handsome palaces. One of them is the Casa Marangoni or **Casa dei Nani**, thought to be the oldest building in Orta. It probably dates from the 14th century and gets its name ('of the dwarves') from the diminutive windows above the wood architrave. At the top of the street is the parish church, with a decorative façade (1941) and an 11th-century doorway. The Baroque interior has interesting frescoes and works by Carlo Beretta, Giulio Cesare Procaccini, Morazzone and Fermo Stella.

A lane to the right of the church (Via Gemelli, signed 'Cimitero Sacro Monte') continues uphill to the cemetery (with an 18th-century wrought-iron gate). From here the road bends left to the monumental gateway of the **Sacro Monte** (*see p. 53;* you can also get there by car from the Via Panoramica). On this low wooded hill (396m), now a park with some rare plants (including palm trees), are 20 pretty little chapels dedicated to St Francis of Assisi, whose life is interpreted here as resembling that of Jesus, inspired by the *De Conformitate* of Bartolomeo da Pisa, a Tuscan Franciscan of the late 14th century, which detects 40 similarities between the life of Christ and that of St Francis. A path beyond the gateway (*usually open 9.30–4; otherwise enquire at the Capuchin monastery at the top of the hill*) continues straight uphill, with good views over the lake, and then leads through the woods past the chapels. Most of them were built between 1592 and 1670, and most of them were designed by Padre Cleto (1556–1619). Each chapel has a different ground plan, usually with a pretty loggia or porch. They contain remarkable groups of life-size terracotta figures illustrating scenes from the life of the saint, as well as frescoes. There are notices in each chapel describing the works of art. Carved wooden or wrought-iron screens protect the sculptures; the best are the earliest (1607–17) by Cristoforo Prestinari (chapels I–VI, XI and XV). The frescoes include works by Antonio Maria Crespi and Carlo Francesco and Giuseppe Nuvolone.

The area around the Sacro Monte is now a nature reserve, of considerable geological and botanical interest: the mountain here is made up of rocks shaped by Quaternary glaciers. The lower elevations are covered with deciduous forests, whereas evergreen species and mountain-dwellers such as bilberry prevail. There is also a beautiful avenue of hornbeam trees overlooking the lake.

A gravel lane at the northern end of the town, beyond the Hotel San Rocco, leads past a few villas and ends at the wrought-iron gate in front of the pink **Villa Motta**, built in the late 19th century in Venetian style and surrounded by a pretty garden (*open by appointment March–Dec; T: 335 611 7702 or 335 274 261*). First laid out in 1880, it has camellias, rhododendrons and azaleas, and some fine trees. A delightful path continues to the left round the headland of **Punta Movero**, following the water's edge past more villas with their boathouses (including an eccentric Art Nouveau villa) and lawns.

ISOLA SAN GIULIO

Isola San Giulio, a picturesque little island, is especially beautiful from a distance (the best view, which changes constantly according to the light, is from Orta San Giulio). With a perimeter of just 650m, it has no cars and hardly any shops. There is only one lane, which circles the island past a few villas. The huge former seminary building, with an overgrown garden, is now a Benedictine convent. The 30 nuns (closed order) run a restoration centre here and offer hospitality for retreats.

Boats dock in front of the **basilica of San Giulio**, traditionally thought to have been founded by St Julius. This saint is supposed to have purged the island of serpents and other dangerous beasts in 390—though the first written document testifying to his cult dates from 590 (Paolo Diacono). The interior of the church is Baroque, though there are 14th–16th-century frescoes. The pulpit, in dark Oira marble, dates from the 11th–12th centuries and the sombre carvings show German influence. A white marble sarcophagus with Roman carvings now serves as an alms-box. Some of the chapels are decorated with 15th-century Lombard frescoes, one of which is attributed to Gaudenzio Ferrari (*see p. 71*).

In 962 the island was defended by Willa, wife of Berengar II of Lombardy, against the incursions of the Emperor Otho the Great: the charter of Otho giving thanks for his eventual capture of the island is preserved in the sacristy. The whale's vertebra here is supposed to be a bone of one of the serpents destroyed by St Julius. Fragments of exquisite marble intarsia panels of the 4th–5th centuries, from the cenotaph of the saint (formerly in the apse, destroyed in 1697), are displayed in a room off the crypt. The body of St Julius, and a Greek marble panel incised with the palm, peacock and Cross (6th–7th centuries), are also preserved here.

OTHER TOWNS ON THE LAKE

Vacciago lies between Orta San Giulio and Gozzano, to the south. A handsome collection of modern art (*open throughout the summer from mid-May; for opening times, see fondazionecalderara.it*) is displayed in the former home of the painter Antonio Calderara (1903–78), a 17th-century villa built in Renaissance-revival style. Nearby Monte Mesma is now a nature reserve, with wetlands at lower elevations, along the Torrente Agogna, chestnuts and oaks on the hillsides, and evergreen species such as holly, boxwood, cherry laurel, and yew, above. At the southern end of the lake is a hill crowned by the tall (24m) Torre di Buccione, a Lombard watch tower; chestnuts rule the forest preserve that surrounds the tower. On the other side of the lake is **Pella**, with a little port. The terraced hills above the town hold some small villages and the sanctuary of the Madonna del Sasso, built in 1748 on a granite spur overlooking the lake (panoramic view).

Omegna, a small manufacturing town at the north end of the lake, retains a few old houses, a medieval bridge, and an ancient town gate. It lies at the foot of the Valstrona, a narrow winding glen that descends from the Laghetto di Capezzone (2104 m), a lovely tarn beneath the Cima di Capezzone (2420m). The Postmodern Forum di Omegna, on the site of a former iron foundry, hosts an interesting collection (*forumomegna.org*) of household items made in the 19th, 20th and 21st centuries by local manufacturers famous for their groundbreaking designs: Alessi,

Calderoni, Girmi, Irmel, Lagostina, La Nuova Faro, Piazza, Tracanzan and others. The permanent collection, assembled by the Fondazione Museo Arti e Industria di Omegna, traces the history of Italian industrial design from the 19th century the present. It is surprising how much well-known kitchen equipment, especially, comes from this tiny corner of Europe.

A byroad leads from Omegna to **Quarna Sotto**, where wind instruments have been made since the early 19th century. The Forni manufactory was succeeded here by the Rampone company at the end of the century. A small museum, Museo Etnografico e dello Strumento Musicale (*museodellequarne.it*) in a bright green contemporary building illustrates the history of the craft and preserves a collection of clarinets, oboes, saxophones, flutes and brasses. Another section is devoted to farm life in the valley.

Another town with a small manufacturing tradition is **Pettenasco**, whre there is a museum of wood-turning in an old water mill (Museo dell'Arte della Tornitura del Legno; *museotornituraperttenasco.it*) and where Pepper Style by Bisetti sells traditional wooden salt and pepper mills. From the main roadside church (dedicated to St Catherine and the locally venerated St Ausenzio, said to have been a companion of St Julius at Orta San Giulio), Via Caduti leads down to the water, from where lakeside paths lead both right and left.

VAL GRANDE

The Val Grande was carved out by the Rio Valgrande, a tributary of Lake Maggiore. In 1992 it was incorporated into the Parco Nazionale del Val Grande. The area is so sparsely populated that there is only one village—Cicogna—which has 17 inhabitants. The valley has become a popular destination for nature lovers and hikers, due to its rugged landscape and the rather eery human evidence of bygone days when the economy flourished here: abandoned roads, broken bridges and tumbledown buildings enveloped by plants. Rarely does one find such evidence of the force of nature and its capacity to reclaim the space once occupied by human activities.

VOGOGNA

The name Vogogna (map B, B2) is first mentioned in the 10th century but may reflect the ancient people who inhabited these lands before the Romans: the Agon Gauls. Vogogna in this case would derive from *Vallis Agonum*, 'village of the Agons'. The town, located on the left bank of the Toce, is dominated by its 14th-century Visconti castle, a remarkable example of medieval military architecture characterised by high walls and an imposing semi-cylindrical tower.

There are numerous churches and oratories scattered over the countryside here, and most are well preserved. Just outside the historic centre is the **Oratorio di San Pietro**, probably of Lombard origin, with some fine 15th-century frescoes. The Chiesa Parrocchiale lost its bell tower in 1975, but the Renaissance portal survived. Cross a bridge and enter the village by the Porta Superiore; the main Via Roma leads past the castle tower to the Palazzo Pretorio, a Gothic building with an arcade resting on squat columns, built in 1348 and the seat of the government of the Lower Val d'Ossola until 1819. Surrounding the 'palace' are the village's most stately mansions, notably Villa Biraghi Lossetti (1650) next to the church of Santa Marta.

The **Castello Visconteo** (*open daily in summer, at weekends and holidays during the rest of the year; for details, see castellodivogogna.it*) probably dates from 1348, when the territory was a fief of the archbishop Giovanni Visconti. In 1446, the feud of Lower Ossola passed to the Borromeo, who retained ownership until 1797. When the village lost its role as a border post, in the mid-16th century, the castle fell into neglect. The oldest documents refer simply to a fortress, using the term both for the castle in the village and for the fortification set on the cliff above. The two are in fact linked: the fortress was almost certainly built to defend the castle, the rectangular towers that characterise both edifices providing formal evidence of their common origin (the semi-cylindrical towers were built during a restoration carried out by the Borromeo in the late 15th century). Despite its decline, the castle retains its massive semi-cylindrical corner tower, whose Guelph battlements served to defend the rampart walk. The castle itself is a solid construction that develops between the tower facing the village and the other, square one, set against the mountain. In 1798, after three centuries of Borromeo rule, it became public property and was used as a prison. Restoration was begun in 1990, with the recovery of the courtyards and garden, and is still underway.

A walk of about 20mins climbs to the old village of **Genestredo**, with its characteristic stone houses rich in medieval decorative motifs. A sign on the path points the way to the Lombard Rocca, a romantic ruin that continues to dominate the Lower Val d'Ossola.

PARCO NAZIONALE DELLA VAL GRANDE

Vogogna is the gateway to one of Italy's newest national parks (established 1992). In the heart of this 14,000 ha reserve is the largest wilderness area in the country, a perfect place for studying the natural evolution of Alpine flora and fauna in regions (practically, or once again) untouched by humans. It is a place of high mountains and deep valleys, dense forests, vast meadows and, above all, silence. Of the plant species that have adapted to the harsh climate of these lands the rarest and most interesting are the Alpine columbine, the mountain arnica, the yellow gentian, the wild tulip and the bellflower. Chamois, deer, marmots, foxes, martens, weasels and numerous rodents inhabit the dense forests, and birdlife includes golden eagles and peregrine falcons. The park also includes the quarries that provided the pink Candoglia marble used in the construction of Milan cathedral. That building project (begun in 1386) also brought about the deforestation of the Val Grande, the timber being used to shore up the mines, build barges and construct the cathedral's scaffolding. The main recreational activities here are white-water rafting and hiking, the latter on trails ranging from very easy to extremely challenging (for trail itineraries, see the park website; *parks.it/parco.nazionale.valgrande*). There are quite a few petroglyphs in the park, and more are being discovered every day. Near the Casa dell'Alpino hut on the Alpe Prà is a particularly large one representing a number of small 'basins' connected by 'channels'. The position of the stone—which faces the rising sun and offers a magnificent view over Lago Maggiore—has led some scholars to suggest it may have been used by a nature cult as an altar.

VAL D'OSSOLA

This alpine district in the northernmost corner of Piedmont is bordered on three sides by Switzerland. The main town is Domodossola, at the entrance to Italy from the Simplon Pass and railway tunnel.

DOMODOSSOLA
Of Roman origin, this town (*map B, B2*) at the confluence of the Ossola valleys became important as a halting place for travellers after the opening of the road over the Simplon Pass by Napoleon in 1805, and again after the construction of the railway tunnel through the Alps in 1906. It is still an important rail junction and preserves a grand station built in 1906.

Corso Ferraris leads from the station to the old part of the town. Beyond Piazza Cinque Vie is the pretty arcaded **Piazza Mercato**, with 15th–16th-century houses, some with balconies and loggias. A market is held here on Saturdays. Just off the Piazza is the handsome grey-and-white Teatro Municipale Galletti.

Via Paletta leads from Piazza Mercato to Piazza della Chiesa and the church of **Santi Gervaso e Protaso**, which has a façade rebuilt in 1953 but retains an old porch with 15th-century frescoes. Palazzo Silva is a handsome building, begun in 1519 and enlarged in 1640, with a frieze, pretty windows and a spiral staircase. It houses the **Musei Civici Galletti** (*open Fri–Sat 10–12 & 3–7; check on museionline. info/musei/musei-civici-gian-giacomo-galletti*), with Etruscan and Roman antiquities, costumes and other ethnographic holdings, and an interesting natural sciences collection. **Palazzo San Francesco**, a handsome town house built around the remains of the early 13th-century church of St Francis, now houses the civic museum (*Piazza Ruminelli; for opening times, see amossola.it*) with sections on archaeology and natural history as well as a picture gallery and material relating to the construction of the Simplon tunnel (*see overleaf*). Via Carina is an attractive old street with wooden balconies and water channelled beneath the paving stones. To the north, on Via Monte Grappa, is an old medieval tower.

To the west of the town in a nature reserve is the **Sacro Monte Calvario**, with a view from the top. The 14 chapels, built from the 17th–19th centuries, each to a different design, contain life-size sculptures representing the Passion of Christ by Dionigio Bussola, Giuseppe Rusnati and others, as well as frescoes. The hill has always had strategic importance because of its dominant position over the Val d'Ossola and for this reason has been fortified since the 11th century. The way to the top leads past the Giardini dei Padri Rosminiani, with venerable old examples of Cryptomeria cypress, Lawson cypress, and Libocedrus and, in the shade of a magnificent cedar, a pond whose shape echoes that of Lake Maggiore.

TWO WAYS ACROSS THE ALPS

Whether you travel by rail or by car, Domodossola is the traditional gateway between Piedmont and Switzerland. The **Simplon Railway Tunnel** is the longest rail tunnel in the world (19.8km); its first gallery was constructed in 1898–1905. It is also the lowest of the great Alpine tunnels, with a maximum elevation of only 705m—which means there are 2134m of mountain overhead where the main ridge is pierced. The **Simplon Pass** (Passo del Sempione, 2009m) is wholly on Swiss soil. It became important when Napoleon chose it, after the battle of Marengo, as the route for the Simplon road connecting the Rhône valley with the northern Italian plain (182km from Geneva to Sesto Calende). It was begun on the Italian side in 1800, on the Swiss side a year later, and was completed in 1805. About 1km below the summit on the south side is the Simplon Hospice (2001m), built by Napoleon as a barracks in 1811 and acquired by the monks of St Bernard in 1825.

THE UPPER VAL D'OSSOLA AND THE SIDE VALLEYS

The **Val Vigezzo**, running east from Domodossola and followed by a spectacular railway line to Locarno, opened in 1923 but has been visited by artists since the 19th century. Santa Maria Maggiore has a little museum illustrating the work of chimneysweeps.

The **Val Divedro**, northwest of Domodossola, leads to the Simplon Pass. At 1275m, the Parco Naturale dell'Alpe Veglia-Devero (*map B, B1*) below Monte Leone (3552m), has beautiful scenery, with meadows and larch woods laced with hiking trails (information from the tourist office in Varzo or on the website (*valdivedro.it*). The park is known for its geology (there are 127 different minerals beneath its soil), its flora (300 species, of which a fifth are rare) and its fauna (chamois, roe deer, deer, ibex, marmots and Alpine hares; eagles, black grouse and ptarmigan). Archaeologists have uncovered a Mesolithic hunting camp (8th millennium BC) on the Alpe Veglia, and a late Neolithic cave painting (4th millennium BC) at the Balm d'la Vardaiola.

The spectacular **Upper Val d'Ossola**, with its vineyards, fig trees and chestnut woods, extends north to Switzerland. The Alpe Devero (1640m; *map B, B1*) is in the centre of a park with fine scenery and Alpine lakes. The beautiful **Val Formazza** is an interesting region colonised in the Middle Ages by German-speaking families from the Valais. The **Cascata del Toce** (1675m) at La Frua (*map B, C1*) is one of the great waterfalls of the Alps (*viewable on Sun June–Sept*).

South of Domodossola, in the **Valle d'Antrona**, is the beautiful little Lago d'Antrona (1083m), formed by a landslip in 1642.

The **Valle Anzasca** also has spectacular mountain scenery. The most important resort here is **Macugnaga** (1326m; *map B, A2*), nestled at the foot of the east face of the Monte Rosa massif, the tallest rockface in the Alps. Many climbers have made their reputations finding new ways to ascend the sheer wall, which is 2600 m high and 4km wide; others have died trying and are buried in the mountaineering cemetery by the 13th-century Chiesa Vecchia. Macugnaga is also a famous winter resort—one can ski into Switzerland via the Passo del Monte Moro, 3000m.

LEPONTINE ALPS PRACTICAL TIPS

GETTING AROUND

• **By rail:** The EuroCity train service from Milan (Central Station) to Geneva, Bern and Basel passes through Domodossola (1hr 18mins). There is also a direct regional service from Milan (Central Station) to Domodossola (1hr 37mins). There are direct regional trains to Domodossola from Omegna (51mins) and Novara (64mins).

WHERE TO STAY

DOMODOSSOLA (*map B, B2*)
€€ **Corona**. Large and comfortable hotel in the heart of the town; wellness centre and swimming pool, and in good weather there is the outdoor restaurant, La Pergola. *Via Guglielmo Marconi 6 .coronahotel.net.*
€ **B&B Il Tiglio**. Small and cosy bed and breakfast with large back garden. Everything is run on sustainable lines: the electricity is generated by photovoltaic panels and the hot water from solar. *Via Deseno 5, bbtiglio.com.*

MACUGNAGA (*map B, A2*)
€ **Alpi**. One of the oldest Alpine hotels in the area, at the foot of Monte Rosa, with its own restaurant. Closed half of Nov. *Frazione di Borca, Centro Abitato Borca 234. T: 0324 65135.*
€ **Girasole**. Small traditional Alpine inn. Good food. *Frazione di Staffa. Via Monte Rosa 41. T: 0324 65052.*
€ **Signal**. This unassuming family-run establishment is close to the ski lifts but far from the noise and traffic, making it a good option for winter; the views of Mt Rosa, and the courtesy and skill of the Meynet family and their staff, make it magnificent in all seasons. *Via Pecetto 118, Macugnaga, hotelsignal.it.*

OMEGNA (*map B, B3*)
€€ **Hotel Croce Bianca**. Family-owned hotel located on the shores of Lago d'Orta. Rooms are basic but comfortable. *Via Mazzini 20, hotelcrocebianca.net.*

ORTA SAN GIULIO (*map B, B3*)
€€€ **Villa Crespi**. An extraordinary late 19th-century folly, a cross between a Moorish kasbah and a Tuscan town hall: the opulent drapes and arabesques may well make you feel you've landed on a silent-movie set. Extensive gardens. 14 rooms. Michelin-starred restaurant. *Via Fava 18, villacrespi.it.*
€€ **Al Dom**. In this 18th-century B&B by the lake, the furniture and decorations harmonise perfectly with the house's coffered ceilings, stone columns and pebble floors. White is the dominant colour here, and natural sunlight the defining element. All rooms are equipped with a large balcony overlooking the lake, and each room has been furnished individually to give it its own, special character. The garden offers magnificent views of the Isola and the surrounding mountains, and you can relax on the lakeside terrace in summer, or take a ride around the lake in the hosts' very own wood-hulled motorboat. Three rooms. *Via Giovanetti 57, Orta San Giulio, aldom57.com.*

WHERE TO EAT

DOMODOSSOLA (*map B, B2*)
€€ **Sciolla**. Traditional trattoria and inn serving good local dishes like *gnocchi dell'Ossola*. They also have a guesthouse with 6 comfortable rooms. *Piazza Convenzione 4, ristorantedasciolla.it.*
€€ **La Meridiana**. Open since 1968, specialising in Italian, French and Swiss cuisine; 150 wine labels. Closed Sun and Mon. (Also has its own residence at Frazione Cadarese, Premia.) *Via Rosmini 11, ristorantelameridiana.it.*

ORTA SAN GIULIO (*map B, B3*)
€€–€€€ **Locanda di Orta**. Upscale *osteria* with a Michelin rosette in the heart of Orta San Giulio, serving traditional dishes reinterpreted with zest and flair. A simpler bistrot operates from April–Oct. Also has rooms. *Via Olina 18 (Piazza Ragazzoni, just off the main square), locandaorta.com.*
€€ **Due Santi**. On the main square, with outside seating in fine weather. An excellent choice for lunch. Good local dishes. *Piazza Motta 18, aiduesanti.com.*
€€ **La Motta**. On the main stepped street leading up towards the Sacro Monte. Cosy interior in winter. Restaurant and bistrot (with different menus). *Via C. Caire Albertoletti 13, lamottarestaurant.it.*
€€–€ **Luci sul Lago**. Outside the centre, close to the main approach road to the peninsula. Relaxed and informal place, good for pizza, with a terrace and tables right on the water. They also offer beach service and you can rent parasols and loungers from them. *Via Domodossola, lucisullago.com.*
€ **Pan e Vino**. Simple, lively place on the main square, serving bread, wine and Piedmontese cheese and salami. It operates an excellent ice cream shop, also on the main square, in the old Monte di Pietà pawnbroker's, with an exterior fresco of the Resurrection. Closed Wed. *Piazza Motta 37. T: 393 858 3293.*

LOCAL SPECIALITIES

The **mortadella** of the Val d'Ossola (also known as 'Mortadella Ossolana') is a *salame* ('sausage') of pork meat to which is added a small amount of pig's liver. It is then cured for two months with herbs and spices and, usually, Barbera wine. Baked in the oven, it is an excellent accompaniment to *polenta*. The region also produces some distinctive Alpine **cheeses**, such as the mild and fragrant Ossalano d'Alpe from the Valle d'Ossola, and Bettelmatt, at around 2000m on the seven mountain pastures of the Valle Antigoro. Both are made from the milk of the Bruna Alpina breed of cow.

For a choice selection of cured meats and cheeses try Ossola Salumi e Formaggi di Antonio & Bruno Del Vecchio at Via de Nicola Enrico 16 in Domodossola.

FESTIVALS AND EVENTS

Domodossola *Ossola Guitar Festival*, an annual feast of classical guitar music, July/Aug (*ossolaguitarfestival.com*). The town also hosts the Settembre Musicale in autumn.

The Pennine Alps

The Pennine Alps (Italian *Alpi Pennine*, French *Alpes Pennines*) are the segment of the Western Alps along the Italian-Swiss border bounded by the Mont Blanc group on the southwest, by the Upper Rhône Valley on the north, by the Lepontine Alps on the northeast, and by the Po River Valley on the south. The range takes its name from the pre-Roman Ligurian word *pen* ('peak'), and indeed includes at least 30 peaks over 4000m high. The ridge line remains very high everywhere, averaging 3000m, but never descending below 2472m (at the Great St Bernard Pass). The highest point is Dufour Peak (Punta Dufour/Dufourspitze, 4634m) in the Monte Rosa group; other important peaks include the Matterhorn (4478m), the Weisshorn (4405m) and the Grand Combin (4317m). Most of the glaciers lie on the northern slopes, including the celebrated Gorner Glacier near Zermatt, Switzerland.

The Swiss portion of the range is sometimes called the *Alpes du Valais* (French) or *Walliser Alpen* (German) by the pastoral population that has inhabited it since antiquity, and who in the 12th and 13th centuries settled the upper valleys of the mountains' southern slopes; there is an interesting reconstruction of a Walser farm in Alagna Valsesia, described below.

THE VALSESIA

The lovely valley of the River Sesia extends for about 70km between the southeastern flank of Monte Rosa and the Po, which it joins at Romagnano Sesia (*map B, B4*). The highest section (the Val Grande, not to be confused with the Val Grande by Lago Maggiore), which stretches for about 40km from the foot of Monte Rosa to Varallo, is steep and winding and blanketed with thick forests. Here (and in the valleys of the rivers Sermenza and Mastellone, which merge from the left) are pretty resorts including Riva Valdobbia, Rima, Fobello and—the best-known and highest of all—Alagna (*map B, A3*).

ROMAGNANO SESIA
The Neoclassical Villa Caccia here (*map B, B4*) was designed between 1840 and 1848 by Alessandro Antonelli, the architect of the Mole Antonelliana in Turin and the Basilica of San Gaudenzio in Novara. It has been beautifully restored to house the Museo Storico Etnografico della Bassa Valsesia (*open April–Oct by appointment,*

museostoricoromagnano.it), with a wonderfully installed collection documenting local material culture, from farming to lace-making. The villa has a lovely two-hectare park with greenhouses, fountains and a scenic terrace. The Cantina dei Santi, located in the ancient district of Contrada della Badia, is the last remaining vestige of the medieval abbey of San Silvano. The monumental cellar consists of two rooms, the largest of which, once possibly the chapter house, contains a 15th-century fresco cycle depicting biblical scenes and stories of chivalry. The town is famous for its Good Friday re-enactment of Calvary, a tradition that reaches back two and a half centuries.

BORGOSESIA

This is the largest town in the Valsesia (*map B, B3*) and one of Italy's leading manufacturing hubs. There are factories everywhere, even in the historic town centre. The main product is textiles (one local firm made the legendary red coats worn by the troops in Giuseppe Garibaldi's Expedition of the Thousand) and some of the old mills are quite handsome. Carnival is a big event here: the high point is the last night, *Mercu Scùrot*, celebrated with a funeral procession in which the townsfolk (men and women) parade through the streets in tails, white tie and top hat, stopping in at the bars along their way; the tradition dates from the 18th century. The Museo Carlo Conti has displays of palaeontology and archaeology devoted to Pleistocene fauna, prehistoric ceramics and artefacts ranging in date from prehistory to the Middle Ages (*Via Combattenti d'Italia 5, museocarloconti.it*). However the best thing to explore, at the east end of the town, is the Monte Fenera Natural Park (*parks.it/parco.monte.fenera*), which has been established to protect the great chestnut and beech forests of Monte Fenera, an area once inhabited by Palaeolithic cave-dwellers. The reserve is home to some 800 plant species (including some rare ferns and Alpine daphnes) and typical alpine fauna, plus the black stork, which began nesting here in 1994. You can also see a unique creation of Valsesia vernacular architecture, the *taragn*, a humble thatch-roofed stable or tool shed whose origins can be traced as far back as the 8th or 9th century.

East of Borgosesia, on the road to Lago d'Orta, is **Valduggia** (*map B, B3*), the birthplace of Gaudenzio Ferrari (1471–1546). The church of San Giorgio has a *Nativity* by him and a *Madonna* by Bernardino Luini.

PRAY

By far the most interesting old textile mill in this historic industrial district is at Pray (*map B, B4*), nestled in the Valle Sessera, 10km west of Borgosesia. The **Fabbrica della Ruota**, formerly the Zignone woollen mill, flanks the Torrente Ponzone. Built in 1878, it preserves one of Europe's first 'telodynamic' power plants—plants for the generation and long-distance transmission of energy. The plant, with large wheels driven by a turbine and a system of belts and axles, is still in perfect working order; the distance from the turbine to the machinery that actually uses the power is over 80m. The property, acquired by the DocBi-Centro Studi Biella, which studies industrial archaeology, has been transformed into a cultural centre. Today it is home to a museum (*open for temporary exhibitions, hours vary, docbi.it*), an archive and a specialised library. The restoration has captured the atmosphere of the factory perfectly, showing in detail the production process that transformed the raw wool into soft fabric. Video installations present virtual simulations of the machinery in motion and recreate the sounds of voices and noises typical of the factory. Many of the workers in the Zignone mill walked up to an hour and a half to reach the workplace from their remote villages; some of the *sentieri del lavoro* they created have been cleared again and marked, and can be hiked.

Pray is the first stop along the **Strada della Lana**, a 50km drive through the Valle Sessera and Valle Strona between Borgosesia and Biella. Abundant, fast-flowing water made this an ideal place for the wool industry; indeed, the valleys are home to Italy's oldest mills, many of which—together with the workers' living quarters that surround them—are still in use.

GAUDENZIO FERRARI

Ferrari (c. 1470–1546), the greatest artist of the Piedmontese school, is barely known outside his native Piedmont, perhaps because he never left it throughout his long life (with the exception of his probable training in Milan and one possible visit to the Rhineland). He was born in Valduggia, and learned his art under old-fashioned masters who preserved their archaic styles against the encroaching rationalist spirit of the Renaissance. Ferrari had no aristocratic patrons: he painted exclusively for churches and convents. There is always something rather homespun about his art, but it is neither naïve nor foolish. His religious beliefs seem to have been sincere, and his art is suffused with an intense lyricism. His greatest works are on the Sacro Monte at Varallo (*see p. 73*), his *Madonna of the Pomegranate* in the church of San Cristoforo in Vercelli (*see p. 146*), and his *Madonna in Paradise* at Saronno, near Milan (Lombardy).

TRIVERO

From Pray, winding roads ascend through the hills west of the Sessia to Trivero (*map B, B4*)—more a cluster of villages than a town, with some interesting frescoes and wooden sculptures in the church of **Santi Quirico e Giulitta**. The church comes with a story.

THE SAGA OF FRA' DOLCINO

Dolcino da Novara, or Fra' Dolcino as he came to be known, was a millenarian preacher, the founder and leader of the Dolciniani. His birthplace is thought to be Prato Sesia, but the date of his birth is uncertain. Accused of heresy by the Inquisition, he was captured and burned at the stake in 1307.

In 1291 Dolcino joined Gherardo Segarelli's Apostolici, a back-to-basics religious movement that was condemned as heresy by Pope Honorius IV and repressed by the Catholic Church, Segarelli being burned at the stake in 1300. Dolcino, who is believed to have been a lay brother, preached primarily in the area of Lake Garda and around Trento. He was a man of great charm and a formidable communicator, and the ranks of the Apostolici grew rapidly under his leadership. He and his followers, now called the Dolciniani, put an even more radical twist on the fundamentalist ideology of the Apostolici; they led a life of fasting and prayer, without compulsory celibacy; they preached obedience to Scripture, affirming the duty to disobey the pope when he strayed from evangelical precepts; they affirmed the right of the laity to preach and spoke of the imminence of heavenly punishment for the ongoing corruption of ecclesiastical customs, and they advocated a life of absolute poverty, working or begging to survive. Their doctrine, and their open hostility to Rome and Pope Boniface VIII, drew the ire of the Church. Dolcino withdrew from the Venetian pre-Alps to the Valsesia, where the villagers, because of their severe living conditions and the Dolcinians' promise of redemption, initially welcomed the group. With the military support of the powerful Visconti family, in 1304 Dolcino decided to occupy the valley and set up a sort of 'free republic' intended to create the kind of community envisaged in his preaching. But in the spring of 1306 the Visconti broke with Dolcino, who withdrew again, to Monte Rubello above Trivero, in the vain hope that his millennial prophecies might materialise under their own impetus. Taking advantage of their precarious position, Raniero d'Avogadro, bishop of Vercelli, backed by the militia of Novara, launched a veritable crusade against the Dolcinians, who to avoid starvation turned to raiding local farms—a move that cost them the support of the populace. They were defeated and captured during Holy Week in 1307; Dolcino was tried and publicly executed on 1st June.

At its peak the movement is thought to have had 10,000 followers, at a time when the population of Novara was 5,000 and that of the Valsesia, 500. Dante mentions Fra' Dolcino in the *Inferno* (*XXVIII, 55–60*); Nobel Prize-winning playwright Dario Fo cites him in *Mistero Buffo* (1977); and Umberto Ecco has two characters in *The Name of the Rose* (1980), Remigio da Varagine and his aide Salvatore, burned at the stake for their past as Dolciniani.

During the siege of 1306–7 the heretics set fire to the church in Trivero; they soiled it with excrement, stole or destroyed its sculptures, paintings and liturgical objects, and razed the bell tower, using the stones to fortify their camp on Monte Rubello. More than a century would pass before reconstruction could begin. The interior holds two paintings recalling the saga of Fra Dolcino: the *Capture of Dolcino and his Companion Margherita* (by Antonio Cianci, 1867) and the *Capture of Dolcino* (a fresco by Pietro Mazzietti, 1880), in addition to a fine wooden *Via Crucis* by Pietro Antonio Serpentiero.

Trivero's economy is tightly bound to the wool industry, and particularly to the Ermenegildo Zegna woollen mill. From 1932 until his death in 1966 the industrialist poured money and imagination into his community, building a trade school, a hospital, an indoor pool and the Bielmonte ski area, as well as a social-service, entertainment and shopping centre. His most ambitious venture, however, was the construction of the scenic parkway that still bears his name.

The **Strada Panoramica Zegna** (1938; *map B, A4; Ronco 1, Trivero*) placed Trivero at the centre of a vast programme aimed at ensuring the ecological, social and cultural sustainability of this remote corner of the Italian Alps, providing for the reforestation of the mountainsides, the restoration of walking paths and mule tracks, and the development of ecotourism—all 60 to 80 years before ideas such as 'sustainability' and 'ecotourism' became fashionable. The parkway, which winds for 65km with an elevation gain/loss of about 700m, starts from Trivero and ends at Andrate in the Alto Canavese, intersecting the roads leading to the shrines of San Giovanni d'Andorno and Oropa.

The **Oasi Zegna** (*oasizegna.com*) is the parkway's most stunning attraction. This nature reserve, begun by Ermenegildo Zegna and developed by his heirs, offers a spectacular balcony over the Po Valley as well as beautiful views of the Upper Val Sessera, an EU Site of Community Importance (SCI). Largely landscaped by the entrepreneur himself, it contains half a million conifers, hundreds of rhododendrons of various species and colours, and spectacular blue hydrangeas. Highlights of the 100sq km reserve include the wonderful Conca dei Rododendri (Valley of Rhododendrons), blossoming from mid-May to mid-June, created by Pietro Porcinai and recently restored by Paolo Pejrone, and the Bosco del Sorriso (Forest of Smiles), a loop trail through the forest demonstrating the bioenergetic benefits of native plants. In 2014, the Oasi Zegna won the patronage of FAI, the Italian Environmental Fund, in recognition of its valuable contribution to the environment and its conservation. The reserve's logo features the *Carabus olympiae*, a rare iridescent beetle endemic to these mountains.

Casa Zegna (*Via Marconi 23, open Sun 2–6 during temporary exhibitions, fondazionezegna.org/casa-zegna*), the seat of the Fondazione Ermenegildo Zegna, is a private institution combining the historic archives of the Zegna Group with an indoor museum and outside sculpture project. The archives and museum occupy a 1930s mansion that was originally the family home; here you'll find a wonderful collection of 19th-century fabric samples, a permanent exhibition telling the story of the Zegna firm from its origins to the present day, and temporary exhibitions showcasing the historical archives and natural environment of the Oasi Zegna. The foundation is the driving force behind a public art project, *All'Aperto*, which involves the whole town, from the Zegna mills, to public spaces, to the charming Conca dei Rododendri in the Oasi Zegni. The project, undertaken with the intent to facilitate the appreciation of contemporary art, brings internationally renowned artists to the Trivero area to create permanent, site-specific installations for the community. At the time of writing there are works by Daniel Buren, Alberto Garutti, Stefano Arienti, Roman Signer, Marcello Maloberti and Dan Graham.

VARALLO

This handsome town (*map B, B3*), the capital of the upper Valsesia, is famous for its **Sacro Monte**, the ascent to which begins at the church of Madonna delle Grazie, where you'll find frescoed scenes of the *Life of Christ* (1513) by Gaudenzio Ferrari (*see p. 71*). The sanctuary (608m; reached on foot in 20mins or by cable railway or road) was founded c. 1486 by the Blessed Bernardino Caimi, a Franciscan friar. The 45 chapels, completed in the late 17th century, recall various holy sites in Jerusalem and are decorated by local artists—Ferrari, Giovanni Tabacchetti, Giovanni d'Errico and Morazzone. Tabacchetti's best chapels are the *Temptation* (no. 38; with a *Crucifixion* by Ferrari) and *Adam and Eve* (no. 1); d'Errico's is the *Vision of St Joseph* (no. 5). The Basilica dell'Assunta, dating from 1641–9, has a façade of 1896.

> **Samuel Butler at Varallo**
> It may be doubted, indeed, whether there is a more remarkable work in North Italy than the Crucifixion chapel at Varallo, where the statues, as well as the frescoes behind them, are (with the exception of the figure of Christ) by Gaudenzio Ferrari.
> *Alps & Sanctuaries*, 1881

Back in the town the **Palazzo dei Musei** (*Via Pio Franzani 2, pinacotecadivarallo.it*) houses a small natural history museum (Museo Calderini) and a large and well-designed picture gallery (pinacoteca), with over 3,000 works ranging in date from the 15th–19th centuries. Here you can see paintings by Gaudenzio Ferrari and Tanzio da Varallo (1582–1633), sculptures from the Sacro Monte, and *bozzetti* by the Neoclassical sculptors Giovanni Albertoni and Pietro della Vedova, all thoughtfully installed and well lit.

ALAGNA VALSESIA

At 1183 m above sea level, Alagna Valsesia (*map B, A3*) is a fashionable summer and winter resort, especially famous for its off-piste skiing. The entire town falls within the Parco Naturale Alta Valsesia, which includes part of Monte Rosa. Here, on the Punta Gnifetti (4559 m), rises the Regina Margherita CAI Refuge Observatory (4559m, begun 1893), the highest inhabited place on the continent; it is still used as a weather station and a laboratory for the observation of the effects of altitude on the human body (as well as providing a refuge for hikers and skiers). The park encompasses the heads of the three main valleys forming the Valsesia: the Val Grande, Val Sermenza and Val Mastallone. The Monte Rosa glacier feeds a number of spectacular waterfalls in deep glacial ravines, collectively known as the Caldaie del Sesia. The park's glacial history is documented (with text panels and other visual aids) along Italy's only *sentiero glaciologico*, leading in two hours via the Acqua Bianca falls and the Vallone del Bors to the high pastures of the Alpe Fun d'Ekku.

Alagna is an important centre of the Walser, the population of Swiss origin and German language and culture that, in its search for pastures new, migrated across the Alps in the 12th and 13th centuries to settle the valleys of the Lys, Sesia and Toce (as well as in areas of Austria, Germany, Liechtenstein, Switzerland and France). The characteristic Walser neighbourhoods are mainly found in the upper part of the town. One of the old wooden houses, at Pedemonte, is occupied by the **Museo Walser** (*alagna.it*). The interior faithfully replicates a Walser home, with the three functions—stables, living quarters and hayloft or granary—on three distinct levels.

The Funivia di Monte Rosa, a cableway in three stages, rises to the Punta Indren ski area (3260m).

BIELLA

A place of rivers (it lies at the confluence of three: the Elvo, Oropa and Cervo), well exposed to the sun, Biella (*map B, A4*) has the ideal degree of moisture for processing wool. Not surprisingly, wool-working is a long-standing tradition here, documented at least from the 14th century. Today Biella is synonymous with firms that focus on the quality of their fabrics (familiar names are Zegna, Barbera and Loro Piana).

Originally settled by Ligurians and Celts, Biella became an important political and religious centre in the 11th century, the town growing up around the bishop's residence on the plain. In the following century a second centre was established on the hill, as the seat of civil authority and of the noble and artisan classes. Today Biella still has two distinct urban centres: the Piazzo, the upper part of the city, and the Piano, on the right bank of the Cervo. A panoramic cable car has connected the two centres since 1885.

PIANO

Biella's **baptistery** (San Giovanni Battista, Piazza del Battistero), built on a Roman burial ground in the early 11th century, is one of the finest examples of Romanesque architecture in Piedmont. The stone-and-brick building follows a central plan with four semicircular apses separated by engaged piers supporting an octagonal lantern, surmounted in its turn by a second, smaller and later lantern. The entrance door is decorated with a Roman marble low relief depicting a pair of cherubs, thought to have been found accidentally when the baptistery was being built. The interior is simple and unadorned, and retains only fragments of its decorative frescoes, including a *Madonna and Child* and a *Holy Martyr* attributed to the Master of Oropa and dated 1318–19. The **cathedral** (Santo Stefano, Piazza Duomo) dates from the early 15th century; it has a Gothic Revival façade and an imposing eight-tiered Romanesque campanile.

Biella has several fine museums and exhibition spaces, some privately managed. The **Museo del Territorio Biellese**, in the former cloister of San Sebastiano (*Via Quintino Sella 54/b, usually open Thur–Sun, for exact time, see museodelterritorio.biella.it*), traces the natural and cultural history of the city and its territory. The archaeology and palaeontology section features a marvellous installation outlining the physical evolution of the region over geological time, and highlighting the epoch, some three million years ago, when the plain of Biella was beneath the sea; in addition to numerous plant and animal fossils there is a full-scale reconstruction of the Isurus shark, a remote ancestor of the tiger shark, and a virtual installation where you can move about under water, rubbing shoulders with the fish. The art-historical collection documents regional art from the 11th to the 19th centuries; in the 19th-century gallery are some stunning landscapes by the local post-Impressionist Lorenzo Delleani: a small Turner-like oil sketch of cattle grazing on the high pastures (1886), and two naturalistic representations of the Punta Gnifetti and Capanna Margherita on Monte Rosa giving a frightening idea of just how precarious the original structure must have been (1900). Here also are works donated to the museum by three private collectors: the connoisseur Enrico Guagno Poma (works by Delleani and fellow Piedmont landscape painter Marco Calderini, by the Tuscan Macchiaioli Telemaco Signorini, Silvestro Lega and Giovanni Fattori, and by the Neapolitan view painter Giuseppe De Nittis—Signorini's *Old Market in Florence* is particularly famous); the industrialist Blotto Balbo (19th-century painters Antonio Mancini, Federico Zandomeneghi, Giovanni Boldini and Giuseppe Pellizza da Volpedo; 20th-century masters Mario Sironi, Felice Casorati, Giorgio de Chirico and Magritte); and the philanthropist Enrico Lucci (paintings from the 15th–20th centuries, with a focus on the Modern avant-gardes: Giacomo Balla, René Magritte, Paul Klee, Salvador Dalí, Joan Miró, Marc Chagall).

At Via Serralunga 27, in woollen mill renovated by Michelangelo Pistoletto, is **Cittadellarte**, home to the Fondazione Pistoletto (*open for guided tours, cittadellarte. it*), a centre for contemporary art with a focus on Arte Povera (*see p. 29*).

The **Fondazione Sella** (*in the Lanificio Maurizio Sella, Via Corradino Sella 10, open for exhibitions and by appointment, fondazionesella.org*), was the home of the photographer, alpinist and explorer Vittorio Sella (1859–1943). Vittorio belonged to a prominent family of scientists, entrepreneurs, bankers, statesmen and, above all, alpinists (his uncle, Quintino, three times Minister of Finance of the Kingdom of Italy, founded the Italian Alpine Club in 1863). The family foundation conserves his remarkable collection of negatives made during mountain expeditions in Europe, Asia, Africa and Alaska, as well as his photographic equipment, and mounts frequent temporary exhibitions.

PIAZZO

The medieval village that became the upper part of the town of Biella was founded in 1160. The village, originally walled, is connected to the rest of the city by steep cobbled streets called *coste* and is characterised by narrow lanes, low arcades, and aristocratic palaces adorned with terracotta friezes. You can reach Piazzo from the lower town by funicular if you don't like steep climbs.

The focus of life in this pleasant quarter is **Piazza Cisterna**, originally home to the Town Hall, the courts, the slaughterhouse and the market. The square is now surrounded by two- and three-storey townhouses with medieval arcades. Palazzo Cisterna (which takes its name from the princes Dal Pozzo della Cisterna) dominates the square with its 16th-century façade over an earlier core on which some terracotta decorations can still be seen. These crop up again on the arches of the oldest building on the square, Casa Teccio. The house's Gothic origins are revealed in the pointed arches of the portico, adorned with Renaissance friezes. The inner courtyard, decorated with terracotta and with a gallery of eleven round arches, like that of Palazzo Cisterna, dates from the Renaissance.

Palazzo La Marmora (*Corso del Piazzo 19*) took half a millennium to build (13th–19th centuries). Within are five courtyards, all from different periods, and beyond, a lovely terraced garden (with an immense, ancient *Ficus repens*) overlooking the countryside. The building and grounds are still in the hands of the Ferrero della Marmora family and are opened for cultural events; the complex is home to the Osservatorio dei Beni Culturali ed Ambientali del Biellese, a watchdog agency for cultural and environmental assets.

ENVIRONS OF BIELLA

Northwest of Biella is Pollone (*map B, A4*) and the **Parco Burcina Felice Piacenza**, noted especially for its rhododendrons, in flower May–June, and its sequoias, which grow alongside native beech, chestnut, maple, ash, oak, and cherry trees.

GRAGLIA

West of Biella, Graglia is one of the minor mountain sanctuaries of Piedmont, not as famous as that of Varallo or Oropa, but nevertheless well worth a visit. In 1615, on returning from a trip to the Holy Land, Nicolao Velotti conceived the ambitious notion of creating a 'New Jerusalem' in Graglia. This was to consist of a hundred chapels, all replete with terracotta tableaux of devotional scenes. Of this bold concept, only four chapels remain, now largely incorporated into the large edifice of the Santuario della Madonna of Loreto. The scenes represented are the Nativity of Christ, Adoration of the Magi, Presentation of Christ in the Temple and Circumcision. The sanctuary buildings themselves largely date from various decades of the 19th century. There are simple rooms and a restaurant-bar (*santuariodigraglia.com*).

SACRO MONTE DI OROPA

The Sacro Monte di Oropa (1181m; *map B, A4*), the most popular pilgrimage destination in Piedmont, is said to have been founded by St Eusebius of Vercelli in 369. Eusebius (d. 371) is thought to be the author of the Athanasian Creed. The sanctuary, the most important Marian shrine in the Alps, consists of a large hospice, a modest church by Filippo Juvarra (*see p. 23*), and a grander church with a large dome, begun in 1885 to an earlier design by Ignazio Galletti and completed in 1960. The museum (*for opening times, see santuariodioropa.it*) displays the sanctuary's gold, liturgical vestments and historical collections. Here are local archaeological finds dating back to the 2nd century BC as well as an altarpiece by Bernardino Lanino (1522) depicting the *Madonna Enthroned with the Christ Child and Four Saints* and the drawings and plans of the architects who worked at Oropa. The liturgical vestments include a blue velvet chasuble that is supposedly made from the mantle of Blessed Amedeo IX, Duke of Savoy (1435–72).

The shrine stands at the heart of a breathtaking nature reserve encompassing 1500 hectares of grasslands, rhododendron, and alder, beech, sycamore, ash, laburnum and rowan forest, ranging in elevation from 800 to 2400m. Within the reserve is a small but enchanting Giardino Botanico (*open May–Sept, for exact times, see gboropa.it*). Carefully tended by the WWF, it is devoted to high-mountain flora from around the world (*Potentilla nepalensis Hook* and *Primula denticulata* from the Himalayas; *Paeonia suffruticosa* and *Paeonia lactiflora* from Tibet), as well as to rare endemic species (*Campanula excisa Schleicher*, native to the Western Alps and depicted in the garden's logo).

SORDEVOLO

This is another town (*map B, A4*) in the wool trade, nestled along the Torrente Elvo at the foot of Monte Mucrone, which divides the Valsesia from the Valle d'Aosta. It has several fine churches, a beautiful open-air theatre, and is widely known for its Holy Week pageant, involving more than 300 costumed actors. The Trappist monastery here (Trappa di Sordevolo) has been restored by a group of volunteers as a working farm. The facility includes a B&B, a restaurant (*by reservation only, coordinatore@ecomuseo.it*), a dairy and riding stables. The buildings and grounds are open for guided tours April–Oct, Sun 10–4.

GAGLIANICO AND CANDELO

Gaglianico, south of Biella (*map B, A4*), has a splendid castle with a well-decorated courtyard and vast Italian garden. The castle had two different phases of construction. During the first an enceinte was built around a central keep to create an impenetrable fortress. During the second phase, which was probably undertaken in the late 15th or early 16th century, it was transformed into a lordly manor. Today the castle is one of the best preserved in the territory of Biella.

Further east, **Candelo** has a remarkable *ricetto*, or communal fortress and storehouse, built in the 14th century as a refuge for the townsfolk. The village merits a visit for its atmosphere: walking through the long *rue* paved with cobblestones, between high walls and vigilant towers, time stands still—which is why Candelo has been used as a set for several costume dramas. The little museum has permanent displays devoted to viticulture and the rural economy.

RISERVA NATURALE ORIENTATA LE BARRAGE

Cerrione (*map B, A4*) is the gateway to this park, which preserves Piedmont's last remaining areas of *baraggia*, a sort of savannah made up of oak, birch, hornbeam and Scots pine growing over an understory of grass and heather, on a soil of quaternary fluvio-glacial clay deposits that are poor in nutrients and virtually waterproof. A patchwork of meadows and moors, sparse trees and wooded vales, the *baragge* are home to lowland flora such as *Gladiolus palustris*, *Centaurea montana*, *Spiranthes aestivalis*, and mountain plants such as *Iris sibirica*, *Hemerocalllis flava* and *Gentiana pneumonanthe*. The entomofauna is characterized by rare endemic species such as the ground beetles *Agnonum livens* and *Bembidion humerale*, the beetle *Catops westi* and the very rare and localised moth *Coenonympha oedippus*. The park includes the **Castello dei Fieschi** at Zumaglia, heavily restored in the 1930s.

PENNINE ALPS PRACTICAL TIPS

GETTING AROUND

- **By road:** Buses run by ATAP (*atapspa.it*) have a variety of services connecting towns in the region.
- **By rail:** There is a fast regional service (approx. 70mins) from Turin (Porta Nuova) to Biella (San Paolo), with one change at Santhià.

WHERE TO STAY

BIELLA (*map B, A4*)
€€€ **Augustus**. Functional and quiet hotel in the city centre. Buffet breakfast. *Via Italia 54, augustus.it*.
€€€ **Michelangelo**. Luxury hotel with friendly atmosphere. Restaurant, café and *pasticceria*. *Piazza Adua 5, hotelmichelangelo.com*.
€€ **Astoria**. Functional and modern. A no frills place to stay. *Viale Roma 9, hotelastoriabiella.com*.

CANDELO (*map B, A4*)
€ **Al Ricetto**. This B&B, with three colourful rooms, is located in the historic centre of Candelo, just five minutes on foot from the Ricetto. Rooms are furnished with genuine antiques, and the relationship between quality and price is quite high. *Via San Sebastiano 35, Candelo, alricetto.it*.

COSSATO (*map B, B4*)
€€ **Castello di Castellengo**. This Rococo country mansion is perched on high ground overlooking verdant farmland, with rolling hills of Biella behind it. Its origins can be traced back to the 10th century; the medieval fortress was turned into a gracious manor house, with stuccoes, frescoes and a terraced garden, in the 17th century. In the 1990s it was lovingly restored by the present owners, who live here year-round, reserving three lovely rooms, a suite and two flats for visitors. The cellars are home to the famous Centovigne winery. *Frazione Castellengo 31, castellengo.it*.

PIODE (*map B, A3*)
€€ **Giardini**. Simple, clean and comfortable rooms, pets welcome, restaurant attached. *Via Umberto I 9, ristorantegiardini.it*.

POLLONE (*map B, A4*)
€ **Villa Tavallini**. A Liberty (Art Nouveau) villa set in a lovely park, surrounded in its turn by forest. The atmosphere is warm and informal, the rooms are airy and light, and the breakfast buffet is a treasure-trove of homemade cakes and jams. Located in the hills 15mins west of Biella and 40mins east of the Valle d'Aosta, it is a good starting point for exploring the Pennine Alps and their foothills. Three rooms. *Via Benedetto Croce 32, Pollone, villatavallini.it*.

VARALLO (*map B, B3*)
€ **Monte Rosa**. Another Liberty-style hotel in a small park, this simple and friendly *albergo* is located in a quiet neighbourhood within walking distance of old Varallo. It has been in the same family since its establishment over a century ago, and the interiors and their furnishings date from that period; patient restoration has brought everything, including the original

colour scheme and the broad-planked wood floors, back to their original splendour. 15 rooms. *Via Regaldi 4, Varallo Sesia, albergomonterosa.it.*

VIGLIANO BIELLESE (*map B, A4*)
€€ **Castello di Montecavallo**. There are two beautiful rooms (with a common sitting room) in the outbuildings of this Gothic Revival castle and winery. The residence was built after 1830 by Filiberto Avogadro, secretary and ambassador of Carlo Felice of Savoy (King of Sardinia 1821-31) over the remains of a fortress that had been in the family since the 13th century. The present lady of the castle is as gracious as can be and welcomes her guests with warmth and enthusiasm. In summer dinner is served in the formal Italian garden with its with boxwood hedges and climbing roses, wisteria, camellias, hortensias and azaleas. There is also a park where exotic palms and cedars of Lebanon grow alongside native holm oaks, chestnuts, maples and ash trees. *Via per Chiavazza 30, Vigliano Biellese, castellodimontecavallo.it.*

WHERE TO EAT

BIELLA (*map B, A4*)
€€ **Ristorante Luca Montersino**. Sinmple restaurant and *pasticceria* in the Hotel Michelangelo. Classic dishes and good pastries. *Piazza Adua 5, hotelmichelangelo.com.*

OROPA (*map B, A4*)
€€ **Croce Bianca**. Restaurant run by the Ramella family for 60 years, set within the precincts of the Santuario di Oropa. Weekly closing day varies. *Via Santuario di Oropa 480, famigliaramella.it/crocebianca.php.*

PIODE (*map B, A3*)
€€ **Giardini**. Small, refined restaurant attached to the hotel of the same name, run by a young couple: good traditional dishes and strong local character. Closed Thur. *Via Umberto I 9, ristorantegiardini.it.*

ROMAGNANO SESIA (*map B, B4*)
€€ **Alla Torre**. Restaurant in the old village watch-tower, offering traditional dishes with a creative twist, and pleasant ambiance. *Via I Maggio 75, ristoranteallatorre.it.*

LOCAL SPECIALITIES

Biella boasts a soft, light yellow-coloured **lager** brewed in the town since 1846 at G. Menebrea & Sons (*Via Ramella Germain 4, birramenabrea.com*), which is also used in the making of the popular local *toma* (cow's milk) cheese *sbirro*. Another particular dish of the region is the dessert **artsumà**, a soft mousse made with sugar, eggs and either milk or wine and usually eaten with the Piedmontese biscuits, *torcetti*.

EVENTS AND FESTIVALS

Biella *Festival Nazionale del Risotto Italiano*. National celebration of one of Biella's staple foods, Oct/Nov; and *Festival Nazionale dell'Agnolotto e del Tajarin*, of two of the region's pasta varieties (similar to ravioli and tagliatelle respectively), April/May.
Candelo *Goloso Medioevo*. Medieval chivalry, archery, acrobatics and banqueting from c. 1374 (when the villagers swore allegiance to the Savoy), end of May.

The Graian Alps

The Graian Alps (French *Alpes Grées* or *Alpes Graies*; Italian *Alpi Graie*) comprise the northern segment of the Western Alps along the French-Italian border. They are bounded by Mont Cenis and the Cottian Alps on the southwest, the Isère and Arc valleys on the west, the Little St Bernard Pass on the north, and the Dora Baltea River Valley on the northeast. These are the highest and most rugged of the Western Alps. The ridgeline rarely drops below 3000m and many of the peaks and massifs are glacier-covered. Between the Little St Bernard (2188m, on the road that connects the Thuile Valley with the Isère), and the Col du Grand Ferret, rises Mont Blanc, the highest peak in Europe (4807m). To the east lies the glacier-covered gneiss massif of the Gran Paradiso (4061m), shared by the regions of Piedmont and Valle d'Aosta.

The name Graian Alps comes from the Celtic Graioceli tribe, who lived in the area of the Mont Cenis Pass and the Viù Valley. The area was conquered by the Romans in the 1st century BC. Following the fall of the Western Roman Empire, it was claimed by various Germanic tribes. Most of the Graian Alps belonged for centuries to the Duchy of Savoy (later the Kingdom of Sardinia). After the sale of Nice and Savoy set forth in the Treaty of Turin (24th March 1860), the western slopes of the southern portion of the chain passed to France.

The Graian Alps have figured prominently in the history of mountaineering since the conquest of Mont Blanc in 1786. Most of the major peaks were climbed in the 19th century, the same period in which the first Alpine guides' associations were born in the shadow of Mont Blanc.

THE BASSO CANAVESE

The Canavese is a subalpine district extending between the Valle d'Aosta, the Valli di Lanzo and the Turin plain. Farming and grazing dominate the lower part, the Basso Canavese, creating a landscape of vineyards, cereal crops, fodder and woods, speckled with dairy cattle and sheep. It has a number of interesting abbeys and castles, some of them open to the public.

ABBAZIA DI SANTA FEDE
This little jewel, with its beautiful brick-and-stone façade and splendidly carved portal, lies in open countryside approximately a kilometre southwest of Cavagnolo

(*map A, D2*). The abbey was once part of a vast system of hospices for pilgrims and travellers, including many coming over the Western Alps from the Rhine River basin along one of the routes of the Via Francigena to Rome. Its origin, which long baffled historians, is now generally attributed to the Benedictine monks of Sainte-Foy de Conques, though the jury is still out on the date of its foundation. Some sources suggest it was established in the 8th century; if this is true, what one sees today is the result of a 12th-century makeover. The namesake was a young Frenchwoman who was martyred in Agen (France) under Diocletian in 303 and whose remains are preserved at the abbey of Conques.

ABBAZIA DI FRUTTUARIA

This grand complex stands on the outskirts of San Benigno Canavese (*map A, D2*), overlooking the Torrente Malone. Founded in 1003 by Abbot Guglielmo da Volpiano, it is dedicated to the Virgin, to Benignus of Dijon and to all the saints. Rebuilt and enlarged many times over the centuries (the campanile is Romanesque, the church is Baroque, the cloister and façade are 18th-century), it is one of the most important monasteries in Piedmont. The church has three short aisles, ending in a transept with five apsidal chapels, following the model of the French abbey of Cluny, which allowed many monks to celebrate the liturgy at the same time, at a certain distance from the main altar. The abbey also preserves the remains of a circular building, on the model of the Holy Sepulchre of Jerusalem. The walls of the transept chapels still have traces of faux-marble decorations. Restoration work has brought to light the remains of the original Romanesque church, whose most important elements are the fine 11th-century mosaics with black and white tiles representing symbolic animals with leaves and ornamental geometric motifs. The paved cloister, with two orders of arches, the upper taller than the lower, was restored after 2007.

The recent round of restoration has created a walk through the abbey's 11th-century spaces, which lie beneath the 18th-century church. These were largely financed by King Arduino of Ivrea, who spent his last years in the abbey; the church was designed by Bernardo Antonio Vittone for Cardinal Vittorio Amedeo delle Lanze. Here are traces of the main altar, the side altars, the rotunda of the Holy Sepulchre and, above all, handsome black-and-white mosaic floors with stylized plant and animal motifs. A historic pageant featuring actors in medieval costume and an archery contest is held at the abbey in June. (*Piazza Cardinale delle Lanze; for opening times, see piemonteitalia.eu/en/cultura/musei/abbazia-di-fruttuaria*)

SAN GIORGIO CANAVESE

Surrounded by low hills, San Giorgio (*map A, D1*) is one of several pleasant towns that has grown up on the vast plain of the River Orco. It was a fief of the Counts of Biandrate, allies of the Valperga (against the San Martino) and fair-weather friends of the marquises of Monferrato in their conflicts with the Savoy—until the Treaty of Cherasco (1631) brought them firmly within the Savoy fold. Shortly afterwards their sombre and formidable medieval fortress began to metamorphose into the luxurious manor house one sees today, wonderfully positioned on a low knoll just above the village rooftops. Within are a spectacular grand staircase and some beautifully decorated rooms (now used for events). The blue-and-white Sala degli Aironi takes its name from the herons who fly amidst the trees and vines adorning the walls. The oldest part of the complex, the 12th-century Castelvecchio, was torn down in the 19th century to make today's formal gardens. The former Foresteria is now a hotel. Traces of the medieval fortifications can still be seen here and there around the village.

San Giorgio is famous in Piedmont for having produced an amazing number of distinguished citizens. Among them are statesmen Carlo Botta and Carlo Ignazio Giulio, opera singer Teresa Belloc (the darling of Rossini), Antonio Michela Zucco (inventor of one of the first shorthand machines), engraver Michele Pechenino and naval engineer Carlo Vigna (co-designer of the first Italian submarine, the *Dolphin*).

CALUSO

The name of this town (*map A, D1*) is associated with two fine wines, Erbaluce and Passito di Caluso, produced by vineyards enjoying a particularly favourable climate. Caluso's mild winters, early springs, breezy summers and mostly sunny autumns, cause the grapes to ripen earlier here than in other towns in the area. Caluso is also an important textile and metallurgical centre, which accounts for the many factories you'll see, especially on entering and leaving the town. The main attractions in Caluso are the lovely park and formal gardens of **Palazzo Valperga di Masino**, with their monumental sequoias, magnolias, tulip trees, camellias, lime and plane trees. The garden was begun in the early 17th century and later enlarged to plans by Filippo Castelli. The view ranges over the Lago di Candida (*see below*) to the Alps. The *palazzo* (also known as Villa Spurgazzi from the name of its last owners) is now the Town Hall and the seat of a publicly owned *enoteca* showcasing wines produced here and elsewhere in the hills around Turin. Caluso also preserves some stretches of its 13th-century walls, particularly around the Porta della Freta, near the 16th-century church of San Calogero.

Lago di Candia, 3km north of Caluso, is a bird sanctuary and nature reserve. The little glacial lake and the surrounding wetlands are fed by underground springs; the lake flora includes white and yellow water lilies and water chestnut. In the wetlands you can find sedge (*Carex elata*), marsh iris (*Iris pseudacorus*), and some rare species such as water violet (*Hottonia palustris*) and frog bit (*Hydrocaris morsus ranae*). The wetlands are particularly important for birds, especially during migration and winter months. Among the species are mallards and coots, great white heron and purple heron, bittern and grebe, the tufted duck, pochard, pintail, gadwall, shoveler, reed warbler warbler and reed bunting, and raptors such as the black kite and osprey. Pike, bream, bleak and chub live in the lake. The local rowing club has hosted a regatta on the lake since 1893.

MAZZÈ

The best thing about this town (*map A, D1*), perched on its moraine hill, is the beautiful open view, which ranges from the plain of Turin over the Monferrato hills to the Vercelli lowlands. The old village developed around its Valperga castle, once a strategic fortress on the border between that family's domain and the lands of

Vercelli. The castle and village were probably built in the 14th century, as a result of the hostilities that opposed the Valperga to the San Martino and more widely in the context of the dispute between the Savoy and the Marquis of Monferrato for control of the vast border with the Canavese. The fortress, which remained in the hands of Valperga until the early 19th century, was extensively remodelled as a comfortable mansion in the Eclectic style, to designs by Giuseppe Bellini Velati. The old cellars and dungeons are now home to a musem of torture (*closed at the time of writing, for updates, see beniculturali.it/luogo/castello-di-mazze-e-museo-della-tortura*).

BORGOMASINO

Set on one of the hills that mark the border between the moraine amphitheatre of Ivrea and the plain of Canavese, Borgomasino (*map A, D1*) offers breathtaking views of the whole area. The 11th-century tower of the ancient castle is now part of a 19th-century mansion used as a hotel. The octagonal church of San Salvatore was designed in the mid-18th century by Bernardo Vittone and then modified in 1773 by Carlo Amedeo Rana. Inside is a wooden choir carved with the *Stories of St Francis*. The Romanesque bell tower of the original church stands in the upper part of the village, whereas in the Lucento neighbourhood, northeast of the historic centre, a megalithic fortress surrounds the *Pera cunca*, thought to be a Druid altar.

Borgomasino has two castles: the *castrum vetus*, in the town, and the *castrum novum*, in the Torrazza neighbourhood, of which only a few ruins remain. Around 1870 Luigi Valperga di Masino had the *castrum vetus* renovated as his mansion. Today's 'castle' only remotely resembles the original fortress; the sole visible sign of fortification is the tall rectangular tower, which rises above the rest of the building.

CARAVINO

Facing out over the Canavese plain, Caravino (*map A, D1*) stands on a hillside opposite the broad moraine amphitheatre of the Serra di Ivrea. It is known primarily for the **Castello di Masino** (*for visiting times, see fondoambiente.it/luoghi/castello-e-parco-di-masino*), for ten centuries the home of one of Italy's great families and now a property of FAI, the the Italian Environment Fund.

The elegant country house occupies the site of an 11th-century castle rebuilt several times during the following centuries. Its present appearance dates largely from the 18th century, when it was the residence of Carlo Francesco II, viceroy of Sardinia, and his brother Tommaso Valperga, abbot of Caluso. At this time the double ramp up to the entrance was constructed, and many of the rooms were furnished. These include the print room with French etchings, the library, the Spanish ambassador's bedroom, and a gallery lined with family portraits. Tommaso Valperga, a friend of the poet Vittorio Alfieri, designed the decoration in the poets' gallery.

The medieval northeast tower was adapted in 1730 as a ballroom. The rectangular keep has a lower room, frescoed in the 1690s with coats of arms, and an upper hall, with numerous 18th-century portraits of the royal house of Savoy. The remains of King Arduino (brought here in the 18th century from the castle of Agliè) are preserved in the little family chapel. The stable block has a collection of carriages, open at weekends. The castle is surrounded by an attractive formal garden (a flower show is held on the first weekend in May), the design of which survives in part from the 17th and 18th centuries, and a large park laid out in 1840.

The **garden** is divided from east to west into two separate sections in keeping with the lie of the land. A majestic avenue flanked by limes leads westwards, on level ground, to the great hornbeam labyrinth, an element typical of Italian formal gardens of the 18th century (not to be missed). Just south of the maze begins the extraordinary *Strada dei ventidue giri*, created 1840–7 to link the nearby town of Strambino to the castle; its 22 hairpin bends on a gradual, constant incline were designed to facilitate the ascent by stagecoach.

The Romantic **park**, where nature is wilder and biological diversity greater, unfolds to the east of the castle: it is distinguished by impeccably tended lawns set at different heights, and there is a small Gothic-Revival temple constructed in the early 19th century. Around it you'll find a surprise or two if you come in spring: Paolo Pejrone, a former student of Russell Page and one of Italy's leading contemporary garden architects, has planted 110,000 daffodils on the lawns and 7,000 white *Spirea Van Houttey* plants in the vicinity of the temple.

IVREA

Situated at the centre of a broad amphitheatre surrounded by the world's highest hills of glacial moraine, the pleasant old town of Ivrea (*map A, D1*) was the Roman *Eporedia*, a bulwark in the 1st century BC against the Salassian Gauls of the Upper Dora. In the Middle Ages its marquises rose to power, and Arduino of Ivrea was crowned King of Italy in 1002. The town expanded as an industrial centre after the establishment of the Olivetti typewriter factories in 1908, and throughout the 20th century it was known internationally as the global headquarters of the firm, which had become a leading manufacturer of business machines (producing Italy's first computer, the Elea 9003, in 1959, and the first desktop computer, Programma 101, in 1965). The Olivetti era ended in 2003 when the firm merged with Telecom Italia, but the firm's historical heritage has been preserved in Ivrea, which—thanks largely to the vision and perseverance of the founder's son, Adriano Olivetti (1901–60)—boasts one of the highest concentrations of Modern architecture in Europe. The finest buildings now constitute the Museo a Cielo Aperto dell'Architettura Moderna (MAAM), an open-air museum roughly two kilometres long (*described below*).

THE CITY CENTRE

The old town unfolds around the **Castello dalle Rossi Torri**, the 'Castle of the Red Towers', a name coined by the poet Giosuè Carducci. It was built by Aymon de Challant (1358) for Amedeo VI and has four tall angle towers, one of which was partially destroyed by an explosion in 1676. Much loved by the Savoy family, who lived here during the war between Piedmont and France, the castle became in 1630 the seat of the Chamber of Representatives, who in 1648 chose it for the coronation of Carlo Emanuele III. Abandoned after the explosion, it served as a prison from

1700 right up until 1970. It has since been restored and is now used largely for special events.

Across the castle square is Ivrea's **cathedral**, dedicated to Santa Maria Assunta and erected probably in the 10th century on the ruins of a pagan temple. All that is left of the Romanesque church is the ground plan (with the sanctuary at the west end), part of the presbytery with the ambulatory, the area west of the crypt and the bottom of the bell towers. The dome was constructed and the bell towers were completed in the mid-12th century. Six centuries later the Romanesque roof was demolished and replaced by masonry vaults decorated with stucco and paintings by Giovanni Cogrossi. The façade of 1854 was built in the Neoclassical style. The cathedral archive contains some precious illuminated manuscripts, including the 10th- or 11th-century *Varmondo Psalter*.

The former monastery of Santa Chiara, on Piazza Ottinetti, houses the **Museo Civico Pier Alessandro Garda** (*closed Mon, for opening hours, see museogardaivrea. it*), featuring collections of archaeology, Asian art and paintings. The archaeological section displays finds from the city and region from the Neolithic period to the early Middle Ages. The Asian art holdings come from the personal collection of Pier Alessandro Garda and include objects in metal, porcelain, lacquer, paper, silk, wood, bamboo, ivory and glass. The painting collection consists of works by Italian masters donated by philanthropist Lucia Guelpa. Among the 50 paintings and drawings on display are a 14th-century *Crucifixion and Saints* by Giovanni del Biondo, an intense *Portrait of a Man* by Annibale Carracci, the famous *Superbiosa* of Filadelfo Simi, and the unusual *Peaches on the Bough* and *Laurel Forest* by Giorgio De Chirico.

MAM: MUSEO A CIELO APERTO DELL'ARCHITETTURA MODERNA

This unique open-air museum of modern architecture is not to be missed. There is no indoor exhibition space; the 'museum' consists of a guided walk. You can upload a map to your mobile device (*http://www.mamivrea.it/collezione/mappa.html*) or print it out, if you prefer a hard copy; NB: website is in Italian only). Well-designed text panels telll you virtually everything you need to know about the architects, the buildings and the Olivetti corporate culture underlying their construction.

The museum was opened in 2001 with the ambitious objective of highlighting Ivrea's extraordinary Modern architectural heritage, of showing how it reflects the values of its time and of demonstrating the firm's contribution to the history of 20th-century Italian architecture and industrial design. The walk unfolds along two kilometres of Via Jervis—the main street of the Olivetti campus on the right bank of the Dora Baltea—and in neighbouring areas. Seven 'information stations' tell of Olivetti's corporate-wide commitment to beauty, from the firm's foundation to its closure—a commitment that made it a global leader in the fields of architecture, urban planning, graphic design and, of course, product design. Here you will find buildings by Gabetti & Isola, Ignazio Gardella and other prominent Italian architects of the 20th century, as well as by lesser-known figures.

The residential neighbourhood of **Canton Vesco** first appeared in Ivrea's 1938 Regulatory Plan, which called for the construction of living quarters for 15,000 inhabitants in fewer than 3,000 housing units. The neighbourhood was built in stages between 1943 and 1967 and is the most complex among those financed by Olivetti. It covers more than c. 400,000 sq m and includes designs by Ottavio Cascio, Annibale Fiocchi, Italo Lauro, Marcello Nizzoli, Gian Mario Oliveri, Ludovico Quaroni, Mario Ridolfi, Ugo Sissa and Emilio Aventino Tarpino, united by a common search for low-cost, high-quality living spaces. The planning documents reference European social housing experiments, particularly the German *Siedlungen*, and their response to the problem of providing adequate accommodation for low-income groups. The neighbourhood has its own nursery (1964, Mario Ridolfi and Wolfgang Frankl), school (1964, Ludovico Quaroni and Adolfo De Carlo) and church (1963, M. Nizzoli and G.M. Olivieri). It was the first to be systematically restored and returned to residents for occupation. The goal was to ensure that the form and appearance of the buildings would remain as close as possible to the original, while allowing the changes required to fit the structures for modern use. In some cases a compromise has been struck: the establishment of a film library (Archivio del Cinema d'Impresa) in the former nursery has involved major changes to the interior, where the original spaces and furnishings were sized (obviously) for 'small-scale' users.

The semicircular **Centro Residenziale Ovest** was intended to provide temporary housing for new employees in 82 residential units. Immediately nicknamed 'The Burrow', it appears to lie underground, thanks to its broad, grassy roof-garden. Designed by Gabetti & Isola, this extraordinary building foreshadows the attention to the natural landscape that has become a concern of much recent architecture. The architects have brilliantly reshaped the slope of the hill that separates the complex from the Olivetti factories, orienting all the apartments towards the wooded summit.

Other points of interest on the campus are the 'red brick factory' (1896, C. Olivetti); the Officine ICO (1934–62, Figini & Pollini); the Social Services Centre (1955, Figini & Pollini), which houses the museum's welcome centre; the Borgo Olivetti neighbourhood (1939–41, Figini & Pollini); the Centro Studi ed Esperienze (1951, Eduardo Victoria); the Olivetti Canteen (1953, Ignazio Gardella); the Castellamonte neighbourhood, which includes seven houses for employee families (1940–2, Figini & Pollini), six villas for executives (1950–2, Figini & Pollini), and single-employee flats (1951–6, Nizzoli & Oliveri); and the office buildings (1960–4, Bernasconi, Fiocchi & Nizzoli; and 1984–8, Gino Valle).

THE ALTO CANAVESE

The availability of energy—first water, then electricity from hydroelectric plants—has enabled the development of important industries in Ivrea and other urban centres of the Alto Canavese, which also boasts some of the prettier Alpine resorts.

PAVONE CANAVESE

The village of Pavone (*map A, D1*) grew up at the foot of its striking castle, set on a hill dominating the road from Aosta to Turin. Its role as a garrison settlement has been documented since the 9th century, with major additions between the 12th and 14th centuries. Remaining in the possession of the bishops of Ivrea until 1706, and probably reinforced on their initiative during the 13th century, the complex was going to ruin when the Portuguese architect, archaeologist and painter Alfredo d'Andrade bought and renovated it in 1885, in the Gothic Revival style (D'Andrade also owned the castle of Rivara; *see below*). The village hosts a famous medieval pageant (*Ferie Medievali*), with duelling knights and dancing damsels, in May–June.

AGLIÈ

The history of this small town (*map A, D1*) is completely bound up with that of its **Castello Ducale** (*check the Savoy Royal Residences website for hours, residenzerealisabaude.com*), one of the grandest of the Savoy country residences. Built in the Middle Ages for the powerful San Martino d'Agliè family, the castle was given its present form in the 17th and 18th centuries. In 1646–57 Filippo di San Martino, counsellor of the regent Christine de France, began to transform the medieval fortress into a comfortable country residence—a project that was taken up again after 1764, when the castle and its fiefs were purchased by Carlo Emanuele III of Savoy for his son Benedetto Maria Maurizio, Duke of Chablais. The first Savoy building campaign was entrusted to the architect Ignazio Birago Borgaro, who enlarged the part overlooking the village and built the church and Galleria delle Tribune. The architect also oversaw the creation of the formal garden with its iconic horseshoe fountain, the first work of the brothers Collino. A second building campaign was undertaken in 1825–49 by King Carlo Felice and Queen Maria Cristina, who created the small theatre and renovated the royal apartments. On the queen's death the castle was inherited by Carlo Alberto, who passed it to his son Ferdinand, the first Duke of Genoa; in 1939 the dukes of Genoa donated the property to the state.

The tour of the interior lasts over an hour (it takes in quite a few of the castle's 300 sumptuous rooms; highlights include the magnificent Teatrino, the frescoed ballroom, the Sala Cinese, the kitchen, the greenhouses and the Sala Tuscolana, a gallery of antiquities from the early 19th-century archaeological excavations conducted by Luigi Biondi at the Villa Tuscolana Rufinella near Rome).

The castle grounds consist of the **Italian gardens** next to the building and the large **Romantic park** designed by Xavier Kürten between 1830 and 1840. A highlight of the formal gardens, which develop on two levels, is the magnificent low box-hedge design with flowering parterres around an elliptical fountain. Also important are the greenhouses, entirely decorated with frescoes and grotesques, and the orangery, made to shelter the citrus plants during the winter season. A small dovecote, its roof covered with Castellamonte ceramic tiles, occupies the northwest corner of the upper garden.

Kürten's Romantic park extends to the northeast of the castle. Built over a Baroque park designed by Michel Benard, it contains archaeological finds placed here and there for the delight of Maria Cristina, a particularly erudite collector of Roman antiquities.

XAVIER KÜRTEN

Born in Brühl, Germany, in the late 18th century, Xavier Kürten became the spokesman of the Romantic spirit in Piedmont. It is largely thanks to his efforts as landscape architect to the Kings of Sardinia that the classic French garden, with its dramatic axial perspectives that speak of a nature dominated by human intellect, yielded to the English Romantic model, in which the seemingly spontaneous interaction of trees and meadows tells of a human will to work in harmony with nature to create a succession of scenes carefully studied to arouse emotion.

Between 1812 and 1840 Kürten designed four gardens for the Savoy (at the castles of Racconigi, Govone, Agliè and Pollenzo) and innumerable others for wealthy Piedmontese patrons. His designs are known for their varied plantings and careful positioning (each plant carefully chosen for the exact point it occupies in the composition). Kürten liked to group trees in curvilinear formations and to create vistas over large expanses of lawn and, where possible, water. His masterpiece is the Park of Racconigi (*see p. 117*), designed with architect Ernesto Melano and sculptor and architect Pelagio Palagi for Carlo Alberto of Savoy (c. 1840).

Also in Agliè is **Villa il Meleto** (*open by appointment; T: 0124 330150*), the home of poet Guido Gozzano (1883–1916). Surrounded by a park and an apple orchard (from which it takes its name) Il Meleto left the Gozzano family in 1912. After Second World War it was purchased by Hedwig Gatti Facchini, who set out to find its missing furnishings and make it as similar as possible to the place described by the poet in his lyrics. On Gatti Facchini's death the villa passed to Francis Conrieri, who restored it in keeping with the Art Nouveau idiom of early 20th-century Piedmont, turning it into a house-museum with the living room, study, library and 'good things in bad taste' that Gozzano celebrated in his Intimist lyrics. Around the house is a small garden combining native plants with the exotics that were common in early 20th-century gardens. The island in the pond, an allegory of the 'garden in the garden' and a place separated from the rest of the world, is a nice Intimist touch. The apple orchard is along the central avenue leading to the villa.

RIVARA

The history of Rivara (*map A, C1*) is also linked to its **castle**, restored by the Portuguese architect, archaeologist and painter Alfredo d'Andrade in the late 19th century, becoming the meeting-place of the 'school' or 'circle of Rivara', which included some of the most prominent Italian writers, painters and architects of the Belle Epoque. The complex is actually made up of two parts, of which the oldest (documented since 1236 and called the Castelvecchio) was commissioned by the Valperga, and the most recent (documented since 1303, but perhaps older) was built by the Discalzi. There is also a *ricetto* (shelter), documented as early as the 13th century, and a village at the foot of the hill on which the two castles stand. D'Andrade's restoration project also covered the medieval village, which became a fashionable holiday spot among northern Italian aristocrats, many of whom built villas here. Examples include the turn-of-the-20th century **Villa Ogliani**, now the Town Hall, and **Villa Colli**, an excellent example of the Rationalist architecture of Gino Levi Montalcini and Giuseppe Pagano Pogatschnig. The church of **San Giovanni Battista** dates from the 16th century and holds a remarkable altarpiece by Martino Spanzotti. The Castel Nuovo hosts a **Centro d'Arte Contemporanea** (*for details of opening times and how to visit, see castellodirivara.it*) with a good permanent collection.

VALPERGA

This (*map A, C1*) was the fief of the powerful Valperga, archrivals of the San Martino of Agliè. Long allied to the marquises of Monferrato, the family switched its allegiance in 1356 to the Savoy, who confirmed their title. The village is still centred around its **castle**, originally made up of three distinct elements (one of which possibly dating from the 10th century), later reduced to two. Of these, the one facing the hillside retains much of its medieval appearance, whereas the one facing the village (now a nursing home) was renovated long ago as a handsome country house.

A *ricetto* was built at the foot of the castle hill in the 14th century, and you can still see parts of its walls and a gate (the Porta Corgnate). Later the village grew toward the parish church of the Santissima Trinità, with a tall 18th-century campanile by Ludovico Antonio Bo, one of the most beautiful examples of Rococo architecture in Piedmont. The oldest church in Valperga, San Giorgio (14th–15th century), stands on the castle hill and is known for its 15th-century frescoes.

A footpath leads from Valperga to the **Sacro Monte di Belmonte** (4hrs round trip including visit to the sanctuary; elevation gain 400m). For the less intrepid, the Sacro Monte can be reached in 20mins by car. The sanctuary sits on a hilltop with stunning views of the Po River basin from the Serra d'Ivrea to the hills of Turin. The summit, forested with chestnut, oak and birch trees and speckled with pink granite outcrops, is of interest to archaeologists for its prehistoric, Roman, Lombard and late medieval remains. The shrine, begun in 1712 on the initiative of the Franciscan friar Michelangelo da Montiglio and finished a full century later, includes a church dating back to the Middle Ages and 13 chapels dedicated to the Passion of Christ. Laid out along a circular walkway, these follow a simple, straightforward design with a square or circular cell preceded by a porch holding polychrome terracotta statues representing the sacred scene. A recent restoration has brought to light a few fragments of frescoes, attributed to Lombard masters.

CUORGNÈ

Spring, autumn or winter, it always seems to be snowing in Cuorgnè (*map A, C1*). Set in magnificent surroundings at the foot of the Gran Paradiso (*see below*), the town claims pre-Roman origins. The Romans built a military stronghold (*Corniacum*) on the right bank of the River Orco, at a point where the valley opens up. The present town is probably the descendant of the 10th-century *Curtis Canava*, destroyed by a flood in the late 11th century. It was once dominated by a Valperga castle, but this was demolished in 1388 by Amedeo VII of Savoy during his repression of the *Tuchini*, groups of farmers who rose up against their lords, protected by the

Marquis of Monferrato and by the Duke of Milan. During the 14th century the town crystallised in two areas, the aristocratic *villa*, around the castle, and the *borgo*, still characterised by its arcaded main street (Via Arduino) its 14th-century towers (the Torre Carlevato and Torre dell'Orologio) and the late medieval Casa d'Arduino.

Cuorgnè's most conspicuous monument is an immense 19th-century mill overlooking the Orco, now a museum and office complex. Here is the **Museo Archeologico del Canavese** (*open Mon–Fri 9–5, cesmaonline.org/museo-archeologico-del-canavese*), dedicated to the prehistory and early history of the district and preserving evidence of human habitation in northwest Piedmont from the Palaeolithic until the Middle Ages. The exhibits trace the development of human habitation of the Canavese from the first tiny communities of Late Palaeolithic hunters, through the more substantial Neolithic settlements to the many permanent villages of the Late Bronze Age. The Roman period is represented by finds mostly from Valperga. Highlights of the collection include square-mouthed vases from c. 3500 BC, biconical urns from a necropolis near Valperga and a Roman sacrificial knife handle, in bronze, found near Cuorgnè.

CERESOLE REALE

The gateway to the Parco Nazionale del Gran Paradiso from Piedmont, Ceresole Reale (*map A, B1*) is one of the most famous resorts of the Canavese. There is no town proper, only a handful of villages scattered through a beautiful valley by the shores of an artificial lake. Surrounded by towering vertical rock face, Ceresole is a favourite destination for free-climbers; but for the less adventurous, the area's streams, waterfalls and flowering meadows are just as attractive. Once the favourite summer retreat of the royal family and their court in the late 19th century, it was here, in July 1890, that Giosuè Carducci wrote his ode 'Piemonte', a poetic tour of the region that begins with a striking description of these mountains, filled with bounding chamois and thundering avalanches, glittering peaks and the lazy flight of the eagle.

PARCO NAZIONALE DEL GRAN PARADISO

Covering nearly 70,000 hectares with an elevation of 800–4061m, the Gran Paradiso National Park (*pngp.it*) is Italy's largest and oldest nature reserve. It was created in 1922, in recognition of the need to conserve a mountain environment suitable for the survival of the ibex, which has come close to extinction several times in recent centuries. Thanks to this park, the species is well on its way to repopulating the Alps.

The protected habitat is split more or less evenly between Piedmont and Valle d'Aosta. The area in Piedmont includes large parts of the Orco and Soana valleys. On the lower slopes forests of larch, pine and spruce prevail, giving way higher up to pastures, alpine meadows and lichens. In addition to the ibex, most of the familiar alpine animals and birdlife can be found—including the bearded vulture, which vanished in 1912 but has now been re-established.

VISITING THE PARK
The park service maintains two permanent exhibits in Ceresole Reale. The **Homo et Ibex** museum, at the visitors' centre in the former Grant Hotel at Prese, traces the past, present and future relationship between *Homo sapiens* and *Capra ibex*, an animal which needs large individual browsing areas. The museum makes a great deal of the argument that sustainable development is a necessity, not a luxury, and stresses the role of parks in protecting species at risk of extinction and in preserving the environments in which they live. There is also archaeological material documenting ibex hunting since the end of the last Ice Age (c. 10000 BC), including finds from excavations in the Orco Valley (Boira Fusca) of an Epipalaeolithic and Mesolithic hunting camp.

Le Torbiere d'Alta Montagna, at Serrù, illustrates the Colle della Losa trail, which connects the Gran Paradiso with the Parc National de la Vanoise in France, and presents the outstanding natural features of the two areas.

GRAIAN ALPS PRACTICAL TIPS

GETTING AROUND

- **By bus:** GTT runs a daily service from Turin (Via Fiochetto 23, Stazione Dora; *www.gtt.to.it*) to Ivrea (c. 1hr 40 mins), as does SADEM (*www.sadem.it*) from the bus station at Corso Vittorio Emanuele II 131 (Ivrea; c. 1hr 20mins).
- **By rail:** There is a regular daily service from Turin (Porta Nuova) to Ivrea (regional 1hr; fast regional, change at Chivasso, 1hr 11mins).

WHERE TO STAY

CERESOLE REALE (*map A, B1*)
€ **Gli Scoiattoli**. The simple, rustic atmosphere of this small hotel in the Parco Nazionale del Gran Paradiso recalls that of a high-altitude Alpine hut. Children are welcome (there are interior and exterior play areas) and the food is delicious and unpretentious, made from the freshest, most genuine local ingredients. A perfect place for young families. *Borgata Barilò 4, Ceresole Reale, hotelgliscoiattoli.it.*

CHIAVERANO (*map B, A4*)
€€ **Castello San Giuseppe**. A magnificently restored and converted former Carmelite convent, on a hilltop with a garden and fine views. Previous house guests have included Eleonora Duse and Ginger Rogers. *Località San Giuseppe, castellosangiuseppe.com.*

COLLERETTO GIACOSA (*map A, D1*)
€€ **Villa Soleil**. This 18th-century country manor, completely restored in 2006, comes with a renowned restaurant and a 5000 sq m park where, for almost three centuries, a tree has been planted for each new male heir. Wisteria and jasmine grow around the pool, and rooms and public areas are warm and filled with light. *Via della Cartiera 13/15, villasoleil.it.*

IVREA (*map A, D1*)
€€ **Sirio**. A family-managed hotel by Lake Sirio. With wellness centre and restaurant (Finch), which specialises in grilled dishes. *Via Lago di Sirio 85, T: 0125 424247.*

ROMANO CANAVESE (*map A, D1*)
€€ **Relais Villa Matilde**. An 18th-century villa with handsome frescoed rooms and meticulously tended grounds, this comfortable hotel is situated in a small town in the Canavese hills. The restaurant is in the former stables and there are more rooms and a few dual-level suites in the ex-dovecote. The hotel is particularly convenient for visiting Ivrea (just 15mins away) and is than an hour from Vercelli and Novara, Biella and the Parco Nazionale del Gran Paradiso. 43 rooms. *Viale Marconi 29, relaisvillamatilde.com.*

SAN FRANCESCO AL CAMPO (*map A, C2*)
€€ **Furno**. An elegant place derived from the careful restoration of a large 18th-century farm, this hotel is just 10mins from Turin's Sandro Pertini Airport. It is also convenient for visiting the Savoy residences at Venaria Reale (20mins), Rivoli (30mins) and Stupinigi (35mins), as well as Turin itself (35mins). Rooms are individually furnished, and dinner is served in relatively small dining rooms with crackling fires (in winter) or by the pool (summer). 33 rooms. *Via Roggeri 2, romantichoteltorino.com.*

STRAMBINELLO (*map A, D1*)
€ **Castello di Strambinello**. This refined country house B&B stands in a quiet, secluded setting overlooking the pristine valley of the Torrente Chiusella, just 15mins from Ivrea. The present owners, a professional restorer and his veterinarian wife, have brought it back to its ancient splendour and furnished it with genuine antiques. They are now working on a garden in keeping with the historic character of the buildings and the ecological integrity of their environs. Three suites. *Via Castello 1, castellodistrambinello.com.*

WHERE TO EAT

IVREA (*map A, D1*)
€ **La Trattoria San Giovanni**. Simple and wholesome Piedmontese fare since 1975. Closed Mon and Tues all day, Wed lunch and Sun dinner. *Corso Vercelli 45, trattoriasangiovanni.it.*
€ **Vecchia Ivrea**. *Osteria* serving good, unpretentious cooking. Plenty of wholesome staples. *Vicolo Cantanara 16. T: 349 780 3324.*

QUINCINETTO (*just beyond map A, D1*)
€€ **Da Giovanni**. The architecture may be contemporary but the cuisine is firmly rooted in the time-honoured traditions of the Canavese. The menu is seasonal and is matched by the views. Closed Tues evening and Wed. *Via Fontana Riola 3, Montellina, Quincinetto. T: 0125 757447.*

SAN GIORGIO CANAVESE (*map A, D1*)
€ **Ristorante della Luna**. Located in the town centre and run by the same family for 80 years, this well-established restaurant offers great local cuisine and a good selection of local and regional wines, simple lunches.

Closed Mon. *Piazza Ippolito San Giorgio 12. T: 0124 32184.*

LOCAL SPECIALITIES

From the Valli di Lanzo and the Canavese come the celebrated **torcetti**, small sweet biscuits made by mixing bread dough with sugar or honey. Also from the Canavese is the winter staple **salampatata**, a mixture of bacon trimmings and pork mince and boiled potatoes (about 50/50), with the addition of salt, pepper, garlic and other spices such as cinnamon and nutmeg, all stuffed into a natural casing and left to cure for a week.

Inextricably tied to the nearby Savoy residence of Agliè, as supplier of the Royal House and of the Duke of Genoa, the venerable **Roletti** pastry shop in San Giorgio Canavese counted among its illustrious customers Queen Margherita and the beautiful Duchess of Pistoia who, with the excuse of buying the biscuits made expressly for her, here met her lovers. The pastry shop, located in a Viennese Secession-style building, was designed in the early 20th century by Antonio Roletti, brother of the founder Giuseppe. It is now run by the fourth generation of the Roletti family, who are upholding the tradition of pastry making in Piedmont very well (*Via Carlo Alberto 28, roletti1896.it*).

EVENTS AND FESTIVALS

Agliè *Sagra del Torcetto*, festival celebrating the 'sweet *grissino*', a small oval biscuit, once popular with humble folk and the Savoy rulers alike, Sept.
Ivrea boasts the most imaginative, combative and messiest festival in the region, the *Storico Carnevale di Ivrea*, for it includes the world-famous *Battaglie delle Arance* ('Battle of the Oranges'), which commemorates the supposed rebellion in the 12th century of a miller's daughter (*mugnaia*), named Violetta in the pageant, and the townspeople against the local marquis (Ranieri di Biandrate) who had demanded *jus primae noctis* (the right of a lord to sleep with the brides of his serfs). The marquis was, apparently, beheaded by the young miller's daughter. It is held in Feb/March, during the three days before Shrove Tuesday.

The Cottian Alps

The Cottian Alps (Italian *Alpi Cozie*; French *Alpes Cottiennes*) are the segment of the Western Alps extending along the French-Italian border between the Maddalena Pass and the Maritime Alps on the south, Mont Cenis and the Graian Alps on the north, and the Dauphiné Alps and Galibier Pass on the west. Monviso (3841m) is the highest point. Other important peaks are the Pierre Menue (or *Aiguille de la Scolette*, 3505m), Mont Chaberton (3131m), Punta Ramiere (or *Bric Froid*, 3303m), Pic de Rochebrune (3325m) and Aiguille de Chambeyron (3409m). Whereas in Italy the Cottian Alps lie entirely within Piedmont, in France they are shared by three departments: Savoy, the Hautes Alpes and the Alpes de Haute Provence. The mountains take their name from the Gaulish chief Cottius, who received the dignity of prefect of Segusium (Susa) from Augustus.

THE VAL DI SUSA

Extending over 80km and with over 90,000 inhabitants, the Val di Susa (*Valsusa* in the dialect of Piedmont, *Val Susa* in Occitan and Arpitan) is the largest and most populated Alpine valley of Piedmont. It takes its name from the city of Susa, located in a central position in the valley, even if its biggest city today is Avigliana. The valley has been traversed by travellers and armies on their way across the Alps for many centuries. It belonged to the Dauphiny until it was transferred to Turin in 1713, and the carved symbol of the dolphin can still be seen in some places in the valley. Three roads across the Alps from France now converge here, the busiest of which is via the Mont Cenis Tunnel.

AVIGLIANA
The town (*map A, B2*) at the entrance to the Val di Susa is known for its lakes, the main attractions of the large **Parco Naturale Regionale di Avigliana**. Located in a moraine valley, the park has a wide variety of ecosystems, including swamps and forests, and varied fauna. The two lakes, called simply Piccolo and Grande, are popular for their beauty, their recreational opportunities (the Lago Grande is best for swimming; the Lago Piccolo, for birdwatching) and their proximity to Turin. The historic centre of the town has some important architecture, including the porticoed medieval buildings on Piazza del Conte Rosso, adorned with terracotta friezes; the 13th–14th-century church of San Giovanni, with paintings by Defendente Ferrari

and a pulpit carved in the late 16th century; and the church of San Pietro, built before the year 1000 but rebuilt in the 13th–15th centuries. On the hill above are the ruins of the castle, destroyed by General Catinat in 1691.

The **Precettoria di Sant'Antonio di Ranverso**, built after 1188 to accommodate pilgrims on the Via Francigena between Avigliana and Rivoli, is one of the finest examples of the International Gothic style in Piedmont. Located in a beautiful natural setting, in the midst of fields and forests 5km east of Avigliana, the abbey appears much as it did when it was last enlarged, in the 13th–15th centuries. The buildings include a church, a monastery (with a small cloister), a hospital where the monks provided assistance to the sick (particularly those suffering from *fuoco di Sant'Antonio*: shingles or *ignis sacris*), and a system of farms. The 15th-century façade of the church has a portico with three arches topped with ornate gables carved with giant leaves, flowers, fruit and rich vegetation and ending in terracotta pinnacles. The brick campanile has three tiers of mullioned windows adorned with glazed ceramic lunettes. Within, on the main altar, is a large altarpiece by Defendente Ferrari representing the *Nativity* flanked by Sts Roch, Bernardino of Siena, Anthony and Sebastian, and the life and miracles of St Anthony in the predella. The presbytery is adorned with an impressive series of 15th-century frescoes by Giacomo Jaquerio, which were hidden until the 20th century by 18th-century overpainting: on the north wall, a *Madonna Enthroned with Sts John the Baptist, Anthony, Martha, Margaret, Nicholas and Martin and Prophets*; on the south wall, *Stories of St Anthony* and *Farmers Offering Pigs to St Anthony*. In the sacristy Jaquerio frescoed the *Four Evangelists* in the crossing and an *Agony in the Garden* and *Road to Calvary* on the walls. The complex passed to the Order of Sts Maurice and Lazarus in the 18th century and is still run by the Fondazione Ordine Mauriziano. Regular exhibitions and events are held here (*ordinemauriziano.it*).

ABBAZIA SACRA DI SAN MICHELE

The most impressive Christian monument in the Val di Susa—and perhaps in all of Piedmont—is the Benedictine abbey of San Michele della Chiusa at Sant'Ambrogio di Torino (*map A, B2; check opning times at sacradisanmichele.com*). It was founded by the Auvergne nobleman Hugh de Montboissier between 983 and 987, on the summit of Monte Pirchiriano, and is one of the oldest shrines dedicated to the Archangel Michael. It was originally garrisoned with troops, whose job it was to control the narrow gorge (*chiusa*) where the Val di Susa meets the Turin plain. Perched on its mountaintop, it took three full centuries to build (and remains unfinished). Master craftsmen from throughout the region, and much of the Po Valley, worked on the architecture and decoration: one of them, a certain Nicolò, who worked in several Po Valley cathedrals, signed the jamb of the Porta dello Zodiaco. The view from the top of the abbey's 243 steps is nothing short of magnificent: the Alpine peaks that surround the valley provide an unforgettable spectacle (best seen on a cold, crisp day in autumn or early spring). In the most recent of the abbey's many building campaigns (1835), Carlo Alberto of Savoy brought a community of Rosminian monks here with the intention of making the abbey a dynastic monument; the campaign ended with the substantial renovation carried out by Ernesto Melano, Arborio Mella and Alfredo d'Andrade half a century later (1888), in which spectacular elements such as the flying buttresses were added. Today the Sacra di San Michele is still in the hands of the Rosminian Order, and hosts frequent cultural events. In 1994 it was chosen as the symbol of the Region of Piedmont.

> **A legend of San Michele**
> The attendant who took us round S. Michele showed us one place which is called *Il Salto della bella Alda*. Alda was being pursued by a soldier; to preserve her honour, she leaped from a window and fell over a precipice some hundreds of feet below; by the intercession there Virgin she was saved, but became so much elated that she determined to repeat the feat. She jumped a second time from the window, but was dashed to pieces. We were told this as being unworthy of actual credence, but as a legend of the place. We said we found no great difficulty in believing the first half of the story, but could hardly believe that anyone would jump from that window twice.
> Samuel Butler, *Alps & Sanctuaries*, 1881

CAPPELLA DEL CONTE (SAN GIORIO DI SUSA)

On a hill on the right bank of the Dora, surmounted by the remains of its magnificent castle, the village of San Giorio (*map A, B2*) lies at the heart of the Parco dell'Orsiera, beneath the five peaks of Villano (Malanotte and Pian Paris, Cristalliera, Pian Reale and Rocciavré) surrounded by majestic chestnut forests that produce the famed *marrone valsusino*. The Cappella del Conte (*or Cappella di San Lorenzo, Via Castello; open July–Aug or by appointment, centroculturalediocesano.it*) was built in 1328 by the local nobleman Lorenzetto Bertrandi, who dedicated it to his patron saint. The chapel, which appears quite ordinary on the outside, was completely frescoed within by a contemporary Franco-Piedmontese painter. Here is a spectacular cycle of theological paintings focused on the themes of Salvation (*Crucifixion*), Redemption (*Legend of the Three Living and the Three Dead*) and the holy life (*Stories of St Lawrence*). The painter's style shows the influence of Giotto, who was active in Milan around 1300.

RISERVE NATURALI SPECIALI DELL'ORRIDO DI FORESTO AND DELL'ORRIDO DI CHANOCCO

An *orrido* (which translates literally as 'horrid' but which derives from the Latin word for bristling or jagged) is quite simply a ravine, gorge, or precipice. The 200ha Foresto Gorge nature reserve features a long canyon carved by the Rio Rocciamelone, which ends in a spectacular waterfall, and the surrounding limestone ramparts alternating with xeric grasslands. It was established to protect a particular kind of juniper (*Juniperus oxicedrus*), a typically Mediterranean plant that is rare in Alpine environments. The canyon is traversed by a magnificent trail, for experienced hikers only (*via ferrata*, difficulty D, elevation gain 250m, total hiking time 3–5hrs). The nearby Chianocco Gorge is a spectacular cleft in the rock barely ten metres wide and more than fifty deep, created by the Torrente Prebèc in its descent to the floor of the Val di Susa. It has a unique microclimate characterised by high summer temperatures, low snowfall and limited rainfall; these conditions, combined with its southern exposure, have favoured the establishment of different plants typical of Mediterranean or steppe climates, such as *Adiantum capillus-veneris*, *Asplenium fontanum* and *Thesium divaricatum*. The most interesting growth is that of holm oak (*Quercus ilex*), the only natural occurrence of this tree in Piedmont, believed to be a relic of past interglacial periods. There is a very challenging trail here, too, and although it is shorter than that of the Foresto Gorge, it is equally risky (*via ferrata*, difficulty D, elevation gain 150m, total hiking time 1–1½ hrs).

SUSA

Susa (*map A, B2*), the main centre in the valley, lies in the shadow of Monte Rocciamelone, at the confluence of the Dora Riparia and the Torrente Cenischia. Here the valley forks: to the north the great expanse of the Val Cenischia extends towards Mont Cenis, and from there into France; to the west, the Guaglione and Gravere gorges lead to the upper valley, the Dauphiné and the territories of Briançon.

There are several Roman monuments here: the amphitheatre; the **Terme Graziane**—arches of the aqueduct that brought water into the city; **Porta Savoia** (symbol of the city); and the **Arch of Augustus**, erected by Cottius in 8 BC, to honour the emperor, and faced with white Foresto marble.

Susa's **cathedral**, consecrated in 1027 and dedicated to San Giusto, was a simple conventual church until the establishment of a diocese here in the 18th century. It abuts one of the great cylindrical Roman towers that flank the Porta Savoia. In the early 12th century the nave and aisles of the original monastery church were extended westward to incorporate the city wall, which is built into the lower part of the façade. Later reconstructions destroyed most of the 11th-century church; only the presbytery, the vaulted transept arms and the nave and aisles as far as the fourth bay from the entrance were left standing (the imposing Romanesque campanile has also survived intact). The marble altar dates from 1724; it was designed by Ignazio Bertola, architect of the fortresses of Alessandria, Exilles and Fenestrelle. The church underwent its last major renovation in the 1860s, when Edoardo Arborio Mella designed, and Giuseppe Guglielmino executed, the interior decorations. The church holds a triptych attributed to Bergognone, a 16th-century polychrome wood statue of a woman praying (popularly called Adelaide di Susa but more probably a Mary Magdalene), as well as finely-carved 14th-century choir stalls. In a chapel on the south side is a copy of a Flemish bronze triptych (the original is in the Museo Diocesano; *see below*). Bonifacio Rotario, a member of the prominent family from Asti that gave its name to the Roero region (northeast Piedmont), is said to have carried it to the top of the Rocciamelone mountain 1358 to thank the Virgin for freeing him from prison in the Holy Land.

Opened in 2000 on the left bank of the Doria Riparia, Susa's **Museo Diocesano di Arte Sacra** (also called Museo di Susa; *Via Mazzini 1, centroculturalediocesano. it*) occupies ten rooms of the rectory attached to the church of the Madonna del Ponte, one of the city's oldest. The collection is divided into three sections: the first includes objects from the cathedral treasury; the second, items from the treasury of the church of the Madonna del Ponte and the third, the treasure of the Diocese of Susa. Highlights include the *Rocciamelone Triptych* (1358), a Lombard reliquary casket in engraved wood and bone (6th–7th century), the bronze door knockers from the abbey of San Giusto (1130), a processional Cross in silver-covered wood (the *Croce di Carlo Magno*), the *Rotario Triptych* (1358; *see above*) and the statue of the *Madonna del Ponte* (12th century).

The **Castello della Contessa Adelaide** (*closed at the time of writing*) overlooks the town from its hilltop. Here in 1046, Countess Adelaide of Susa welcomed her betrothed, Otto, Count of Savoy, offering as her dowry the Marquisate of Susa and the County of Turin. Their marriage, which established the rule of the Savoy dynasty in Piedmont, is celebrated in the July *Torneo Storico dei Borghi*, a tournament in costume.

The castle, several times rebuilt since Adelaide's time, is now the seat of the **Museo Civico**, which holds the municipal collections of archaeology and natural history. Here are prehistoric and Roman archaeological finds mostly from within the city, a coin collection, relics of the Risorgimento and a collection of weapons from the Middle Ages to the 19th century, a small collection of Egyptian artefacts (fragments of sarcophagi, bronzes and beetles, remains of mummies) and exotic objects from private collections arranged in the style of an 18th-century *Wunderkammer*. There is also a zoological collection, donated in the 19th century by the Alpine Club, featuring samples of local fauna, minerals and fossils. Two rooms on the ground floor are dedicated to petroglyphs in the valley.

NOVALESA

This charming village (*map A, B2*) with its slate-covered roofs is located in the Val Cenischia along the Via Francigena, which followed the Dora Riparia and the Cenischia upstream to cross the Alps at Mont Cenis. In the Middle Ages it was one of the most heavily trafficked routes between Rome and France. On the main street, where the Francigena crosses the town centre, stands the parish church of Santo Stefano, built on the site of a Romanesque chapel and enlarged several times, but taking its present form in 1684. Inside are some paintings donated by Napoleon to the prior of the Mont Cenis hospice and the Teca di Sant'Eldardo, which according to tradition contains the saint's relics. On this same street is the Museo Etnografico, which displays tools, furniture, costumes and other items of daily use. Although Novalesa is now mainly a tourist destination, agriculture and pastoralism are still an important part of the local economy.

In the midst of meadows and forests high above the village to the southwest, stands the **Abbazia di Novalesa** (*visits by appointment, abbazianovalesa.org*). Founded in 726 by Abo, governor of Susa, and dedicated to Sts Peter and Andrew, the abbey is one of the most important Benedictine houses in Europe. Charlemagne stayed at Novalesa in 773, and the abbey gave food, shelter and medical care to legions of pilgrims over the centuries. The surviving buildings include the church, largely reconstructed in the 18th century, as well as its Romanesque cloister and a system of chapels scattered about the woods and meadows. One of these, the Cappella di Sant'Eldrado, has a remarkable cycle of 11th-century frescoes depicting episodes from the lives of Sts Nicholas and Eldrado (the latter an 8th-century abbot of Novalesa). Another 11th-century fresco, the *Stoning of St Stephen*, can be seen in the abbey church.

The modern history of the abbey has been rough, to say the least. In 1802 Napoleon evicted the Benedictines and assigned the abbey, together with the hospice on the Mont Cenis Pass, to Trappist monks from Savoy, to assist the French troops in transit. In 1855 the abbey was secularised: the Trappists were forced to leave, the buildings were sold at auction (they became a hotel and spa), the library was moved to the seminary in Turin and the collection of manuscripts transferred to the State Archive. It was not until 1972 that the monastic complex was bought by the Province of Turin, which entrusted once again it to the Benedictines.

The former refectory holds a small museum displaying artefacts found during archaeological excavations conducted at Novalesa after 1980. There are also exhibits devoted to the history of monasticism, the monastic life and the restoration of books.

EXILLES

This town (*map A, A2*), thanks to its location halfway between two major routes across the Alps (the Mont Cenis and Montgenèvre passes), has always been considered strategic. Hence the **Forte** (*closed at the time of writing*), a huge complex on the top of a rocky outcrop that dominates the entire Val di Susa.

This is one of the oldest monuments in the area: the first documented fortification dates from the 12th century, when it assured France strategic control of the Montgenèvre Pass. In the 14th century the first fort was enlarged to include a keep and two circuits of walls, and in the early 17th century it was given new ramparts, to withstand the shock of modern artillery. It is at this time (1681-7) that the fort of Exilles held prisoner the mysterious figure known to history as the Man in the Iron Mask. Only in 1708, during the War of the Spanish Succession, the armies of Vittorio Amedeo II of Sardinia managed to occupy the valley of and seize the fortress. With the Treaty of Utrecht (1713) and the subsequent passage of the Duchy of Savoy into the Kingdom of Sardinia, the fortress underwent massive renovation and modernisation, including the reversal of the defensive front, which was now turned towards France: the plan was designed by the military engineer Ignazio Bertola between 1728 and 1733. The Peace of Paris (1796) mandated the demolition of the structure, but because of its strategic location the fort was rebuilt between 1818 and 1829 at the behest of King Vittorio Emanuele I of Sardinia. It was equipped with 22 modern artillery pieces, but like the other fortresses on Italy's western frontier it was disarmed in 1915 to transfer weapons to the Eastern Front. It was decommissioned in 1943, acquired by the Region of Piedmont, and restored as a museum hosting part of the military-history collections of the Museo Nazionale della Montagna of Turin. The museum is divided into two sections: one with drawings, prints and photographs telling the history of defensive architecture in the Western Alps, the other dedicated to the Alpine Corps and high-mountain combat.

At the foot of the fort lies the small **village**, with its characteristic stone houses and the 11th-century church of San Pietro Apostolo, rebuilt in the late 15th century.

SAUZE D'OULX

The story of this small mountain town (*map A, A2*) in its green basin in the upper Val di Susa took an unexpected turn when Adolfo Kind, a Swiss entrepreneur, introduced skiing to Italy and founded the Ski Club Torino in Sauze. The first ski lift was opened in 1936, and since that time the construction of hotels and winter sports facilities has continued non-stop, transforming Sauze into a busy and fashionable resort. Today the town, its skyline marked a bit too clearly by new buildings, is part of the vast Via Lattea ski area and attracts visitors from all over Europe. Piero Gros, World Cup champion in 1974 and Olympic gold medallist in 1976, is a native. During the 2006 Winter Olympics, Sauze d'Oulx hosted the freestyle skiing events.

Sauze is also attractive as a summer destination. There are two interesting natural sites in the immediate environs, in addition to some of the most beautiful peaks in the Western Alps. The 80ha **Riserva Naturale Speciale dello Stagno di Oulx**, 1100m above sea level, surrounds a small lake that was once a bog from which large amounts of clay were taken to make bricks for the Fréjus Tunnel. The depression this created was quickly filled by the waters of the springs at the base of Mt Cotolivier, and colonised by wetland plants and animals. Today the Stagno di Oulx, also known as Lago Borello, is home to rare Alpine plants, including Roman garlic and black swamp reed. The surrounding forest is composed of birch, Scots pine and creeping willows. The waters are home to rare crayfish, rare dragonflies including *Sympetrum vulgatum*, and numerous waterfowl and migratory birds.

The peculiarity of the **Parco Naturale Regionale del Gran Bosco di Salbertrand** is its expanse of silver and red fir, which covers 700 of the reserve's 3,775 hectares, between 1300 and 1800m above sea level. It is the only place in the Western Alps where red fir grows abundantly, as the tree is not suited to the region's continental climate with its long summer droughts. Salbertrand fir trunks were used in the 18th century to make the beams of the Basilica of Superga (*see p. 27*) and the Castello della Venaria Reale (*see p. 30*). The park is home to about 80 nesting species, including many birds of prey, and four species of ungulates: chamois, wild boar, deer and roe deer. Hikers can retrace a part of the Sentiero dei Franchi, the route Charlemagne's armies probably took into Italy, or follow the trails of the Grande Traversata delle Alpi (GTA), which meet at the Rifugio Arlaud.

BARDONECCHIA

A popular holiday resort (*map A, A2*) in the middle of a sunny valley, Bardonecchia (1300m) is surrounded by four different ski areas (Campo Smith–Colomion, Melezet, Jafferau and Les Arnauds), offering over 140km of downhill slopes and about 20km of cross-country trails. The town is divided into two distinct parts: the new village, made up almost exclusively of hotels and self-catering flats, is connected by the central Via Medail to the old village, spread out around the parish church of **Sant'Ippolito** (where there are a late 16th-century baptismal font and 15th-century carved wooden choir stalls). The former **Colonia Medail** of 1939, considered one of the most important works of the architect Gino Levi Montalcini and a masterpiece of Rationalist architecture, was restored for the 2006 Winter Olympics.

A turning off SS335 on the southern outskirts of the village winds its way up to **Forte Bramafam**, on a ridge at the southeastern edge of Bardonecchia's little valley. This immense, irregular polygon is the largest modern fortification in the Cottian Alps; it was built in the 1870s to defend the new Turin–Modane railway line and the Fréjus tunnel. Partially disarmed during the First World War, when it was used as a camp for Austrian prisoners, it was upgraded in the 1930s by the addition of two underground cave systems to become part of the Vallo Alpino, the system of fortifications erected along Italy's 1851-km northern frontier. During the Second World War it was occupied by the Germans, who remained there until 1945. Decommissioned after the war, after decades of neglect the fort was entrusted to the non-profit Associazione per gli Studi di Storia e Architettura Militare in 1995. It now houses the **Museo del Regio Esercito** (or Museo Forte Bramafam), featuring more than 2,000 exhibits related to military life and the fortifications of the Val di Susa (*fortebramafam.it*).

PINEROLO

Pinerolo (*map A, B3*), the historic capital of the Princes of Acaia (or Acaja), ancestors of the Savoy kings, is in a beautiful position at the foot of the hills where the Chisone and Lemina valleys merge into the Piedmontese plain. The fortress of Pignerol was under French control from 1630 to 1706 and, because of its remoteness from Paris, was used as a state prison. Nicolas Fouquet, Louis XIV's disgraced former Finance Minister, died in captivity here in 1680. Today the town has two historic centres— one on the hill of San Maurizio, and another on the plain. Its temperate climate and its rich historical and artistic heritage make it a pleasant place to visit, or even to live: in recent years many Turin professionals whose job doesn't require a daily presence in the office have chosen to telecommute from Pinerolo.

The most important religious monuments are the cathedral of **San Donato** and the church of **San Maurizio**, the two main hubs around which the city has developed. The former, with its 15th-century Gothic façade, is located on the plain; the latter, a late Gothic edifice with Romanesque campanile, stands at the top of the hill. The nearby Via Principi d'Acaja and Via al Castello are lined with 15th- and 16th-century houses.

The 15th-century **Casa del Senato** (*Piazzetta d'Andrade 2–4*), a crenellated building with mullioned windows, terracotta decorations and free-standing sculptures on the façade, still appears much as it did when it was built by Lodovico d'Acaja as the seat of the Curia Pineroliensis, his court. In 1713 Vittorio Amedeo II of Sardinia seated the Senate of Pinerolo here, giving the legislators jurisdiction over the whole of Piedmont. A small museum devoted to the necropolis of Doma Rossa, a trove of some 30 tombs and 500 burial objects accidentally discovered during the construction of the Turin-Pinerolo motorway is open by appointment (*T: 3450 868633*). Three reconstructed graves occupy the ground floor hall; other funerary objects, including precious glass and items in metal and ceramic, are shown upstairs.

Palazzo Vittone, overlooking Pinerolo's market square, was designed in 1740 by

Bernardo Vittone for King Carlo Emanuele III as the seat of the Hospice of the Catechumens—Waldensians who had chosen to convert to Catholicism. Today the building is home to three museums: the **Collezione Civica d'Arte, Museo di Scienze Naturali** and **Museo Etnografico** (*Piazza Vittorio Veneto 8, amarte1999. it*). In the art gallery are works by local, regional and national painters of the 19th and 20th centuries: Lorenzo Delleani, Giacomo Grosso, Felice Carena and Enrico Reycend. The natural science museum is known for its extraordinary mycological collection, with thousands of specimens of fungi from around the world. There are collections of insects and molluscs, an entire room devoted to mineralogy with beautiful specimens from around Piedmont, as well as a collection of mammals, birds, fish, amphibians and reptiles of Pinerolo. There are several large models (Rocca di Cavour, Susa, Sangone, Po, Pellice and Chisone valleys), and a small and rare biospelaeological collection with specimens collected in various caves in Piedmont. The ethnographic collections, displayed in the basement beneath a beautiful vaulted brick ceiling, include extensive documentation of popular culture of the countryside and mountains of Pinerolo and the Alpine valleys in general. There are reconstructions of a typical kitchen, stable, bedroom, craft shops etc.; scale models of buildings; a collection of music, musical instruments and folklore and a collection of dolls.

Across the square is the former royal riding school, moved to Pinerolo from the Castello di Venaria Reale by Vittorio Emanuele II, ostensibly to take advantage of the mild climate and the abundance of water and fodder here, but really to get the school away from Turin, where the (republican) political atmosphere was considered inappropriate. The building now houses the **Centro Studi e Museo d'Arte Preistorica** and **Museo Civico di Archeologia e Antropologia** (*Viale Giolitti 1; under rearrangement at the time of writing, munus.com*). The Centro Studi conducts archaeological and anthropological research on rock art in the Western Alps and around the world and possesses an extraordinary collection of rock-art casts, the result of half a century of scientific expeditions. Also here is the **Museo Storico dell'Arma di Cavalleria** (*Viale Giolitti 5, museocavalleria.it*). Almost nothing in this museum comes from the army itself: almost all the objects have been donated over time by individual officers, soldiers and admirers. On the ground floor are carts, wagons, carriages, saddles and saddle-cloths; on the upper level are banners, flags, bronzes, drawings, prints and photographs, and uniforms. A special section is devoted to Italy's colonial campaigns and the two world wars.

ENVIRONS OF PINEROLO

SUBURBAN VILLAS

The immediate surroundings of Pinerolo hold some interesting surprises. The most unusual is certainly the **Cascina la Tegassa**, 4km southeast of the city centre (*Stradale Baudenasca 118, comune.pinerolo.to.it*). In 1994 the art collector Elena Privitera decided to turn her 18th-century farmhouse in the peaceful countryside of Pinerolo into a contemporary art centre. The centre shows new and emerging, as well as internationally renowned, artists.

At the entrance to the Chisone and Pellice valleys, 3km southwest of the city centre, is the **Fondazione Cosso–Castello di Miradolo** (*Via Cardonata 2, San Secondo di Pinerolo, for opening hours, see fondazionecosso.com*). The castle, mentioned in documents of the 17th and 18th centuries, was renovated in the Gothic Revival style in 1866. Purchased by the Fondazione Cosso in 2008, it is now devoted to the cultural and social promotion of the Pinerolo area and the rediscovery of its history. The park covers more than six hectares and is listed among the historic gardens of Piedmont; it features exotic plants—a tall sequoia, a vast bamboo wood, historic ginkgo biloba, roses, hydrangeas and camellias—and a large oval lawn. Along the castle's southwest façade extends a Gothic Revival greenhouse used for concerts, exhibitions and events.

PARCO NATURALE DEL MONTE TRE DENTI–FREIDOUR

This nature reserve, entered at Cumiana, 15km northeast of Pinerolo (*map A, B3*), has magnificent forests of beech, chestnut, oak and Scots pine. In spring the park explodes with primroses, pulmonaria, periwinkle, white and pink anemones, crocuses and gentians. There are large populations of deer, chamois, wild boar and roe deer, and birds of prey such as buzzards, peregrine falcons and ravens.

PIOSSASCO

Adjoining the Parco Naturale del Monte Tre Denti–Freidour, at the foot of Mt San Giorgio, Piossasco (*map A, C3*) consists of a number of different parts. In the Middle Ages the highest ground was fortified, and some ruins, called the **Gran Merlone**, can still be seen above the castle, halfway up the hill. A second fortification was built in the 12th century. Next came the construction of the feudal castle, later converted into a mansion. Lower down stood a second system of fortifications and walls, which together with the first formed one of the largest defensive complexes in medieval Piedmont. The fortifications survived intact until the 18th century, but have since been partially dismantled, being a cheap source of good building stone.

Though several times altered, Piossasco's parish church of **San Vito**—formerly dedicated to the martyrs Vito, Crescentia and Modesto, portrayed in the statues on the façade—preserves frescoes dating from the mid-15th century and attributed to Giacomo Jaquerio, who was active at the same time at Ranverso, Avigliana and Manta. The finest attraction in Piossasco, however, is the garden of **Casa Lajolo**, at the west end of the town (*Via San Vito 24, for opening hours, see casalajolo.it*). The villa took on its present appearance in the mid-18th century, probably at the behest of Count Aleramo Chialamberto. With the extinction of the Chialamberto line, around 1850, the property was inherited by the counts of Cossano Lajolo, who still own it. The formal garden develops on three levels, connected by stone steps: the highest level consists of a large parterre in front of the house, with slender palms (*Trachycarpus fortunei*), boxwood hedges, lemon trees (in spring and summer) and sculpted yews. *Buxus sempervirens 'Suffruticosa'* reigns supreme on the second level, which is divided into two parts: a symmetrical Italian garden characterised by carefully shaped geometric hedges and a grove of yews, which creates wall of greenery, and an English garden. The third level hosts a fruit orchard where the trees and plants (cherries, currants, raspberries, peaches, pears, plums, figs, grapes) are neatly arranged in staggered rows and separated by a central path, bordered by *Stachys byzantina*, which ends in a rustic pergola overlooking the surrounding landscape.

PARCO NATURALE DEL MONTE SAN GIORGIO
This park, northeast of Piossasco, offers panoramic views of the whole of the Western Alps and the plain below. Its forests are mostly made up of oak, holm oak and hornbeam and are a refuge for about 60 species of bird. These include species typical of mountain forests, such as crested tits, and Mediterranean species, such as the Sardinian warbler and Western Orphean warbler, and there are birds of prey such as the harrier and peregrine falcon. On the summit is the **Cappella di San Giorgio**, built around the year 1000 by Benedictine monks. The park has trails for hiking, biking and horseriding.

CAVOUR
South of Pinerolo is Cavour (*map A, B3*), ancestral home of the great statesman's family. Giovanni Giolitti, five times prime minister of Italy, died here in 1928. The Museo Archeologico Caburrum, in the former Abbazia di Santa Maria, displays finds from a nearby Roman site known as *Forum Vibii Caburrum*.

THE VAL CHISONE

The name Chisone comes from the Latin *Clausum*, which means closed. The valley was called *Vallis Clusii*, then *Clausonia*, *Cluxinis* and finally Chisone, possibly because to enter it one must pass through a deep, narrow gorge. It is a place of great natural beauty, frequented by summer hikers as much as by winter skiers.

FENESTRELLE
This village (*map A, B2*), located roughly halfway up the valley at an elevation of 1154m, is famous for its pleasant walks—to the Colle dell'Assietta, Pra Catinat, Mount Albergian, and other destinations. The history of the former French frontier post, however, is tied to that of a Waldensian community (*see p. 108*) that lived in the valley from the 12th century until 1685. In that year Louis XIV revoked the freedom of worship granted to Protestants by Henry IV's Edict of Nantes (1598) and, to prevent Protestants from entering the valleys of the Chisone and its tributaries, ordered the construction at Fenestrelle of a Jesuit monastery, a church and a fortress.

The latter was the precursor of the present *Forte di Fenestrelle* (*check website for hours; T: 0121 83600, fortedifenestrelle.it*), one of the largest and most complex fortresses in Europe. Over 3km long from end to end, it covers an area of 1,350,000 square metres and encompasses an elevation gain of nearly 650m, negotiated via a covered stairway of 4,000 steps that extends along the ridge line.

The French fort was already one of the most important strategic points on the border between France and the Duchy of Savoy. In 1692 it served as a base for the French troops commanded by General Catinat in the Nine Years' War (fought between King Louis XIV of France and the Grand Alliance of Spain, Holland, England, the Holy Roman Empire and Savoy). The upper Valle Chisone remained under French rule until the conclusion of the War of the Spanish Succession, when Vittorio Amedeo was ceded the area by the Treaty of Utrecht (1713). At this time the king asked the military architect Ignazio Bertola to design a new fortress; construction began in 1727, but it took more than a century to complete the imposing structure, consisting of three major strongholds (San Carlo, Tre Denti, Valli), three minor strongholds (Carlo Alberto, Santa Barbara, Porte) and two batteries (Scoglio, Ospedale), connected by the covered staircase. The fort never saw action and was eventually abandoned.

Today, restoration is gradually bringing it back to life. The Palazzo degli Ufficiali houses a museum on the history of the Italian army from 1861 to 1945. Dozens of mannequins (including three with their horses) illustrate the evolution of military uniforms, weapons and decorations; the displays include rare items such as the uniform of one of Garibaldi's Thousand, and two suits—one ceremonial and the other civilian—worn by the last king of Italy, Umberto II.

Fenestrelle is one of the gateways to the **Parco Naturale dell'Orsiera-Rocciavré**, which covers nearly 11,000 hectares ranging in elevation from 900 to 2890m in three valleys: Susa to the north, Chisone to the south and Sangone to the east. The first two are characterised by extreme seasonal variations in temperature and precipitation. The intense exposure and high summer temperatures favour a sub-Mediterranean or steppe flora. The Val Sangone has a cooler climate more suited to plants such as beech. Native birds include buzzards, sparrowhawks, golden eagles, kestrel, black grouse, ptarmigans, boreal owls and various species of woodpecker. Where the woody vegetation gives way to meadows and rock, ermine, mountain hare, marmots, chamois, wild sheep and ibex can be found. Prehistoric petroglyphs and artefacts dating from the Neolithic to the Bronze Age have been found in the park. The Certosa di Montebenedetto dates from the 12th century.

USSEAUX

This cluster of five alpine villages (*map A, B2*) in enchanting surroundings is one of the few places where you can still speak *Patouà*, a variant of Alpine Occitan, in its turn a variant of the Langue d'Oc once spoken in southern France. The name is probably Celtic (*uxellos* = high). The place was known to Julius Caesar, who in *De Bello Gallico* mentions a village named *Occellum*.

Usseaux is an outstanding example of a rustic high-mountain farming town. The five villages—Usseaux, Balboutet, Laux, Pourrieres and Fraisse—are among the oldest in the valley; their tightly-huddled stone and wood houses, and the culture, language and traditions of the inhabitants, have staunchly resisted change. Each village has something distinctive about it, although the homogenising effect of recreational tourism is increasingly evident. The houses of **Usseaux** are painted with murals dealing with themes from country life, nature, myth and legend.

Balboutet has some 20 sundials on the walls of its houses and a Piazza del Sole, where text panels and hands-on exhibits explain ways of measuring time. **Laux** has a little lake, an ancient sundial on its church and a Piazza della Preghiera ('Prayer Square') in the Waldensian tradition. **Pourrieres** has a charming old church and small cemetery and is the starting point for walks in the Vallone di Cerogne and on the Colle dell'Assietta. **Fraisse**, at the top of the valley, is a town of wood surrounded by forests and divided by the River Chisone into two distinct neighbourhoods.

Dairy farming is the main agricultural activity here and Usseaux is famous for its cheeses, particularly *Plaisentif*, locally the 'cheese of the violets', which is made from the milk of the first days of pasture and matured for at least eighty days. *Calhiette*, a rich plate of potatoes, sausage, onion, butter and cheese, is the local delicacy.

PRAGELATO

The ancient capital of the Val Chisone (*map A, A2*), located at the centre of a natural basin surrounded by pastures and woods, is a favourite destination for cross-country skiers and hikers—thanks especially to the many trails that wind through the enchanting scenery of the **Parco Naturale della Val Troncea**. This 3300-hectare park, ranging in elevation from 1650 to 3280m, encompasses a working landscape as well as a wilderness area. The Val Troncea, along with the rest of the upper Val Chisone, was settled by Waldensians from France in the 12th and 13th centuries. In the 17th century the forests began to be harvested to provide timber for the fortifications of Fenestrelle and the tunnels of the Beth chalcopyrite mines, which closed in the early 20th century. Today the forests are confined to small areas, usually along the steeper rocky slopes, and consist of larch, sometimes alongside Swiss pine and, more rarely, mountain pine. The colourful blooms that characterise the broad pastures in spring and summer have given Val Troncea the nickname *Valle dei Fiori*. All the Alpine ungulates are present in large numbers, while the most typical birds are the golden eagle, goshawk, kestrel, boreal owl, black grouse and ptarmigan.

SESTRIERE

Located in between the Val Chisone and the upper Val di Susa, at over 2000m, **Sestriere** (*map A, A3*) consists of three main sections: the ancient villages of Champlas Seguin and Borgata, once mainly devoted to sheep raising; and the recently formed Sestriere Colle. The ski resort was established in the 1930s on the initiative of Giovanni Agnelli, founder of the Fiat car works, who built the two hotel towers and the first two lifts to the Banchetta and Sises slopes. Today Sestriere is one of the most famous winter-sports and summer resorts in the Alps: with its 120km of slopes it is the main centre of the Via Lattea ski area, and its magnificently-sited 18-hole golf course and modern athletics facilities make it a popular summer destination too.

West of Sestriere is **Cesana Torinese**, where the painter Cézanne spent much time. His family originally came from here, although they moved to France in the 18th century and Cézanne himself was born in Aix-en-Provence.

THE VALLE PELLICE

TORRE PELLICE
This pleasant town (*map A, B3*) is the largest municipality of the Waldensian valleys. Its congenial air belies a history marked by persecution and violence. There are numerous Waldensian monuments in the city: the 17th-century **Tempio dei Coppieri** (in the town of Tagliaretto), the first Waldensian religious building to be built here; the Tempio Valdese of 1850, which each year hosts the opening ceremony of the Synod; and other structures including the Foresteria, the Casa Valdese, which serves as the administrative centre, and the Collegio.

The **Museo Valdese** (*Via Beckwith 3, museovaldese.org*) was established at the initiative of the Waldensian Church in 1889 to preserve Waldensian heritage and cultural memory. It presents two collections, one historical and the other ethnographical. The former traces the history of the Waldensians from the first migrations (1170) to the present day, through Bibles, liturgical objects, historical documents, weapons, furniture and material from African missions. The latter has reconstructed rooms representing life at home, at school and at work, and depicts the agricultural cycle in the Waldensian Valleys in the late 19th century. The museum is managed by the Fondazione Centro Culturale Valdese, which administers a system of museums and cultural institutions scattered throughout the Pellice, Chisone and Germanasca valleys.

THE WALDENSIANS
The Val Chisone and the Valle Pellice, also known as the Valli Valdesi, have been inhabited for centuries by the Protestant Waldensians or Vaudois. This religious community originated in the south of France around 1170, under the inspiration of Peter Waldo, a Lyons merchant who sold his goods and started preaching the gospel. His adherents were formally condemned by the Lateran Council in 1184, and persecution drove them to take refuge in these remote valleys. In about 1532 the Vaudois were absorbed by the Swiss Reformation. When renewed persecution broke out in 1655 under Carlo Emanuele II, assisted by the troops of Louis XIV, a strong protest was raised by Cromwell in England, and Milton wrote his famous 'Sonnet—On the Late Massacre in Piedmont (May 1655)', *Poems* 1673):

Avenge, O Lord, thy slaughter'd saints, whose bones
Lie scatter'd on the Alpine mountains cold;
Ev'n them who kept thy truth so pure of old
When all our Fatheres worshipt Stocks and Stones,
Forget not: in thy book record their groanes
Who were thy Sheep, and in their antient Fold
Slayn by the bloody Piemontese that roll'd
Mother with Infant down the Rocks...

Still further persecution followed the revocation of the Edict of Nantes (1685), but the remainder of the Vaudois, about 2,600 in number, were allowed to retreat to Geneva. In 1698 Henri Arnaud led a band of 800 to the reconquest of their valleys; following a rupture between Louis XIV and Vittorio Amedeo of Savoy, the Vaudois were given recognition as subjects of Savoy, in a spirit of religious tolerance. By the beginning of the 19th century Protestant countries were taking keen interest in the Vaudois, and an Englishman, General Charles Beckwith, helped them personally, building their church in Turin (1849). Since 1848 they have been allowed complete religious liberty. Towards the end of the 19th century large colonies emigrated to Sicily, Uruguay and the Argentine Republic.

The **Civica Galleria d'Arte Contemporanea Filippo Scroppo** (*Via Roberto d'Azeglio 10, galleriascroppo.org*) was founded by Filippo Scroppo (1910–93), an artist, teacher, critic and curator who in 1959 invited a group of artists to participate in the first Autunno Pittorico di Torre Pellice. The criterion for participation required guest artists to donate one of their works to the municipality. Over the years the collection has grown to include nearly 500 paintings, sculptures, drawings and prints.

BOBBIO PELLICE
This little resort (*map A, B3*) at the foot of the Alps, on the upper rim of the Val Pellice, is the gateway to the Oasi del Barant, an important wildlife reserve 2250 m above sea level. The main draw here is the **Giardino Botanico Alpino Bruno Peyronel**, a small but fascinating treasure chest of rare flora (*giardinopeyronel.it*) that can be reached only by foot (1.5hrs from the Rifugio Jervis at Conca del Prà, or from the Rifugio Barbara at Comba dei Carbonieri). Here, in an area of 17,000 sq m, are more than 300 marked species in a variety of habitats: scree, various types of pasture, wetlands, brush and sheer rock.

Bobbio's Tempio Valdese was rebuilt in the 18th century after severe persecutions destroyed the earlier structure.

THE ALTA VALLE DEL PO

The entire Piedmont section of the Po Valley is under environmental protection, but the management of this great ribbon-like nature reserve is divided between three different authorities. The first stretch of the Parco del Po includes the river's course through the mountains and the plain at their base. The river actually originates in a system of high-altitude lakes and bogs in the Monviso group and the source is historically identified at Pian (or Piano) del Re, in the municipality of Crissolo (*map C, A1–B1*), at an elevation of 2020m. The transition between mountain and plain environments is such that the young Po crosses a large number of different natural habitats with a wide variety of landscapes, fauna and flora. The vegetation along the banks consists of larch, beech and fir at higher altitudes, and willow and poplar on the plain. In the area of the Riserva Naturale Speciale del Pian del Re, a peat bog is home to residual glacial flora, which came to the area more than 200,000 years ago. As for the fauna, ibex, chamois, marmots, eagles and ptarmigans thrive in the mountains; choughs and snow finches nest on the rocks. Brown trout swim in the cold alpine lakes. Down in the valley, one encounters deer, roe deer and squirrels, especially in the larch groves. Near Saluzzo the river slows its course and flows between gravel bars that offer an ideal nesting place for the common kingfisher and for the small river swallows called *topini*. Mallards, egrets, black-winged stilts and white storks live amid the riparian vegetation.

ABBAZIA DI SANTA MARIA STAFFARDA

Map C, B1. Revello-Staffarda, Piazza Roma 2. To visit, see ordinemauriziano.it/abbazia-maria-staffarda.

Established between 1122 and 1138 on land donated by the Marquis of Saluzzo, the Cistercian Abbey of Staffarda was the fulcrum of a vast project to improve agriculture on the Po river plain and the Alpine foothills in western Piedmont. In just a few decades it attained immense economic importance as the central point for gathering, processing and trading produce from the surrounding countryside. This in turn brought civil and ecclesiastical privileges that made the abbey a major player in regional political and social life. By the end of the 15th century, however, its influence had begun to decline, and on 31st July 1690 it was severely damaged in a bloody battle fought in its fields by Vittorio Amedeo II of Savoy and the French general Nicolas Catinat. The buildings were restored at the expense of the King of Sardinia, but the abbey never recovered its former stature. In 1750 a papal bull of Benedict XIV transferred its assets from the Cistercian Order to the Order of Saints Maurice and Lazarus, revoking its status as an independent abbey.

The church, built in a transitional Romanesque–Gothic style, has three aisles with cross vaults resting on differently shaped piers, its austere atmosphere in perfect keeping with reformed Cistercian monastic rule. Above the main altar is a remarkable 16th-century altarpiece in painted and gilded wood by Pascale Oddone: open, it shows scenes from the life of the Virgin; closed, it bears representations of St Benedict, the Archangel Gabriel, St Bernard of Clairvaux and the Virgin Annunciate. The well preserved cloister, dating from the mid-13th century and partially rebuilt after 1690, has a regular colonnade of white columns surmounted by the massive buttresses that diffuse the lateral thrust of the church vaults. The *concentrico*, or lay brothers' village, still retains farm buildings including the 13th-century covered market.

REVELLO

The town of Revello (*map C, B1*), 9km south of the abbey described above, is built around an interesting historic core which includes a 14th-century tower, the Loggia del Mercato, 15th-century porticoes, and houses with mullioned windows, terracotta decorations and devotional frescoes on their façades.

Its prime attraction is the **Cappella Marchionale**, located within what remains of the Palazzo Marchionale (*Piazza Denina 2, for information and to book a visit, T: 327 780 4528*). At the time of its construction (16th century) the palace was an elegant square castle with three cylindrical towers at the corners. The chapel, a late Gothic construction with a nave and semicircular apse, is in the only surviving tower, on the west side. The walls and ceiling are adorned with a beautiful cycle of frescoes illustrating episodes from the lives of Sts Margaret of Antioch and Louis IX of France; in the apse lunettes, the marquis and marquesse are presented to the Virgin by their patron saints. On the west wall is a *Last Supper* inspired by Leonardo da Vinci's masterpiece in Milan. The paintings are attributed to the court painter of the Marquis of Saluzzo, Hans Clemer.

Revello is the seat of the **Museo Naturalistico del Fiume Po** (*Piazza Denina 5; T: 0175 257358 or email info@parcodelpocn.it*). The large exhibition space presents full-scale reconstructions of natural environments, representing the main ecosystems of the park and its landscapes: alpine, subalpine and river plain.

The collegiate **church of Santa Maria**, a Gothic construction of the late 15th century, has a beautiful Renaissance marble portal. The interior, with three aisles and a polygonal apse, preserves 16th-century works including the *Raspaudi altarpiece*, painted by Hans Clemer in 1503.

CASTELLAR

A fief of the Marquis of Saluzzo, this town (*map C, B1*) grew up at the foot of a rocky outcrop around its 14th-century **castle**. The latter is first mentioned in an act of 1138 by which Henry of Brondello gave it and its lands to Staffarda Abbey. Transformed into a stately home, then renovated several times over the centuries, it was reconstructed in the early 20th century by Count Ludovico of Saluzzo on the basis of medieval drawings found in Paris. It now appears as a solid fortress surrounded by a massive enceinte with cylindrical towers and Ghibelline battlements. Recently restored as a cultural centre, it houses a museum of Royal Army uniforms and (in the stables) a small ethnographic collection.

SANFRONT

What is now the **Borgata Museo Balma Boves** at Sanfront (*map C, B1; Località Balma Boves, Frazione Rocchetta; exterior always open, interior visitable by guided tour; for times, see balmaboves.it*) was a pueblo-like farming hamlet until the 1960s. Huddled beneath a huge rock in the upper Po Valley (*balma* means 'rock shelter' in local dialect), it includes houses, barns, stables, a bread oven and a wash house. The two-hour walk from the car park by the Po at Rocchetta leads past other *balme*, touching upon a natural overlook with prehistoric petroglyphs (Roca d'la Casna). The view alone is worth the hike.

OSTANA

The most common interpretation dictates that Ostana (*Oustano* in Occitan; *map C, B1*) derives from Augustana, with reference to the month of August in the Occitan form, *oust*. If so, the name may have early medieval origins associated with transhumance: Ostana may have been an area for summer grazing. Today it is a cluster of scattered hamlets in a panoramic position on the sunny side of the Po Valley, with splendid views of Monviso. The Po here is little more than a trickle. A four-hour circular walk touches on all the hamlets—La Villo (Villa in Italian), Champanho (Ciampagna), Marquét (Marchetti), La Ruà (Bernardi), Miribrart (Sant'Antonio), San Bernardo, Samicoulàou (San Nicolao)—and is best done in winter (on snowshoes), stopping from time to time to drink something warm and alcoholic. Autumn is also pleasant, the beech and larch woods turning bright yellow and gold, and in summer the forest floor is paved with blueberries. The vernacular architecture of the place is all wood and stone—including the roofs, which are covered in flagstones. Although some houses are sadly abandoned, a recent 'back to the land' movement has led to some very fine, and sensitive, restorations. An extension of the walk (6hrs total) leads up to the Punta Sellassa (2036 m), affording a breathtaking view of the entire western arc of the Alps, from Monviso to Monte Rosa and the Matterhorn. A few farmers still produce Ostana's special cheese, the rich, creamy *toma d'alpeggio*, and you won't have a lot of trouble finding the signature dish, *polenta di patate e grano saraceno*, an oven-baked delight made with equal amounts of mashed potatoes and buckwheat flour, served piping hot with cheese, *banho dë cousso* (pumpkin sauce) or *banho dal jòous* ('Thursday's sauce', using the dregs of butter, which was normally made on Thursday to bring to market on Friday).

SALUZZO & ENVIRONS

This lovely small city of Saluzzo (*map C, B1*) is located on the spur of Monviso, which separates the Val Varaita from the upper Po Valley. It is divided into a medieval upper town, originally enclosed within walls, and a lower town extending onto the plain. The upper town is particularly attractive.

History of Saluzzo
Notwithstanding archaeological finds from the Roman era that suggest an ancient origin for the settlements in this area, no one knows exactly when Saluzzo was founded. The existence of the city is attested for the first time only in 1028, in an act that mentions a *castrum* of the Marquis of Turin Olderico Manfredi. Fourteen marquises succeeded one another at the head of this small border state, which maintained its independence thanks to its political and cultural ties with France, going so far as to dispute the Savoy domination of Piedmont and the construction of a regional state.

The Marquisate of Saluzzo reached its apogee in the 15th century, under the successive rules of Ludovico I and Ludovico II, whose tenure saw a period of economic prosperity, political peace, and a flourishing of the arts and letters. In 1511 Pope Julius II granted the city episcopal status, and in the following years Saluzzo took on its present appearance. Decadence set in during the next century, however; overwhelmed by Franco-Imperial contention, the small state was finally annexed to the Duchy of Savoy (Treaty of Lyon, 1601), to which it would remain inextricably bound. In the 18th century it experienced an economic and demographic recovery, growing to become a provincial capital of the Kingdom of Sardinia. During the Napoleonic period (1796-1814) it was annexed to France in the Department of the Stura; with the establishment of the kingdom of Italy, it was made a district capital—so even in the worst of times it has always been a place of some importance.

EXPLORING SALUZZO

The **cathedral** of Maria Vergine Assunta was built in the late 15th century by Marquis Ludovico II, in the hope of demonstrating the importance of his family in the religious as well as the civil sphere—a first step toward shaking off all subjection to the Savoy. Designed in the Lombard Gothic style, it is a large church with an imposing brick façade whose central portion was once adorned with frescoes by Hans Clemer, the well-known Flemish artist in the service of the marquis in the late 15th and early 16th centuries (some fragments remain). Three large portals, the central one surmounted by a tall terracotta gable, lead into to the three-aisled interior; among the highlights here are a 14th-century wooden Crucifix high up in the nave, a polyptych by Clemer in the 18th-century chapel of the Santissimo Sacramento, and the Baroque high altar decorated with statues by Carlo Giuseppe Plura.

Casa Cavassa is a fine example of a stately Renaissance town house. Dating from the 15th century, it was the residence of the Marquis of Saluzzo until 1464, when Marquis Ludovico II gifted it to the Vicar General Galeazzo Cavassa. It now houses the **Museo Civico** (*Via San Giovanni 5; closed at the time of writing, T: 0175 41455, casacavassa.it*). The museum fills 15 magnificent rooms with painted wooden ceilings and decorated walls, and houses works of great historical and artistic importance. There are two interesting paintings created in the late 15th or early 16th century by Hans Clemer: the *Labours of Hercules* in grisaille in the wooden interior loggia, and an altarpiece depicting the *Madonna della Misericordia*. The museum also houses the late Gothic choir stalls from the Cappella Marchionale in Revello, a cradle of 1560 from Lagnasco Castle, and 16th-century portraits of the Duke (Carlo Emanuele I) and Duchess of Savoy. The building is considered one of the finest examples of a Renaissance aristocratic home in Piedmont, and there is an interesting tale behind its transformation into a museum. The idea came in the late 19th century to Marquis Tapparelli d'Azeglio (the grandson of writer Massimo d'Azeglio), who personally curated each room in an attempt to recreate the atmosphere of the Cavassa family's era. He searched the antiques market for furniture and artworks that in some way documented the history of the Cavassa family or that of the marquisate of Saluzzo in its glory years (1400-1500). In addition, he commissioned skilled craftsmen to make new furniture in a Renaissance style, sometimes using bits and pieces of antiques. In 1888 Tapparellli bequeathed Casa Cavassa (and everything in it) to the city of Saluzzo with the proviso it be used as a museum. Unfortunately the project was still unfinished at the time of his death (1890), so some artworks do not have an assigned room, some rooms have no furniture or artworks, and the basement is still full of material set aside during the renovation.

The Gothic church of **San Giovanni** was begun in 1300 and enlarged in the late 15th and early 16th centuries. It has a very simple façade and a beautiful campanile with mullioned windows, whose form is echoed in the tall **Torre Civica** (1460) down the street. Within, the Cappella dei Santi Crispino e Crispiniano (left) has 15th-century frescoes attributed to Pietro da Saluzzo; the apse, in a late French Gothic style, dates from 1504. It contains beautiful carved-wood choir stalls of the same period, and the tomb of Marquis Ludovico II (1508), by Benedetto Briosco. In the Gothic cloister (now a hotel) is the 16th-century Chapter House with the tomb of Galeazzo Cavassa by Matteo Sanmicheli.

Salita al Castello, flanked by 15th-century houses with mullioned windows, terracotta friezes and grisaille frescoes, is perhaps the most interesting street of the upper town. Here is the **Antico Palazzo Comunale** (*at the time of writing open at weekends; comune.saluzzo.cn.it/monumento/antico-palazzo-comunale-6*), built between 1440 and 1462 and recently restored to its ancient splendour, its façade adorned with terracotta decorations and frescoes (by Cesare Arbasia, 1601). The adjoining **Torre Civica**, built in 1462 (the belfry was added in 1556), is 48m high and was a symbol of the fierce independence of the marchisate. From the top of its 130 steps one has a wonderful view over the town, the plain and Monviso and the Alps. Inside the Palazzo Comunale the first-floor Sala delle Congregazioni del Marchesato has a coffered ceiling with mythological, symbolic and heraldic decorations dating from the 15th century. It is currently used for conferences, exhibitions and concerts. The second-floor **Pinacoteca**, dedicated to Matteo Olivero, a prominent exponent of Italian Divisionism, includes a hundred paintings, drawings and sculptures. Olivero exhibited in Paris, Brussels and Munich, and from 1905–30 kept a studio on Salita al Castello, a few steps from the new museum.

The hilltop **Castiglia** was the fortified residence of the Marquis of Saluzzo. Originally built as a fortress by Marquis Tommaso I between 1271 and 1286, along with the first circuit of city walls, the castle was enlarged over the centuries, over time acquiring four towers, ramparts, a drawbridge and a moat. The name *castiglia* probably comes from the Latin plural *castella* ('castles') and may allude to the fact that the complex combines several fortified buildings that were fused together over time. During the 15th century it was converted into an aristocratic home, with garden, by Marquis Tommaso III and his grandson Ludovico II. Following the decline of the marchisate it was used as a barracks and a prison. Recently renovated and revitalised as a cultural and exhibition centre, it once again symbolises the small but magnificent capital that was Saluzzo for four centuries. Several museums are planned here; the first two opened in 2014. The **Museo della Civiltà Cavalleresca**, dedicated to aristocratic life in the Marquisate of Saluzzo in the late Middle Ages, and, in the former prison, the **Museo della Memoria Carceraria**, a museum of prison life (*Piazza Castello; museodellamemoriacarceraria.it*). A contemporary art museum is also planned.

Lower down in the village, **Casa Pellico** is a building of medieval origin located in the scenic Piazzetta dei Mondagli, one of the prettiest squares in the old town. Here the poet and anti-Austrian patriot Silvio Pellico was born in 1789 and spent the first years of his childhood. The house is currently set up as a house museum (*open

March–Oct, T: 0175 46710) with memorabilia and manuscripts, mostly donated by the writer's sister in 1858. A room on the first floor is dedicated to reproductions of title pages of *Le mie prigioni*, one of Pellico's most popular works, published in hundreds of editions and recounting his experiences as a prisoner (he had been jailed for seditious activity). There is also a remarkable room with Neoclassical décor in which the writer's study, including his original desk, has been reconstructed.

MANTA

The town of Manta (*map C, B1*) is known for its splendid castle, **Castello della Manta** (*Via de Rege Thesauro 5, T: 0175 87822*), a 13th-century fortress remodelled in the second decade of the 15th century by Valerano, first Count of Manta and Verzuolo, who received the town and the fortress in fief. Transformed and expanded in the late 16th century, it became one of the most important stately homes in Piedmont. It was acquired by the Fondo Italiano per l'Ambiente (FAI) in 1989, which has overseen its restoration and opened it to the public. The interior is decorated with frescoes dating from the epoch of Valerano (c. 1420) and unanimously considered among the most important pictorial documents of the late Gothic period in Piedmont. The best of these are the nine *Heroes* and nine *Heroines* depicted in the Sala Baronale, and the fresco depicting the *Fountain of Youth* by an unknown pupil of Giacomo Jaquerio, known simply as the Master of La Manta.

The parish church of **Santa Maria del Castello** dates from the same period. The presbytery holds a cycle of frescoes depicting the Passion of Christ, and the burial chapel of Michele Antonio, Marquis of Saluzzo is also richly decorated. More 15th-century frescoes can be seen in the Romanesque church of **Santa Maria del Monastero**, an ancient Benedictine priory of the abbey of Pedona (Borgo San Dalmazzo).

FOSSANO & SAVIGLIANO

Fossano (*map C, C2*), on the left bank of the River Stura in a position strategic for trade between Piedmont and Liguria, was founded in 1236 by a league of Guelph cities that was formed to fight Ghibelline Asti. It passed in 1304 to the Marquis of Saluzzo but, after a brief Angevin occupation, came within the sphere of influence of Prince Filippo I d'Acaja and then, after 1418, the Savoy.

The city is known for its porticoed streets and 18th-century Baroque architecture (the cathedral of San Giovenale, the churches of San Filippo Neri and Santissima Trinità, and the Palazzo del Comandante, now a bank) but is famous most of all for its magnificent **Castello degli Acaja** (*visitfossano.it/portfolio/castello-fossano*), one of the most impressive in northern Italy. The rectangular fortress has four corner towers turned out diagonally and a moat that forces access over a massive drawbridge. It was erected as a fortress after 1324 by Filippo di Savoia, Prince of Acaja, and rebuilt as an aristocratic residence in the late 15th century by Carlo I of Savoy, who added the loggias and porticoes; and again in the late 16th and early 17th centuries under Carlo Emanuele I of Savoy. It is now home to the town library and archives.

SAVIGLIANO

Though the approach to the town (*map C, C1*) is marred by recent urban sprawl, Savigliano preserves a pleasant historic centre. First mentioned in 981, in the 13th century Savigliano was a member of the Lombard League of free communes that opposed the rule of Holy Roman Emperor Frederick I Hohenstaufen in northern Italy. In the 15th century the Dukes of Savoy decided the city would be new seat of the University of Turin, but the experiment lasted only two years (1434–6). The art of printing has been practised here since its invention: in 1470 the opening of the press of Christopher Beggiami marked the first use of movable type in Piedmont and inaugurated what is now a tradition that has lasted more than half a millennium.

The heart of the city is the medieval **Piazza Santorre di Santarosa**, a long, irregular rectangle surrounded by porticoed buildings on sturdy pillars and overlooked by the imposing Torre del Comune, with its ogival mullioned windows, and the Mannerist triumphal arch, erected in 1585 for the festivities in honour of the Dukes of Savoy, and by which the square is entered from the south. The nearby Collegiata di Sant'Andrea probably harks back to the 11th century (although what you see today dates from the early 18th), whereas the handsome little Teatro Milanollo, with a Neoclassical façade graced by statues of *Comedy*, *Tragedy* and, at the very top, *Glory crowning Music and Poetry*, was built in the early 19th century. The town's architectural heritage also includes several stately palaces, notably **Palazzo Muratori Cravetta**, (*Via Jerusalem 4*) and **Palazzo Taffini d'Acceglio** (*Via Sant'Andrea 53; visitsavigliano.it*).

There are two interesting museums in the town. The **Museo Civico Antonino Olmo & Gipsoteca Davide Calandra** (*Via San Francesco 17/19, museocivicosavigliano.it*) occupies two floors in the 17th-century convent of San Francesco. On the ground floor are a display tracing Savigliano's urban development, and the *gipsoteca*, which brings together over a hundred casts, sketches and maquettes by the 19th-century monumental sculptor Davide Calandra (among his most famous works are the Bartolomé Mitre equestrian monument in Buenos Aires and the frieze celebrating the Savoy dynasty in Italy's Chamber of Deputies at Palazzo Montecitorio in Rome). Upstairs is the municipal art collection, with works ranging from the 16th–18th centuries and including the Attilio Bonino bequest of paintings and sculptures, arranged as though in the collector's home.

The **Museo Ferroviario Piemontese** (*Via Coloira 7, for opening times, see museoferroviariopiemontese.it*), by the railway south of the historic centre, is a must-see for train buffs, being home to one of the finest collections in Europe of working locomotives (in a former roundhouse), vintage carriages, models, photographs and documents. Some of the historic trains are taken out for excursions in summer. There is also a 10m-long digitally controlled train table.

LAGNASCO

This town (*map C, C1*), located just south of the road from Saluzzo to Savigliano, is known for the **Castelli Tapparelli D'Azeglio** (*Via Castelli 4, castellidilagnasco. it*), a complex of three castles. When they were begun is not known, but they were completed in the 16th century by Benedetto I Tapparelli, the chief magistrate of Saluzzo under Francis I of France. It was he who had the interior decorated with paintings and sculptures, by Cesare Arbasia and Giacomo Rossignolo (who painted the Sala della Giustizia with scenes from Classical myth) and Pietro Dolce and his school (who drew their inspiration from Norse grotesques). In the late 19th century Emanuele d'Azeglio Tapparelli, the last scion of the family, bequeathed the castles to the community. The complex is now home to a small but fine collection of early Modern painting featuring works by local artists such as Reycend and Delleani, and internationally renowned masters such as De Chirico, Carrà, De Pisis, Severini and Sironi.

SAVIGLIANO TRAINS

The completion in 1853 of the Turin–Savigliano railway, one of the first lines in the Kingdom of Sardinia, gave new impetus to the local economy. A few years later the Società Nazionale delle Officine di Savigliano was established for the production of rolling stock and railway infrastructure. This is where the first, elegant Wagon Lits carriages were made. Although the works have changed hands several times over the years they have never shut down. In the past two decades the plant has turned out nearly 500 high-speed trains in use in twelve countries, from Italy to Finland, the United Kingdom and Russia. Now operated by Alstom, the Savigliano works also host the First Train Workshop, where the French multinational develops and tests its prototypes before they go into production.

RACCONIGI

At Racconigi (*map C, C1*) you can visit the castle (Castello di Racconigi; *http://polomusealepiemonte.beniculturali.it*), originally built in the 14th century by the marquises of Saluzzo and later a favourite royal residence of the kings of Italy. Its park and garden (Parco Reale) is the masterpiece of Xavier Kürten (*see p. 89*).

THE VALLE VARAITA

COSTIGLIOLE SALUZZO

Three castle-mansions dominate the narrow streets of this late-medieval village (*map C, B2*), whose history is linked to local factions. It has always been a farming town, its climate being particularly good for fruit and vines. The typical product is Quagliano wine, which together with Pelaverga is grown in a small area stretching from Costigliole Saluzzo to Busca. The recent trend of valuing even minor grape varieties has given rise to a new DOC appellation, 'Colline Saluzzesi-Quagliano Costigliole'. Costigliole is also known for its apples and the typical round apricots called simply *tonde di Costigliole*.

Among the main things to see is the **Palazzo dei Conti Giriodi di Monastero**, now the Town Hall, built after 1740 to plans by Bernardo Vittone. It has a majestic entrance portal and a monumental staircase leading to the main public rooms, decorated frescoes by Luigi Vacca, set designer and painter at the court of Carlo Felice di Savoia. In the lower part of the village is the **Palazzo Sarriod de la Tour** (*Via Vittorio Veneto 109, visitcuneese.it*), with medieval walls, a double loggia and crenellated tower. Purchased in 1734 by Count Tommaso Alberto Saluzzo together with the surrounding hamlet, it has been enlarged and restored several times over the years and is now a library and cultural centre.

PIASCO

Piasco (*map C, B2*) was a Roman customs station on the road to Gaul. Today it boasts a medieval tower and a 17th-century castle designed by Amedeo di Castellamonte, but its greatest claim to fame is its harp collection, the world's largest. The **Museo dell'Arpa Victor Salvi** (*Via Rossana 7, museodellarpavictorsalvi.it*) was established in 2005 by the Italian-American musician and harp-maker Victor Salvi, born in Chicago in the 1920s. The collection includes more than a hundred harps from around the world, ranging in date from the 18th century to the present; a large window opens onto the Salvi workshop below, where skilled craftsmen continue to assemble harps.

CASTELDELFINO

The name of this village (*map C, A1*) derives from the presence of the *Castrum Delphini*, the 'Castle of the Dauphin', the heir to the throne of the kingdom of France, Humbert II de Viennois. The castle was destroyed in 1690, and only a few ruins remain. Today the economy of Casteldelfino is based on farming and tourism: there are several walks on the slopes of Monviso and through the **Foresta d'Alevè**, the largest forest of stone pine (*Pinus cembra L.*) in Europe. Covering 824 hectares between 1500 and 2500 m, the forest is strictly protected and is listed among the biotypes of European importance. The fragrant pink wood of the stone pine (which termites loathe) is traditionally used by local artisans to make sculptures, carvings and furniture. There is a forest information centre in Casteldelfino.

BELLINO

Bellino (*map C, A1*) is a small, scattered settlement (1572m; pop. 156) located near the French frontier. Occitan is still the main language here. The town, composed of nine villages (*ruas*), preserves a strong Alpine character, with ancient fountains, covered walkways, stone houses with flagstone roofs and stone façades with devotional paintings and sundials. Bellino has more than 30 of the latter, dating back as far as 1735. A 'solar walk', beginning and ending at the **Museo del Tempo e delle Meridiane** in Celle, just west of Bellino (*comune.bellino.cn.it*), has been devised to show them off.

COTTIAN ALPS PRACTICAL TIPS

GETTING AROUND

• **By bus:** Local services in the region are run by Arriva (*torino.arriva.it*), Cavourese (*cavourese.it*) and Grandabus (*grandabus.it/orari*) .
• **By rail:** From Turin (Porta Susa) there are direct services to Pinerolo (49mins). There is an hourly train from Turin (Porta Nuova) to Oulx-Cesana-Claviere-Sestriere (1hr 11mins). To reach Susa, take the train from Turin (Porta Nuova) to Bussoleno (43mins/56mins). There are stops at Grugliasco, Collegno and Avigliano. A branch line connects Cuneo to Saluzzo.

WHERE TO STAY

BARDONECCHIA (*map A, A2*)
€ **Villa Myosotis**. Attractive 1930s villa with garden, in a quiet street in the centre of Bardonecchia. A family-run establishment offering B&B, or half or full board accommodation in cosily furnished rooms. *Via Generale Cantore 2, biovey.it.*
CAVOUR (*map A, B3*)
€ **Locanda La Posta**. A historic coaching inn dating back to 1706, with comfortable, unfussy rooms. *Via dei Fossi 7, locandalaposta.it.*

COSTIGLIOLE SALUZZO (*map C, B1*)
€€ **Castello Rosso**. In a Romantic garden overlooking a village not far from Cuneo, this large 15th-century manor house with finely appointed rooms, a restaurant with garden seating in summer, and a spa, offers a good starting point for excursions on the plain of Saluzzo and in the Val Varaita. *Via Ammiraglio Reynaudi 5, castellorosso.com.*

PINEROLO (*map A, B3*)
€€ **Il Torrione**. The Neoclassical villa of the Marquis Doria Lamba of Pinerolo was originally a medieval fortress with a tall central keep, from which it takes its name, 'great tower'. It seems that Alessandro Antonelli, architect of the Mole Antonelliana in Turin and San Gaudenzio in Novara, had a hand in its redesign. Now used for events, it preserves a Baroque entrance hall, a beautiful elliptical ballroom and rooms adorned with mythological paintings, stuccoes, grotesques and zodiac signs. The adjacent Bigattaia, once used to breed silkworms, is now a warm and charming *Maison d'Hôtes* B&B, where the Doria family invites guests to share their peaceful *vie de château* and its amenities: pool, tennis courts and park designed by Xavier Kürten (*see p. 89*). *Via Galoppatoio 20, iltorrione.com.*
€ **Hotel Regina**. Modern-style hotel in the town centre, eight studio apartments and good restaurant. *Piazza Barbieri 22, albergoregina.net.*

SALUZZO (*map C, B1*)
€€ **Griselda**. Agreeable and convenient. *Corso XXVII Aprile 13, hotelgriselda.it.*
€€ **San Giovanni Resort**. Originally a monastic complex built by Cistercian monks in the late 13th century. In 1320 it passed to the Dominicans, who gave it its present appearance between the 14th and the 16th centuries. In 1826 it was taken over by the Servants of Mary,

who leased it to the municipality. It is now a hotel, warm and welcoming without betraying its simple and austere monastic vocation. The rooms are comfortable but sober, making extensive use of natural materials (wood, terracotta) and colours (earth tones); the strategy is echoed in the vaulted halls of the Castellana restaurant, as well as in the sober meeting hall—the former refectory—with its coffered wood ceiling and frescoed *Crucifixion*. Seating is extended outdoors to the cloister in summer. 13 rooms. *Via San Giovanni 9a, sangiovanniresort.it.*

€ **Antico Podere Propano**. Country hotel on Saluzzo's northern fringe, originally a farm donated by Marquis Michele Antonio of Saluzzo to the Cistercian monks of Monbracco in 1525. The rooms are a bit impersonal, despite the efforts made to preserve original elements such as fireplaces and beamed or vaulted ceilings; on the other hand, they are larger than in most hotels at this price and the views of Monviso and old Saluzzo are exceptional. 30 rooms. *Via Torino 75, anticopoderepropano.com.*

€ **Antiche Mura**. Completely renovated rooms in the centre of town. Functional, clean, welcoming. *Via Palazzo di Città 75, antichemurasaluzzo.com.*

SAUZE D'OULX (map A, A2)
€€ **Il Capricorno**. A cordial, family-run place with just seven rooms, in a historic chalet in the forest at 1800 m. Lots of old wood, thick duvets and crackling fires in winter—plus an extraordinary gourmet restaurant. *Via Case Sparse 21, Le Clotes, Sauze d'Oulx, chaletilcapricorno.it.*

SESTRIERE (map A, A3)
€€€ **Principi di Piemonte**. *The* place to stay in the resort in Piedmont, set in a beautiful larch grove outside the town. This historic hotel was built in the 1930s in a style blending audacious Modernism (curved walls and bold geometries) with vernacular elements (rooftop pinnacles and massive wood panelling inside). A real monument to the architecture of luxury tourism in the early 20th century. Worth stopping in for a look even if you don't stay there. *Via Sauze di Cesana 3, principidipiemonte.it.*

TORRE PELLICE (map A, B3)
€€ **Maison Flipot**. Lovely old farmhouse with beautifully appointed B&B accommodation, and a restaurant attached. *Corso Gramsci 17, maisonflipot.com.*

WHERE TO EAT

BARDONECCHIA (map A, A2)
€ **Biovey**. In a quiet street in the centre of Bardonecchia, a warm family-run establishment in the Villa Myosotis Inn, with good atmosphere and excellent mountain cuisine (venison carpaccio with red cabbage and porcini mushrooms, rye gnocchi with *toma* (ewe's cheese) sauce). *Via Generale Cantore 2, biovey.it.*

CAVOUR (map A, B3)
€ **Locanda La Posta**. Restaurant and hotel in a characteristic old coaching inn, proudly in business since 1706. *Via dei Fossi 7, locandalaposta.it.*

PINEROLO (map A, B3)
€€ **Taverna degli Acaja**. A warm, quiet restaurant bringing creative

imagination to bear on traditional recipes, particularly fresh egg pasta, fish and meat. Across the street from the Museo della Cavalleria. Closed Sun and midday Mon. *Corso Torino 106, tavernadegliacaja.it.*

SALUZZO (*map C, B1*)
€€ **Casa Pellico**. The name references poet and patriot Silvio Pellico, who was born in Saluzzo, and the cuisine of chef Marco Roberto is similarly tied to the place and its tradition. Snails au gratin, potato panzerotti and hazelnut tart are as traditional as the come, but the cooking is inventive too, as exemplified by the sea bream and sea bass burger. Closed Mon. *Piazzetta Mondagli 5, casapellico.com.*
€€ **Taverna dei Porti Scür**. Located beneath the porticoes in the centre of town and known for its creative interpretations of traditional recipes, its quick and cordial service and its very reasonable prices. *Via Palazzo di Città 75, T: 0175 219483.*

TORRE PELLICE (*map A, B3*)
€€ **Maison Flipot**. Excellent regional cooking in a lovely old farmhouse, which also offers B&B accommodation. *Corso Gramsci 17, maisonflipot.com.*

USSEAUX (*map A, B2*)
€ **Lago del Laux** (also a hotel). Small and delicious, on the lakeside 1km south of the town, this mountain inn serves outstanding dishes from the *terroir*, prepared with passion from the finest ingredients. Reservations suggested. *Via al Lago 7, hotellaux.it.*

LOCAL SPECIALITIES

The best **chestnuts** in Piedmont come from the Valle di Susa, the so-named *marrone della Valle di Susa*, and the eight varieties of antique **apples** from the Valle del Pellice (*grigia di torriana, carla dominici, calvilla bianca, buras, gamba fina, magnana* and *runsè*), protected by the Slow Food movement.

EVENTS AND FESTIVALS

Pinerolo *La Maschera di Ferro*. The famous 'Man in the Iron Mask', immortalised in Alexandre Dumas's *The Three Musketeers* (1844), is 'revealed' by the residents of Pinerolo in Piazza Vittorio Veneto at the culmination of a festival celebrating this mysterious figure who was imprisoned here, 1st weekend of Oct.
Saluzzo *Storia Arte Saluzzo*, a festival of antique and contemporary applied art, held in April/May (*startsaluzzo.it*).
Susa *Castagna d'Oro, Festival Internazionale del Folklore*. The communes of the Valle di Susa unite in the Roman arena of Susa to celebrate past and present culture and traditions, end of Aug.

The Maritime Alps, with Cuneo & Mondovì & the Alpi Liguri

The Maritime Alps (Italian *Alpi Marittime*; French *Alpes Maritimes*) are the segment extending along the French–Italian border between the Ligurian Alps on the east and the Cottian Alps (west). Punta Argentera (3297m) is the highest point. The name provides a clue to the mountains' most distinctive feature: together with the Ligurian Alps, they are the portion closest to the sea, thus enjoying the mildest climate. Their extremes are considered the two passes of Colle della Maddalena (1996m) on the northwest, and Colle di Tenda (1871m) on the east-southeast. The Maritime Alps possess many of the features typical of the Western Alps: sharp crests and peaks, deep canyons and narrow valleys of fluvial origin, accompanied by more open glacial valleys, numerous lakes and a fairly high ridgeline. Geologically they combine soft, light-coloured limestone and dolomite (in the Valle Stura) with darker, harder granitic rock (notably the Argentera massif in the Valle Gesso), both shaped by thousands of years of glacial erosion.

The broad Valle Gesso forms a sort of hinge on which the chain turns gradually from east–west to south–north; it is here that one finds the Maritime Alps' highest peaks: Monte Clapier (3045m), at whose feet nestle the southernmost glaciers of the Alps; Mont Gelàs (3143m), with its perpetual mantle of snow; Cima Ghilè (2998m), Cima di Nasta (3108m), Monte Argentera (south peak 3297m, north peak 3286m), Monte Gelàs Lourousa (3261m) and Monte Stella (3262m). Between the latter two peaks, on the north side of the range, is the striking Lourousa ice rill, beneath the imposing north face of the Corno Stella (3050m), one of the most daunting rockfaces in Europe. From Cima Ghilè, when the sky is clear, the view stretches over the Mediterranean and the French Riviera, from Nice to Cap d'Antibes.

CUNEO

Located on a wedge-shaped alluvial terrace created by the confluence of the rivers Gesso and Stura di Demonte, Cuneo (*map C, B2*) enjoys good views of the whole southwestern arc of the Alps, from Monviso and Monte Argentera to Rocca dell'Abisso and La Bisalta. The town was founded in the 12th century by farmers, merchants and artisans who fled the neighbouring countryside to escape oppressive landlords, and its strategic location has deeply marked its historical development.

From the 14th century it was used as a defensive outpost by the Savoy armies crossing the Alps. Having just one direction in which it could grow (to the southwest), it long remained enclosed within its original walls. It was only after the demolition of these, under Napoleon in the early 19th century, that the city began to expand. The first urban plan, dated 1802, set the scheme for the city's growth towards Borgo San Dalmazzo and the base of the plateau, along an orthogonal street pattern. Piazza Galimberti was built in the 19th century and Corso Nizza, the heart of an elegant middle-class neighbourhood, in the early 20th. Urban development took on a particularly rapid pace after the Second World War as the city extended to occupy the whole plateau, right up to the avenues built on the ramparts of the ancient fortifications overlooking the Gesso and the Stura.

Today Cuneo is a lively city, as much as ever a crossroads for ideas and goods. It is also one of the gourmet capitals of Piedmont. Its inhabitants are very fond of the *caffè salotto*, a very old Piedmont institution combining conviviality with the consumption of fine sweet and savoury pastries. Cuneo has given its name to a very delicate kind of rum chocolate, the *cuneese*, and is the site of Italy's grand chestnut fair (Oct).

The oldest part of Cuneo was given its street plan, a chessboard pattern with a strong central axis (Via Roma), in the Middle Ages, a fact that contradicts the conventional wisdom which would have rectilinear street plans be either modern (Manhattan, Barcelona) or antique (Roman). In such an old context one would expect to find an equally ancient religious centre, but Cuneo's **cathedral**, dedicated to Santa Maria del Bosco, is relatively new. It was built over a medieval church, to a design by Giovenale Boetto of Fossano, in the late 18th century, but its present appearance is the result of a major restoration carried out a century later. Surmounted by a dome, the church has an elegant façade with tall Corinthian columns supporting a Classical pediment. The rather dark and heavy interior holds numerous 17th-century paintings, notably a *Madonna and Child, St Michael, St John the Baptist and Angels* by Andrea Pozzo (1685) in the apse.

The **Museo Diocesano San Sebastiano** (*Contrada Mondovi, museodiocesano cuneo.it*) is located in the heart of old Cuneo. The collection is laid out thematically and focuses almost entirely on the complex of San Sebastiano and the ancient Brotherhood of St James and St Sebastian. The visit starts with the dedication of the complex to St James and the importance of Cuneo as a stage on one of the major pilgrimage routes from southern Europe to Santiago de Compostela. It then deals with the patronage of St Sebastian, protector against the plague, in an epoch during which the city closed its doors to foreigners, no longer seen as imitators of Christ to be sheltered, but as hostile bearers of illness and death. Other salient themes are the Counter-Reformation and the Napoleonic period, which brought an end to the dominance of religious institutions in civil affairs and laid the foundations of modern secular society. The museum also boasts an escape room, with a maximum capacity of nine.

The **Museo Civico** likewise occupies a religious complex, the 15th-century Romanesque-Gothic church and 17th-century cloister of the former monastery of San Francesco (*Via Santa Maria 10, www.comune.cuneo.it/cultura/museo*). It is devoted to regional archaeology, art and ethnography. The first section presents antiquities from prehistory to the Middle Ages; the second houses a remarkable 14th-century fresco of the *Madonna with Child* and other paintings; the third displays typical costumes of the Alpine valleys, furniture, objects related to farming, weaving and everyday life, and a unique collection of Lenci dolls, the elaborately dressed pressed-felt dolls of the mid-20th century made in Turin by Elena Scavini and her firm, Ars Lenci.

Cuneo is the gateway to the **Parco Fluviale Gesso e Stura**, which extends over 4500 ha in the hills south and west of the city and links up with the Parco Naturale delle Alpi Marittime (around Monte Argentera) and the Parc National du Mercantour in France to make a single vast protected area.

The spectacular **railway line** through the mountains between Cuneo and Ventimiglia is a remarkable feat of engineering, with numerous tunnels and viaducts. Inaugurated in 1928, it was finally reopened in 1979, having been put out of action in the Second World War. Between Limone Piemonte and Ventimiglia it traverses 46km of French territory. The 96km ride takes just over 2hrs.

ENVIRONS OF CUNEO

CARAGLIO

Caralh in Occitan, *Caraj* in Piedmontese, Caraglio (*map C, B2*) was an important Calvinist centre until the strict Counter-Reformation laws of the Savoy compelled residents to renounce their faith. Today its name is linked to its historical silk industry. Though silk-making is a thing of the past, its memory survives in the beautifully restored **Filatoio Rosso** (*Via Matteotti 44, filatoiocaraglio.it*), thought to be the oldest extant silk mill in the world. Built in just two years (1676–8) by entrepreneur Giò Gerolamo Galleani, it is a symmetrical edifice with two courtyards, cylindrical corner towers, and rich stucco and terracotta decorations inside and out. The mill was shut down on the eve of Second World War and remained closed until a few years ago, when it was completely overhauled to make a silk museum and modern art centre.

Other sights of historical significance in Caraglio are the 13th-century church of **San Giovanni** with its green lawn, pink façade and steep-spired 14th-century campanile, and the six-tiered 13th-century campanile of the former church of San Paolo. The **Convento dei Cappuccini** was founded in 1698 just outside the town (*Via dei Cappuccini 29, T: 0171 618260*). Its present appearance is largely the result of later extensions and renovations, and although the church, dedicated to Santa Maria degli Angeli, still has its original wooden altars, the convent and gardens are now a cultural centre and contemporary art space.

DRONERO

During the Second World War, Piedmont was one of the chief areas of resistance, and Dronero (*map C, B2*) was a focal point of **Partisan activity** in Piedmont. Here, following the armistice of 8th September 1943 (when Italy broke off its alliance with Germany), the local anti-Fascists took to the hills to form the first Partisan groups. Dronero paid a heavy price, with deportations, shootings and eight aerial bombardments, from 12th–27th February 1945, which caused death, destruction and the flight of the population. Liberation finally came on 26th April 1945. With the establishment of the Italian Republic, Dronero was awarded the War Cross for Valour for the sacrifices of its residents and for its activities in the Partisan Resistance Movement.

Today it is a pleasant place surrounded by wooded mountains. The small but fascinating **Museo Sòn de Lenga**, (*Via Val Maria 19; open winter by appointment, for summer hours, see espaci-occitan.org*) provides an effective approach to Occitan culture through the study of the Occitan language and its oral traditions. A sequence of 'sound stations' in four languages (Italian, Occitan, English and French) illustrate Occitan literature, music, history, material culture and social customs. The **Museo Civico Luigi Mallé** (*Via IV Novembre 54, museomalle.org*) is the house-museum of a well-known native 20th-century art historian, collector and connoisseur. His collections are arranged chronologically and include a wide variety of artists and works ranging from Flemish paintings of the late 16th century to modern masters such as Lucio Fontana and Graham Sutherland, and Asian and European ceramics.

THE OCCITAN LANGUAGE

Occitan or the *languedoc* (originally: *occitan, lenga d'òc*), in Italian also called *lingua provenzale alpina* because it is the autochthonous language of the Cottian and Maritime Alps, is a Gallo-Romance language spoken in a specific area of Mediterranean Europe that is not limited by national boundaries and which is coarsely identified with the South of France. Occitan is not be confused with the Franco-Provençal (or *arpitan*) of the Graian Alps, nor with the French *patois* or the *patois* of the Valle d'Aosta, two other Gallo-Romance idioms. These languages grew up during the gradual Romanisation of Gaul in late antiquity and the early Middle Ages (from the 4th–12th centuries or so), mixing Latin phrases with Franco-Gallic terms. Today they are recognised alongside the official languages of the nations in which they are spoken. The *langue d'òc* was not only a standard language distinct from the *langue d'oïl* spoken in north-central France (the Gallo-Romance predecessor of modern French), it was a literary language in France and northern Spain in the 12th–14th centuries and was widely used as a vehicle for poetry; it was the primary language of the medieval troubadours (some scholars believe Dante was the first to draw the distinction). The modern dialects of Occitan are spoken by more than a million people in southern France and northern Italy; they have changed little with respect to their medieval counterparts, although they are being affected by their constant exposure to other European languages.

BUSCA

Busca (*map C, B2*) is a farming town not far from the River Maira. Though probably pre-Roman in origin, it did not attain any sort of renown until the 17th century, when the cultivation of wheat, grapes and fruit brought its inhabitants regional fame and fortune. The town still retains its medieval street plan and there are a couple of interesting monuments—the Baroque church of the **Santissima Trinità** (locally 'La Rossa') and the church of **Santissima Annunziata** ('La Bianca'), by Francesco Gallo.

The main thing to see, however, is outside the town, to the northwest, towards Saluzzo. The **Castello del Roccolo** (*Frazione San Quintino 17; open May and Oct Sun 2.30–7; June–Sept Sat 2.30–7, Sun 10–7; T: 0171 618260; www.castellodelroccolo.it*) was built over an earlier structure by Marquis Roberto d'Azeglio Tapparelli after 1831. The marquis designed the building himself, in a then-fashionable style combining Gothic Revival, Romantic and Moorish elements. The result is eclectic, to say the least, but it was considered sufficiently stately to host King Umberto I and Queen Margherita. The marquis hired the landscape architect Xavier Kürten (*see p. 89*) to lay out the grounds, with their terraces, lakes, waterfalls and scenic trails. Lately the large greenhouses, built between 1846 and 1850, have been used for flower shows and cultural events. The curious name is derived from *roccoli*, nets used to hunt small birds.

Five minutes north by car, on the road to Costigliole Saluzzo, is the ruined Romanesque **chapel of San Martino**, with three apses and a frescoed lunette over the main portal.

Another fine castle can be seen at **Rocca de' Baldi** (*map C, C2*). This one is an urban fortress, later transformed into a comfortable home. Towering over the centre of the town, its Ghibelline-crenellated keep bears witness to its strategic importance as a checkpoint on the royal road that linked Mondovì and Cuneo. Captured and burned by the Spanish in 1543, it was rebuilt and enlarged in subsequent centuries, most notably by Marquis Gaspare Filippo Morozzo, who added the pink wing, designed by Francesco Gallo. Today the castle is home to a unique collection of votive offerings and the **Museo Etnografico Augusto Doro** (*museodoro.org*), which has well-designed interactive displays documenting rural life and agrarian practices in the Cuneo region. You should leave time to stroll through the park, where there are two extraordinary specimens of *Sophora japonica* and 130 heirloom fruit trees (*open for guided visits May–Oct Sun 2.30–6.30*).

THE VALLE STURA

The valleys of the rivers Stura and Gesso, respectively west and southwest of Cuneo, are visited for their natural beauty and their year-round recreational opportunities, but the villages have retained a degree of authenticity that is difficult to find in other Alpine regions.

DEMONTE

One of the prettiest places in the Valle Stura, this small village (*map C, B3*) is surrounded by verdant mountains where vast fields of lavender bloom in summer. Its chief monument is the 18th-century **Palazzo Borelli**, built for Count Giacinto Borelli, a signatory of the Albertine Statute, a constitutional covenant. Inside the palace are decorated wooden ceilings and frescoes from the 18th and 19th centuries; outside is a 19th-century terraced garden, with fountains and grottoes. The palace hosts a small museum devoted to poet and journalist Lalla Romano (*for details and opening times, see visitdemonte.com*).

VINADIO

This Occitan town (*map C, A3*), founded by the Romans, was troubled throughout its history by territorial disputes between the Anjou, the Visconti, the marquises of Saluzzo and the Savoy—all engaged during the Counter-Reformation in the repression of Calvinism, which had taken a foothold in the area. Now a popular holiday resort, Vinadio is known for its spa, the Bagni di Vinadio (1300m), built in the mid-18th century, aas well as for its skiing.

The **Forte Albertino** here (*for opening times see fortedivinadio.com*) is among the most impressive examples of military architecture in the Alps. The construction of the fortress, undertaken by King Carlo Alberto to control traffic in the valley, began in 1834 and ended in 1847. The fort measures 1200m on its longest side. The complete visit, which unfolds on three levels of walkways, is c. 10km long and is divided into three 'fronts' where the garrison could be assembled for battle: the Upper Front, Attack Front and Lower Front. The fort also houses two small museums: a mutimedia display of mountain culture, *Montagna in Movimento*, and a display on the fort's carrier pigeons, *Messageri Alati*. In summer the fortifications host cultural events and entertainments.

PIETRAPORZIO

This pretty village (*map C, A3*) lies at the very top of the Valle Stura just 15km from France. It has an older part, Saretto, and a Romanesque bell tower in the cemetery, called the **Campanile dei Catre Loupes** for the wolves carved on the corners of the cusp. At the nearby hamlet of Pontebernardo is an **Ecomuseo della Pastorizia** (*for opening times, see visitstura.it or T: 0171 955555*) where cheese is made daily and some nicely designed exhibits take you on a pleasant journey through the cheese-making process.

THE VALLE GESSO

VALDIERI

This amenable resort (*map C, B3*) is spread over an expansive valley on the left bank of the Gesso, beneath the limestone walls of the fortress of San Giovanni. It was the town of the *lousatier*, the slate-quarriers who provided the stone for so many roofs in rural Piedmont, and was also known for its grey-striated *bardiglio* marble.

The natural beauty of the Maritime Alps led the Savoy to establish yet another hunting reserve in the Valle Gesso and to spend their summers either in the village of Sant'Anna di Valdieri or at the nearby **Casa di Caccia** (1865), surrounded by the splendid fir forest of Pian del Velasco. King Vittorio Emanuele II laid the cornerstone of the **Terme di Valdieri** in 1855, and the spa has been frequented ever since for the therapeutic properties of its hot springs and mud. The very pretty **Giardino Botanico Alpino Valderia** is home to about 450 species of plants; the sanctuary of the **Madonna del Colletto** offers excellent views of the valley (a plaque recalls that Italy's famous Giustizia e Libertà partisan brigades were founded here in September 1943); and an archaeological park protects one of the largest prehistoric necropolises in Italy. A two-hour marked walk takes you through the **Ecomuseo della Segale**, or museum of the rye plant, which documents the harsh living conditions of local farmers. Some houses with thatched-rye roofs have been restored in the villages of Tetti Bariau and Tetti Bartola and evocations of everyday life have been reconstructed in their interiors. More reconstructions are planed in the village of Sant'Anna (*ring walk always open, for access to the interiors, see ecomuseosegale.it*).

Valdieri lies at the foot of an important nature reserve. The **Riserva Naturale Speciale-Stazione Juniperus phoenicea**, located on the rock walls of the limestone Pissousa, Saben and San Giovanni peaks, was established to protect an unusual colony of a plant that really has no business being here. The particular sedimentary soil of this protected area, and its unique microclimate (determined by its southern exposure and the verticality of the mountain sides, which hinders the accumulation of snow), have made this Alpine environment very similar to that of the Mediterranean. This has provided favourable conditions for Phoenician juniper, a shrub typical of the Mediterranean coast, to form its northernmost and highest colony here. The reserve is also home to other species of juniper (*Juniperus thurifera, Juniperus communis* and dwarf juniper); its birds include the peregrine falcon, harrier, golden eagle and kestrel and there are a number of rare and endemic species of insect.

ENTRACQUE

This picturesque village (*map C, B3*) has 800 year-round residents and a summer/winter population of 5,000 to 6,000, most of whom own second homes here. The economy was originally based on farming and grazing; then the 18th and 19th centuries brought several textile mills to the town and a sharp increase in population. With the advent of modern industry and the consequent abandonment of the small-scale, water-driven mills, and with the establishment of the Royal Hunting Reserve in the upper Valle Gesso, Entracque became a resort. Today summer tourism is mostly based on the proximity of the national park (*see below*), whereas winter visitors come to ski. Entracque is also known for its DOP potato, which is the centre of attention at the annual feast of St Anthony (*August*).

The **Centro Faunistico Uomini e Lupi** (*Piazza Giustizia e Libertà 3 and Strada per San Giacomo 3; for opening times, see centrouominielupi.it*) is a natural-science museum with a clear mission: to paint a truthful, unbiased portrait of the wolf, a predator humans have always viewed as a competitor. Two exhibition spaces, one at Entracque and the other at Casermette, are dedicated to the relationship between humans and wolves and to the animal's behaviour—here exemplified by Ligabue, a young male tracked throughout his journey from the Parma Apennines to the Maritime Alps. The Casermette facility houses specimens, born in captivity or injured in road accidents, in an enclosure of about eight hectares. An underground tunnel leads to the middle of the area, where there is a three-storey platform for wolf-watching. It's easy to think this is for children...until you realise you've spent an hour waiting for a glimpse.

PARCO NATURALE DELLE ALPI MARITTIME
By far the greatest attraction in the Valle Gesso, the Parco Naturale delle Alpi Marittime (*map C, B3*) coordinates its efforts with those of the adjacent French Parc National du Mercantour, to create a single, immense entity. In Italy the protected area covers some 28,000 ha (making it the largest in Piedmont); together, the two nature reserves cover 100,000 ha along a 30km frontier. The Parco Naturale delle Alpi Marittime encompasses the uppermost stretches of the Gesso, Stura and Vermenagna valleys—a landscape deeply shaped by the action of glaciers and abounding in streams, waterfalls and lakes due to the low permeability of the underlying rock—in the shadow of the 3297m peak of Mount Argentera, the roof of the Maritime Alps. The park is known for its wide variety of microclimates, a consequence of having of 3000-m peaks right next to the sea. One outcome of this unusual combination is a floral heritage consisting of more than 2,600 different species. In certain cases (for example, orchids), the park contains half the species found in Italy. The fauna includes all the usual Alpine mammals (marmots, hares, ermine, weasels and martens; chamois, ibex, deer, wild boar and mouflon), all the birds typical of the Western Alps (plus many migratory species) and, of course, wolves.

MONDOVÌ

Located in the foothills of the Maritime Alps, Mondovì (*map C, C3*) is a small city with two centres: an upper one, Piazza, on a hill and a lower one, Breo, on the plain of the Torrente Ellero, 150m lower down. Piazza is the oldest part of the town and the traditional seat of civic and religious power. Breo, together with the neighbouring Pian della Valle, Borgato and Altipiano, are the centres of the city's industrial and commercial life.

Mondovì was established in 1198 when the inhabitants of Carassone, Vasco and Vico (now Vicoforte) rebelled against the bishop of Asti, the district's largest landowner. A free commune after 1290, in 1418 it entered the domains of the Savoy. By the 16th century it was the most populous city in Piedmont and the seat of the region's only university. From that time until the Second World War it was home a small but thriving Jewish community, evidence of which remains in the old ghetto with its synagogue, and in the 18th-century cemetery in Breo.

Mondovì has been a leading ceramics centre for more than a century: the skilled hands of its potters paint tableware and other objects in bright colours with simple designs and subjects (flowers, birds, landscapes). Today the tradition is carried on in various craft shops, mainly located in Piazza.

The architect Francesco Gallo (1672–1750), a native, designed numerous buildings in the town. Mondovì is also the birthplace of Giovanni Giolitti (1842–1928), who was five times prime minister from 1892 to 1921 and introduced universal suffrage to Italy.

A funicular was added in 1880 to improve the connection between the upper and lower town. The ingenious mechanism initially used a counterweight of water to move the cars up and down the hill (rather than having ascending and descending cars balance one another). The completely rebuilt line reopened in 2006.

THE UPPER TOWN: PIAZZA

The heart of the town on the hill is the arcaded Piazza Maggiore, overlooked on the south by the **Chiesa di San Francesco Saverio della Missione**. This Jesuit church was begun in 1665 to plans by the architect and engraver Giovenale Boetto and completed in 1676. The sandstone façade has superimposed orders of columns and niches and a large triangular pediment; the window surround and balcony above the door are the work of the architect and painter Andrea Pozzo, a lay brother of the Society of Jesus. Pozzo, born in Trento, was well known for his illusionistic and trompe l'oeil frescoes. As well as in Mondovì, he worked in Rome and Vienna.

The interior has an aisleless nave with a plethora of pictorial and architectural elements (red faux-marble columns, pilasters, entablatures, broken pediments, stucco friezes) that blend to create a grand effect: it was created between 1675 and 1679 by Andrea Pozzo. The architect and painter transformed the flat ceiling into a *trompe l'oeil* dome open to the sky, taking up and continuing the architectural elements of the interior in what may be his most spectacular perspective painting. The dome shows the *Glorification of St Francis Xavier*, accompanied by a procession of angel musicians. In the apse is another powerful scene, *St Francis Baptising the Infidels, Princess Neachile, daughter of Almanzor, and all the Nations*. Pozzo also designed the spectacular *macchina* (scenic surround) of the main altar, a decorative wooden structure that was intended to be provisional (the image of St Francis is painted on sheet metal). This may be the only surviving *macchina* in Europe.

The **Museo della Ceramica**, in the prestigious Palazzo Fauzone di Germagnano across Piazza Maggiore, displays nearly 600 pieces of local ceramic ware (2,000 more are in storage), produced over nearly two centuries. The museum (*museoceramicamondovi.it*) is conceived as a journey through a craftsman's workshop; multimedia displays introduce the various stages of the creative process—from the composition of the raw clay and the techniques of shaping and decorating the unfired objects to the presentation of the finished pieces. The history of ceramics in Mondovì is traced through its major stages and the presentations are all really quite ingenious.

North of the square is the **cathedral** (San Donato), built between 1743 and 1753. It is the last work of the Baroque architect Francesco Gallo, who died before finishing it. It stands on the site of a Romanesque church dedicated to St Francis; the crypt holds the tombs of civil and religious figures of local eminence.

Set in the midst of a large green garden, the **Torre Civica del Belvedere**, also called the Torre dei Bressani, was built in the 13th or 14th century in the Gothic style and altered over the centuries. Nearly 30m tall, with mullioned windows and battlements, it is all that remains of the church of Sant'Andrea and, as a plaque explains, in 1762 was used by Giovanni Battista Beccaria as a trigonometric point for determining the length of a meridian arc. The climb to the top of the tower (*open at weekends, see visitmondovi.it*) leads past the working mechanism of the original (1859) one-handed clock, surrounded by other vintage clocks brought here to form a little museum. The tower, along with the Giardini del Belvedere and Palazzo di Giustizia, make up the **Parco del Tempo**, an educational park devoted to the measurement of time; panels on the outside of the Torre Civica illustrate the operation of sundials and trace out a walk past the old sundials of the historic centre. Three new solar clocks designed by Giuseppe Viara have been installed in the garden; there is an analemmatic sundial, a horizontal clock for telling true local time combined with an equatorial clock indicating the true time of Central Europe, and a clock calibrated for Italic and Babylonian time.

The last of Piazza's attractions lies in a quiet corner of the town, south of Piazza Maggiore. The **Museo Civico della Stampa** (*Via della Misericordia 3; usually open Fri–Sun, museostampamondovi.it*) is the most comprehensive public collection of presses and other items of printing equipment in Italy. Through its collections it illustrates the development of the printer's art as well as its more creative expressions, such as intaglio printing and lithography. The oldest press is a 17th-century example used by the Royal University of Turin, but there is also the press that printed the first issue of the *Gazzetta del Popolo* (1848), the Turin daily newspaper that helped spark the Risorgimento. The museum is housed in the 17th-century Collegio delle Orfane, once a convent-school of the Discalced Carmelites.

A TOWN OF PRINTERS

On 24th Oct 1472, just two decades after Gutenberg made his mechanical metal movable-type printing press, the first book to be published in Piedmont was printed in Mondovì by the Flemish typographer Antonius Matthiae with the financial support of the local merchant Baldassarre Cordero. *De Institutiones Confessorum* by St Antoninus of Florence (1389–1459) set in motion a local industry that has survived to the present day, thanks to the knowledge and experience handed down from generation to generation by families of skilled printers, notably the Vivalda (active 1476–95) and the Berruerio (1508–21).

THE LOWER TOWN: BREO

The main street of the lower town is Corso Statute, a long tree-lined stretch of which follows the Ellero. Here are the parish church of **Santi Pietro e Paolo**, built in 1489 and remodelled in the 17th century, and the church of **San Filippo**, built in 1734–57 by Francesco Gallo, who also designed the convent finished in 1796 by Bernardo Vittone.

THE ALPI LIGURI

CHIUSA DI PESIO
This lovely village (*map C, C3*), in a magnificent setting at the mouth of the Valley Pesio, is now a quiet, restful resort, though its name suggests it may once have been a military outpost (*chiusa* means 'fort'). Its chief monument is the great Carthusian monastery, which has been a hub of the region's spiritual and economic life for centuries.

The **Certosa di Santa Maria**, founded in 1173 as the third monastery of the Carthusian Order in Italy, immediately became a paragon of wise land use. It is thanks to the sound management of the area's forests by the monks here that today one can see tree species now rare in other parts of Italy. The monastery, located a short distance from Chiusa, beyond the villages of Vigna and San Bartolomeo, has a 16th-century cloister open on one side to the mountain and an abbey church dating from the 12th century. In the 19th century it acquired a reputation as a health resort, attracting guests of the stature of Count Camillo Benso di Cavour and Massimo d'Azeglio. The wall-less **Ecomuseo dei Certosini nella Valle Pesio** retraces the most important stages of Carthusian colonisation of the Valle Pesio, taking visitors on a journey through local ethnography and religious history with a particular regard to the Carthusians' view of the environment and of the relationship between the religious community and local farmers. Spiritual and material culture comes alive on numerous marked walks in the area leading to churches, chapels, votive pillars, frescoes and Carthusian granges. There are also itineraries showing the different economic activities developed over time, including the cultivation of medicinal herbs.

The immediate availability of immense quantities of wood and water made Chiusa a good place to produce glass and ceramics. In the Antico Palazzo Comunale, the **Complesso Museale e Centro Studi Cavalier Giuseppe Avena** (*Piazza Cavour 10; closed Mon, check precise opening times at comune.chiusadipesio.cn.it*) displays artefacts, tools for working glass, antique glass objects and glass produced at the Royal Manufactory of Glass and Crystal (established in Turin and modelled on the Manufactures Privilégiées et Royales de France, then moved to Chiusa di Pesio in 1759 by Carlo Emanuele III); numerous ceramic artefacts from donations and private collections; the so-called *Bronzes of Mount Cavanero*, documenting the discovery of a store of bronze, amber and glass items created in the 8th century BC on Mount Cavanero; and historical documentation of the Second World War Resistance movement (*see p. 125*), which was extremely important in southern Piedmont.

Chiusa is also the gateway to a major nature reserve. The 6770-ha **Parco Naturale dell'Alta Val Pesio e del Tanaro** encompasses the valleys of the Pesio and Alto Tanaro, which originate on opposite sides of Mt Marguareis, the highest peak of the Ligurian Alps (2651m). An impressive alpine karst system, second only to that of Trieste, runs underground, with caves exceeding 150km in length and reaching depths of up to 1000m. This part of the Maritime Alps is known as the Piccole Dolomiti because of its pale limestone substrate and extensive fir, beech and larch forests. Unlike the Dolomites, however, the area enjoys a particularly diverse variety of flora and fauna, due to its seaside location and relatively mild climate.

The **Collezione Fotografica Michele Pellegrino** (*Via Sant'Anna, 34; check opening times at the Tourist Office or T: 0171 734021*), displayed at the park's headquarters, is intended to highlight the importance of the area's natural and cultural heritage, but the power and beauty of the images go far beyond that. The collection, which counts 300 striking black-and-white photographs, is divided into sections devoted to the Alta Langa, the high-mountain landscape, springs in the Valle Pesio, vernacular architecture, the monks and the nuns of Chiusa, and moments in everyday life. The photographer's technique is impeccable, his approach to his subjects at once objective and poetic.

FRABOSA SOPRANA

This ancient village (*map C, C3*) of 800 residents, now a summer and winter resort, lies in a beautiful natural setting, on the slopes of Monte Moro between the Val Maudagna and the Valle Corsaglia—an area that has been under special protection since 1939. The village is home to a particular strain of the Occitan language, *Kyé*, which exists in oral form only, and it is one of just nine towns producing *raschera* DOP cheese (celebrated together with *brus* at the annual *Sagra dei Formaggi Raschera e Brus*, in August). The parish church of San Giovanni Battista (1701) is one of the earliest works of Francesco Gallo.

The most spectacular attraction here, however, is not manmade. The **Grotta di Bossea** (*open daily for guided tours; at the time of writing pre-booking was required, grottadibossea.com*), the terminal section of an underground karst stream system, extends for 2km (with an elevation loss of 200m) in the upper Valley Corsaglia. It is rightly considered one of the most beautiful and important caves in Italy. The underground chambers reach dizzying heights, with huge stalagmites and stalactites, sharp cliffs, giant boulders and deep ravines. Water is everywhere, rushing through roaring rapids and over majestic waterfalls, or dripping and oozing from ceilings and walls. In the active area (where karst phenomena are still taking place) the water removes 750–800 tonnes of rock per year and the vast underground chambers host an extraordinary ecosystem with at least 50 species of flora and fauna. The Torino Polytechnic University and the Italian Alpine Club jointly operate a research station here, and there is a now consolidated custom of performing classical music in the cave in the winter holiday season.

VICOFORTE

This pretty hilltop village (*map C, D3*) retains the battlemented tower of an 11th-century fortress destroyed by the French in 1545. It is best known, however, for the religious shrine in the valley below. The great sanctuary, intended by Duke

Carlo Emanuele I to be the pantheon of the House of Savoy, stands on the site of a shrine of the Virgin that had long been a centre of popular devotion. The **Santuario Regina Montis Regalis** was begun by Ascanio Vitozzi in the 17th century but work on the complex soon ceased; it was resumed in the 18th century by Francesco Gallo. Vitozzi had imagined a monument in local sandstone but Gallo preferred brick, so you can clearly see who built what. Vitozzi gave the sanctuary its semi-octagonal forecourt, the 'Palazzata', initially used to accommodate pilgrims. Gallo designed the great cupola, the largest elliptical dome in the world (37.15 by 24.9m) and still today an impressive feat of engineering (it also hosts the world's largest fresco cycle devoted to a single theme: the *Assumption of the Virgin and her Role in Salvation*, by Mattia Bortoloni and Felice Biella. Construction of the complex continued until the early 20th century, when the four tall campanili were completed. The visit (*hours are different according to season, see santuariodivicoforte.it*) includes the church and the adjacent monastery, with a fine cloister, monk's choir and refectory, splendidly decorated with illusionistic paintings by Bortoloni and Biella.

MOMBASIGLIO

This historic village (*map C, D3*) is dominated by its 11th-century castle. Set in a park with splendid views of the surrounding valleys, the castle is now home to the **Museo Generale Bonaparte** (*open by appointment; T: 0174 780268, galmongioie. it*), showing prints of Napoleon's first Italian campaign (1796) based on the drawings and watercolours he commissioned from the architect, topographer and landscape artist Giuseppe Pietro Bagetti to celebrate his early victories. Explanatory texts and scale models give a broad overview of the Napoleonic period, and the 44 copper engravings document both the fighting and the area in which it took place, accurately depicting the rural landscape of the time. There are also collections of uniforms, lead and tin soldiers, artefacts, busts, arms and documents, which together with the prints cast a great deal of light on the First Italian Campaign of 1796.

GARESSIO

Spa waters and winter sports (notably the Garessio 2000 ski area) are the main attractions of Garessio (*map C, D3*) and its mountainous environs. The town is divided into four villages: Borgo Maggiore, Borgo Ponte, Borgo Poggiolo and Borgo Medievale. In Borgo Maggiore, which has preserved its medieval appearance, are the church of the **Assunzione della Beata Vergine Maria**, designed by Francesco Gallo (1717–27), demolished and rebuilt in 1868 according to the original plan, and the church of the **Confraternità di San Giovanni**, with 18 lunettes portraying the life of the saint, dating from the late 17th century and recently restored. The square at the foot of the beautiful staircase here is paved in black and white cobblestones on a design by Giorgetto Giugiaro (b. 1938), a native of Garessio. Best known, perhaps, as an automobile designer (Fiat, Lancia, Maserati, Volkswagen), Giugiaro has also produced successful designs for trains, yachts, aircraft and other forms of transport.

In Borgo Ponte the parish church of **Santa Caterina** is an important work of Francesco Gallo (1723–40), with a campanile of 1786 designed by Bernardo Vittone. In Borgo Poggiolo are the **Fonti di San Bernardo**, with their weakly mineralised diuretic waters, bottled here and sold throughout Italy. In the Borgo Medievale are some old houses with terracotta friezes.

The name Garessio derives from the Provençal for ilex, an evergreen oak—whence *garriguo*, 'field covered with oaks', a term medieval statutes use to describe the plain of Garessio and especially the hill of San Costanzo.

CASTELLO REALE DI CASOTTO

This Savoy hunting lodge (*map C, D3*) was originally Carthusian monastery, founded in the 12th century high in the hills 17km (30mins) west of Garessio. It had an upper part, with church and guesthouse and a lower, with grange and service buildings. The suppression of religious orders in the Napoleonic era led to the sale of the property, which eventually ended up in the hands of Carlo Alberto of Savoy. In 1837 the king asked the architect Carlo Sada to remodel it as a hunting retreat and summer residence. Sada made the Carthusian church into a royal chapel, giving it a central plan and removing all traces of the earlier decorative scheme, and in the former monastery struck just the right balance between Carthusian simplicity and the monumental style that befitted a royal residence. It was Vittorio Emanuele II, the hunter-king, who used the retreat the most, organising grand hunting expeditions and summering here with Princess Maria Clotilde (*for opening times, see www.comune.garessio.cn.it*).

MARITIME ALPS PRACTICAL TIPS

GETTING AROUND

- **By bus:** Services around the region are operated by Grandabus. For routes and timetables, see the website (*grandabus.it/orari*).
- **By rail:** There is a fast regional service every two hours from Turin (Porta Nuova) to Cuneo (1hr 11mins). There are regional trains from Savona to Cuneo with a change at Fossano (2hrs 19mins). Branch lines connect Cuneo to Mondovì, Saluzzo, Ventimiglia and Nice.

WHERE TO STAY

BOVES (*map C, B1*)
€ **La Casa Arancione**. Everything about this delightful B&B is warm, from the colour scheme and the style of hospitality to the wonderful reading room with shelves and shelves of books in Italian, French and English. There are just two rooms (Wisteria and Mulberry), but the living area is quite large and the garden (where breakfast is served, weather permitting), covering some 1500 sq m notwithstanding the house, is just a few paces from the village square. *Via Peveragno 13, T: 0171 388244.*

CUNEO (*map C, C3*)
€€€ **Palazzo Lovera**. A restored elegant Renaissance *palazzo. Via Roma 37, palazzolovera.com.*
€€ **Hotel Principe di Piemonte**

Comfortable place in the heart of town. In business since 1932. *Piazza Tancredi Duccio Galimberti 5, hotel-principe.it*.
€€ **Ligure**. Small hotel in the historic centre of town, in the hands of the same family since 1939. *Via Savigliano 11, ligurehotel.com*.

MONDOVÌ (*map C, C3*)
€€ **Park Hotel**. Centrally-located hotel, modern and functional, with its own restaurant, Villa Nasi. *Via Pietro Delvecchio 2, parkhotelmondovi.it*.
€ **Sant'Agostino**. This B&B is located in the town centre, just 100m from the cable car that connects Breo (the historic centre on the plain) to Piazza (the historic centre on the hill), on the main shopping street, Via Sant'Agostino. On the first floor of a registered building it has three quiet, refined bedrooms, a common area for guests, a live-in kitchen and a large, flowery terrace where breakfast is served in summer. The service is excellent and the breakfasts exceed expectations. *Via Sant'Agostino 10, bbsantagostino.it*.

TERME DI VALDIERI (*map C, B3*)
€€ **Hotel Royal**. A few years before creating the Kingdom of Italy—in 1857—Vittorio Emanuele II laid the cornerstone of this grand hotel and spa in the heart of his Maritime Alps hunting reserve. Though they are now endowed with every modern comfort, the great white hotel and the wood-and-stone Casino di Caccia still have a distinctly 19th-century air about them, which is the essence of their charm. The rooms in the Casino di Caccia, with plank floors and great beamed ceilings, are warm and cosy; the hotel rooms, a little less so. The sulphurous waters of the Valdieri springs are alkaline (pH 9.4) and hypothermal (64°C at the source), and there are natural Turkish baths in caves fed directly from the thermal aquifer. Hotel and spa are open May–Sept. *Terme di Valdieri, termerealidivaldieri.it*.

WHERE TO EAT

BOVES (*map C, B1*)
€€ **Osteria della Luce**. Simple homely restaurant serving excellent comfort food. *Via Ing. Capello 5, T: 348 796 2580*.
€€ **Osteria Pizzeria La Quercia**. Friendly unpretentious place serving familiar staples, local dishes and piazza. *Piazza Italia 18, T: 0171 380374*.

BRIAGLIA (*map C, D2*)
€€ **Marsupino**. East of Mondovì. Getting here is an adventure, regardless of where one starts out. The bends in the road seem endless, and when one arrives, the first impression of this *trattoria*, entered through a humble village *caffè*, can be disappointing. Don't be deceived. The welcome is cordial and the food superb. Delicious agnolotti and ravioli and Barolo veal shank. They also offer comfortable rooms in the adjacent *palazzo*. *Via Roma 20, trattoriamarsupino.it*.

CUNEO (*map C, C3*)
€ **Caffè Bruno**. The shop window, nestled beneath the arcades of the main street of old Cuneo, still bears the sign, *Pietro Bruno Confettiere Liquorista* and the emblem of the official suppliers of the House of Savoy. Beneath the café's vaulted ceilings and chandeliers unfolds one of Piedmont's

most elegant old interiors (est. 1864), in rich, warm wood and shiny black marble. Created by the Swiss Raiter family, this was one of the few places where the poor could buy the crumbly maize biscuits *paste di meliga*. Today it is the café of choice of the artists from the nearby Teatro Toselli and the city's cultural, political and social élite. It stays open late. *Via Roma 28, caffebruno.it.*

€ **Caffè Pasticceria Arione**. The founders of this local institution, beneath the arcades of 19th-century Piazza Galimberti, invented the famous chocolates, *cuneesi al rhum*. In 1954 Hemingway, on the advice of his publisher, Arnoldo Mondadori, stopped here to buy two pounds' worth to give to his wife Mary, who was on holiday in Nice: witness a photo jealously preserved. In 1963, Mario Monicelli filmed scenes of *The Companions* here with Marcello Mastroianni and Annie Girardot. Now run by the third generation of the founding family, it has kept intact the original display cases and furniture. *Piazza Galimberti 14, arionecuneo.it.*

€ **Osteria della Chiocciola**. Excellent restaurant and wine bar in the historic city centre, offering creative and traditional dishes using local ingredients: risotto with eggplant and mint, cream of asparagus, Barolo braised beef, and *bonet*, the rich pudding made from amaretti, cocoa, eggs and milk, and covered with caramel. The wine list is long and varied. Closed Sun. *Via Fossano 1, osteriadellachiocciola.it.*

MONDOVÌ (map C, C3)

€€ **Il Baluardo**. Built into the walls of Mondovì, this excellent restaurant offers expertly prepared dishes from land and sea. All are made from only the freshest ingredients; the best combine the culinary traditions of Piedmont and France. Closed midday Mon and Tues. *Piazza d'Armi 2. T: 0174 330244.*

€ **Croce d'Oro**. An informal, family-run place in a former stable just outside the town, serving delicious local fare with a personal touch: eggplant with chives, tomino cheese with truffle, fondue, gnocchi, filetto al Barolo and a delicious hazelnut cake, accompanied by regional wines Closed Mon. *Via Sant'Anna 83. T: 0174 681525.*

€ **Grigolon**. A fine example of Liberty, the Italian Art-Nouveau style that took its name from the London fabric shop, Grigolon preserves much of its original (1912) walnut woodwork, carved with floral motifs and monograms, marble-topped wrought-iron tables and vintage jars. A landmark in town, it was the first unofficial headquarters of the Italian Alpine Club in southern Piedmont, and it was here that *Rakikò*, the signature bitter of Mondovì, was created. Born as the 'Confetteria, Liquoreria Comino', from the name of the founder, it now bears the name of the family that has owned and managed it for two generations. Exquisite traditional sweets, including *paste di meliga* maize biscuits and *Monregalesi al rum*, the local answer to *cuneesi*. *Corso Statuto 2e. T: 0174 43564.*

€ **Ristorantino Michelis**. Michelis has been producing pasta, grissini and maize biscuits since 1919. As well as a shop, they also have a tiny snack bar offering homely dishes made from their pastas. *Via Vigevano 12, michelis.it.*

FESTIVALS AND EVENTS

Cuneo *Festival della Montagna*. A programme of events centred on the past traditions and future direction of mountain culture, May/June, *festivaldellamontagna.it*. Cuneo also hosts an important chestnut fair, the *Fiera Nazionale del Marrone*, in Oct. The potatoes of **Entracque** have their own festival, the *Fiera della Patata*, in Aug. **Frabosa Soprana** celebrates its rare cheeses (*raschera* and *brus*) at the annual Sagra dei Formaggi Raschera e Brus, Aug.

LOCAL SPECIALITIES

Cuneo is known for its chocolate. The chocolatier Venchi, founded in Turin in 1878 and which now has shops across Italy, is headquartered in Cuneo.
Caraglio is locally renowned for its *torta amara della Vallera*, an almond or hazelnut cake made without leavening (but with plenty of eggs).
Garessio is known for its Gabbiana chestnuts, and for its mushrooms, potatoes and leeks. *Garessini* are delicious sweets made with hazelnuts and cocoa.

Piedment on the Plain

Piedmont is one of the most productive agricultural regions in Italy. Its lowlands are famous for their rice, which in addition to being the prime ingredient of one of Italy's best-loved dishes, risotto, provides high-value farmland, ideal for the conservation of biodiversity (the rice fields are home to nesting and migratory birds as well as to countless other forms of wildlife). The hills bounding the Po river plain to the south enjoy an ideal climate for the cultivation of stone fruits, particularly apricots, peaches and cherries. The traditional markets for this produce are the four small cities (or large towns) that dominate Piedmont on the plain: Alessandria, Novara, Tortona and Vercelli. All have an air of subdued wealth, which translates into serene city centres, dignified (if not spectacular) monuments and interesting little museums. Naturally, the food and wine are of the highest quality.

ALESSANDRIA

Alessandria (*map D, B3*) stands on the alluvial plain formed by the rivers Tanaro and Bormida, near their confluence. It was founded by seven castellans of the duchy of Monferrato who rebelled against Frederick Barbarossa in 1168 and named their new city after Pope Alexander III. It became the episcopal see seven years later, in 1175. It was eventually ceded to the emperor, who attributed it to the Milanese Visconti family in the 14th century, and it was awarded to the house of Savoy by the Treaty of Utrecht in 1713. From 1796 to 1814 it was the capital of the French *département* of Marengo, which was named after the site of Napoleon's victory of 1800, on the plain south of the city. In the following years it became a focal point of the Risorgimento: the red, white and green *tricolore* was first raised over its great Savoy citadel in 1821, in an early insurrection celebrated by Giosuè Carducci in his poem, 'Piemonte'. Always a place of strategic importance, it was garrisoned by the Austrians after their victory at Novara (1849).

Industrial development began in the late 19th century (when the Borsalino hat works, among other industries, were established here) and boomed again in the late 20th century. Today Alessandria is a cheerful place with a fine cathedral, a Romanesque-Gothic church, several interesting museums and a handful of stately mansions.

MUSEUMS AND MONUMENTS OF ALESSANDRIA

Alessandria's first **cathedral** was built from 1170 on today's Piazza della Libertà, but it was torn down by Napoleon in 1803 to make way for a parade ground. A new cathedral was erected after 1808 using the church of San Marco and the adjacent Dominican convent; these were adapted to their new role by Cristoforo Valizzone, and the Napoleonic cathedral—dedicated, like its predecessor, to St Peter—was consecrated two years later. The 106m campanile, one of the tallest in Italy, was completed in 1844. The Neoclassical exterior has a fascinating façade with muted colours, double columns and pilasters and low reliefs; its resemblance to a triumphal arch is anything but accidental. The ornate buff-and-blue interior holds a fine wooden statue of the Madonna della Salva, patron saint of the city, and paintings by Guglielmo Caccia.

Palazzo Cuttica di Cassine forms part of Alessandria's **Museo Civico** (*Via Parma 1; for opening times go to asmcostruireinsieme.it/palazzo-cuttica*), a municipal museum system which also includes the Sale d'Arte, the Museo del Cappello Borsalino and several minor museums. The palace was built in the 18th century by Marquis Cuttica di Cassine and it immediately became a focus of social life in Alessandria. During the Napoleonic period it was occupied by the generals Chasseloup and Despinois. The collections arranged in its sumptuous Baroque interior range from pre-Roman and Roman antiquities (mainly from the areas of Alessandria and Tortona, and including the private collection of 19th-century enthusiast Cesare Di Negro Carpani) to sculptures and liturgical items (notably the vestments and illuminated choir books of St Pius V, shown in beautiful antique cases), Flemish tapestries (in the entrance hall), works regarding Napoleon and the Battle of Marengo, and 16th–17th-century paintings. Of the latter the most remarkable is undoubtedly the immense polyptych of the *Crowning of the Virgin* (c. 1510), by Gandolfino da Roreto (also known as Gandolfino d'Asti). There are modern works by Carlo Carrà, Giuseppe Pellizza da Volpedo, Aligi Sassu and Bruno Cassinari, among others, and an especially good print and drawing cabinet with beautifully displayed works by old and modern masters.

A selection of works from the municipal collections is displayed in the **Sale d'Arte** (*Via Macchiavelli 13; for opening times, see asmcostruireinsieme.it/sale-darte*). The 'art halls' are divided into four sections. The first is dedicated to medieval Alessandria, represented by a 14th-century fresco cycle inspired by the legend of King Arthur, from the farmhouse known as Torre di Frugarolo, and by sculptural fragments from local churches. The second explores the 19th century, taking as a key the life and work of Giovanni Migliara (1785–1837), a local painter known for his views of Lombardy, Piedmont and Liguria, as well as for his fascinating industrial interiors. The third covers the 20th century, especially as seen through the life and work of the local landscape painter Alberto Cafassi (1894–1973). The last section holds temporary exhibitions.

Alessandria's city hall (*Piazza della Libertà 1*) is known as the **Palazzo Rosso** because of the colour of its arcaded façade. Its most distinctive feature is the astronomical clock at the top of its pediment, showing the night sky, the time and the phases of the moon (best after dark when the dials light up). The clock is so important that the area in front of the palace is known informally as Piazza dell'Orologio.

At the very top of the wrought-iron belfry is the *Galletto*, a weathercock stolen by Alessandria from Casale Monferrato during a war of 1215.

The fulcrum of political, administrative and judicial life in the medieval city, the **Palatium Vetus** (*Piazza della Libertà 28*), was built around 1170—just two years after the founding of Alessandria. The building you see today is an early modern reconstruction; it has recently been acquired by a local community foundation and renovated, to plans by Gae Aulenti, to host offices, events and exhibitions.

The **Palazzo delle Poste e Telegrafi** (*Piazza della Libertà 23–24*) was designed and built in the late 1930s by Franco Petrucci. Its bare-bones Modern design caused some dismay when it was unveiled; to enliven it a colourful mosaic cycle was commissioned from the Futurist painter Gino Severini. Completed in 1940–1 and installed on the main façade and in the atrium, the cycle illustrates the evolution of postal and telegraphic communications. The large wall painting in the original writing room (1941) is by Giulio Rosso.

Palazzo Ghilini (*Piazza della Libertà 21*), built after 1732 for Marquis Tommaso Maria Ghilini, was designed by Benedetto Alfieri and Giovanbattista Gianotti with two atria—the first octagonal, the second rectangular—and a central courtyard with a scenographic double staircase. The Savoy acquired the palace in the mid-19th century, later devoting it to public offices.

Occupying a former barracks and its stables, the **Museo Etnografico C'era Una Volta** (*Piazza Gambarina 1, comune.alessandria.it t*) explores peasant society on the plain of Alessandria in the late 19th and early 20th centuries. A special space is dedicated to the two world wars, with a display of weapons, tools and furnishings largely from 1915–18. The section devoted to labour has tools and furnishings from the workshop of a shoemaker, a blacksmith and a carpenter, as well as abundant farm implements. A late 19th-century library and early 20th-century classroom have been set up on the first floor, and there is a marvellous collection of dolls and vintage toys.

The **Museo del Cappello Borsalino** (*Via Cavour 84, comune.alessandria.it*) tells you everything you need to know about the Borsalino hat and its 150-year history. Borsalino is one of the world's most prestigious milliners and Alessandrians are fiercely proud of the firm. Located in the historic factory showroom, the museum displays examples of all the hats produced by the company since 1857, the year the firm was established. You can spend a very enjoyable hour or two here: there are about 2,000 hats of different styles in historical cabinets, designed by Arnaldo Gardella, which alone are worth a trip. Arnaldo Gardella designed the building in the 1920s, and his son Ignazio Gardella designed the restoration and extension 60 years later. The basement housed steam generators; the intermediate floor, offices; the top floor, the workshops where the hats were actually made. The warehouses were torn down to make the new wing with its shopping centre and apartment block.

Among the most important examples of 18th-century Italian military architecture and one of the largest fortresses in Europe, the **citadel** of Alessandria was born when Vittorio Amedeo II, Duke of Savoy, switched his allegiance from France to Austria in the War of the Spanish Succession (1703). It was designed by the military engineer Ignazio Bertola and its construction began in 1728, during the reign of Vittorio

Amedeo. Work on the immense brick hexagon continued under Carlo Emanuele III and was completed in the late 19th century. The walls have a perimeter of three kilometres and form a complete enceinte with hexagonal bastioned fronts; a public competition calling for projects for the restoration and reallocation of the interior followed its recent demilitarisation, but at the time of writing no decision had been announced. Giuseppe Garibaldi was imprisoned here in 1867 shortly before the Rattazzi government sent him into exile in Caprera.

To the south of Alessandria is the battlefield of **Marengo** (*map D, B3*), where Napoleon defeated the Austrians on 14th June 1800, in a battle that he regarded as the most brilliant of his career. The Marengo Museum is in the middle of the battlefield (*for opening times, see asmcostruireinsieme.it/marengo-museum*).

NOVARA

Novara (*map D, B1*), a Roman town, was occupied in 569 by the Lombards and became a free city state in 1116. Important battles were fought here throughout the town's history. Lodovico il Moro, Duke of Milan, was taken prisoner by the French after one of them, in 1500. The last famous battle, in 1849, resulted in the defeat of the Piedmontese by the Austrians under the 82-year-old Field Marshal Radetzky. That same evening Carlo Alberto of Savoy abdicated in favour of his son, Vittorio Emanuele II, marking the beginning of the Risorgimento movement in Italy.

Today Novara is an extremely pleasant and well-kept city. Its streets are paved in granite and porphyry, quarried locally, and it has particularly good 19th-century architecture.

MUSEUMS AND MONUMENTS OF NOVARA

In the arcaded Via Fratelli Rosselli is the **duomo**, rebuilt by Alessandro Antonelli in 1865–9 with a Neoclassical colonnade. Six Brussels tapestries (1565) by Jan de Buck hang in the gloomy interior. Behind the huge orange stucco columns, on the south side, are a 14th-century carved wooden Crucifix, an altarpiece (c. 1525–30) by Gaudenzio Ferrari (*see p. 71*), and works by his pupil Bernardino Lanino. The chapel of San Siro, which survives from the earlier church, contains damaged late 12th-century frescoes; the *Crucifixion* dates from the 14th century. The adjoining 18th-century room contains frescoes by Bernardino Lanino (1546–53) from the old cathedral, and paintings by Gaudenzio Ferrari and Callisto Piazza.

Remarkable black-and-white mosaic panels from the original cathedral, dating from the 12th century, with symbols of the Evangelists, Adam and Eve, and other biblical subjects, are displayed in the sacristy. The Neoclassical high altar is by Antonelli and Thorvaldsen. On the north side are a reliquary bust (1424) of St Bernard of Aosta (after whom the St Bernard dog is named).

The **baptistery** is a centrally planned octagonal building of the late 4th century, with 1st-century Classical columns and an 11th-century cupola. High up above the windows are very worn 11th-century frescoes of the Apocalypse, one of them covered with a 15th-century *Last Judgement*. The funerary monument of Umbrena Polla (1st century AD) was once used as a font.

Opposite the duomo is the entrance to the finely paved courtyard of the **Broletto**, a medley of buildings dating from the 13th and 15th centuries with terracotta windows and remains of frescoes above Gothic arches. The main buildings are the Palazzo Arengario (north), Palazzo del Podestà (with fine terracotta decoration), Palazzetto dei Paratici and Palazzo della Referendia (largely rebuilt in medieval form). The complex is used for exhibitions and cultural events. Here too is the **Galleria d'Arte Moderna Paolo e Adele Giannoni** (*galleriagiannoni.it*) with painting and sculpture by Italian artists of international renown, mainly of the late 19th and early 20th centuries (members of the Macchiaoli and Posilippo schools as well as the modern artists Pietro Marussig and Achille Funi, and the Divisionist Plinio Nomellini).

Via Fratelli Rosselli, with its porticoes, leads east to the arcaded Piazza delle Erbe, the old centre of the town. In the other direction, Classical colonnades continue past a statue of Carlo Emanuele III to **Piazza Martiri della Libertà**, with an equestrian statue of Vittorio Emanuele II by Ambrogio Borghi (1881). Here are the handsome Neoclassical buildings of the huge Teatro Coccia (1888) and Palazzo del Mercato (1817–44). You can see some remains of the Sforza castle on the south side of the piazza. In Via Dominioni is the yellow building of the former **Collegio Gallarini** (restored as a music conservatory), with remarkable late-19th-century terracotta decoration and a coloured roof. There are also stretches of Roman walls here, in a little park.

Leave the courtyard of the Broletto by Corso Italia. Via San Gaudenzio, on your left, continues north to the church of **San Gaudenzio**, built in 1577–1690 from a design by Pellegrino Tibaldi. The church has a fine brick exterior. The cupola, crowned by an elaborate spire 121m high, is by Alessandro Antonelli (1844–80). The campanile (92m) is another exceptionally original work by Benedetto Alfieri (1753–86). Within, on the south side, are works by Morazzone, Fiammenghino and Gaudenzio Ferrari. The Baroque chapel of San Gaudenzio opens off the south transept. On the north side are works by Ferrari (a polyptych of 1514 in a beautiful frame), Paolo Camillo Landriani, Tanzio da Varallo and Giacinto Brandi.

In the nearby Via Ferrari, Novara's large and fascinating natural history museum, the **Museo di Storia Naturale Faraggiana Ferrandi** (*Via G. Ferrari 13mrsntorino. it*). This is the most important such collection in the Piedmont region after the one in Turin. It was bequeathed to the city of Novara, together with the zoo, by Catherine Faraggiana Ferrandi and her son Alessandro. Enlarged by the donation of another family enthusiast, explorer Ugo Ferrandi, today it displays specimens of native and exotic vertebrates, mostly birds and mammals, plus an entomological collection. The animals are posed with unusual dynamism and the dioramas are superb.

Via Fratelli Rosselli is continued east by **Via Canobio**, in which are two fine old palaces—Palazzo Natta-Isola, attributed to Pellegrino Tibaldi, and the Casa dei Medici by Seregni.

ENVIRONS OF NOVARA

SAN NAZZARO SESIA
This little farming town (*map D, B1*) developed around the abbey of **Santi Nazario e Celso**, from which it takes its name. The abbey was founded in the 11th century by Bishop Riprando of Novara, fortified in the 13th and 14th centuries (when Novara was at war with Vercelli) and largely rebuilt in 15th-century Gothic forms, leaving only the tall campanile in the original Romanesque style. Suppressed in 1801, it was used as a farm until its late 20th-century restoration. Today the fortified abbey has an 11th-century portico forming a sort of open narthex before the three-aisled church; the west façade is finely decorated with terracotta tiles, a beautiful example of 15th–century ornamentation you find again in the cloister.

Santi Nazzaro e Celso is located inside the **Parco delle Lame del Sesia**, protected wetland abounding in reeds (*lame*). There are common reeds and rushes (especially *Juncus inflexus*), as well as water-loving trees such as white and grey willow, white poplar, black alder, elm and English oak. The marsh is an ideal habitat for an astounding number of migratory and nesting birds (the Eurasian teal, common moorhen, little grebe, grey and white heron, great bittern, little bittern, little egret, white swan, common spoonbill and black-winged stilt).

BELLINZAGO NOVARESE
On a knoll between Bellinzago and the Torrente Terdoppio, where Alessandro Antonelli spent his last months working on the parish church of San Clemente, stands the **Badia di Dulzago** (*map B, C4*). Founded in the early 12th century by the Canons Regular of St Augustine, perhaps on the remains of an ancient Roman town, it originally consisted of a church (San Giulio), the canons' residence, the abbot's residence and farm buildings. During the 16th century the abbey lost its canonical community and was transformed into a rich and productive farm: the monastery was adapted to accommodate the farmers; the cloister to house offices and storerooms. The farming community was perfectly self-sufficient: food was stored in an underground vault and there was even a primary school. During the French occupation the land and the buildings were confiscated and sold, and today the signs of the past survive only thanks to the few families who live and work there. The church of San Giulio has been restored to show the three semicircular apses of the original Romanesque foundation and the beautiful capitals of the nave. The chapter house preserves a small cycle of 14th–16th-century frescoes, whereas the 15th- and 16th-century buildings, the stables and the cloister are still in ruins. Notice the Roman sarcophagus beneath the cloister portico, converted to a watering trough for farm animals.

TORTONA

For millennia at the centre of one of the most important road networks of northern Italy, Tortona (*map D, C3*) succeeds the ancient *Dertona*, re-founded by the Romans during the construction, in 148 BC, of the Via Postumia between Piacenza and Genoa. One of the first cities in Italy to become a free commune, it was destroyed by Emperor Frederick I Barbarossa in 1155. It fell to the Visconti in 1347 and passed to the Savoy in 1738. The skyline is dominated by the immense golden statue of the Madonna and Child on the campanile of the Sanctuary of the Madonna della Guardia, built in 1931 at the behest of Don Orione, who in Tortona in 1893 founded his first school for boys, the Piccola Opera della Divina Provvidenza.

MUSEUMS AND MONUMENTS OF TORTONA

Tortona **cathedral**, dedicated to the Assumption and St Lawrence, was built to replace an earlier church destroyed to make room for new fortifications on the hill, made necessary when the Duchy of Milan, of which Tortona was part, came under Spanish rule. The construction of the new church started in 1574 and ended in 1592, but the Neoclassical edifice you see today dates from 1877. It follows a three-aisle plan with a raised presbytery ending in a semicircular apse. The ceiling vaults were frescoed in the third quarter of the 19th century, although near the altars you can glimpse some fragments from the 15th–16th centuries. The Palazzo Vescovile was built after 1584 and restructured in the 18th century.

The church of **Santa Maria Canale** may date from the 9th or 10th century; it was altered in the 13th–14th century. The Museo Civico (*open only for special exhibitions*), in the 15th-century Palazzo Guidobono, contains relics of ancient Dertona, including the sarcophagus of Elio Sabino (3rd century AD), medieval works of art, and a 16th-century terracotta *Pietà*.

The most extraordinary sight in Tortona is the small but wonderful **Quadreria della Fondazione Cassa di Risparmio** (*Corso Leoniero 6, fondazionecrtortona.it*). The collection here is entirely devoted to Divisionism is a technique of neo-Impressionist painting which, like Pointillism, uses tiny dots of pure colour that are blended in the viewer's eye. It was seen by the artists of the 1890s, and by the early 20th-century Futurists, as the language of Modernity. There are more than a dozen works by native artist Giuseppe Pellizza da Volpedo (*Fiore reciso*, 1903; *Sacra Famiglia*, 1892; *La donna dell'emigrato*, 1888; *L'annegato*, 1894), who was born near Tortona (*see below*), and masterpieces by other Italian Divisionists such as Plinio Nomellini (*Piazza Caricamento a Genova*, 1891; *Festa al villaggio*,1912–13), Carlo Fornara (*Ultimi pascoli*, c. 1904), Raffaello Gambogi (*Cantiere*, 1897), Angelo Morbelli (*Mi ricordo quand'ero fanciulla*, 1903), Giovanni Segantini (*La raccolta del fieno*, c. 1889, *Ave Maria a trasbordo*, 1890–3; *Malvoni*, 1881), Gaetano Previati (*La via del calvario*, c. 1900) and Giacomo Balla (*Paesaggio*, 1900).

VOLPEDO

More early Modern art is to be seen in the hills 12km east of Tortona, at Volpedo (*map D, C3*). This pretty village, with its pronounced 19th-century air, is the birthplace of Giuseppe Pellizza di Volpedo (1868–1907), perhaps the best known Italian Divisionist, who built his studio here in 1888. Eighteen large-scale reproductions of his paintings are scattered around the village in the places where the artist stood when painting them; together they compose a fascinating trip through time, in which past and present are fused. The walk touches upon the **artist's studio** (*Via Rosano 1/a, 1888–96*), with its neutral-toned walls and large skylight, and the **Museo Didattico Pellizza** (*Palazzo del Torraglio, Piazza Quarto Stato 1, pellizza.it/il-museo-didattico*), with material and multimedia displays detailing the artist's life and work; his **house** (*Via Garibaldi*); the 10th–15th-century **Pieve Romanica di San Pietro**; the walls of the medieval **castrum**; and the **Piazza Quarto Stato** and **Palazzo Guidobono Cavalchini Malaspina Penati**. In the square, between 1892 and 1901, Pellizza di Volpedo created his most famous works—large, socially engaged paintings using farmers as models; the palace was built in the Middle Ages but profoundly altered in the 18th and 19th centuries.

Volpedo is known also for its peaches and strawberries, grapes, cherries and apricots, all grown without irrigation thanks to a particularly mild microclimate.

VERCELLI

Vercelli (*map D, B1*) was a Roman municipium founded in 49 BC. It was noted in the 16th century for its school of painters, including Giovanni Martino Spanzotti, Sodoma, Gaudenzio Ferrari and Bernardino Lanino. It is now the largest rice-producing centre in Europe.

MUSEUMS AND MONUMENTS OF VERCELLI

Piazza Cavour is the old market square, with attractive arcades and the battlemented Torre dell'Angelo rising above the roofs. In Via Gioberti is the tall, square **Torre di Città**, dating from the 13th century. Corso Libertà is the main street of the old town. **Palazzo Centoris** (*no. 204*) has a delightful interior courtyard with frescoes and arcades in three tiers (1496). In Via Cagna is **San Cristoforo**, with crowded scenes frescoed in 1529–34 by Gaudenzio Ferrari (*see p. 71*), and the *Madonna of the Pomegranate* (1529), considered his masterpiece. The church of **San Paolo** (begun c. 1260) has a *Madonna* by Bernardino Lanino.

The **Civico Museo Borgogna** (*Via Antonio Borgogna 4-6, museoborgogna.it*) preserves the most important collection of paintings in Piedmont after the Galleria Sabauda in Turin. Founded by Antonio Borgogna (1822–1906), it was donated to the city by him together with the handsome Neoclassical palace and first opened to the public in 1907. It is especially representative of Renaissance and Baroque painting from Italy, Holland and Flanders. Highlights include the original Borgogna collection (works by Antonio da Viterbo, Francesco Francia, Marco Palmezzano, Bergognone and Bernardino Luini; a *Deposition*, a replica by Titian of his painting in the Louvre; early 16th-century altarpieces by Defendente Ferrari and Lanino; 18th- and 19th-century works by Angelica Kauffmann, Girolamo Induno, Filippo Palizzi and others; a 16th-century *Madonna and Child* by Hans Baldung Grien and works by Jan Brueghel the Elder; a *Holy Family* attributed to Andrea del Sarto and a collection of Meissen, Doccia and Ginori porcelain.

Nearby **San Francesco** is a restored church of 1292 containing a *St Ambrose* by Girolamo Giovenone (1535).

The **Museo Leone** (*Via Verdi 30; closed Mon, museoleone.it*) is an unusual museum housing the collection of Camillo Leone (1830–1907), first opened to the public in 1910. The entrance is through the lovely courtyard of the 15th-century **Casa degli Alciati**, which has early 16th-century frescoes and wood ceilings. Rooms built in 1939 to connect the house with the Baroque Palazzo Langosco have a display illustrating the history of Vercelli, interesting for its arrangement dating from the Fascist period. The 18th-century **Palazzo Langosco**, once the residence of Leone, retains part of its original decorations. The library contains more than 1,200 precious incunabula and a fine collection of illuminated manuscripts and scrolls. The renovated Salone di San Martino displays arms and armour from the Middle Ages to the 19th century and the Palazzo Langosco rooms show jewellery made in the Vercelli area. There are also some mementos of the Risorgimento.

In front of the station is the basilica of **Sant'Andrea** (1219–27), a largely Romanesque church showing Cistercian Gothic elements at a very early date for Italy. It was founded by Cardinal Guala Bicchieri with the revenues of the Abbey of St Andrew at Chesterton (Cambridgeshire, England) bestowed on him by his young ward, Henry III of England. The fine façade, combining Lombard–Emilian motifs (gabled roof, rounded portals, double order of loggias) with Provençal and Norman elements (door embrasures, lateral towers and their cusps, capitals), is flanked by two tall towers connected by a double arcade; the cupola is topped by a third tower, in the manner of Benedictine and Cluniac churches. The two lunettes hold sculptures by the school of Antelami. The detached campanile dates from 1407. Inside, the pointed arcades are carried on slender clustered piers, with shafts carried up unbroken to the springing of the vaults. The crossing and cupola are particularly fine. At the east end are intarsia stalls of 1514. The remains of the Cistercian abbey include a lovely cloister and chapter house.

Via Bicheri leads to the huge **cathedral**, begun in 1572 to a design of Pellegrino Tibaldi, but preserving the Romanesque campanile of an older church. The octagonal chapel—built in 1698 and decorated in 1759—of the Blessed Amedeo IX of Savoy (who died in the castle 1472) contains his tomb and that of his successor Charles I (d. 1490). The chapter library includes the 4th-century *Evangelistary of St Eusebius* (in a 12th-century binding); some Anglo-Saxon poems (11th century); the Laws of the Lombards (8th century); and other early manuscripts, perhaps relics of the Studium, or early university, which flourished here from 1228 for about a century.

The presence of a small Jewish community in Vercelli has been documented since 1446 but it is only after the emancipation of 1848 that its size became such as to require the construction of a place of worship suited to accommodate 600 people. The first small temple was replaced at that time by the present **synagogue** in the Moorish style, built in 1878 by the architect Giuseppe Locarni. The façade is characterised by great bands of pale blue and white sandstone and domed gazebo turrets. The recently restored interior, decorated with geometric motifs, has three naves and a luminous apse with stained glass by Michele Fornari.

PIEDMONT ON THE PLAIN PRACTICAL TIPS

GETTING AROUND

- **By bus:** Buses in the region are operated by ATAP (*atapspa.it*), STP (*stpalessandria.it*). Check the websites for routes and timetables.
- **By rail:** Trains link Turin (Porta Nuova) with Vercelli in 55mins. There are also regional services (55mins) between Milan (Central Station) and Vercelli operated by the Ferrovie Nord Milano (*www.trenord.it*). Alessandria is on the main Turin–Genoa rail line. Intercity and fast regional trains run from Turin direct to Alessandria (c. 55mins); and from Genoa (Piazza Principe) to Alessandria (fast regional, c. 45mins; Intercity 1 hr). There are trains from Alessandria to Asti (fast regional c. 20mins; regional 30mins) and to Acqui Terme (30mins). Novara is on the main Milan–Turin line; from Milan (Central Station) to Novara (40mins); from Turin (Porta Nuova) to Novara (60mins). There are also regional services (60mins) between Milan (Porta Vittoria) and Novara operated by the Ferrovie Nord Milano (*www.trenord.it*).

WHERE TO STAY

ALESSANDRIA (*map D, B3*)
€€€ **Alli Due Buoi Rossi**. Hotel, restaurant and bar in late-19th century building, rather insensitively restored but clean and comfortable. *Via Cavour 32, hotelalliduebuoirossi.com*.
€€€ **Hotel Lux**. Large, modern hotel in a quiet area of the city centre. Ample buffet breakfast. *Via Piacenza 72, hotelluxalessandria.com*.
€€ **Europa**. Sleek and modern city-centre hotel. Clean lines, no frills, marble floors. *Via Palestro 1, hoteleuropaal.it*.

NOVARA (*map D, B1*)
€€€ **Albergo Italia**. Modern and comfortable business hotel in the city centre. *Via Generale Solaroli 8, albergoitalia.novara.it*.
€€€ **Europa**. Modern hotel with renovated rooms, all with standard comforts. *Corso Cavalletti 38/a, hoteleuropanovara.it*.
€€ **La Torre dei Canonici**. Eleven rooms and suites, a comfortable living room and beautiful spa make this farm a good starting point for exploring Novara, Vercelli, Alessandria and the surrounding countryside. The farm is immense (350ha, of which 300 are planted with rice and 50 with seed crops). The rice is stone husked, a traditional process that ensures that the nutrients contained in the outer part of the grain are preserved intact. Three kinds of rice are grown— Carnaroli, ideal for *risotti*; and Pantera and Cardinale, respectively black rice and red rice, which go well with fish and vegetables. All are sold on the premises. Meticulous care has been invested in choosing the furniture and fabrics for the rooms, each of which is unique. *Via San Rocco 17, Lumellogno (in the southwest outskirts of Novara), latorredeicanonici.com*.
€€ **Croce di Malta**. Small and conveniently located, a short walk from the castle and cathedral. Closed Aug. *Via Giulio Biglieri 2/a, crocedimaltanovara.it*.

QUARGNENTO (*map D, B3*)
€€ **Colle Aperto**. On a hill surrounded by verdant famland, this attractively restored farmhouse 15km northwest of Alessandria offers three lovely rooms with beautiful views, warm public areas, a gorgeous pool and delicious breakfasts. Good for exploring the Basso Monferrato as well as Alessandria and its plain. *Strada Vallerina 12, T: 335 677 2386.*

TORTONA (*map D, C3*)
€€ **Casa Cuniolo**. The house was built in the 1930s as the home and studio of painter Gigi Cuniolo and its white geometry stands proudly amidst the greenery. Now his daughter Gabriella, an interior designer who also owns a restaurant and inn in town, has turned it into an oasis of tranquility for a small number of fortunate guests. There are just four bedrooms, but you have the run of the house, including the little rooftop spa and the ground-floor dining room, where sensational breakfasts are served. *Viale G. Amendola 6.* Also part of the same outfit are the **Residence Perosi** (*Via Calvino 4*) and the **Ristorante San Giacomo** (*Via Lorenzo Perosi 42*). All share the same webiste: *gabriellacuniolo.com*

VERCELLI (*map D, B1*)
€€ **Hotel Matteotti**. Pleasantly decorated and welcoming small city-centre hotel, a good choice for its three stars. *Corso Giacomo Matteotti 35, hotelmatteotti.it.*
€€ **La Terrazza Vercelli**. This bed and breakfast in the very heart of old Vercelli bills itself as shabby-chic, but the shabbiness is a complete illusion: rooms and living spaces are bright and well appointed, with rigorously black white furniture and fabrics, and small colourful artworks. The breakfast room is small, but the buffet is more than adequate and there is a nice terrace (whence the name) overlooking the little piazza. *Via San Paolo 18, laterrazzavercelli.it.*
€€ **Casa Bona 1910**. Liberty-style palazzo built in 1910 and still in the hands of the same family. Now a delightful little guest house with just two beautifully appointed rooms. *Via San Paolo 23, casabona1910.it.*

VOLPEDO (*map D, C3*)
€€ **Tenuta Terensano**. This 18th-century farm in Monleale, in the hills 2km west of Volpedo by the beautiful Val Curone, produces Volpedo peaches and other fruits, and Cortese, Barbera and Timorasso grapes, which are served up in breakfast jams and in the evening meals. The farm buildings are arranged around a gated court with a cool green pergola, and the simple but pretty rooms are scattered here and there: upstairs in the main house, and in the ground-floor stables. There is a very nice swimming pool, plus a billiard room, and you can borrow a bike to explore the neighbourhood. *Corso Roma (SP100) Km 4.5, Monleale, terensano.it.*

WHERE TO EAT

ALESSANDRIA (*map D, B3*)
€€ **Ristorante Duomo**. Evocative little restaurant next to the duomo which serves delicious stewed squid stuffed with wild rice and cream of Jerusalem artichokes. *Via Parma 28, ristorante-duomo.com.*

€ **Le Nouveau Bistrot**. Cristina and Ermanno opened their bistro when the number of friends they invited to dinner began systematically to exceed the capacity of their flat. They serve simple but plentiful regional cuisine, with a limited (unprinted) menu and a high standard of quality. Their aim is to bring the flavours of the countryside to the city—and this includes freshly baked bread and *focaccia*. Lunch and dinner Mon–Fri; dinner only Sat. *Via Piacenza 80, T: 335 573 1244.*

€ **Cappelverde**. Excellent value, cosy city-centre *trattoria* with a good range of alpine cheeses and Piedmontese wines. Open evenings only. *Via San Pio V, T: 388 981 9989.*

NOVARA (*map D, B1*)
€€€ **Tantris**. Michelin-starred gourmet restaurant which offers classy but unfussy fare. *Corso Risorgimento 384. T: 0321 657 343, ristorantetantris.com.*

TORTONA (*map D, C3*)
€ **Derthona**. It calls itself a *vineria* (in Italian slang, a hole-in-the-wall wine bar) even though the cooking is on a par with anything you'll find in a sophisticated 'gastronomic' restaurant and the cellar holds more than 400 labels. Specialities include *bagna cauda*, beef stewed in red wine and *vitello tonnato*. Lunch and dinner Tues–Fri; dinner only at weekends. *Via Lorenzo Perosi 15, T: 0131 812468, vineriaderthona.it.*

VERCELLI (*map D, B1*)
€ **Il Giardinetto**. Fine, elegant overlooking a lovely, quiet garden. The menu features some good local delicacies and superb risotto. Closed Mon. *Via L. Sereno 3, ilgiardinettovercelli.it.*

€ **Ristorante Il Paiolo**. Excellent local fare (*paniscia* and pig shin), good selection of local wines (Cerotto) and grappa. *Viale Garibaldi 72, T: 0161 250577.*

LOCAL SPECIALITIES

Although widespread in Piedmont, *bagna cauda* (literally 'warm bath') is especially associated with **Alessandria**. A winter staple of vineyard workers for centuries, it is a hot sauce of anchovies, garlic, butter and olive oil in which one dips raw vegetables. Otherwise, there are some delicious cakes and biscuits in the province, such as *polenta di Marengo*, a simple and versatile cake made with cornmeal or maize and almonds. As for sweets, there are *baci di dama* ('the lady's kisses') from **Tortona**, so named because the two halves resemble lips about to kiss. Between them is hazelnut cream and melted chocolate.

Rice is the staple ingredient of many dishes in **Novara**, the most famous being *paniscia* (though Vercelli claim it as their own, too). Originally hearty peasant fare made with a type of millet (*panigo*), it is a delicious rich risotto made with rice, lard, butter borlotti beans, red wine, sausage meat, vegetables, salt and pepper. To be tried at **Circolo della Paniscia SOMS San Martino**. Closed Mon evening and Tues (*Via Perazzi 1/f, circolodellapaniscia.com*). The vineyards on the hills of Novara also yield some excellent wines, such as Ghemme, Boca and Fara

Like Novara, **Vercelli** is famous for *paniscia*. However here it can be made with rice or beans, in which latter case it is referred to as *fagiolata*, an even more robust dish. Vercelli is also home to the spiced *pasta frolla* (shortbread) biscuits with a Renaissance heritage, called *bicciolani*, which are the gastronomic highlight of the Vercellese carnival. Good wines to be found in this province are Gattinare, Bramaterra, Canavese and Brachetto.

EVENTS AND FESTIVALS

Novara The *Patronal Feast Day of San Gaudenzio* (22nd Jan), first bishop of Novara, sees the town set out its market stalls with produce typical of the province, including the *biscotti di novara* and the delicious *pane* ('bread') of Saint Gaudenzio (a sweet pastry filled with vanilla and sultanas and covered with chopped pine nuts or hazelnuts); a special service in the basilica of the saint and a visit to the patron saint's tomb, end of Jan–beginning of Feb; a *re-enactment of the Battle of Novara* (or Battle of Bicocca) commemorates the defeat of the Piedmontese army under the leadership of Carlo Alberto during the First War of Italian Independence of 1849; it includes guided tours of the battlefield, educational activities, music concerts, theatre performances, and historical cuisine, 23nd–23nd March.

Vercelli *Patronal Feast of Saint Eusebius*. Celebration (with classical music and fireworks) of the Sardinian-born Eusebius (c. 283–371), bishop of Vercelli (from 340), who combated the Arian heresy, first week of Aug; *Sagra d'la Panissa*. Week-long festival devoted to Vercelli's version of the lusty rustic dish, 3rd week of Aug (*sagrapanissa.it*); Sagra della Rana. All manner of frog-based dishes (risotto and fried) are available to try at Vercelli's longest running festival, beginning of Sept.

The Wine Country

The Langhe, Roero and Monferrato were added to the list of UNESCO World Heritage Sites in June 2014 under the collective name 'The Vineyard Landscape of Piedmont'. The area produces the finest wines in Piedmont—and according to some, the finest wines in Italy, from the rich red Barolo to the dry yet fragrant Gavi white (although strictly speaking, the Gavi wine district lies outside the World Heritage site). As might be expected, the area's world-class wines go hand in hand with a culinary tradition that is second to none.

THE LANGHE

The collective term *Le Langhe* is used to designate the rolling landscape traversed by the rivers Tanaro, Belbo, Bormida Millesimo and Bormida di Spigno. It is often divided into the Alta Langa, the area bordering with Liguria (famous for its forests and its hazelnuts), the Bassa Langa, the area between the Tanaro and the Belbo (famous for its red wines and truffles) and the Langa Astigiana, the area south of Asti (known for its white wines). The hills are typically marked by badlands—tracts of heavily eroded, uncultivable land with little vegetation—caused by the easily erodable clay, sandstone and blue marl of which they are constituted. The region is home to the *pecora delle Langhe*, a prized breed of Bergamo sheep from whose milk excellent cheeses are made. The local wine road, the Strada del Barolo e Grandi Vini di Langa, touches on all the main winemaking towns.

THE BASSA LANGA, WITH ALBA AND BAROLO

ALBA
This delightful small city (*map C, D1*) is one of the oldest places in Piedmont: the Roman *Alba Pompeia*, traces of which continue to surface, is grafted onto an earlier, pre-Roman settlement of the Ligurian Stazielli, which came under Roman control around 100 BC. One of the earliest episcopal seats (4th century), the city was the capital of a county in the Carolingian era and a free commune in constant conflict with Asti after the 11th century. Later a fief of the Anjou, then of the Visconti and the Gonzaga, it was separated from the territories of Monferrato with the Treaty of Cherasco (1631), which gave it to the Duchy of Savoy. Today vestiges of medieval Alba include the cathedral (extensively altered by the 19th-century restorations and

reinterpretations of Edoardo Arborio Mella), part of the street plan (superimposed on that of the Roman town), the recently restored Gothic church of San Domenico and a large number of brick towers that rise here and there around the city centre. Home to the 15th–16th-century painter Macrino d'Alba, the city holds some of his best works. The 19th-century city is organised around the new urban centre of Piazza Savona, starting point of the road to the sea (Corso Langhe). The 20th-century urban design focuses on the town's world-class industries—Miroglio for textiles and Ferrero for food produce (notably the chocolate-and-hazelnut spread, Nutella)—which drive the economy of the Langhe, along with the extraordinary wines and truffles of which Alba is the undisputed capital.

Located in the spacious Piazza Risorgimento, the **cathedral of San Lorenzo Martire** has undergone several transformations over the centuries, which have changed its appearance and ground plan. Built according to Romanesque canons in the 10th century, it was rebuilt for the first time in 1486 at the behest of Bishop Andrea Novelli and later altered several times. The present façade dates from 1878, when the church underwent its last significant renovation, which gave it the regular, symmetrical appearance it has today. Inside is a beautiful wooden choir carved and inlaid by Bernardino Fossati between 1512 and 1517. Another extraordinary work of woodcarving is the great Baroque cabinet of the sacristy, made in the 18th century (the date is inscribed at the foot of relief depicting San Lorenzo). Also in the sacristy is an elegant polychrome bas-relief of the *Madonna and Child, St. John the Baptist and St. John the Apostle*, a work of 1507 by the Lombard sculptor Giovanni Lorenzo Sormani. The Romanesque bell-tower with its mullioned windows dates from the early 13th century and incorporates the original campanile.

Entered from the campanile, the **Museo Diocesano di Alba–Museo della Cattedrale** (*check website for hours, visitmudi.it*) takes you beneath the present church to discover the ancient history of the building and of the city as a whole, revealing its Roman and early Christian foundations. It also provides a panoramic view over the rooftops through the mullioned windows of the medieval bell-tower. Archaeological excavations conducted in 2008 have made it posible to study the different phases of the cathedral's construction. The finds range in date from Roman times, when the area on which San Lorenzo now stands was occupied by the basilica, to the Renaissance reconstruction under Bishop Novelli. One of the best discoveries is the baptismal font of the early Christian church. The cathedral museum is located in the crypt, dedicated to St Peter, and houses the lapidary of the cathedral and a diverse collection of old and new finds.

San Domenico, a Gothic edifice of the 13th–14th century, several times restored, has a graceful portal and polygonal apse; the interior, with its unusual chequered columns and rust-red vaulted ceiling, is used for concerts and events.

Built in the 14th century on the remains of Roman walls, the **Palazzo del Comune** stands at the opposite end of Piazza Risorgimento, the ancient forum. The council chamber preserves a valuable painting of 1501 by Macrino d'Alba, depicting the Enthroned Madonna and Child clutching an apple, St Francis, St Thomas and two ladies praying.

The **Museo Civico Archeologico e di Scienze Naturali Federico Eusebio**

(*Via Vittorio Emanuele 19; T: 0173 292473, comune.alba.cn.it*), established in 1897 on the initiative of historian and archaeologist Federico Eusebio, was enlarged in the 1970s with a natural history section, and renovated and re-installed in 2001. In the new arrangement, the holdings of the old archaeological museum have been supplemented by finds from recent excavations.

At the northwest edge of the city centre (*Piazza Medford 1*), the Modern **Tribunale** by Gabetti & Isola (1982–7) has low stone walls and grass roofs that recall both the great fortresses of the Western Alps and the terraced hillsides of the Langhe. The architects, in addition to establishing formal ties between their new courthouse and the historical architecture and landscapes of southwestern Piedmont, foreshadow several distinctive features of the 'green' architectural revolution of the 21st century—including the use of natural insulators, such as stone and grass.

RODDI

By the Tannaro southwest of Alba is the medieval successor of the ancient *Castrum Rhaudium* (*map C, D1*), its houses clustered at the foot of its castle on a hilltop enjoying views of the Langhe, the Monferrato and the Alps. The vineyards here produce Nebbiolo, Barolo and Dolcetto di Alba DOC reds. Roddi's Piazza del Municipio, overlooked by the late-Baroque façade of the Chiesa dell'Assunta, is considered one of the most beautiful squares in Piedmont. The **castle**, an 11th-century Benedictine foundation enlarged in the 14th century and made over as a hunting lodge in the 19th century by Carlo Alberto of Savoy, still appears massive and forbidding despite the large windows and other refinements. Entered through an outer courtyard, it has two cylindrical towers built in the 12th century and modified in the 15th, and interiors with handsome coffered ceilings. The castle is the property of the municipality, which uses it for temporary exhibitions and special events.

Roddi is probably the only town in the world that can boast a special training school for truffle dogs (est. 1880).

POLLENZO

At the same time he bought Roddi castle, Carlo Alberto acquired the property now known as the Tenuta Reale di Pollenzo (*map C, D1*), transforming its 14th-century castle into a comfortable private residence and the vast estate—nearly 700ha—into a hunting reserve and model farm. He entrusted the design of the new complex to the Gothic Revival architects Pelagio Palagi and Ernesto Melano, who, in addition to remodelling the castle in their favourite idiom, built the village from scratch. The royal landscape architect Xavier Kürten (*see p. 89*) designed the gardens. The title of Count of Pollenzo, often used by Vittorio Emanuele III, testifies to the bond that he, too, felt with the property: it was here that he devoted himself to his beloved studies on agricultural techniques. Pollenzo is now home to Slow Food's Università degli Studi di Scienze Gastronomiche, possibly the only university in the world to come complete with a hotel, restaurant and wine cellar. The tradition of excellence in agriculture and food science continues.

CHERASCO

This very pretty town (*map C, D1*) stands on a natural terrace at the confluence of the Stura di Demonte and the Tanaro Cherasco on the border between the Langhe and the Roero. It is a regular quadrilateral, with orthogonal arcaded streets and an extraordinary number of religious and civic buildings built between the Middle Ages and the 18th century. Established in 1243 as a *villanova* (new town) by the common folk and lesser nobility of the surrounding lands, it was intended as a centre of defence against the militias of Alba, Asti, Saluzzo and the Marquis of Monferrato.

The Romanesque **church of San Pietro** (*Via della Pace*) dates from the 12th–13th centuries and is the oldest monument in Cherasco; it has an unusual façade with blind arcades adorned with reliefs and majolicas and a fine campanile. Flanking the church on the north is a wonderful **garden** of medicinal herbs and other plants of historic interest. It was created in 2004 to exemplify the kind of gardens cultivated by monastic communities in the Middle Ages. Surrounded by a cobblestone-and-brick wall, the garden consists of four beds in a cross-shaped layout. Walking along the paved paths you can examine a typical medieval herb garden, a rose garden, a flowering lawn with aromatic plants, and a teaching garden illustrating farming techniques of the past, using vegetables that were known before the discovery of America. Four trees—an apple, a pomegranate, a medlar and a holly—represent the seasons and the passage of time.

Currently owned by the city, **Palazzo Salmatoris** (*Via Vittorio Emanuele II 3*) was built between 1616 and 1620 by Giovanni di Audino Salmatoris, a rich silk merchant. In 1631, while war and pestilence raged elsewhere, the Salmatoris gave refuge to Vittorio Amedeo I and his wife Christine of France, and in 1706, the Holy Shroud was brought here from Turin for fear it might end up in the hands of the French. Ironically, perhaps, in this symbolic place Napoleon signed the Armistice of Cherasco in 1796. Today it is an important cultural and artistic centre, a busy venue for exhibitions and cultural events.

Via Vittorio Emanele II ends at the **Triumphal Arch of the Madonna del Rosario**, built in the late 17th century to a design by Giovenale Boetto.

Cherasco's **castle**, surrounded by shady plane trees in the town's southeastern corner, was built in 1348 by order of Luchino Visconti, Duke of Milan, who after defeating the Savoy and taking the city, thought it wise to fortify it. Today the huge square structure still has a tower at each corner and a smaller central tower with drawbridge over the entrance. Over the centuries the building followed the fortunes of the Visconti family; in 1559, after the Treaty of Cateau Cambrésis, it returned to the Savoy who used it to escape the plague in 1630 and the French in 1706. Renovated at the end of the 19th century by Alfredo d'Andrade, it offers superb views of the surrounding countryside.

The **Museo Civico Giovan Battista Adriani** (*Via Ospedale 40; open Sun and holidays in March–Dec, enquire at the Tourist Office*) was founded in 1898 following a donation by the local historian, archaeologist and coin collector Giovanni Battista Adriani. It is located in the 17th-century Palazzo Gotti Salerano and preserves archaeological finds (mainly from local digs), a lapidary collection, a collection of seals, and various historical documents. There are also paintings, drawings and prints ranging in date from the 17th–19th centuries, medals, furniture and a small part of the important numismatic collection of the founder. The rooms themselves (Salone della Sapienza, Sala della Grazia, Alcova del Sonno, Cappella e Saletta dello Stemma) are magnificently decorated with frescoes by Sebastiano Taricco.

Other interesting sights are the church of Sant'Agostino, designed and built by Giovenale Boetto in 1672 and decorated with frescoes by Sebastiano Taricco and Aliberti; the Santuario della Madonna del Popolo, designed by Sebastiano Taricco with an elaborate façade and even more exuberant interior; and the synagogue, housed on the top floor of a private house in the Jewish quarter.

JEWISH HISTORY AT CHERASCO

The duchy, and later the kingdom, of Piedmont was the nearest realm in southern Europe where Jews fleeing eastward from persecution in France (beginning in the 14th century) or Spain (15th century) could settle in relative freedom. It is therefore not surprising that the region hosts one of Italy's largest Jewish populations even today. The Jewish community of Cherasco has always been small (it peaked at just eleven families in the 18th century), so the synagogue is also tiny. It is a typical 'ghetto synagogue', built on the top floor of a residential building and invisible from the street.

Cherasco's 'ghetto' initially was just one house at the corner of Via Marconi and Vittorio Emanuele. Established around 1725, it was not strictly segregated: during the French occupation many families moved elsewhere and did not return even during the Restoration. The characteristic long balconies that connected one house to another and made it possible to reach the synagogue without leaving the ghetto can still be seen.

The oldest mention of Jews in Cherasco is a document of 1543 attesting the arrival of one Benedictus Debenedetti. The community became stable only in the 17th century, however, as other families settled under the protection of the Debenedetti, who by this time had established a bank sanctioned by the papacy in the 16th century and by the Savoy in the 17th. The Jews of Cherasco, in addition to lending money (the Banca Segre Leone, which granted peasant farmers interest-free loans, was especially famous), were active in the production and sale of locally-made silk.

The present synagogue dates from the 18th century but is probably built over an earlier temple. At the centre of the small rectangular room is an ornate octagonal *teva* (from which the celebrant reads Torah in the Sephardic tradition) with a baldachin on spiral columns; the gilded wood *aron* (or container for the Torah) stands against the east wall. Both date from the 18th century. Hebrew inscriptions adorn the walls, several beautiful lamps hang from the ceiling and the small, raised matroneum is behind a wood screen. Adjoining rooms host an exhibition devoted to Jewish life and culture in Piedmont (*Via Marconi 4; open for guided visits by appointment, torinoebraica.it*).

Cherasco's Jewish cemetery is on the northern outskirts of town, at the junction of Via Sant'Iffredo and the main road to Bra.

Cherasco is famous for its *baci*, exquisite chocolates made with dark chocolate and hazelnuts, and it is recognised as the Italian capital of snail farming. The Istituto Internazionale dell'Elicicoltura, established here some 30 years ago, promotes recipes using snails—accompanied, of course, by fine wines. Cherasco is also a centre of the antiques trade—and in fact an extraordinary number of shops offering antiques, paintings, furniture and *objets d'art* can be found beneath its arcades. For more than 15 years Italian and French antique dealers and collectors have gathered at Cherasco's famous street markets of antique furniture and books, vintage ceramics and glass, toys and models, and other collectibles.

BENE VAGIENNA

This town (*map C, C2–D2*) of narrow streets, wide porticoes and lovely churches and palaces is the successor of the Roman *Augusta Bagiennorum*, which was founded near the oppidium of the Ligurian Bagienni at the same time as *Augusta Taurinorum* (Turin) and *Augusta Praetoria* (Aosta) in the late 1st century BC. Together with *Pollentia* (Pollenzo) and *Alba Pompeia* (Alba) it was a focal point of Roman territorial control, urbanisation and land use. Excavations, set in a nature reserve a half-hour's walk (or a five-minute drive) northeast of the town, have revealed traces of a temple, a bath complex and an amphitheatre and are still ongoing. The Roman town was abandoned for reasons that remain unclear, and the refugees established the present settlement at the confluence of the Mondalavia and Cucetta torrents, a place that offered better natural defences and, perhaps, a higher quality of life given the abundance of water.

The old town, almost entirely surrounded by walls, is mostly medieval, though many buildings were renovated in the Baroque style in the 17th and 18th centuries. A good example is the parish church of **Santa Maria Assunta**, rebuilt in the 17th century by Giovenale Boetto and again in the 19th century, but still preserving its Gothic bell-tower with single- and double-light mullioned windows and octagonal spire. The frescoes inside are by Luigi Morgari.

In the central Via Roma is the **church of the Confraternita di San Bernardino**, documented in the 15th century and rebuilt in the 18th century with the addition of stuccoes and the main Porta dei Desideri or Porta del Paradiso.

The **Museo Civico Archeologico** (*Via Roma 125; check website for hours, archea.info/museo-archeologico-benevagienna*) was established at the beginning of the 20th century in the 18th-century palace of Lucerne Rorà by Giuseppe Assandria and Giovanni Vacchetta, who discovered the site of the Roman Augusta Bagiennorum and conducted the first excavations between 1892 and 1925. A significant part of the present installation deliberately reflects the original 19th-century display, creating a museum-within-a-museum. Highlights are the marble jambs of two of the three stage doors of the theatre, some delicately carved cornices and capitals, everyday objects including glass and pottery, and jewellery and other burial treasures from the south necropolis (1st century AD). Three new rooms on the ground floor focus on the city's public monuments—the theatre and amphitheatre (I); the Forum, Capitolium and Basilica (II); and daily life (III), including an interesting section on building techniques.

The **Museo di Casa Ravera** (*Via Vittorio Emanuele 43, T: 0172 654969*), a temporary exhibition venue, also displays objects ranging in date from the Roman age to the Baroque. Here are the artist Giovanni Vacchetta's 19th-century sketches and drawings of the excavations of Augusta Bagiennorum, and a collection of paintings, wood sculptures and silver liturgical items—notably two inlaid tabernacles by Pietro Piffetti (18th-century) and a monstrance made for Emperor Leopold I of Austria. The town house was built in the early 15th century and enlarged in the 17th century.

The perimeter of the medieval castle is still intact, with the exception of the southern tip and one of the two adjacent sides. The fortress was made into a hospital in the 19th century and further modified in the 20th.

DOGLIANI

In the 16th century this seemingly insignificant farm town (*map C, D2*) was occupied first by the French and then by the Spanish, in the long and tremendously expensive Italian Wars between Francis I and Charles V, who both wanted dominance over Europe. With the Treaty of Lyons in 1601, France ceded Dogliani and other towns in southwestern Piedmont to the Savoy, who in turn gave the fief to the Solaro di Moretta and the Solaro del Borgo. After the Napoleonic interlude Dogliani entered a period of prosperity that it still enjoys today, thanks to its cherries, and the grapes from which its renowned Dolcetto di Dogliani is made (respective harvest festivals are held in late spring and early autumn). Its citizens have played important roles in Italian civic and intellectual life; the most famous native is Luigi Einaudi, first President of the Italian Republic.

Dogliani is always a pleasant place to visit, with an atmosphere of relaxed wellbeing in the old Borgo, heightened in autumn by the warm colours of the surrounding forests and vineyards. The little **Civico Museo Storico Archeologico Giuseppe Gabetti**, located on the first floor of the Palazzo Comunale (*Piazza San Paolo 10, doglianiturismo.com/museo-storico-archeologico-giuseppe-gabetti*) has a respectable collection of local paleontological and archaeological material, ranging in date from the Neolithic, Bronze and Iron Ages to Roman antiquity and the Middle Ages. There is an especially rich collection of fossils, funerary inscriptions and Roman epigraphs from Dogliani and neighbouring towns, and there are some fine medieval capitals and stone sculptures. The museum also houses paintings, prints and documents of the 16th and later centuries, and an archive of local interest.

Nearby **Monforte d'Alba** (*map C, D2*) also has a pleasant village centre and a 15th-century fresco in the Cappella delle Sette Vie.

BAROLO

The fame of the medieval village of Barolo (*map C, D1*) is quite disproportionate to its tiny size. This is just one of eleven municipalities in the Langhe hills that is authorised to grow the Nebbiolo grapes from which Italy's finest red wine (Barolo) is made. The shape of the village, its streets and houses spread out at the foot of its castle, probably dates from the 13th century, though the image was largely crafted in the 19th. The village and the surrounding hills were long a fief of the Falletti, a noble family that had found fortune as bankers and merchants in Alba. It is they who were responsible for the mid-19th-century revival of Barolo wine. More specifically, it was Juliette Colbert de Maulèvrier, wife of Marquis Carlo Tancredi Falletti di Barolo, and her French oenologist Alexandre-Pierre Odart, who developed what many consider the epitome of the winemaker's art. Juliette was also a generous philanthropist: a direct descendant of the finance minister of the Sun King, she donated an estimated 12 million lire to charity—a sum equal to the annual budget of many states of the time. She left the 10th-century **Castello Falletti** to her foundation with the intention of creating a girls' school. In 1870, six years after her death, it was renovated and enlarged with this mission in mind by Carlo Trocelli, in the then-fashionable Medieval Revival style. Today the castle still holds a school, as well as the **Enoteca Regionale del Barolo** and the Museo Enologico ed Etnografico (*see below*). The main public rooms, on the first floor, can be visited during exhibitions and events: they are the Sala delle Quattro Stagioni, named after the paintings of the four seasons over the doors; the Sala degli Stemmi, whose ceiling bears the Falletti arms; the Stanza della Marchesa Colbert and the Stanza di Silvio Pellico (the poet and patriot was a frequent guest) with *trompe-l'œil* wall paintings imitating fabrics; and the Biblioteca, whose 3,000 volumes were undoubtedly one of the reasons Pellico spent so much time here.

WiMu is the catchy new name of the Museo Enologico ed Etnografico, occupying no fewer than 25 rooms on all five floors of the castle (*wimubarolo.it*). The name comes with a smart new installation, by celebrity exhibition designer François Confino, aimed at underscoring the cultural dimension of wine rather than the technical aspects of winemaking. Light and darkness, sound and colour are used to create an 'emotional journey' through the myth and reality of wine (wine in the history of art, cuisine, cinema, literature, folk traditions, etc.), through the salient moments of the agricultural year, and through the history of Barolo the place, and Barolo the wine. The visit ends in the Enoteca Regionale del Barolo, located in the cellars of the castle, where you can linger for a glass or two and, of course, purchase some Barolo to take home. The rooftop terrace offers unmatchable views of the surrounding hills.

Across the street from the castle is the quaint little **Museo dei Cavatappi** (*Piazza Mazzocchi 4, museodeicavatappi.it*), with a nicely displayed collection of 500 corkscrews of various types, shapes and materials, some dating back to the 18th century.

La Morra, a 15-minute drive north of Barolo (*map C, D1*), has a fan-shaped medieval centre around the Piazza Castello, from where you can enjoy stunning views of the Langhe and the Alps. Just outside the town, at Brunate, stands the little chapel of the **Madonna delle Grazie** (also called Cappella del Barolo), built in the early 20th century by the Ceretto, a family of wealthy landowners, as a shelter to be used by local farm workers in the case of severe weather. At the end of the century the chapel was restored and given an audacious new decorative programme, with bright, colourful wall-paintings by David Tremlett (interior) and Sol LeWitt (exterior).

GRINZANE CAVOUR

Grinzane Cavour (*map C, D1*) is home to another massive castle. This one was built in the 13th century over an earlier fortification, was expanded and remodelled in the 16th century and renovated as a comfortable country house in the 19th century. Its most famous tenant was Camillo Benso, Count of Cavour, a founding father of the Kingdom of Italy and mayor of Grinzane from 1832 to 1849. The **Museo delle Langhe** (*castellogrinzane.com/il-museodelle-langhe*) is full of memorabilia (as well as rooms devoted to daily life in town and country); the Enoteca Regionale Piemontese, in the cellars, bears his name. The ground-floor rooms of the castle are entirely given over to the display of fine wines selected by the Ordine dei Cavalieri del Tartufo e dei Vini di Alba, a very serious confraternity devoted to hunting down and tasting excellent food and wine, especially products of the Langhe. Since 1982 the castle has also been the seat of the Premio Letterario Grinzane Cavour, a world-class literary award for young writers.

SERRALUNGA D'ALBA

Castello di Serralunga, the severe fortress of this picturesque hilltop village (*map C, D1–D2*) was built for the powerful Falletti family in the mid-14th century. The building has few windows, almost no decorations, and is markedly vertical in shape. One of the finest and best preserved hilltop castles in Piedmont, it absolutely dominates the pretty *borgo* that spreads out, ringlike, at its foot. The castle consists of several parts: the *palacium* or keep, a compact vertical block containing large rooms stacked one above the other; a cylindrical tower (a distinctive innovation of 14th-century military architecture); and a chapel with a barrel vault and frescoes dating from the mid-15th century. Because it was not the object of major attacks and was rarely renovated, its original medieval structure has survived intact. Purchased by the Italian State in 1949 at the request of President Luigi Einaudi, it was meticulously restored and is now used for exhibitions and events (*castellodiserralunga.it*).

While in Serralunga you might like to taste its signature product, Barolo Chinato, a spicy 19th-century cure-all developed by local pharmacist Giuseppe Cappellano, based on Barolo wine laced with *China calisaia*, rhubarb root, and gentian and cardamom seeds.

CASTIGLIONE FALLETTO

Castiglione, another hilltop village (*map C, D1*) just a stone's throw from Serralunga and Barolo, was originally a *castrum et villa* (fortified farm) held in fief by the Marquis of Saluzzo. Over the centuries the vast manor changed hands several times, eventually coming into possession of the Falletti, whose name it still bears. The fortress has an irregular footprint that follows the lie of the land, with two cylindrical corner towers and an even larger cylindrical tower at its centre. In the 19th century it was renovated as an aristocratic home, so today's castle appears considerably less forbidding than the original. In the past the castle square was used to play *pantalera*, the traditional ball game of southern Piedmont and northern Liguria, which can be imagined as lying somewhere between tennis and volleyball. In the same square is the municipal *crota* (cellar), where you can pick up local growers' Barolo, Barbera and Dolcetto d'Alba wines, or get information on the area's hiking, riding and cycling trails.

NEIVE

This picturesque village (*map C, D1*) owes its name to an aristocratic Roman family, the *gens Naevia*, of whom it was a possession. Old Neive rises above its anonymous modern surroundings and is considered among the best preserved medieval towns in the area. Originally accessible by just two gates, the circular core holds the village's most prestigious buildings, the homes of wealthy middle-class families. The 13th-century *casaforte* of the Cotti banking family is the oldest building in the village. The 18th-century palace of the counts of Castelborgo has a magnificent garden gate designed by local architect Giovanni Antonio Borgese (1751), who also designed the church of the Confraternita di San Michele (1759–89), with its tall dome. Other points of interest are the 18th-century church of Santi Pietro e Paolo, designed by Francesco Gallo; the 16th-century chapels of San Rocco and San Sebastiano; the tall Torre Comunale; the Palazzo Cicito; and Casa Bongioanni, also by Borgese (1750). The 10th-century Torre del Monastero is all that remains of the Romanesque Benedictine monastery of Santa Maria del Piano, on the road to Mango.

It was in Neive that the French oenologist Louis Oudard first experimented with the vinification of Nebbiolo grapes to produce Barbaresco (1854). To show off its wine heritage Neive has set up the Bottega dei Quattro Vini (Barbera, Dolcetto d'Alba, Barbaresco and Moscato) in the cellars of the Town Hall.

MANGO

Located on the ridge between the valleys of the Tinella and Belbo, Mango (*map D, A4*) enjoys magnificent views of the surrounding hills. Its castle was built in 1630 by the Marquis of Busca on the ruins of a 13th-century tower. A four-square fortress with a tower at each corner, it passed first to the Dukes of Mantua and then, after 1714, to the Savoy. Plain and simple in its lines but Baroque in feeling, it now houses the Enoteca Regionale Colline del Moscato (which promotes the hundred-odd growers who produce Moscato d'Asti, Asti Spumante, Moscato passito and Moscato grappa), a restaurant and events spaces. The writer Beppe Fenoglio spent several months in Mango as a partisan during the Second World War and wrote more than a few pages about the village. In his memory a 'cultural park' has been established in the village and its immediate surroundings, with signs and panels marking the places mentioned in his novels and short stories.

THE ALTA LANGA

SANTO STEFANO BELBO

Santo Stefano Belbo (*map D, A4*) is a very old place. The 10th-century abbey of San Gaudenzio, some remains of which can be seen on the left bank of the River Belbo, probably stands over a Roman temple; it is thanks to its Benedictine monks that the hills here were planted with muscat grapes more than a millennium ago. Santo Stefano is best known, however, as the birthplace of Cesare Pavese, one of the great Italian authors of the 20th century. Many of the places mentioned in his books are to be found in the village and the surrounding hills. The **Casa Natale Cesare Pavese** (*Via Cesare Pavese 20, open Tues–Sat, guided tours can be booked, fondazionecesarepavese.it*), Pavese's birthplace, displays the complete works and their translations, photographs of the writer and of the places where his novels are set, as well as scholarly studies of his works. There is also a collection of household items and tools used in agriculture and related activities. The deconsecrated church of Santi Giacomo e Cristoforo hosts the Centro Studi Cesare Pavese, with archives and a library, and rooms for meetings and exhibitions.

CORTEMILIA

The main town of the Alta Langa, Cortemilia (*map D, A4*) was probably founded in the 1st or 2nd century BC as *Cohors Æmilia*. By the 10th century it was considered one of the most important towns between the sea and the rivers Tanaro and Bormida. Its strategic location, along a major axis connecting landlocked Piedmont with the ports of Liguria, has contributed quite a bit to its economic development, which is now tied to the cultivation and processing of hazelnuts. The local hazelnut, the *nocciola tonda gentile delle Langhe*, is protected by an IGT designation; you can taste it in the traditional cakes made here and in almost every town of the Alta Langa.

The Bormida divides the town into two neighbourhoods, which take their names respectively from the 16th-century parish churches of San Michele and San Pantaleo. The ruined castle has a 10th- or 11th-century enceinte and a tall, cylindrical 13th century tower. A legend says that St Francis preached at the 10th-century Romanesque church while journeying to France in 1213.

Sandstone is prominent in traditional buildings in Cortemilia, such as in the truly impressive terraces covering the hill of Monte Oliveto. The terraces are the object of a living museum, the excellent small **Ecomuseo dei Terrazzamenti e della Vite** (*Via Dante Alighieri 4, ecomuseodeiterrazzamenti.it*). The idea behind this museum is to draw attention to the cultural heritage behind the technique of terracing—a conservation method that enhances soil quality and moisture while preventing erosion. The most interesting feature of the museum is the Strada dei Terrazzamenti, a series of walks on trails and country roads, each designed to focus on a particular trait of the agricultural landscape, such as the cylindrical hazelnut-drying towers known as *scau*.

BERGOLO

With just 74 inhabitants, Bergolo (*map D, A4*) may be the smallest village in Piedmont; it is certainly one of the most attractive. Perched on a ridge top between the Bormida and Uzzone valleys, it commands stunning views over beautiful bucolic landscape. Its position on the border between Piedmont and Liguria puts it within range of day-trippers from the Mediterranean beaches, which means that tourism has replaced farming as the chief source of revenue, putting a dent in the village's authenticity. On the other hand the arrival of tourists has permitted the conservation and restoration of the village's beautiful stone buildings and given the last handful of residents a reason to stay. The Romanesque church of San Sebastiano, with its plain pitched roof and semicurcular apse with blind dwarf arcading, dates from the 12th century.

LEVICE

This pleasant village (*map C, D2*) occupies a hillside in a landscape criss-crossed by the Belbo, Bormida and Uzzone, likewise on the border between Piedmont and Liguria—the landscape of the narratives of Cesare Pavese and Beppe Fenoglio. From the Middle Ages until the 18th century its castle was part of a system of fortifications that included the castles of Cortemilia, Perletto, Prunetto, Bergolo and Cravanzana and was intended to provide a common defence for the towns of the Uzzone Valley. In 1796, however, a fierce battle between the French and the allied forces of Austria and Piedmont reduced the castle to a pile of rocks (though part of one circular tower can still be seen). Fortunately a number of interesting churches in the village and its environs have kept Levice on the map for Italians and foreigners alike. These include the 18th-century Madonna del Bricco, Sant'Antonio Abate and Cappella della Madonna Addolorata; the 20th-century San Callisto Papa with its decorative stone façade; the little chapels of San Rocco (14th-century, with frescoes), Sant'Anna, Sant'Antonio, San Bernardo, Santa Lucia and Sant'Ermete (17th century).

In recent years an effort has been made to increase tourism in Levice and **Bergolo** (*map D, A4*) by commissioning mural paintings from local artists. For the time being the highest achievements of contemporary art in the villages remain their *murazzano* and *castelmagno* cheeses served with *cugnà* (grape mustard) and honey, and *bunet*, the signature pudding made with cocoa and *amaretti*.

THE LANGA ASTIGIANA

MONASTERO BORMIDA

This town (*map D, A4*) stretches along the left bank of the river Bormida. For centuries its history was closely linked to that of the Benedictine monastery founded here in the 9th century and later fortified to provide a refuge for the population of the surrounding countryside. The old town is dominated by its castle, flanked by a 27m tower probably added in the 11th century. The Baroque façade was added in the 17th century. The interior has frescoed rooms and mosaic floors.

ROCCAVERANO

This little town (*map D, A4*) draws quite a few visitors for its calm, relaxing atmosphere and beautiful views. Set in an isolated position on a broad hill between two branches of the Bormida and surrounded by a bucolic landscape of woods, farms and pastures, it is home to a real gastronomic treasure: *robiola*, a soft, creamy crustless cheese. All that is left of its 13th-century castle is a cylindrical tower and a section of the curtain wall with three elegant windows, but a recent restoration has made the top of the tower accessible and the views are magnificent. A trail along the ridgetop leads to the little church of San Giovanni, a 12th-century Romanesque construction with a 19th-century façade; in the apse is the most complete cycle of Gothic frescoes in southern Piedmont, painted by an unknown artist around 1480.

The paintings on the walls show *Stories of St John*, the *Apostles* (eight in imitation marble niches), the *Crucifixion* (in which the figure of Christ on the Cross was lost when the window was opened in the east wall). In the vaulted ceiling is the *Blessing Christ with Mary and St John*, and *Evangelists*; and there are saints beneath the arches. Somewhat later frescoes by a different painter, in the south aisle, represent the Virgin, the *Pietà* and fragments of saints.

MOMBALDONE

Surrounded by badlands, like an oasis in a desert of tufa softened by gorse, Mombaldone (*map D, A4*) is the only village in the Langa Astigiana that still has its original walls. To stroll down the single main street, with its lateral alleyways and passages, arches and courtyards, is to journey back in time. The old fortified village, whose medieval character is well preserved, grew up in Roman times near the Via Æmilia Scauri, which connected the Ligurian coast to the Po River basin. The village consists of two distinct neighbourhoods separated by the now-ruined castle. Most of the houses are made of bare grey stone; some have finely carved windows and doorways dating from 15th–17th-century renovations.

Via Cervetti enters the fortified *ricetto* through an ogival archway, beyond which you soon reach the central Piazza Umberto I and the village's main monuments. The oratory of **Santi Fabiano e Sebastiano**, built over the castle moat in 1764 to a design by Pietro Barozzi and restored in 1995-7, now hosts conferences, exhibitions, meetings and cultural events. The church of **San Nicola**, a hexagonal church by Giovanni Matteo Zucchi (1790), contains 17th-century paintings by Giovanni Monevi and other local masters and a huge organ of 1885, made by Fratelli Collino of Turin.

Beyond the square the street climbs to the highest part of the village, where the houses gradually give way to the countryside, passing what remains of the 13th–14th-century castle. The latter was demolished in 1637, then used as a quarry for stones to build the Mombaldone–Spigno railway. The Del Carretto family, to whom Mombaldone was given in feud in 1209, still own the castle and are active in the preservation of the village and its historical and cultural identity.

BRA & THE ROERO

This small, hilly district is known for its wines, but even more, perhaps, for its fruit: particularly the peaches of Canale and the local variety of pear known as Madernassa, which originated in the late 18th century in Guarene. Strawberries are also grown. The name comes from a family of merchants and bankers—variously called Roero, Rotari, Roveio or Roure—who were prominent in the political life of Asti and who dominated the area for a number of centuries during the Middle Ages.

The family is still alive and well and deserves a word of introduction. The Roero maintained neutrality between Ghelphs and Ghibellines and with the wealth gained from trade and banking, dramatically increased their political power locally and in

Europe. The many family lines (there were more than 20 in the 16th century) either received or purchased most of the large properties in the area that still bears their name. According to legend, the Roero descended from the Lombard king Rotari, or were privileged to carry his name, abandoning that of Troia. Another, more credible story, suggests they may have been Flemish in origin. Their business activity was concentrated mainly in Flanders, Brabant, Hainault, Cologne, Bonn, Freiburg and Lucerne.

The success of the Roero enterprises in Europe was due in part to the family's refusal to participate in ventures that might tarnish their name: in a sense the Roero conglomerate was one of the first firms in Europe to practise corporate social responsibility. The family gained immensely by this decision: Emperor Henry VII, in 1330, granted them the privilege to pardon prisoners and to consider their homes inviolable places of asylum to any person—at that time a privilege exclusive to religious edifices. Many Roero castles have vanished; others were taken over by the Savoy in the 17th and 18th centuries. The best preserved is the castle of Monticello.

Today the territory of Roero encompasses 24 municipalities on the left bank of the Tanaro. It does not include Asti, which is associated instead with the Monferrato.

BRA

Bra (*map C, C1*) was established around the 11th century by inhabitants of Pollentia (modern Pollenzo; *see p. 154*), who settled at the foot of a fortified hill. A free commune in the 12th century, it came under the sovereignty first of the Visconti, then of the dukes of Orléans and finally, after 1552, of the Savoy. In 1760 Carlo Emanuele III granted it the title of city, sparking a period of rapid economic and cultural development. In the mid-19th century Bra gained international renown for its leather industry, which diversified in the 20th century to include the processing of synthetic fibres and plastics. Today winemaking and fruit and vegetable farming are also important components of the economy.

MUSEUMS OF AND MONUMENTS OF BRA

The modern gateway to Bra is the **Movicentro Brauno**, an innovative transport facility occupying 6500 sq m right next to the station. The design, by Simona Dabbene, involved the redevelopment of the area adjacent to the train station with the creation of a car park and a new coach terminal as well as a service structure with shops, ticket offices and a cafeteria in a former goods depot. The award-winning design (2004; construction completed 2007) makes ingenious use of materials, leaving the wood-truss roof, steel beams and girders, and stainless-steel climate-control systems in full view; the large floor-to-ceiling windows and thoughtfully designed lighting keep the space cosy and luminous on even the darkest winter day. The extensive use of glazing also enables travellers to keep coaches and trains in view without leaving the building. There is also a convenient rental-bike rack.

The centre of city life is the sloping Piazza Caduti della Libertà. The church of Sant'Andrea Apostolo, on the north side of the square, was built between 1672 and 1687 on a design ascribed to Guarino Guarini (*see p. 23*). Adjacent to the church are the Monte di Pietà, originally a pawn broker's, and the Palazzo Civico—the Town Hall, attributed to Bernardo Vittone. The latter is a medieval building (some traces of the earlier structure can be seen on the side facing Via Monte di Pietà) although the main façade overlooking the square consciously echoes that of Palazzo Carignano in Turin. The nearby Palazzo Traversa, a 15th-century Gothic building with crenellations, mullioned windows and terracotta decorations, is home to the Museo Civico di Archeologia Storia e Arte (*Via Parpera 4, museidibra. it/museotraversa*), with an archaeological section displaying Etruscan and Roman remains (including a great deal of material from the Roman Pollentia) and a section focusing on the history of painting and sculpture from the 17th–20th centuries.

The **Museo Civico di Storia Naturale Federico ed Ettore Craveri** (*Via Craveri 15, museidibra.it/museocraveri*) displays the natural history collection of Federico Craveri, one of the first scientists to ride across North America on horseback, in the mid-19th century. Among its many curiosities is a large ornithological section with an important collection of hummingbirds; material that illustrates the prehistory of the Ténéré desert; and meteorological instruments used by Craveri. Over time the collection has been augmented with exhibits on the natural history of Piedmont.

Further examples of Baroque architecture are the churches of the Santissima Trinità and Santa Maria degli Angeli and the Palazzi Garrone and Mathis (both medieval, but remodelled in the Baroque period). **Santa Chiara**, considered one of the most important churches of Bra, was built between 1742 and 1748 to a design by Bernardo Vittone in a transitional style uniting Rococo and Neoclassical elements. Perched at the top of Monte Guglielmo, the highest point in the city, is the **Zizzola**, an octagonal *villa delle delizie* built in 1840; it has a lovely park and beautiful views.

Bra is the birthplace of the Slow Food movement, which here hosts the biennial gourmet cheese fair, Cheese. Slow Food's Università di Scienze Gastronomiche, the first university in the world dedicated wholly to the culinary arts, is in nearby Pollenzo (*see p. 154*).

OTHER TOWNS AND VILLAGES OF THE ROERO

MONTICELLO D'ALBA
Located in the hills on the left bank of the Tanaro, Monticello (*map C, D1*) is divided into a lower and an upper town, respectively called Borgo and Villa. Towering over both is the great 13th–14th-century Roero castle, renovated as an elegant country house in 1786–7 (*roerodimonticello.it*). Among the most impressive of the area, it is square with corner towers (one square, one cylindrical and one octagonal), its ramparts crowned by parapets. Xavier Kürten (*see p. 89*) designed the beautiful Romantic park, with its winding paths, small ponds and grassy meadows; it commands good views over the Roero hills, their forests and fields interspersed with vineyards growing Barbera and Nebbiolo grapes. The castle and park still belong to the Roero family and can be visited on Sundays.

GUARENE
This ancient fief (*map C, D1*) of the bishops of Asti and Alba, an afterwards of the

Roero, lies in a panoramic position dominating the Tanaro Valley and the valley of Alba. Its Baroque castle was built by order of Carlo Giacinto Roero (1726–8) over a pre-existing 13th-century fortress. Completed by Filippo Castelli (1778), it appears as an elegant and refined palace. It is now a hotel. In the main square is Palazzo Re Rebaudengo, an 18th-century building that preserves rooms with finely decorated ceilings. Completely restored in the late 20th century, it is now home to a contemporary art space run by the Fondazione Sandretto Re Rebaudengo per l'Arte, in Turin (*open for temporary exhibitions*).

GOVONE

This one-time fief (*map C, D1*) of the convent of Nonatola later belonged to the bishops of Asti and then to a branch of Solaro family. It is known for its **Castello Reale** (now the Palazzo Comunale), a gorgeous Baroque edifice erected over a 14th-century fortress. This was a royal residence of the Savoy; Carlo Felice spent his summers here, redecorating the interior (*for details of when it is open to the public, see residenzerealisabaude.com*) with spectacular frescoes and *trompe-l'œil* paintings (those inspired by Greek myth, in the reception hall, are particularly beautiful). The statues, brought from the Venaria Reale, and the 18th-century Chinese tapestries that hang in many rooms, were added by the Solaro. The castle has a beautiful park (1819), designed like those of so many Savoy residences by Xavier Kürten (*see p. 89*). It is famous for its blue grape hyacinths and periwinkles and for its red tulips—the latter the object of a special celebration, Tulipani a Corte. The orangery is used for conferences and cultural events.

Nearby is the parish church of **San Secondo**, a 14th-century Romanesque–Gothic building extensively rebuilt in the 18th and 19th centuries. Govone produces excellent Barbera, Nebbiolo, Arneis and Bonaria wines.

THE MONFERRATO

This historical region of Piedmont extends between Asti and Alessandria. It is bounded on the south by the courses of the Tanaro, Belbo and Bormida, and on the north by the Po. Residents speak of an Alto and Basso Monferrato—respectively the southern and northern parts of the region—and there is some topographical evidence to support the distinction of a third district, the Monferrato Astigiano. All are devoted to farming and forestry, especially cultivation of the vine, which produces some very fine local grape varieties (Barbera, Freisa, Grignolino, Cortese etc.).

The Marquisate of Monferrato was formed in the 10th or 11th century by the dismemberment of the vast Aleramic March: made up almost entirely of imperial fiefs, it was governed by Aleramicis of the line of Otto until John I, upon whose death (1305) it passed to the descendants of Violante, sister of John I and wife of the Greek emperor Andronicus Palaeologus. The Palaeologan dynasty ruled until 1533, when Giangiorgio died without direct heirs. The unity of the marquisate had been preserved, until that time, by the principle of indivisibility and primogeniture. Its administration was no different from that of all great fiefs: the head was the marquis, assisted by a staff of counsellors (the curia), replaced in the 15th century by a senate. The seat of government was Moncalvo, then Chivasso, and finally, after 1435, Casale.

Forced to defend itself in the 12th–15th centuries from the expansionist intentions of the neighbouring *communi* (Asti, Alessandria and Vercelli) and later of the Savoy and the Visconti, an exhausted Monferrato was disputed in the 16th century by Federico II Gonzaga of Mantua and Carlo III of Savoy. In 1536, Emperor Charles V intervened, entrusting the marquisate to the Gonzaga, who took possession only after the Peace of Cateau Cambrésis (1559). Hated by the *monferrini*, the Gonzaga sold many fiefdoms to the highest bidder—Mantuans, Genoese and Lombards). The insistent ambitions of the Savoy led to two bitter wars (1612–17 and 1627–31), brought to an end by the Peace of Cherasco, which awarded the regions of Alba and Trino to the Savoy and the Monferrato, which in 1575 had been made a duchy by Emperor Maximilian II, to the Gonzaga-Nevers. The last Duke of Mantua and Monferrato was Ferdinando Carlo, who twice (1681 and 1701) surrendered Casale to the French, causing the emperor to declare him guilty of felony and assign the Monferrato to the Savoy (1708)—a move confirmed by the treaties of Utrecht (1713) and Rastatt (1714). Briefly under French occupation as the Department of Tanaro (1798), in 1814 the Monferrato was united with the Kingdom of Sardinia.

CASALE MONFERRATO

The mighty ramparts that made Casale Monferrato (*map D, A2*) one of the most important strongholds in Europe are gone, but the 14th-century castle still remains to testify to the city's past grandeur. Casale was the capital of the small but powerful Marquisate of Monferrato for 800 years, from the 10th–18th centuries. Today it is known for its industries, for its antiques market and for a local invention of 1878—*krumiri*, the arched and ribbed biscuits inspired by the handlebar moustache of Vittorio Emanuele II.

MONUMENTS AND MUSEUMS OF CASALE MONFERRATO

The old town is largely Baroque in character, having been rebuilt from the ground up in the Savoy era. The hexagonal **Castello dei Paleologi**, the city's largest and most imposing monument, is kept closed most of the time (its halls are opened for temporary exhibitions) though you can get a glimpse of its brick-vaulted cellars by peeping into the **Enoteca Regionale del Monferrato**. The castle is strategically sited between the historic town centre and the Po; the oldest part dates from the 14th century and was built for John II Palaeologus. It was fortified, in the 15th and 16th centuries, with massive walls, towers and ramparts. When the Monferrato was absorbed by the Kingdom of Sardinia, a garrison was stationed here. The fortress remained a military base until the third quarter of the 20th century, when it was devolved to the municipality. It now houses offices, spaces for exhibitions and events, a children's library and the enoteca.

The **Torre Civica** rises to a height of 60m beside the church of Santo Stefano, on Via Saffi. It probably dates from the 11th century but was built higher in 1512 by Marquis William IX Palaeologus (who commissioned Matteo Sanmicheli to top it with a belfry) and again in the Savoy period (with the addition of an elegant Baroque dome).

A bronze equestrian statue of King Carlo Alberto stands in **Piazza Giuseppe Mazzini**, Casale's main square. His 'commanding' pose, with one hand extended towards the Bar Savoia, known for its outstanding chocolate and pastries, makes residents smile.

The **cathedral** (Sant'Evasio), consecrated in 1107, preserves a remarkable narthex whose roof, carried by huge intersecting arches, recalls the architecture of French, Mozarabic and Armenian churches. The façade has tall sandstone and brick arches between tall corner towers—a design without parallel in Romanesque religious architecture. Its sheer size leads scholars to believe the church was intended to reflect the importance of Casale even before it became the seat of a bishop; the boldness of its architecture suggests its builders may have been brought from Constantinople, with which city the Paleologi would certainly have had ties. A number of artworks grace the five-aisled interior. Above the main altar hangs a magnificent silver-leafed wooden Crucifix made in the 12th century by Lombard artists. The saints and angels in the choir and the dome of the apse were added by Costantino Sereno during a restoration of 1860. In the chapel on the north side of the high altar is the High Renaissance tomb of Bernardino Tibaldeschi, by Matteo Sanmicheli. In the north aisle is the 18th-century chapel of Sant'E-vasio, designed by Benedetto Alfieri; the low reliefs are the work of Giovanni Battista Berber and the ceiling fresco is by Giovanni Battista Ronchelli. The Sacrestia Aperta–Tesoro del Duomo (*open weekend afternoons*) is the cathedral treasury, holding a small collection of paintings, sculptures and liturgical items. Highlights are a *Baptism of Christ* by Gaudenzio Ferrari and an altarpiece of the *Madonna and Child with Saints* by Giorgio Alberini. Some remains of the 12th-century floors are displayed in the ambulatory, together with 14th- and 15th-century statues. A staircase here leads to the attic (*Percorso archeologico dei sottotetti*), where a metal catwalk brings the bold face to face with the structure and decoration of the original nave, aisles and transept; a spiral staircase leads back to ground level via the narthex.

The **synagogue** (*Vicolo Salomone Olper 44, casalebraica.info*), established 1595, is the oldest in Italy and one of the most elegant and refined in Europe. A splendid example of Piedmontese Baroque architecture, it abounds in decorative stuccoes and Hebrew inscriptions with quotations from the Psalms and refernces to historical events. The rectangular hall was enlarged in 1700 and again in 1787, when the *aron* (the cabinet in which the Torah scrolls are kept) was also redesigned. The synagogue was renovated agin in the mid-19th century, when the Venetian-style mosaic floor was added. Later it was semi-abandoned, as Casale's Jewish community dwindled. In 1968 it was completely restored by the architect Giulio Bourbon and, although the congregation is too small to support continuous use, it is open for worship on Jewish holidays. There are two museums: the Museo di Arte e Storia Antica Ebraica, in the former women's gallery, displays one of Europe's largest and finest collections of Jewish ceremonial objects: lamps, medallions, chalices and historical documents concerning Casale's Jewish community; the Museo dei Lumi, in what was once the bakery where the congregation's unleavened bread was made, displays more than 150 menorahs by contemporary artists, architects and designers, Jewish and non-Jewish.

The **Museo Civico e Gipsoteca Bistolfi** (*Via Cavour 5, comune.casalemonferrato.al.it/museo*), in the 15th-century convent of Santa Croce, is entered from a cloister frescoed in the early 17th century by Guglielmo Caccia (il Moncalvo). The *gipsoteca*, dedicated to the famous symbolist artist Leonardo Bistolfi (1859–1933), a native of Casale, documents his career with plaster, marble and bronze sculptures. The museum preserves works by artists active between the 16th and 20th centuries. The Levi Grazioli bequest of ceramics, Italian majolica and wooden sculptures, a collection of paintings by locally-born Divisionist painter Angelo Morbelli, and the archaeological section displaying Bronze Age material found in the Monferrato, are also on display.

The **Palazzo Gozani di San Giorgio** (*Via Mameli 10*), built for the Gozani di San Giorgio family and rebuilt after 1775 for Count Filippo Nicolis de Robilant, is now the city hall. It has a three-tiered façade with stucco-framed windows and a monumental doorway surmounted by a balcony with a stone balustrade. In the courtyard, beneath a portico enclosed by a wrought-iron gate bearing the Gozani emblem, are busts of past mayors, by Leonardo Bistolfi, and a bronze tondo by his contemporary Odoardo Tabacchi. The first-floor state rooms are adorned with 18th-century frescoes by Francesco Lorenzi and Pietro Francesco Guala.

The **Palazzo Gozani di Treville** (*Via Mameli 29*), begun in 1710 by Giovanni Battista Scapitta and completed by his grandson Vincenzo for the Gozzani di Treville family, was considered particularly advanced for its time, a model for later residences in Casale. The Neoclassical façade was designed by the Vicentine architect Ottavio Bertotti Scamozzi. The palace is now the seat of several organisations, notably the Accademia Filarmonica.

Casale is the administrative centre of the ribbon-like **Parco Fluviale del Po e dell'Orba** (*visitor centre at Viale Lungo Po Antonio Gramsci 8/10*), where the Po first flows through a fairly tame landscape of low hills and flat rice fields, then enters wilder country, making sinuous loops and creating bars and islets of gravel as it goes. There are eight marked cycling trails along the river's banks, whose woodlands and gravel flats are home to numerous nesting birds and raptors. Nearly all the villages overlooking the river have splendid castles, most of which are now private homes.

SACRO MONTE DI CREA

This Marian shrine (*map D, A2*) stands at one of the highest points in the Monferrato hills. Built on the site of an earlier sanctuary, it was begun in 1589 by Prior Costantino Massino. It consists of 23 chapels built in two phases: the first in the 16th–17th centuries, the second in the 19th. With the exception of the first two, which are dedicated to St Eusebius, the chapels recount the life of Mary—with the kind of passionate exuberance that only popular religious feeling can achieve. The earlier chapels are particularly fine, with colourful frescoes (some by Moncalvo) and polychrome terracotta statues forming exquisite tableaux; the largest and most complex, the *Crowning of the Virgin* (or *Paradiso*) has more than 300 statues. *The Way to Calvary*, painted by the Symbolist Leonardo Bistolfi, is the best of the later chapels. On a clear day the view from the Sacro Monte over the Basso Monferrato and across the Po to the Alps is stunning.

The 47ha park surrounding the shrine offers some beautiful walks. The nature reserve is an ecological niche where certain plant species, such as wild saffron, have survived more than one glaciation. The hill's temperate south slope is covered with oak and manna trees, while the steeper and cooler north slope is forested mainly with elm, cherry, hornbeam, oak, chestnut, Norway maple and sycamore. The north slope also hosts some relict ice-age mountain species, such as Turk's cap lily, aconite and various orchids.

VIGNALE MONFERRATO

The name *Vinealis*, 'land of wine', makes its first appearance in a 12th-century document and effectively sums up the economic history of this charming town (*map D, A3*), set on a hill between the valleys of the Grana and Rotaldo. The 17th-century Palazzo Callori, approached by a great staircase, is the seat of an **Enoteca Regionale del Monferrato**, in whose tufa cellars you can taste the best local wines and grappas. Other important buildings are the 18th-century parish church of **San Bartolomeo**, from which there are marvellous views over the surrounding countryside, and the late Gothic church of the **Addolorata**, built for Marquis William VIII Palaeologus in 1470, with finely carved 16th-century choir stalls. The village is famous for its views, and for its summer dance festival (*Vignaledanza*, July), which draws companies from all over the world.

ACQUI TERME

Originally a settlement of the Ligurian Stazielli, in the 2nd century BC, Acqui Terme (*map D, B4*) was re-founded under the name of *Aquae Statiellae*. At the time it was an important stop on the road between the ports of Liguria and the Alpine passes, but it was also famous as a spa with sulphurous thermal waters (a large Roman bath has recently been discovered beneath the Nuove Terme, near the city centre), which the Romans mixed with fresh spring water brought in by the great arched aqueduct whose ruins can be seen on the south bank of the River Bòrmida di Spigno.

Acqui was the seat of a bishop as early as the 4th century. After 1277 it became the capital of the Alto Monferrato, first under the Anjou, then under the Visconti, Gonzaga and (after 1708) the Savoy. The city retains substantial traces of its historic heyday. The Castello dei Paleologi was built in the 11th century as the bishop's palace; two centuries later it became the seat of the marquis. Enlarged around 1480 and severely damaged in 1646 (by the Spanish) and 1746 (by the French), since the 1960s it has been the seat of the Civico Museo Archeologico (*acquimusei.it/il-museo*). The musem contains a wealth of material ranging from prehistory to the Renaissance. The effectively displayed, well-lighted exhibits include a fine collection of prehistoric stone and iron tools, numerous burial treasures and funerary stelae, a reconstruction of a Roman fountain, a large Roman mosaic, Lombard tomb finds and medieval polychrome ceramics.

The **cathedral** (Nostra Signora Assunta), consecrated in 1067 and rebuilt several times afterwards, retains several 13th-century Romanesque features, notably the transept, the brick campanile and three semicircular apses. The façade, with a large central portal of 1481, is preceded by a 17th-century portico on double columns. The five-aisled interior has finely carved Baroque wooden furnishings and a crypt with an aisled nave and transept and vaulted ceilings carried by slender columns. In the sacristy is the Madonna di Montserrat, a triptych by the 15th-century Spanish painter Bartolomé Bermejo. Attached to the church is the 14th-century cloister of the Canonica, with some Roman remains.

The **Palazzo Robellini** (*Piazza Levi 12*), built in the late 16th century and remodelled in the 18th century (when it was given its grand staircase and elaborate staterooms), today houses the municipal exhibition hall as well as the **Enoteca Regionale del Brachetto d'Acqui**, where you can taste Acqui's signature sparkling red wine.

The basilica of **San Pietro**, an Early Christian church extensively rebuilt by Bishop Primo in 989–1018, was later attached to a Benedictine abbey. The apse dates from the original 5th–6th-century edifice.

No visit to Acqui would be complete without a moment's pause before **La Bollente**, the hot spring that has become the symbol of the city, its steaming water constantly gushing forth beneath a little octagonal marble aedicule in the pretty, sloping piazza to which it gives its name. There are two spas in Acqui, the Nuove Terme, at the end of the main Via Giuseppe Saracco, connecting Piazza Italia with Piazza della Bollente (flanked by a contemporary fountain of cascading waters along Corso Vigano), and the Antiche Terme, across the Bormida.

AROUND ACQUI TERME

The **Villa Ottolenghi Wedekind** at Monterosso, 2km north of Acqui Terme, is unique among the many villas of the Monferrato, and famous for its gardens, which can be visited, along with the villa, on a guided tour by appointment (*villaottolenghiwedekind.com*). The modern architectural complex—which includes a house, two gardens, a block of artists' studios and a mausoleum—was begun in the 1920s and completed in the 1970s. The initial idea of Herta Von Wedekind and her husband Arturo Ottolenghi was to design a house and garden complex inspired by the great *ville all'antica* of the Renaissance. The architectural design was entrusted to Rationalist architects Federico d'Amato, Marcello Piacentini and Ernesto Rapisardi. The painter Ferruccio Ferrari was chosen for the interior décor and he also created the designs for the mosaics of the mausoleum. Arturo Martini made several large sculptures for the park—*The Lions of Monterosso, Tobias, Adam and Eve, The Dream*, the *Wounded She-wolf*—and about 80 smaller works, most of which are unfortunately no longer *in situ*. The artists involved in the project lived and worked in the studio block across the garden from the villa, an arcaded structure worthy of the Metaphysical painting of De Chirico. Work was suspended during the Second World War, but in 1955 Astolfo Ottolenghi, Herta and Arturo's son, asked the eminent landscape architect Pietro Porcinai to complete the garden begun by Giuseppe Vaccaro. Porcinai's design unified the previously separate areas of the property, creating the undulating lawn, the rock garden, the long flowerbed and the pergola between the villa and the artists' studios, and laying out the stunning skewed grid of grass, flowerbeds and stone echoing the design of Amerigo Tot's panoramic terrace overlooking the valley of Acqui. The villa is now a Relais de Charme, with fine rooms and a restaurant.

OTHER TOWNS OF THE ALTO MONFERRATO

In the hills east of Acqui Terme are several privately owned castles, opened for summer exhibitions and other special events (*details at castelliaperti.it*). **Morsasco castle**, dating originally from the 13th century, towers over the stone houses of its medieval *ricetto*, now a pretty village enjoying good views over the surrounding countryside. The Gothic Revival **castle of Trisobbio** is now a hotel and restaurant. **Prasco castle**, a 12th-century fortress rebuilt in the 19th century, has a 17th-century *neviera* (ice-house) in its park, for cold storage of food. The **Castello Malaspina** at Cremolino was built as a watch-tower in the 11th century and enlarged over time to become the large, elegant manor you see today; it is the highest of the Alto Monferrato and 14 of the area's 28 castles can be seen from its grounds. The little town of Molare boasts two aristocratic residences: **Castello Chiabrera** (or Gajoli Boidi) was built for Tommaso Malaspina before 1278, the year he moved the family seat to Cremolino. What you see today is a Gothic Revival creation of the 19th century, but a few original elements (notably the two towers, one square in plan, the other circular) can still be distinguished; the interior holds several paintings by Giuseppe Pellizza da Volpedo (*see pp. 145–6*). The Neoclassical **Palazzo Tornielli**, in the heart of the old town centre, has a spectacular staircase and handsome rooms with paintings by by Ignazio Tosi (1811–61).

OVADA

This pleasant small city (*map D, B4*) has strong ties with the history and culture of Liguria. Typically Ligurian are the sunny colours of the palaces and houses of the old town centre and the narrow streets they overlook, called *carrugi*, in the Genoese tradition. The local cuisine also layers the flavours of two regions: the typical products are ravioli and white truffles (Piedmont), focaccia and farinata (Liguria). At least one thing, however, is unique here, and distinctly local: Dolcetto di Ovada, the signature doc wine.

Ovada's main streets meet in front of the **church of the Assunta**, where there is a large painting of the *Ecstasy of St Theresa* by Luca Giordano. The little, striped **Oratorio della Santissima Trinità e di San Giovanni Battista**, the chapel of a confraternity established in the Middle Ages, holds a wooden crucifix by Domenico Bissoni and the wooden processional group representing the *Beheading of St John the Baptist* by Anton Maria Maragliano. Both are carried in procession every 24th June. Another processional sculpture by Maragliano (*Annunciation*) can be seen in the Oratoria della Santissima Annunziata.

The 14th-century church of Sant'Antonio houses the **Museo Paleontologico Giulio Maini** (*Via Sant'Antonio 17, museopaleontologicomaini.it*). The museum is named after the local naturalist who assembled the carefully researched and documented collection. There are numerous crustaceans, including a species of crab discovered by Maini, *Calappilia mainii*, as well as shellfish, corals and fossils of extinct warm-climate plants.

The **Loggia di San Sebastiano**, the oldest building in Ovada, is all that remains of the collegiate church built around the year 1000, where St Ambrose is said to have preached. An inscription on a stone at the base of the tower tells that the building was restored in 1391. By the late 18th century, however, it had deteriorated to the point that it was deconsecrated and turned into a covered market for fruit, vegetables and silk cocoons. It is now used for exhibitions and events.

TAGLIOLO MONFERRATO AND ROCCA GRIMALDA

The hills of Ovada are speckled with castles much like those around Acqui Terme. At **Tagliolo Monferrato** (*map D, B4*), the Castello Pinelli Gentile dates from 967, although the present building was constructed largely in the 16th and 17th centuries. It was restored in the Gothic Revival style in the late 19th century and again in 1931; the vineyards produce the excellent Castello di Tagliolo wines, sold on the premises. At **Rocca Grimalda** (*map D, B4*), the old Malaspina fortress (of which a cylindrical 14th-century tower remains) was made into a comfortable country house by the Genoese Grimaldi family in the 18th century; it is they who built the little chapel of Santa Limbiana, decorated with *trompe l'œil* paintings. The lovely park has a formal Italian garden with beds of herbs and flowers and trees trimmed with meticulous precision, and a larger Romantic garden.

GAVI

The Gavi area (*map D, C4*), on the right bank of the Torrente Lemme at its confluence with the Rio Neirone, is best known for its white wine made from the Cortese grape, a docg since 1998. Winemakers here also make good Dolcetto and Barbera reds; all go well with the local cuisine, which, like that of Ovada, reflects the influence of Liguria.

No one knows just when the imposing **Forte di Gavi** (*closed for restoration at the time of writing*) was established, as there are several oral traditions and few supporting documents. It seems reasonable to suppose that some sort of fortification stood on the cliffs above Gavi even in pre-Roman times. The first written evidence dates from 973, after which the fort was rebuilt several times, most notably in 1540 by Giovanni Maria Olgiati, a military engineer in the service of the Republic of Genoa. Another flurry of rebuilding in the 17th and 18th centuries transformed Olgiati's fort into the mighty fortress of today: the enceinte was redesigned to withstand the assaults of modern artillery; outside, to the east, the Monte Moro redoubt was built, connected to the main fortifications by a tunnel; inside, barracks for the garrison and its officers, cisterns, powder magazines, guardhouses and parade grounds were constructed.

During the Napoleonic wars it was the only French fortress in Italy not to capitulate to the Austro-Russian army before Napoleon's victory at Marengo (14th

June 1800); nevertheless, in 1859 Vittorio Emanuele II decommissioned the fort and recast it as a prison—first for common criminals, then, during the First World War, for prisoners of war and deserters. In the interlude between the First and Second World Wars, experimental vines were planted within its walls by the Italian anti-phylloxera consortium. With the onset of the Second World War the fortress again became a place of detention, initially for English prisoners and then, after 8th Sept 1943, for Italians. In 1946 the fort passed to the Piedmontese authority for environmental and architectural heritage, which now looks after its fabric.

The most important monument in the historic centre of Gavi is the Romanesque **church of San Giacomo**, with a sculpted portal on the west front, a door with fragmentary 14th-century frescoes and weather-worn Romanesque reliefs on the north side, and a lantern with mullioned windows, enlarged in the Baroque period. Inside are a panel painting of the *Madonna and Child with Saints* by Gandolfino d'Asti and a small statue of the Madonna and Child by Francesco Schiaffino.

A 15-minute drive southeast of the town, on the border between Piedmont and Liguria, is **Voltaggio** (*map D, C4*), where the secluded Capuchin monastery (*Via Provinciale 1, pinacotecadivoltaggio.it*) holds an astonishingly good collection of 15th–18th-century paintings by artists from Liguria, Piedmont and Lombardy. The collection was put together in the 19th century by Father Pietro Repetto da Voltaggio and includes paintings by Luca Cambiaso, Domenico Fiasella, Giovanni Benedetto Castiglione (Grechetto), Sinibaldo Scorza, Bernardo Strozzi, Augine Bombelli, Mattia Preti, Paolo Pagani, and wood sculptures by Anton Maria Maragliano.

SERRAVALLE SCRIVIA

A crossroads between Genoa, Turin and Milan, Serravalle (*map D, C4*) welcomes thousands of visitors each year to the largest outlet mall in Europe, a New Urbanism 'village' where one can shop endlessly in a meticulously created replica of an 18th-century town. This is one of many outlet malls in Europe commissioned by the British McArthurGlen Group to be 'architecturally-designed retail environments that elevate the shopping experience'. Demand for this kind of structure is high: the firm has recently reported an increase in turnover in all major centres as well as an increase in non-European customers.

The **Area Archeologica di Libarna** (*map D, C4; libarna.al.it*), one of the most important archaeological sites in Piedmont, in contrast, is almost always deserted. By the river, midway between Serravale and Arquata Scriva, it was found by chance during construction of the Strada Regia dei Giovi and the Turin–Genoa railway in the early 19th century. It has been excavated to reveal some major public buildings and much of the street plan of the Imperial-era Roman city. There are private homes, a forum, a bath complex, two city gates, an amphitheatre, and (across the railway tracks) a theatre believed to have seated nearly 4,000 spectators. The area is planted as a park, with neatly kept lawns and shady cypress trees, the ruins rarely rising more than a metre above the grass. Some of the finds are displayed in the library of the Palazzo Comunale in Serravalle.

NOVI LIGURE

Once you get past its busy industrial outskirts, Novi (*map D, C4*) is a very pleasant town with a low-key, country feel. The historic centre is a delightful place to stroll around. There are no breathtaking monuments here, just an extraordinary abundance of colourful old palaces, some with frescoed façades, built when Novi was a possession of Genoa, and exuberant Baroque churches overlooking cobbled streets or quiet little squares. This is not to say there is no good reason to visit Novi. In fact there are at least four: chocolate, nougat, the delicate little *canestrelli* biscuits, and white truffles—and if you are at all interested in cycling, there is a fifth: the town is the birthplace of Costante Girardengo (1893–1978) and Fausto Coppi (1919–60) was an honorary citizen. The city has dedicated the **Museo dei Campionissimi** to the two competitive cycling champions. The museum, which occupies some 3000 sq m in a former factory on the town's northwest outskirts (*Viale dei Campionissimi, T: 0143 322634*), traces the history of the bicycle and bicycle racing and is also the best place to go for information on cycling in the area.

BOSCO MARENGO

This village (*map D, B3*) on the lowlands by the Torrente Orba is known for its Renaissance convent of Santa Croce, located at the north edge of the historic centre. The complex was commissioned by the Dominican Michele Ghislieri, the only native of Piedmont to be elected Pope (as Pius V, in 1566), and was intended as his burial place. The church is one of the earliest examples of Counter-Reformation architecture inspired by the Council of Trent, and its severe simplicity faithfully reflects the pope's own character. Inside are two colourful and dramatic paintings by Giorgio Vasari (*Adoration of the Magi* and *Martyrdom of St Peter*), both dated 1566 and made for *macchine* (decorative, quasi-architectural surrounds) that are no longer extant. The church also holds finely carved wood choir stalls and, in the side chapels, works by Moncalvo and Lombard painters. Pius V was canonised in 1712. His tomb is in Santa Maria Maggiore in Rome.

SEZZADIO

On the southern edge of this peaceful farming town (*map D, B3*) is one of the most important medieval monuments of Piedmont: the **Abbazia di Santa Giustina**. A church was founded on this site in 722 by the Lombard king Liutprand; in 1030 Otbert, Marquis of Sezzadio, added the Benedictine abbey, whose prestige grew steadily until the 12th century and then declined. First it was assigned to the abbots of Sant'Ambrogio in Milan; then, during the Napoleonic period, the buildings and farms were confiscated, broken up, and distributed to Napoleonic veterans. In 1863, what remained of the complex was purchased by the locally eminent Frascara family, who made it into a country house called L'Abbadia. It was restored in the 20th century and is now an events venue known as Villa Badia. You can see the Romanesque-Gothic church, with an imposing brick façade and a three-aisled interior with 15th-century vaulted ceiling and fragmentary frescoes in the apse, and part of the abbey. The remarkable three-aisled crypt preserves a beautiful mosaic floor dating from the 11th century and bearing an inscription that recalls Otbert as its founder.

ASTI

Asti (*map D, A3*), on the left bank of the Tanaro, was founded by the Romans as *Hasta Pompeia*. It was an important market town in the 13th century and became a possession of the house of Savoy after 1532. In 1558 Emanuele Filiberto of Savoy gave the community a small medieval building next to the collegiate church of San Secondo in order to move the Town Hall there, so that it would be close to the market square, the commercial heart of the city. In 1727 the medieval building was completely redesigned by Benedetto Alfieri to make the **Palazzo Municipale** (*Piazza San Secondo 1*), which originally included temporary stores for merchants and a covered cattle market, as well as public offices

One block north of the long, central Corso Alfieri, the **Torre Troyana** (*Piazza Medici*), or clock tower, affords an excellent vantage point for viewing the city from above. It was erected in the late 12th century and acquired by the Troya family in the mid-13th century. It was completed between 1250 and 1280, when the upper battlements were added. Throughout the 19th century its bell rang out the hours and signalled the opening of schools and the closing of shops. A staircase of 199 steps climbs to the top of the battlements. The bell, which still marks the passage of time, is one of the oldest in Piedmont.

THE CATHEDRAL

Overlooking a quiet square at the western end of the Recinto dei Nobili, the oldest part of the city, Asti's cathedral of **Santa Maria Assunta** is the largest church in Piedmont and the most important example of Gothic architecture west of Milan. Originally built in the Lombard-Romanesque style, in the early 14th century it was rebuilt in spectacularly vertical Gothic forms. The cathedral is entered by door in the south flank, preceded by an elaborate porch. In the late 17th century, the interior was renovated in the spirit of the Counter-Reformation; the Milan-born Venetian painter Federico Cervelli was summoned to paint the frescoes with stories from the life of the Virgin. The floral decoration of the interior dates from the 18th century, as does the imposing marble altar by Benedetto Alfieri.

The **Museo Diocesano San Giovanni** (*Piazza Cattedrale, museo.sicdat.it*) occupies the nave and crypt of the church of San Giovanni, the city's first cathedral. The early Christian building probably dates from the 6th century but was rebuilt several times: after Countess Adelaide of Susa burned the city to the ground in 1070, and again in the 15th century, when Archdeacon Giacomo de Gentis reversed the orientation, destroying the apse and part of the crypt; the cross-vaults and their decorations were added in the 19th century. The visit consists of a very interesting archeological walk through the Roman and early medieval remains beneath the cathedral square, revealing the foundations of the first cathedral of Santa Maria Assunta, which like San Giovanni seems to date from the 6th century. Baldino di Surso's beautifully carved choir stalls from the cathedral (1477) have been installed here, and there are also collections of liturgical silver and fabric, and temporary exhibitions of contemporary art.

MUSEUMS ALONG CORSO ALFIERI

Asti's main street is the long Corso Vittorio Alfieri, extending the whole length of the town. At its western end, the Torre San Secondo (*Corso Alfieri 426*), a Romanesque tower on a Roman base, serves as bell tower for the **church of Santa Caterina** (1773). A popular legend has it that San Secondo, patron saint of Asti, was imprisoned here before his execution in AD 119.

The **Museo Paleontologico Territoriale dell'Astigiano e del Monferrato** (*Corso Alfieri 381, astipaleontologico.it*) has fossils and skeletons of whales and dolphins dating from the Pleiocene (5 to 2 million years ago), when the entire Po Valley was covered by the sea. Some of these finds are very important: the Valmontasca Whale, found in 1959 near Vigliano d'Asti, is perhaps the most complete example of its kind, whereas the Tersilla Whale of San Marzanotto d'Asti is the only representative of its species.

The **Museo Alfieriano** (*Corso Alfieri 375; closed Mon, T: 530403*) is the house museum of Asti's favourite son, the poet and dramatist Vittorio Alfieri (1749–1803). As an orphan, Vittorio was entrusted to his cousin and guardian Benedetto Alfieri, the first royal architect of Vittorio Amedeo II of Savoy, who took him into his home in this medieval building. The museum also houses several mementos and curiosities collected by Alfieri's long-time lover Louise, Countess of Albany, the wife of Bonnie Prince Charlie the Young Pretender. The pair had met in Florence and remained faithful to each other until Alfieri's death.

The **Cripta e Museo di Sant'Anastasio** (*Palazzo del Collegio, Corso Alfieri 365/a, museidiasti.com/cripta-di-santanastasio*) is an archaeological site and museum rolled into one. The west wing presents a fascinating layering of archaeological remains, all connected with the church of Sant'Anastasio, demolished in 1907. Constructed in the 8th century as part of an influential Benedictine nunnery, the church was enlarged and rebuilt up until the 17th century; some remains of the early church are still clearly distinguishable in the ruins. The most interesting and best preserved element is the crypt, a basilican edifice with three aisles beneath cross vaults. Its 11th-century builders reused Roman and early medieval columns and capitals, unlike the masons of the later extensions to the east and west, who fashioned new sandstone columns and capitals. Near the crypt are fragmentary Roman pavements, traces of late antique houses, 8th–10th-century tombs, the foundations of the façade of Sant'Anastasio, remains of the 11th-century and 12th-century churches and a wall of the 17th-century edifice. The convent is documented since 1008, though it was probably founded in the Lombard period. Suppressed by the Napoleonic government in 1802, it was for centuries a centre of economic and political power, being one of the largest landowners in the area and closely allied with the aristocracy of Asti, from whose ranks the abbess usually came. The east wing of the museum preserves stone elements belonging to Sant'Anastasio and its neighbourhood, dating mainly from the 8th–17th centuries.

Palazzo Mazzetti (*Corso Alfieri 357*) was the home of a family of noble origins that made its fortune by managing the mint, as well as by making shrewd real-estate purchases. The building occupies the site of the fortified house of the Del Turco, bought by the Mazzetti in 1442 and joined with the medieval buildings purchased by

Marquis Giovanni Battista Mazzetti after 1693. In 1751–2 the architect Benedetto Alfieri planned the east wing and the renovation of the façade. James Stuart, pretender to the throne of England, stayed here, as did the Prince of Piedmont and future king Carlo Emanuele III, and Napoleon. Since 2011 Palazzo Mazzetti has been home to the **Museo Civico e Pinacoteca** (*museidiasti.com/palazzo-mazzetti*), which combines the palace's lavishly decorated period rooms with collections of paintings and sculptures assembled in the 19th and 20th centuries. Here you'll find old-master paintings, early Modern art, Asian ivories, lacquer work, armour and porcelain, and antique fabrics and garments, all impeccably displayed. The highlight of the collection is the fascinating collection of micro-sculptures by the locally-born cabinet-maker Giuseppe Maria Bonzanigo (1745–1820). Bonzanigo made the tribune, organ and tabernacle for the church of San Rocco and all the woodwork for Asti's synagogue, including the magnificent *aron*, before being appointed court cabinet-maker to Vittorio Amedeo III in 1787. Everything in this collection is magnificent; some pieces (*Three Graces*, early 19th century) are truly minuscule.

The little **Museo del Risorgimento** (*Corso Alfieri 350; T: 0141 399555*) occupies the elegant grey-and-white Palazzo Ottolenghi. Multimedia aids inform visitors without being intrusive, and the material itself is nicely displayed and well lit. In addition to paintings, documents, flags, weapons and various memorabilia, the museum includes a meticulously restored Second World War air-raid shelter in the sub-basement, and educational displays in the rooms of the first underground level telling the story of the city in the First and Second World Wars. The palace originally belonged to the Gabutti family, who hired Benedetto Alfieri in 1754 to make a single large residence from two adjoining houses. Today it bears the name of Asti's wealthiest Jewish family, who acquired it in 1851 and completely renovated the main floor, giving it the décor you see today. In 1932 the Ottolenghi donated it to the city, which used it initially as the seat of the prefecture.

Asti's 18th-century **synagogue** (*Via Ottolenghi 8; just off Corso Alfieri*) may be the least impressive of the four major temples of Piedmont (the others are in Turin, Casale Monferrato and Alessandria), but it is the only one with an *aron* crafted by Giuseppe Maria Bonzanigo (1809). The eight delicately carved and gilded panels represent symbolic subjects—a menorah, the ark of the covenant, a table with the twelve loaves of the Presence, an altar with flame, a censer, vessels with holy water, fruit, and a hand pouring purifying water from a jug into a basin. The **Museo Ebraico** (*open Sept–July by appointment i; T: 0141 399466*) occupies what was once the winter temple, next to the synagogue. The museum displays liturgical objects and books dating from the 14th century onward.

PIAZZA ALFIERI AND SAN PIETRO

The **Casa Littoria e Palazzo del Governo** (*Piazza Alfieri*), was built as the seat of the Fascist Party and municipal offices to designs by Ottorino Aloisio in 1933–4. Aloisio's Rationalist design was praised for its 'modern clarity of conception and harmony of masses, which give the whole work Italian power of expression and monumentality'. The complex, divided into two parts—the Casa Littoria and Palazzo del Governatore—was left unfinished at the outbreak of the war. Only the Casa Littoria was completed, the part on Piazza Alfieri being added later by Mario Passanti as the seat of the Province of Asti. The building you see today was finished in 1961. Aloisio's design divided the complex into two parts around a large trapezoidal courtyard. To the Casa Littoria, with its 'M' (for Mussolini) footprint dominated by a triangular tower, corresponds the more massive volume of the Palazzo del Governatore, facing Piazza Alfieri. Passanti chose a different strategy, using ordinary materials to give his building an anti-rhetorical, 'civic' character.

The **Complesso di San Pietro e Musei Paleontologico e Archeologico** (*Corso Alfieri 2, museidiasti.com/complesso-di-san-pietro*) includes two centrally-planned buildings—a church and a chapel—and a cloister and priory. From the 12th century until 1798 the complex belonged to the Knights of St John of Jerusalem. The round church was built between 1110 and 1130. Its original dedication to the Holy Sepulchre and its form make it one of the most significant examples of churches constructed in imitation of the rotunda of the Holy Sepulchre of Jerusalem, built in the 4th century over the burial place of Christ. The Cappella Valperga, a perfect square, was built between 1446 and 1467 and preserves 15 panes of the central window and carved-mask corbels from which the vault ribs spring. All the terracotta decorations are attributed to Francesco Filiberti of Alessandria. The cloister, with cylindrical columns and cross vaults, took on its present appearance only in the 15th century. The appearance of the priory is largely the result of a restoration of 1930–1. The premises house archaeological and paleontological museums. The latter has a collection of fossil shells from the Valle Andona and Valle Botto; the first, a rich collection of Egyptian materials, prehistoric metals, Greek and Etruscan ceramics, and numerous Roman remains.

The **Domus Romana** (*Via del Varrone 30, off Corso Alfieri; museidiasti.com/domus-romana*) preserves remains of a dwelling belonging to the ancient Roman Hasta, precursor of modern Asti. Sections of 1st–2nd-centuruy mosaic floor are preserved.

OUTSKIRTS OF ASTI

The former Certosa di Valmanera, an old monastery on the outskirts of Asti, is the charming home of a 'high warp' tapestry museum and workshop, and for the cleaning and restoration of antique tapestries. In the **Museo degli Arazzi Scassa** (*Via dell'Arazzeria 60, arazzeriascassa.it*) you can admire tapestries by Joan Miró, Giorgio de Chirico, Vassily Kandinsky, Felice Casorati, Mario Sironi and other modern masters. During the visit you can learn the secrets of the high warp, which is the noblest form of tapestry weaving, and also the most time-consuming and expensive: to weave one square meter with this technique requires, on average, 500 hours of labour.

The **park of Villa Badoglio** (at San Marzanotto, 6km south of Asti) covers 30,000 sq m and slopes down from the crest of the hill towards the north. The park's interest derives not only from its exceptional size but also from its botanical value, both for the monumental size of certain trees and the overall variety of its flora. The 18th-century villa was enlarged and radically altered in the final years of the 19th century. The park took on its present form at the same time.

Located 8km west of Asti, at Valleandona, the **Riserva Naturale Speciale Valle Andona, Val Botto e Valle Grande** is one of the few nature reserves in Italy to protect paleontological heritage. These places preserve fossils dating back to the Pleiocene age (5–2 million years ago) in sedimentary strata along the valley walls—geological memories of when the sea occupied the Po Valley right up to the Alps. Among the fossils that have come to light are hundreds of species of molluscs, brachiopods, corals, echinoids, and arthropods, and a few skeletal remains of marine mammals. In addition, a 7m-long fossilised whale has been discovered in an area adjacent to the reserve. Vineyards once covered the hillsides, but lately forests have taken over.

OTHER TOWNS OF THE MONFERRATO ASTIGIANO

CALOSSO
Calosso (*map D, A4*) extends along a ridgetop surrounded by vineyards and cereal crops. Its castle, over which the Roero di Cortanze family held title in the 14th century, retains certain features typical of 16th century fortresses (gun ports and loopholes) on the north side, but the rest of the complex was made over in the late 17th century as an elegant country mansion. The parish church of San Martino probably dates from the 12th century, though it was enlarged in the late 17th century and is now Baroque in appearance.

CANELLI
This (*map D, A4*) is one of the most widely renowned winemaking centres in Piedmont. The profound influence of viticulture and œnology is evident everywhere—in the landscape, economy, history and the life of the community. Canelli's signature wine is Asti Spumante, the delicately aromatic sparkling white, and the local growers have created a fascinating introduction to their produce—a walk from cellar to cellar, embracing no fewer than 13km of brick and stone chambers in the tufa beneath the city. You can easily spend hours in the historic Bosca, Gancia, Contratto and Coppo cellars. Barrels and casks, and racks and racks of bottles, are meticulously aligned beneath magnificent brick or stone vaults, connected here and there by narrow tunnels. The four **Cantine Storiche—Cattedrali Sotterranee** are open on consecutive Sundays (each on a different Sun), or by appointment (*for information, visit canellieventi.it*).

The historic town centre clings to the hillside at the foot of its castle, built to defend the trade route from Asti to the sea, and refined over time to make the aristocratic palace you see today. The castle is now owned by the Gancia family of winemakers, who have gone to great lengths to bring the Italian garden back to life, and established a small museum.

NIZZA MONFERRATO
Built around the abbey of San Giovanni in Lanero in the early 1200s, Nizza (*map D, A3*) has a long history. Its tumultuous past ranges from the feudal struggles of the 13th–18th centuries to the dramatic experience of the wartime Resistance. Farming

has always been the main economic resource: the city is now a major centre for the production of the highly prized Nizza wine (a Barbera d'Asti Superiore produced in a very restricted area), and the Nizza cardoon, treated locally with the respect reserved elsewhere for truffles and called the *spadone* because of the sword-like shape of its leaf and stem. These and other local products are presented periodically in the specialised markets and food and wine events held at the **Foro Boario**, a long brick loggia of the 19th century covered with a truss roof carried on round arches, on the wooded Piazza Garibaldi.

The **Palazzo Comunale** (*Piazza Martiri d'Alessandria 19*) was built in the 14th century, its crenellated tower originally a fortification. On Via Pio Corsi is the **Palazzo Crova di Vaglio**, a fine 18th-century aristocratic residence designed by Giovanni Battista Nicolis Robilant with a brick façade and narrow ground-floor portico. On the north façade botanic and anthropomorphic friezes act as string courses and ornaments for windows.

MASIO

From this hill town (*map D, A3*) overlooking the Tanaro, the Percorso Naturalistico della Poiana winds its way through vineyards, over hills and along ancient farmers' paths. From almost everywhere you can see the 13th-century tower, some 30m high, that was part of the town's extensive fortifications and is now a national monument. Inside is the museum, called simply **La Torre e il Fiume** (*latorreeilfiume.it*), presenting the history, culture and environment of the Tanaro Valley. The displays tell the story of the tower of Masio and of the great towers of Piedmont generally. The view from the little terrace at the top is breathtaking. The Gothic church of San Dalmazzo and the medieval castle of Redabue, a short distance from the village, are also interesting.

WINE COUNTRY PRACTICAL TIPS

GETTING AROUND

- **By bus:** The main companies serving the region are GTT (linking it to Turin; *gtt.to.it*), Bus Company (*buscompany.it*), Benese (*benese.it*) and Gunetto (*gunettoautolinee.it*).
- **By rail:** A fast regional service (change at Cavallermaggiore) connects Turin (Porta Nuova) and Alba (1hr 27mins) via Bra (59mins). There are also rail services to Asti.

WHERE TO STAY

ALFIANO NATTA (*map D, A2*)
€€ **Castello di Razzano**. On a beautiful estate in one of the most picturesque corners of the Monferrato, this 17th-century manor offers elegantly furnished suites consisting of sitting room and bedroom, bathroom and balcony. There is a spectacular cellar producing excellent wines, and an in-house wine museum. Even the pool is surrounded by vineyards. The

landscape is exquisite in all seasons, and in summer the sun sets behind Monviso. *Strada Gessi 2, Frazione Casarello, castellodirazzano.it.*

BAROLO (*map C, D1*)
€ **La Giolitta**. The Volpi family's, cosy, tasteful B&B in the heart of the village where Piedmont's finest wine is made offers three simple but comfortable rooms. The atmosphere is warm and informal and the breakfast buffet provides the ideal flavours (and calories) for a tough day of touring. The lovely 19th-century house is just a few steps from the Falletti castle. *Via Cesare Battisti 13, lagiolitta.it.*

CANELLI (*map D, A4*)
€€ **I Tre Poggi**. A wonderfully peaceful biodynamic farm with pool and wellness centre. The restaurant (closed Wed) strikes a perfect balance between innovation and tradition. The flavours are traditional: dishes from Piedmont and the Langhe, Roero and Monferrato are paired with biodynamic wines from the farm's own cellars and from other regional vintners. *Regione Merlini 22, itrepoggi.it.*

CHERASCO (*map C, D1*)
€€ **Campanile della Veglia di Cherasco**. Before becoming a hotel, this Rococo convent was known as *il palazzo delle anime*, the 'palace of souls', and there is certainly something spiritual about it. Far from the hustle and bustle (but near historic sites of great interest), it is quiet and peaceful. Several of the 15 rooms have antique furniture, some dating back to the time of the convent's foundation. The restaurant, offering *cuisine du terroir*, occupies several small rooms, which keeps the noise level delightfully low. In chilly weather, a fire crackles away in one of the dining rooms. *Frazione Veglia 56, hotelilcampanile.com.*

CIOCCARO DI PENANGO (*map D, A2*)
€€€ **Relais Sant'Uffizio**. This large farm was once a possession of the Holy Office—the Supreme Sacred Congregation of the Roman and Universal Inquisition, created in 1542 by Pope Paul III—and the 17th-century villa was the residence of the Dominican Inquisitor of Casale. Now the stately brick palace and the farm buildings at its foot host elegant rooms and suites, a fine restaurant and a spa, all in one of the most gorgeous locations in the Monferrato. There is also a beautiful formal garden. *Strada del Sant'Uffizio 1, relaissantuffizio.com.*

COSTIGLIOLE D'ASTI (*map D, A3*)
€€ **Villa Pattono**. Costigliole d'Asti is home to the Barbera wine auctions and the Italian Culinary Institute for Foreigners (offering courses for professionals and amateurs)—which means the focus here is very much on food and wine. This neo-medieval manor 3km west of the village has 13 elegantly furnished rooms and suites, many with private terraces and frescoed walls or ceilings. The villa was sited to enjoy stunning views and furnished with a wooded park to ensure privacy, on the side facing the village. There is no restaurant (but there is no lack of good restaurants in nearby Costigliole and Canelli). Wellness area and an impressive cellar (at La Morra) selling estate-grown wines. *Strada Drotte, Frazione Annunziata, villapattono.com.*

DOGLIANI (map C, D2)
€€ **Poderi Luigi Einaudi**. The family estate of economist, academic and president of the Italian Republic Luigi Einaudi (1874–1961), this beautiful winery is one of the most pleasant places to stay in southern Piedmont. The décor is elegant and restrained, the welcome is warm and genuine, and the food and wines are superb (guests can request a personal chef). *Cascina Tecc, Borgata Gombe 31, relaiseinaudi.com.*

FRASSINELLO MONFERRATO (map D, A3)
€ **Castello di Frassinello**. A farming town, Frassinello is dominated by the castle of the Counts Sacchi Nemours, a brick-and-sandstone Gothic Revival edifice (very popular for weddings; check when you book) built over a fortress of the 11th century. The interior retains many of its Baroque and Rococo decorations, including colourful *trompe-l'œil* frescoes and exuberant stuccoes. The guest rooms, arranged around the sitting room and library, have period furniture and, in some cases, frescoed ceilings; there is also an apartment with its own kitchen in the Gothic Revival Fioriera. The area is famous for the production of Barbera and Grignolino. *Via Garibaldi 1. T: 338 907 9406, castellodifrassinello.it.*

GABIANO (map D, A2)
€€ **Castello di Gabiano**. Built in the 13th century, then destroyed in the 17th, this immense castle was rebuilt in the Gothic Revival style by Alfredo d'Andrade in the early 20th century. Today it is one of the most beautiful in Piedmont. Its position, dominating the village of Gabiano on the right bank of the Po, is made even more dramatic by the vineyards that surround it on three sides, producing excellent wines. The castle park holds one of the few labyrinths to be seen in the historic gardens of Piedmont. *Via San Defendente 2, castellodigabiano.com.*

GUARENE (map C, D1)
€€€€ **Castello di Guarene**. Built in 1726 by Count Carlo Giacinto Roero over an austere fortress of the 13th century, this majestic palace is a paragon of Baroque elegance. Designed personally by Count Carlo Giacinto in a style strongly resembling that of Filippo Juvarra, it has a rectangular plan with two lateral wings that project into the garden. The interior is equally magnificent, its rooms richly furnished with antiques. The garden is on two levels. The upper, laid out in the formal Italian manner, occupies an artificial plateau surrounding the building on three sides. The lower level, facing the Tanaro Valley, has low hedges of hornbeam around symmetrically arranged beds of different shapes. The 12 large rooms are regal in atmosphere, and the spa features a swimming pool in a natural cave. *Via Alessandro Roero 2, castellodiguarene.com.*

MOMBARUZZO (map D, B3–B4)
€€ **La Villa**. Mombaruzzo is a small village known for its narrow lanes, Renaissance portals and spectacular views. This refined hotel in the countryside 4km west occupies a 17th-century villa that has been painstakingly restored by an English couple who have gone to great lengths to preserve original floors and ceilings, beginning with those of the impressive vaulted wine cellar. Amenities include an excellent restaurant, a pool, a

rooftop terrace—even a small library, where you can wile away the hours. *Frazione Casalotto, Via Torino 7, lavillahotel.net.*

MONCALVO (*map D, A2*)
€€ **Spinerola**. A lovely 18th-century villa on a hilltop overlooking the village of Moncalvo, at once a sophisticated small hotel and a working farm. The pool commands one of the best views in southern Piedmont. *Strada Casale 15, Località Berna, en.cascinaspinerola.it.*

NIZZA MONFERRATO (*map D, A3*)
€€ **Casa Isabella**. This small B&B offers four beautifully furnished rooms in an old farmhouse on the crest of a hill at Vaglio Serra, 5km north of Nizza Monferrato, with forests on one side and vineyards on the other. It is the creation of two smart young professionals from Turin—Monica, an architect and designer, and Alessandro, an IT specialist—whose dream it was to create an island of sophistication in the countryside. The rooms are large and airy; the furniture ranges from Art Deco to Liberty (the Italian Art Nouveau) and contemporary, and colours are warm and captivating. Monica prepares delicious dinners, and breakfast is served in the garden, weather permitting. *Via La Pietra 5, casa-isabella.com.*

NOVI LIGURE (*map D, C4*)
€€ **Tenuta La Marchesa**. Surrounded by vineyards and woods, this historic home has 12 rooms with antique furniture, a swimming pool, restaurant, formal garden, fruit orchard and herb garden. The estate covers 76ha, 58 of which are planted with grapes—making it today, as in the 18th century when it was established, one of the largest vineyards in the Gavi district. The atmosphere makes it a perfect place to relax—as you stroll out to the little lake 10mins away from the house (thick with flowering waterlilies in summer) or while sipping extraordinary wines in the garden. *Via Gavi 87, tenutalamarchesa.it.*

OVADA (*map D, B4*)
€€ **Villa Schella**. The three rooms in this delightful B&B are in the frescoed orangery of the Belle Epoque villa at the centre of a large, wooded park in suburban Ovada. The décor is at once elegant and informal, and breakfast is served in the light-filled winter garden. The park is a listed monument with many tall old trees, including a 200-year-old cedar of Lebanon, and there is a secluded pool on a hilltop amid the vineyards. Breakfast is continental. *Via per Molare 8, villaschella.net.*

ROCCA GRIMALDA (*map D, B4*)
€€ **Castello di Rocca Grimalda**. This castle on a rocky spur was built to control the road between Liguria and the Alessandria plain. The oldest part is the cylindrical tower, dating from the 12th and 13th centuries. The Genoese Grimaldi family bought the castle in 1570 and lived there for 200 years, adding the Classical west façade. Today the Rocca is a charming B&B offering four large, comfortable rooms and apartments furnished with family heirlooms. Breakfast is continental. There is no pool, but the recently restored gardens (there are three: a formal Italian garden, a wooded Romantic garden and a secret garden with culinary and medicinal herbs) are

so lovely, it won't be missed. *Piazza Borgatta 2, castelloroccagrimalda.it.*

SANTO STEFANO BELBO (*map D, A4*)
€€€€ **Relais San Maurizio**. The view from this hilltop location takes in all of the surrounding landscape. Founded as a monastery in 1619 by the Franciscans, who held it until 1802, this luxury spa resort retains as much as possible of the original architectural structure. The public areas are frescoed, as are several of the 36 rooms and suites; 10 rooms have private gardens. The restaurant is one of the finest in Piedmont; it overlooks the flower garden, with summer dining outdoors. The historic park enjoys a special microclimate that enables Mediterranean arbutus and olive, and Alpine firs, larches and beeches to grow alongside the native elms and oaks. There is an immense swimming pool, and the heart of the very impressive spa is the Grotta del Sale, a natural cleft in the rock where the monks of San Maurizio established detoxifying salt baths centuries ago with salt brought from Sardinia. *Località San Maurizio 39, relaissanmaurizio.it.*

TAGLIOLO MONFERRATO (*map D, B4*)
€€ **Castello di Tagliolo**. There was a fortress on this hilltop dominating Ovada and the Orba Valley at the end of the first millennium; over the centuries it changed hands several times, belonging to the Genoese Spinola and Doria families, the Republic of Genoa, the Duke of Milan, and the Spanish Crown, among others. It has been in the family of the Pinelli Gentile, Marquis of Tagliolo, since 1750 and is now home to one of the finest wineries in southern Piedmont. The castle was renovated in a Gothic Revival style by Alfredo d'Andrade in the 19th century, but the *borgo* at its foot has retained its medieval air. Restoration has produced five large suites here, all with direct access to the castle garden. *Via Castello 1, castelloditagliolo.it.*

WHERE TO EAT

ACQUI TERME (*map D, B4*)
€-€€ **I Caffi**. On the first floor of the former Palazzo Comunale, an elegant gourmet restaurant occupies the frescoed mayor's room and offers the finest traditional Piedmontese cuisine. Michelin-starred. Dinner only Tues–Sat, lunch only on Sun. *Via Scatilazzi 15, icaffi.it.*

ALBA (*map C, D1*)
€€-€€€ **La Piola & Piazza Duomo**. La Piola and Piazza Duomo are two restaurants under one roof, in Alba's central Piazza Risorgimento. La Piola is an informal *trattoria* offering traditional regional dishes, with the menu written up on a chalkboard. There is outside seating on the piazza, and the souvenir plates are designed by contemporary artists (John Baldassari, Kiki Smith, among others). Upstairs, at Piazza Duomo, Enrico Crippa offers creative cuisine in a candy-pink dining room. Piazza Duomo has three Michelin stars. *Piazza Risorgimento 4. lapiola-alba.it and piazzaduomoalba.it.*
€€ **Locanda del Pilone**. A charming inn and prestigious restaurant in a meticulously restored old farmhouse surrounded by Barbera and Dolcetto vineyards, 5km from Alba. The inn has period furniture and lots of charm. In

the restaurant, chef Federico Gallo, a native of Turin, concocts gourmet marvels. *Strada della Cicchetta/Località Madonna di Como 34, locandadelpilone.com.*

€ **Osteria dell'Arco**. Renowned for its warm friendly atmosphere and excellent, creatively prepared regional cuisine, Osteria dell'Arco was born as an *enoteca* and has an excellent wine list. Conveniently set beneath the arcades of Alba's central Piazza Savona, it offers a high standard of service and great food. Closed Sun except in Oct–Nov. *Piazza Savona 5, boccondivinoslow.it.*

BENEVELLO (*map C, D1*)
€€€ **Villa d'Amelia**. It takes time to reach this restaurant deep in the hills of the Alta Langa (unless you're staying at the attached luxury hotel), but it's well worth the trouble. The young chef Dennis Cesco cut his teeth in multiple-Michelin-starred restaurants in Paris before working here under Damiano Nigro, from whom he took over this restaurant in 2021. The focus is on regional ingredients sourced from small producers. *Fraz. Manera 1, villadamelia.com.*

BOSCO MARENGO (*map D, B3*)
€ **Locanda dell'Olmo**. This warm, informal, family-run establishment offers a seasonal menu of classic dishes from southern Piedmont and Liguria, a good cheese selection and excellent desserts. The menu is built around local produce and the focus is on quality. The *corsetti novesi* (a home-made pasta from the area of Novi Ligure) and *rabattoni della fraschetta* (a main course made with spinach and ricotta grilled with butter and parmesan cheese) are worth a trip. *Piazza Mercato 7–8, bondivini.it.*

BRA (*map C, D1*)
€€ **Battaglino**. Heritage is all-important in this restaurant founded in 1919 and still in the same family. The philosophy is traditional, the menu is seasonal, the wines are classic, the dining room is luminous and bright and the warm-weather seating in the garden courtyard best in spring, when the wisteria is in bloom, making everything look and taste better. Closed Sun evening and Mon. *Piazza Roma 18, ristorantebattaglino.it.*

€ **Boccondivino**. This excellent *osteria* serving traditional dishes of Piedmont is the historic meeting place of the founders of Slow Food and the prototype for the *osteria* of the 21st century. The summer *tartrà*, a medley of vegetables with fresh basil sauce, is a good starter, and the *tajarin* in a sauce of sausage of butter and sage is a good pasta choice; main courses and desserts are equally delicious. The *osteria* occupies fine old rooms stacked floor-to-ceiling with wines, plus a quiet courtyard—here too with cascading wisteria in spring. Closed Sun (in some months) and Mon. *Via Mendicità Istruita 14, boccondivinoslow.it.*

€ **Converso**. This café and pastry shop (est. 1902) has two elegant rooms with vaulted ceilings—one for coffee, the other for pastries. Both preserve their Liberty windows, wainscoting, bar, mirrors, tables and decorations. Past customers include a number of famous painters and writers, and King Umberto of Savoy. The confectionery and *marrons glacés* are superb. *Via Vittorio Emanuele 199, converso.it.*

CALAMANDRANA (*map D, A4*)
€€ **Bianca Lancia dal Baròn**. Bianca
€€ **Violetta**. Maria, Carlo and Silvana Lovisolo's little restaurant, named after the farm carts (*viulette*) once made on the premises, strikes a perfect balance between quality, quantity and price. The cuisine follows the traditions of Piedmont and all the pasta is homemade. *Fraz. Valle San Giovanni 1, ristorantevioletta.it.*

CANALE (*map C, D1*)
€€ **All'Enoteca**. David Palluda is the award-winning young chef at this restaurant above the Enoteca Regionale del Roero; his strategy is to respect tradition without being trapped by it. As you might expect from a restaurant above a wine shop, the wine list is phenomenal, with about 400 labels from Roero, Piedmont and (to a lesser extent) the rest of the world. There is a *ristorante* here and a more down-to-earth, relaxed *osteria*. *Via Roma 57. T: 0173 995857, davidepalluda.it.*

CANELLI (*map D, A4*)
€ **San Marco**. In the old days this fine restaurant was an *osteria* serving hot soup to weary travellers. Today you'll find gourmet recipes of the Monferrato, prepared with special flair by chef Mariuccia Ferrero and matched with fabulous wines. Do leave room for dessert, Mariuccia's strong point. *Via Alba 136, sanmarcoristorante.net.*

CAPRIATA D'ORBA (*map D, B4*)
€ **Il Moro**. Capriata d'Orba is a small town in the Alta Monferrato not far from Ovada and Gavi. The restaurant, café and *enoteca* that make up Il Moro occupy the ground floor of a historic building in the main square. The style of young restaurateurs Simona and Claudio combines influences from Piedmont and Liguria, and the menu is seasonal. In summer it includes zucchini blossoms stuffed with *brandacujun* (a stockfish and potato paté typical of the Ligurian riviera); in winter, homemade pasta with fresh anchovies and artichokes. The stuffed capon and mixed stewed meats are particularly good. You can sit outside in summer. *Piazza Garibaldi 7, T: 0143 46157.*

CASALE MONFERRATO (*map D, A2*)
€ **Bar Savoia**. The best place in town for a light lunch, with warm and cold dishes, sandwiches and excellent cakes and pastries, all reasonably priced and served with elegance. *Piazza Mazzini 17. T: 0142 452173.*

CERVERE (*map C, C1*)
€€ **Antica Corona Reale-da Renzo**. This fine Michelin-starred restaurant first opened its doors at the turn of the 18th century and has been a paragon of regional cooking ever since. It is the last word in recipes involving white truffles, snails, Barolo-braised beef, hazelnuts, etc. The menu follows the seasons, making use of the freshest ingredients. Vittorio Emanuele III was known to stop in for the fish, frogs and snails, the preparation of which is now rightly considered intangible cultural heritage. *Via Fossano 13, anticacoronareale.com.*

CHERASCO (*map C, D1*)
€€ **La Torre**. Cherasco is famous for its snails, and this may be the best place to try them, thanks to the skill and panache of chef Marco Falco. There's

a wide selection of other traditional Piedmontese dishes, too. Outdoor seating in summer. Closed Mon. *Via Dell'Ospedale 22. T: 0172 488458.*
€ **Barbero**. Vittorio Emanuele III admired the same Liberty interior when he visited this confectioner in 1923. Founded in 1881, it is the classic place to go for traditional chocolates, notably *baci di Cherasco, gianduiotti, tartufi, damine* and *dragées*. Order one of each to sample. *Via Vittorio Emanuele 74, bacidicherasco.it.*

CISSONE (*map C, D2*)
€€ **Locanda dell'Arco**. Delicious traditional fare and excellent wines characterise this warm, quiet restaurant attached to a small inn on the outskirts of a tiny village. Come in autumn for mushrooms and truffles, which are expertly prepared and beautifully presented. *Piazza dell'Olmo 1, locandadellarco.it.*

CRAVANZANA (*map C, D2*)
€€ **Da Maurizio**. An excellent *trattoria* (with rooms) specialising in regional dishes, especially cheeses. Locally renowned and absolutely packed on Saturdays but relatively calm at other times. *Via Luigi Einaudi 5, ristorantedamaurizio.net.*

GAVI (*map D, C4*)
€€ **La Gallina**. A lovely restaurant attached to a four-star country hotel between Gavi and Novi Ligure, with beautiful views from its panoramic terrace and fine interpretations of the Monferrine culinary tradition. Chef Graziano Cacciopolo earned his first Michelin star in Genoa in 2021. *Villa Sparina Resort, Frazione Monterotondo 56, la-gallina.it.*

LEQUIO BERRIA (*map C, D2*)
€ **Dei Bersaglieri**. The village is next to non-existent and the hotel is as modest as they come, but this very down-to-earth family restaurant offers delicious cuisine and conscientious service at reasonable prices. The pasta is home made and the meat dishes are nothing short of exquisite. *Via Riale 4, deibersaglieri.com.*

MONASTERO BORMIDA (*map D, A4*)
€€ **Madonna della Neve**. In this country kitchen the philosophy is to make the most of the area's traditional cooking. Starters range from simple carpaccio to rich artichokes stuffed with porcini mushrooms; among pasta dishes the small Monferrato beef ravioli, *agnolotti del plin*, rule supreme. The meat menu varies depending on the season; in spring you will find the famous kids of Roccaverano; in autumn, boiled meats and game. Everything is prepared on a wood stove and flavoured with aromas from the family garden. Country inn attached. *Regione Madonna della Neve 2 (2km southeast of Cessole, 8km west of Monastero Bormida), ristorantemadonnadellaneve.it.*

MONTEU ROERO (*map C, D1*)
€ **Cantina dei Cacciatori**. This country restaurant in a former farmhouse offers traditional dishes of the Roero (Carmagnola grey rabbit in olive and cherry tomato sauce, braised Fassone beef in Nebbiolo sauce) in delightfully verdant surroundings, 10km east of Canale. The style is simple, the atmosphere warm, and the food is absolutely delicious. *Localita' Villa Superiore 59. T: 0173 90815.*

OLIVOLA (*just west of Frassinello Monferrato, map D, A2–A3*)
€€€ **Due Buoi**. One of the historic restaurants of Alessandria, formerly in the hotel of the same name in that city, and now in the countryside in this beautiful old building, Villa Guazzo Candiani, built in the 16th century by the Marquises of Monferrato. Chef Marco Molaro serves up refined dishes in the fine dining tradition. The attached Olivola Apartments are also a lovely place to stay. *Via Vittorio Veneto 23, iduebuoi.it.*

OVIGLIO (*map D, B3*)
€ **Donatella Bistrot**. In 2015 Donatella Vogogna and Mauro Belotti turned in their Michelin star and shut down their gourmet restaurant because they were losing the local clientèle to whom they felt an obligation to provide fine food. Thus was born this bistrot, where the average price of a meal has been cut in half. The kitchen staff remain unchanged. There is garden seating in summer. *Piazza Umberto I 1, donatellabistrot.it.*

PRIOCCA D'ALBA (*map C, D1*)
€€ **Il Centro**. Country flavours and urban sophistication in yet another restaurant famous for its seasonal cuisine. In the kitchen, chef Elide Mollo respects a tradition handed down by her mother and grandmother while also showing the greatest regard for quality ingredients. The restaurant is located at the north end of Prioco's long main street. They also have rooms. *Via Umberto I 5, ristoranteilcentro.com.*

SAN MARZANO OLIVETO (*map D, A4*)
€ **Del Belbo da Bardon**. It's easy to drive right past this modest family-run place in the countryside midway between Nizza and Canelli. But when you do get there, it's hard not to have a memorable meal; the menu is rigorously local, everything is prepared with the utmost finesse and the service couldn't be more cordial. *Valle Asinari 25. T: 0141 831340.*

SANTA VITTORIA D'ALBA (*map C, D1*)
€€€ **Savino Mongelli**. This excellent fish restaurant midway between Alba and Bra enjoys a substantial following among local gourmets. The sea of Liguria is only 90mins away, and the menu is kept short to take full advantage of the catch of the day. A curious twist: each dish is matched with a specific olive oil. The wine cellar is well stocked with delicious whites, and there is garden seating in summer. Open evenings only. *Via Cagna 4. T: 0172 478550.*

SERRALUNGA D'ALBA (*map C, D1*)
€€–€ **Guido & Disguido**. The Villa Reale was the hunting lodge of King Vittorio Emanuele II and Rosa Vercellana ('la Bela Rosin'), his second wife. Guido, an upmarket restaurant offering a contemporary take on traditional recipes, occupies the first-floor dining rooms and ballroom. On the ground floor is Disguido, '*osteria del vino libero*', offering light lunches (and dinners Sun and Mon) at affordable prices. The *foresteria* has recently been renovated to make 11 pretty rooms. *Villaggio di Fontanafredda, Via Alba 15, guidoristorante.it.*

SERRAVALLE LANGHE (*map C, D2*)
€ **La Coccinella**. A fine small

restaurant established by three brothers. The ingredients are all bought from local farmers (and the fish is from nearby Liguria). The menu is seasonal, with truffles and mushrooms taking leading roles in autumn. Closed Tues and midday Wed. *Via Provinciale 5, trattoriacoccinella.com.*

TIGLIOLE D'ASTI (*map A, D3*)
€€ **Ca' Vittoria**. In the kitchen are three generations of the same family—Gemma, Alessandra and Massimiliano—and the ten-room country inn is run by Valentina, Massimiliano's wife. Located in an old house in the midst of an extraordinary forested landscape (grapes and grain usually dominate the horizon), both restaurant and inn command magnificent views. The cooking has a strong base in tradition but is creative and elegantly modern (and Michelin-starred). The wines are excellent. *Via Roma 14, ristorantevittoria.it.*

TREISO (*map C, D1*)
€€ **La Ciau del Tornavento**. Another of the famed restaurants of the Langhe: chefs Maurilio Garola and Marco Lombardo have won many plaudits. There is outdoor summer seating overlooking the vineyards and they also offer rooms. *Piazza Baracco 7, laciaudeltornavento.it.*

LOCAL SPECIALITIES

Wine is the obvious speciality here, as well as **truffles**. The Alta Langa is particularly known for its **hazelnuts** and for the **cheeses** of Levice and Bergolo. Robiola cheese is the speciality of Roccaverano. The Roero is famed for its **peaches and pears**, while Dogliani (in the Bassa Langa) prides itself on its **cherries**. From Casale Monferrato come the ***krumiri biscuits***, their shape inspired by the curvy moustache of King Vittorio Emanuele II. Nizza Monferrato is proud of its **cardoons**: look out for *spadone* in markets and on menus.

The Valle d'Aosta

The mountainous Valle d'Aosta lies on the borders of alpine France and Switzerland. It is the smallest and least populated region in Italy, and also one of the most independently minded, with a strong tradition of home rule. The region's principal attractions are its magnificent mountain scenery, its Roman remains and its castles.

The valley lies at the meeting point of the Graian and Cottian Alps and is crowned by Europe's highest peaks: the Gran Paradiso (4061m), Mont Blanc (4807m), the Matterhorn (Monte Cervino, 4478m) and Monte Rosa (4634m). Ivrea is its southern gateway; the Little St Bernard Pass (from France) and the Great St Bernard Pass (from Switzerland) are its northern entrances. Both are named after Bernard of Menthon (d. 1081), who built guest houses for mountain travellers here. The specially trained dogs that bear his name helped track down wayfarers lost in the snow.

The climate is cold and snowy in winter and warm and relatively dry in summer. The lower slopes of the mountains are covered with trellised vineyards and broadleaf forests; higher up are magnificent conifer forests and above this, to the limit of the perennial snows, the ground is covered with high-altitude grasses and shrubs, including stunning rhododendron. Wine-making, cattle raising and dairy farming are the main agrarian activities; the brown-and-white cows (with loud bells) are taken up to high pasture from May to the end of September. The wealth formerly generated by the lignite mines at La Thuile and the iron mines at Cogne, both now exhausted, has been replaced by revenue from hydroelectric power. The real driving force behind the economy, however, is tourism. The region's population increases six times during the peak winter and summer seasons.

HISTORY OF THE VALLE D'AOSTA

Historically, the valley's earliest inhabitants were the Salassi, a Celtic-Ligurian people who were well established by the 5th century BC. Pliny the Elder describes them as proud farmers, but they may also have engaged in mining and—given their proximity to the Alpine passes—in trade. They conducted a long, bitter struggle against Rome, finally capitulating in 25 BC. The Romans celebrated their conquest by founding Augusta Praetoria Salassorum, the present-day Aosta, and then settled throughout the region, bringing with them their systems of land management and town planning and, above all, their roads.

Aosta became an episcopal city in the 5th century, but was overwhelmed as waves of invading tribes, among them Goths and Lombards, swept through the region. The bishops of Aosta re-established their sovereignty in the 10th century, reviving earlier ties with the kings of Burgundy. It was the French royal house that gave the title of Count of Aosta to Umberto Biancamano, the first of the Savoy dynasty, in the 11th century. Control of the region was shared between the Savoy overlord and local barons, who in the 16th century obtained considerable political autonomy, based on a parliament and on a code of laws, the Coutumier. The balance between the Savoy rulers and the local lords—among them the powerful Challant family—remained substantially stable until the establishment of the Italian Republic in 1946.

Under the Italian Constitution of 1948 the valley was granted a statute of administrative and cultural autonomy—which means, among other things, that revenues from taxes are invested locally. This accounts for the region's many fine schools, hospitals, museums, monuments and public infrastructure (the latter, indeed, can be rather invasive, making the valley floor appear as one continuous, linear city). Another consequence is the protection of intangible cultural assets, such as language. Although never for long under French dominion, the valley had a long tradition of bilingualism under the Savoy kings and French is now an official language of the region (though Italian is the language most heard, and is the language common to all). Patois, a French-Italian dialect, is spoken in the villages. An interesting relic of the colonisation of the valley from the Swiss Valais remains in the German dialect that survives at Gressoney.

Tourists first discovered the Valle d'Aosta in the early 19th century, when British alpinists and excursionists came to explore and admire the mountain scenery. Murray's guide of 1838 was the first guide to the region in any language, and many alpinists who made ascents in the mountains published illustrated descriptions of their travels. Today the region is known for its ski resorts, Courmayeur and Breuil-Cervinia being the most famous. Just south of Aosta itself is the Parco Nazionale del Gran Paradiso, Italy's first national park (created in 1922). The casino at Saint-Vincent is the second most important in Europe after Monte Carlo.

The official tourist website (*lovevda.it/en*) has up-to-date opening times for sights and monuments in the region.

The City of Aosta

Aosta (*map E, B2*) is a small, pleasant city surrounded by snow-capped mountains. Once the capital of the Gallic Salassi, it was captured by Terentius Varro in 24 BC and renamed Augusta Praetoria. You can still see the Roman influence in its regular, grid-like street plan—a characteristic evolved from the Roman battle camp. The Roman road passed over the bridge over the Buthier and entered the city by the Porta Paetoria. Here travellers could follow the decumanus, which crossed the city from east to west, continuing to the pass of Alpis Graia (Little St Bernard); or the cardo, which crossed the decumanus at right angles and, running north–south, led to the Alpis Poenina (Great St Bernard).

The character of the later city, however, is French rather than Italian. The architecture is essentially Burgundian, and the people speak a French dialect. Throughout the later Middle Ages, town and valley owed allegiance to the house of Challant, viscounts of Aosta. It was they who built the most important of the valley's castles, in the 14th and 15th centuries. Later, as mentioned, the dukedom was a prized apanage of the house of Savoy. The most famous native of Aosta is the Benedictine monk St Anselm (1033–1109), who became Archbishop of Canterbury in 1093 and strove with all his might against King William Rufus' habit of using religion for political ends.

Aosta's town centre, less than 2km square, is still enclosed by Roman walls and contains many Roman monuments. Saint-Ours and the cathedral are both interesting medieval buildings with remarkable 11th-century paintings, and the cathedral museum has numerous works of art.

AROUND THE CATHEDRAL & ROMAN FORUM

Piazza Emile Chanoux (*map Aosta 1*) is the centre of the town, site of the Hôtel de Ville, the grand Town Hall of 1837. The square is named after local hero Emile Chanoux (1906–44), founder of the Jeune Vallée d'Aoste, a movement in defence of local language and culture at a time when Fascism was working hard to Italianise the region. Conscripted in 1943, he escaped to France, returning to Aosta after the Armistice of 8th September to fight with the Partito d'Azione and other partisan groups. The Nazis captured his wife and daughters in May 1944; Chanoux surrendered on the condition that they be released, was tortured and executed.

THE CATHEDRAL

Via Hotel des Etats leads north to Via Monsignor de Sales, where remains of Roman baths dating from the 1st century AD have been excavated. To the left is the cathedral (*map Aosta 1*), founded in the early Christian age but rebuilt in the Romanesque and Gothic styles and given a sculptured west portal in 1526, now framed by a Neoclassical façade of 1848. Inside you can see remains of the early-Christian baptistery and traces of the original 3rd–4th-century church. The stained glass dates from the late 14th and early 15th centuries. Sixteenth-century frescoes and a 16th-century painted lunette illustrating the legend of St Grato adorn the south side. St Grato, a local saint, was a 5th-century bishop of Aosta. His protection is invoked against locusts, caterpillars and other farm pests.

The treasury is beautifully arranged in the deambulatory (*open daily 3–5.30; the sacristan will open if closed; check cattedraleaosta.it for changes*). It contains precious objects from the cathedral and from churches in the valley. The 15th-century tombs include that of Count François de Challant (c. 1430). The bishop's missal, illuminated around 1420 by Giacomo Jaquerio (the foremost Savoy artist of the first half of the 14th century), is also displayed. There is also the wood-and-silver tomb of St Grato, exquisitely decorated between 1415 and 1458. Nearby is a crucifix of 1499, removed from below the Arch of Augustus (*see below*).

In the choir are interesting mosaic pavements dating from the 12th and 14th centuries, one with the Labours of the Months, the other depicting lively animals and the Tigris and Euphrates; 15th-century stalls and a crucifix dating from 1397. The crypt has a miscellany of Roman and medieval columns.

The Ottonian frescoes in the roof, discovered in 1979, have been meticulously restored (*open Sat 3–5.30; last entry 30mins before closing; check cattedraleaosta. it for changes*). Illustrating the story of St Eustace and biblical scenes, they are the upper band of a fresco cycle that once decorated the nave and was covered when the 15th-century vault of the church was constructed. They date from 1030 or 1040 and are rare survivals in Italy of mural paintings of this date.

FROM THE ROMAN FORUM TO THE MEDIEVAL MARKET

The forum of Augusta Praetoria was on a slope and was terraced to create an upper and a lower area. The upper area was a sacred precinct, where two temples rose surrounded by a marble colonnade; the lower area was the civic centre, with an open space (platea) surrounded by shops, tabernae and offices.

The Roman cryptoporticus (Criptoportico forense)

In a sunken garden beside the cathedral façade are some remains of the forum, with the base of a temple now part of the foundations of a house. From here you can enter a splendid underground Roman cryptoporticus (*open daily; usually closes for 1hr at lunchtime in winter*), a double corridor with vaulted ceilings supported by sturdy pillars of travertine limestone blocks, finely plastered and lit by ground-level windows. The structure dates from the time of Augustus and is thought to have served as a warehouse and military granary, as well as a support for the sacred precinct. Restoration carried out in the early years of the present century have made the monument—which was found already in an excellent state of preservation—almost entirely accessible.

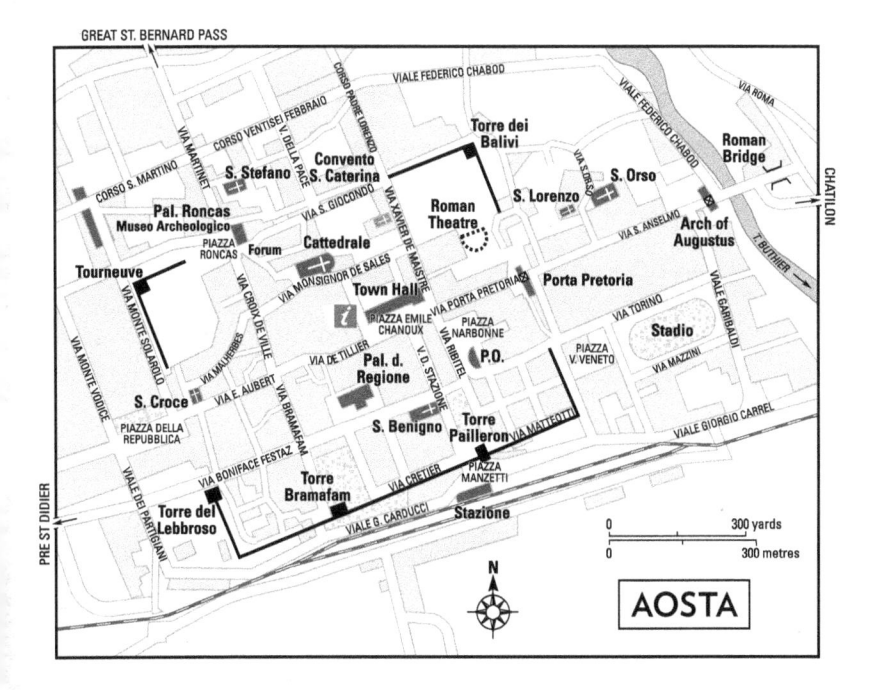

Archaeological Museum

Via Forum and Via San Bernardo lead northwest to Piazza Roncas, where a 17th-century palace houses the Museo Archeologico Regionale (*Piazza Roncas 12; map Aosta 1; open daily; usually closed for 1hr at lunchtime in winter*), documenting human presence in the Valle d'Aosta from prehistory to the Middle Ages. The installation makes extensive use of reconstructed architectural environments and interactive multimedia supports, and many of the showcases have been fitted with drawers that can be opened for 'hands-on' viewing. Prehistory and protohistory are represented by the findings from the first human settlements in the valley and the anthropomorphic stelae found at Saint-Martin-de-Corléans. The large Roman section is divided into displays devoted to Augusta Praetoria, funeral rites and epigraphy, cults, public architecture, the domestic sphere and personal care: the best exhibit here is an exquisite bronze of the 2nd century AD, once part of a horse's bridle, showing a battle scene between Romans and barbarians. The medieval section is largely dedicated to the advent of Christianity. A highlight here is an 8th-century marble altar found in two pieces in the cathedral.

The museum also contains two private bequests unrelated to Aosta. The Aurelio Carugo Collection of Near Eastern, Ancient Egyptian and Etruscan artefacts is installed in a replica of the donor's study. The remarkable numismatic collection of Andrea Pautasso is particularly notable for its Celtic coins found in northern Italy (many of them, in gold, silver and bronze, in imitation of Greek coins). There are also examples from the Roman, Byzantine and medieval periods, as well as the 19th century.

Santo Stefano and San Grato

Via Martinet leads to the church of **Santo Stefano** (or Saint-Etienne; *map Aosta 1*), with a lovely frescoed façade, an elaborate high altar and a striking 15th-century wood statue of St Christopher.

Via Croix de Ville, on the line of the cardo maximus of the Roman town, leads south to the medieval marketplace and a cross set up in 1541 to commemorate the expulsion of the Calvinists from the town. **Via de Tillier** (*map Aosta 3*) leads back to Piazza Chanoux past the **Galleria d'Arte San Grato**, a deconsecrated 15th-century chapel of San Grato, with remains of frescoes on the façade. The interior hosts temporary art displays.

ROMAN REMAINS

Via Porta Pretoria leaves Piazza Emile Chanoux on the east side. Under an archway on the left, an alley leads to a terrace overlooking the Roman theatre (*described below*), near excavated houses with pebble pavements on a Roman road once lined with a portico. At no. 41 is the house of Philippe-Maurice de Challant (1724–1804), the last descendant of the family who built numerous castles in the valley.

The **Porta Praetoria** (*map Aosta 2*), a massive, well-preserved double Roman gateway of three arches, stands at the end of the street. This was the main gate of the city. The two fortified gates, built in pudding-stone, are separated by a small square defended by two towers. The side facing away from the city was originally faced in grey-green Aymavilles bardiglio marble, bits of which can still be seen. The side arches were used by pedestrians and the central one by carriages. The level of the Roman road was 2.6m below the present pavement. The gate was incorporated in a medieval fortress until the 18th century, and the main arches and those on the right were blocked up. This explains why the axis of Via Porta Pretoria is not aligned with the gate.

Beside the gate is the entrance to the **Roman theatre** (*map Aosta 2; open daily*). The most striking part of the monument is the tall façade, 22m high, decorated with arched windows. Behind it are remains of the seats in the cavea and the foundations of the scena.

The Arch of Augustus and Roman bridge

Via Sant'Anselmo continues to the **Arch of Augustus**, a triumphal arch erected in 24 BC to commemorate the defeat of the Gallic Salassi. Decorated with ten Corinthian columns and low reliefs, probably of trophies, the arch was drawn and engraved many times in the 19th century, and before that by Sir Roger Newdigate, who gave his drawing to Piranesi when he reached Rome. The roof was added in 1716. The arch was restored by the famous historian of antiquity Ernesto Schiaparelli ('father' of the Egyptian Museum in Turin) in 1912–13.

Further on, beyond the modern bridge over the Buthier, is a remarkable single-arched **Roman bridge**, still in use, over a dried-up channel. It consists of a single lowered arch composed of radial stone blocks springing from very wide bases, 17m in diameter and nearly 6m wide.

THE ROMAN WALLS

The city walls of Augusta Paetoria, forming a rectangle 724m long and 572m wide, had 20 towers: two for each gate, four at the corners, and eight distributed along the enceinte. Their number, the appearance of might they project towards the exterior, and the presence of double arched windows on all four sides, make scholars think that the towers, and the walls along which they were strung, had not been built for defence alone but were also meant to create a monumental boundary of the urban area and to communicate an Aosta 'brand' expressing both strength and beauty. In Aosta as elsewhere the urban population fled following the fall of the Roman Empire, and when it returned, in the Middle Ages, the aristocracy erected its fortified homes along the old walls. Many towers were razed or turned into feudal residences and the outer face of the enceinte was quarried for building stone. Today, notwithstanding the pillage, you can still see fine stretches of walls on the southern and western sides of the town, as well as the Porta Praetoria and Torre dei Signori (Via Porta Praetoria), Porta Decumana (Via Aubert), Port Principalis Dextera and Torre Bramafam (Viale Carducci, Via Stevenin and Via Bramafam), Tour du Pailleron (Piazza Manzetti), Torre del Lebbroso (Via Festaz), Tourneuve (Via Tourneuve), Torre dei Balivi (Via Guido Rey) and Tour Fromage (Via Baillage).

THE SANT'ORSO COMPLEX

In Via Sant'Orso (*map Aosta 2*) are the priory and collegiate church of Sant'Orso (or St-Ours), founded by St Anselm (*church and cloister open daily; early-Christian chapel closes mid-afternoon in winter*). The church has a campanile finished in 1131 and a late-Gothic façade, 16th-century stalls and an 11th-century crypt with twelve plain Roman columns. In the roof vaulting are remarkable Ottonian frescoes, dating from 1030 or 1040, and thought to be by the same hand as those in the cathedral. A custodian shows them at close range from a system of platforms and walkways. Two of the scenes represent the *Miracles on Lake Gennesareth* and the *Marriage at Cana*; they were damaged in the 15th century by the construction of the nave vault. These frescoes, together with those found beneath the cathedral roof (*described above*), are among the very few mural paintings of this date to have survived in Italy. Recent excavations unearthed a late-Antique mosaic of Samson slaying a lion, now in the choir.

To the right of the church façade is the cloister, with fascinating Romanesque capitals, carved in white marble but covered at a later date with a dark patina. Placed at the top of unusually low columns, they date from c. 1132. They illustrate biblical scenes (*Story of Jacob, Childhood of Christ, Raising of Lazarus, Noli Me Tangere, Stoning of St Stephen*), fantastic and stylised animals, a fable of Aesop (*The Wolf and the Stork*) and prophets. This and the cloister of Monreale in Sicily are the only surviving examples in Italy of large Romanesque cloisters with representations of historical and legendary scenes.

A passage opposite Sant'Orso leads round the deconsecrated church of San Lorenzo to the 5th-century chapel excavated beneath the church's east end. The Latin-cross chapel, with apses at the end of each arm, was the burial place of the first bishops of Aosta. It was destroyed in the Carolingian era.

VILLA DELLA CONSOLATA

On the northern outskirts of the town (*beyond map Aosta 1*) lies the ancient Roman Villa della Consolata (*closed at the time of writing; check lovevda.it for updates; bus 4 or 10 from Piazza Manzetti, map Aosta 4*). Located on a branch of the ancient road to the Alpis Poenina (Great St Bernard) the rectangular villa has a relatively large residential area (*pars urbana*), reserved for the *dominus* and his guests, and smaller areas for processing and storing agricultural produce (*pars rustica* and *pars fructuaria*). The presence of the latter, albeit limited, suggests the villa was connected with a *fundus* (farm, estate).

AOSTA PRACTICAL TIPS

WHERE TO STAY

€€ **La Rêve Charmant B&B**. In the historic centre of Aosta, a warm, refined establishment with just six rooms. Great care has gone into decorating the interiors and cultivating a sense of personal flair. The young proprietors are relaxed yet professional and breakfast is memorable. *Via Marché Vaudan 6, Aosta, T: 0165 238855, lerevecharmant.com.*

€€ **Le Coffret 1779**. Four years were needed to restore this large country house in the hills 20mins east of Aosta, but the restoration has produced a building that is nothing less than stunning, blending contemporary and historic architecture in a way that enhances the effect of both. Wood and stone, glass and steel, smooth white and rough stone surfaces work together in perfect consonance to make a place that is on a par with the finest public architecture in Aosta. The name, Le Coffret (the jewellery box), is in homage to grandfather Gino, a cabinetmaker, whose house this was. *Lieu-dit Jayer, Saint Marcel, T: 0165 778 751, 340 498 5568, lecoffret.it.*

€€ **Le Petit Relais**. The lovely Valpelline is 'the most solitary and pleasantly wild' of the Valle d'Aosta, in the words of novelist Edmondo de Amicis, who (together with numerous English enthusiasts) here pioneered the fine art of Alpine hiking in the third quarter of the 19th century. The tradition is continued with style at this small B&B, which opened in 2012. Two stone cottages of the 17th–18th centuries have been meticulously restored to form a cosy retreat just half an hour north of Aosta. The Ratatouille restaurant serves delicious meals using only the best local ingredients (including produce from the garden), and there are a small spa and heated pool. *Loc. Cheillon 16, Valpelline; T: 0165 713002, petitrelaisvalledaosta.it.*

€€ **Milleluci**. A beautiful, rustic family-run establishment on a sunny hillside just 1km from the centre of town. The only drawback is, the atmosphere so relaxed, the breakfast so copious and the pool so inviting you may abandon your ambitious plans for the day. *Località Porossan Roppoz, T: 0165 235278, hotelmilleluci.com.*

€ **Trois Couronnes**. La Salle is a quiet little village at the foot of Mont Blanc, close to the ski resorts of Courmayeur and La Thuile and roughly midway between Aosta and Chamonix. This 17th-century house is a carefully restored medley of stone and wood just outside the historic town centre. Views range over a magnificent landscape dominated by Mont Blanc, and you can sun yourself in the garden and fruit orchard during summer. *Via Cesar Ollietti 47, La Salle, T: 338 424 3249, troiscouronnes.it.*

WHERE TO EAT

€ **Caffè Nazionale**. Established in 1886, this attractive café offers a superb architectural setting, which includes a circular Gothic hall (a relic of a Franciscan monastery that once stood here), for the Michelin-starred cooking of chef Paolo Griffa. *Piazza Chanoux 9, paologriffa.com.*

€ **Degli Artisti**. This little trattoria in the historic city centre lives up to its name: creative cuisine, good ambience, and prices even a starving artist could afford. *Via Maillet 5–7, T: 0165 40960, trattoriadegliartisti.it.*

€€€ **Veccio Ristoro**. Fine dining at its height. The menu is seasonal, everything is tied to the terroir, and the wine list is excellent. Michelin-starred. *Via Tourneuve 4, T: 0165 33238, ristorantevecchioristoro.it.*

Exploring the Main Valley

The most distinctive architectural trait of the Valle d'Aosta is its high number of fortified feudal residences, military garrisons and royal retreats—an exceptional heritage even for a place close to Alpine passes. This description of the region's most extraordinary castles, as well as the Roman road and bridges, follows the valley upstream from its entrance, on the Piedmont Plateau to its end, at the foot of Mont Blanc.

PONT SAINT-MARTIN, DONNAS & BARD

Pont Saint-Martin

Pont-Saint-Martin (*map E, D3*) lies on the southernmost border of the Valle d'Aosta. Above are the ruins of a 12th-century castle. It has a well-preserved single-arch **Roman bridge** (1st century BC) over the Lys, which can be crossed on foot. It is one of the most magnificent and best preserved Roman bridges in northern Italy and was used continuously until 1836, when it was replaced by its modern successor. The bridge is made from a single segmental arch of 31.5m, composed of 87 radial wedges in five parallel and independent rings 32cm apart from one another, the interval filled with small chips of stone cemented with mortar. The shoulders are formed by large stone blocks laid side by side without the aid of mortar. The track above, 5m wide from parapet to parapet, is mostly cobblestone, but the left side still preserves some polygonal plates, spaced by horizontal incisions to prevent slippage of the animals' hooves.

Donnas

At nearby Donnas (*map E, D3*) you can see the best surviving stretch of the **Roman road to Gaul**. It is the best known stretch of Roman road in the whole Valle d'Aosta, at the western end of the village, above the SS26 (the modern road) and the railway. It was built just above the level of the river, to avoid flooding, and ran mostly along the left bank, where the warmth of the sun (stronger here than on the other side) helped to melt the snow in winter. Here the rocky spur that prevented the passage of the road was cut vertically for 222m, the cut reaching a height in some places of almost 13m. The road surface, the round column serving as a milestone marking XXXVI *milia passuum* from Aosta (about 53km) and a vaulted passage are entirely cut into the rock itself—a demonstration of the skill required by the stoneworkers, who in places had to construct the road out of the sheer rockface. The road surface, 4.75m wide, shows deep, regular and parallel ruts from wear (it was in used up to the 19th century). Are also evident the remains of the parapet, 1.20m high. The most striking feature is the exceptional technical ability underlying the verticality and regularity of the cut, designed according to a definite plan, as is evidenced by the smoothness of the chiselled surfaces and by the elevation line of the road surface, at a constant height of 2.37m.

AUGUSTA PRAETORIA AND THE CONSULAR ROAD TO GAUL

The Valle d'Aosta is schematically represented in the *Tabula Peutingeriana*, a 12th–13th-century copy of an *itinerarium pictum* (road map) dating from the 3rd–4th century AD. The Tabula shows the roads, with an indication of the distances in miles between the various stages, from Eporedia (Ivrea), through Augusta Praetoria (Aosta), to the transalpine provinces. Aosta is depicted with the conventional sign of a city: two towers side by side. The itinerary also documents the presence, along the way, of places of rest and refreshment, mansiones and mutationes. From Eporedia to Augusta Praetoria only Vitricium (modern Verrès) is mentioned. On the road to the Alpis Graia (the Little St Bernard Pass) it lists the intermediate stations of Arebrigium (Arvier) and Ariolica (La Thuile), whereas towards the Alpis Poenina (Great St Bernard) it reports only Eudracinum (Saint-Rhémy-en-Bosses). The route followed by the road is described also in two *itineraria scripta* (travel guides): those of 'Anthony' (early 3rd century) and of the 'Anonymous Ravennate' (early 7th century).

From Eporedia (Ivrea), the Roman road ran through the lower valley closely following the lie of the land. The roadway, between 3.5 and 5m wide, was built well above the course of the Dora, to avoid possible flood damage. The severe climate of the Valle d'Aosta made it keep the orographic left (called the adret), the sunnier side of the valley, where snow melted more rapidly. Generally speaking the road had few curves, proceeding as far as possible in rectilinear segments, like other Roman roads. In the section between Donnas and Bard, especially, you can see how this was possible: substructures cut into the rock, arches and bridges testify to the great skill and expertise of Roman technicians. At Donnas the road is cut into the rock for 221m, with a wall that reaches, in some points, 12m in height. Other important archaeological remains along the ancient route are the majestic bridge over the River Lys in Pont-Saint-Martin, the remains of the road in Montjovet, the cyclopean substructures at Bard and the remains of the bridges of Saint-Vincent and Châtillon.

Bard

The imposing **fortress of Bard** (*map E, D3*), an 11th-century foundation, was largely reconstructed in the 19th century. The Savoy seized the castle and its lands from Bard family in the 13th century, after Ugo di Bard's excessive taxation of residents and travellers on the road that passes beneath it. In the 17th century the Savoy made it the principal fortress of the Valle d'Aosta, concentrating here the artillery (and troops) that had previously been stationed throughout the valley. In 1800 Napoleon's progress was halted here for a week by the castle's defenders, but in the end he managed to pass unnoticed with his army during the night; they went through the narrow gorge in silence, having protected the wheels of the gun carriages with straw. As an over-liberal young officer, Camillo Cavour was despatched to this remote garrison by Carlo Felice of Savoy, King of Sardinia and Piedmont, in 1830–1.

The fortress (*fortedibard.it*) is now home to the Museum of the Alps, a brilliantly conceived and thoughtfully arranged interactive, multimedia showcase of the region's natural and cultural history; the Children's Alps Museum, featuring a virtual climb up Mont Blanc; a Frontier Museum, exploring the concept of boundaries as well as actual geopolitical frontiers; and a Fortress Museum, dealing with the building's history. Changing temporary exhibitions are also held here, as well as open-air concerts, film screenings and theatre performances. Reaching the fortress's three main buildings—the Opera Ferdinando, Opera Vittorio and Opera Carlo Alberto—requires that you take a breathtaking ride in an all-glass exterior lift and negotiate a glass-and-steel staircase.

At the foot of the fortress, by the cemetery, is a characteristic **glacial site** with sheepbacks (glaciated bedrock surfaces, here in the form of rounded knobs), erratic boulders and large cylindrical potholes formed by the erosive action of sub-glacial waters (called *marmitte dei giganti*). Two sloping schist rocks here bear Neolithic petroglyphs and 'women's slides' (*scivole delle donne*), thought to be relics of an ancient rite linked to female fertility. Most of the incisions are arranged around a boulder about 2m high at the centre of the main rock. On the west side there are at least 18 'cups' carved into the stone and a grid pattern measuring c. 60 by 80cm. On the north is an enigmatic design, about 1.2m long, possessing two lines that are sinuous at the ends and parallel in the middle. It is the only known drawing of its kind in Alpine rock art. The incisions are made with the *martellina* technique, which involves repeatedly tapping the rock with a sharp stone that serves as a chisel and a larger stone used as a hammer.

Several stretches of the **Roman road** are also still visible here. From north to south along the SS26 one can see an impressive stretch of road bed cut through solid rock on the right bank of a small stream, over which is a stone arch once belonging to a Roman bridge. Proceeding through the village towards the fort one encounters some more rocks cut for the passage of the road, with stone support walls on the downhill side. The most impressive of these is perfectly preserved in the stretch above the fort's underground car park: huge blocks of stone, perfectly shaped and set in place, hold the road at a height of 16m, for 58m. In the stretch between the Bard town hall and Donnas, finally, the road is cut into the rock face on the uphill side, with huge supporting walls in large polygonal blocks downhill.

ARNAD, VERRÈS & ISSOGNE

Arnad
The church of Arnad (*map E, D3*), founded in the 11th century and restored in the early 15th century, is one of the oldest churches in the valley. The exterior frescoes in late-Gothic style are part of the 15th-century restoration.

Verrès
The castle of Verrès (*map E, D3; for info, see lovevda.it*), built on a rocky outcrop, commands the mouth of the Val d'Ayas. A road leads up to the car park (or a path ascends in 15mins from Piazza Chanoux in Verrès village), from where a steep path continues uphill, taking you to the entrance in 5–10mins. This four-square castle, with sheer walls 30m high, was founded by the Challant family in 1390 and strengthened by them in 1536 (it was acquired by the state in 1894). Never a residence, it was used purely for defensive purposes and its bare interior has huge fireplaces, an old kitchen built into the rock, and an imposing staircase, all arranged around a central court.

Issogne
On the opposite side of the river is the castle of Issogne (*map E, D3; for info, see lovevda.it*), rebuilt by Georges de Challant in 1497–8. This splendid example of a late medieval residence retains some of its original furnishings and lovely Gothic double doors carved in wood. Particularly noteworthy are the 16th-century frescoed lunettes with scenes of everyday life, including a guardhouse with a game of backgammon in progress and various shops, beneath the arches in the courtyard. The unusual wrought-iron fountain, in the form of a pomegranate tree (the Challant family emblem), was made in the 16th century. The little walled garden has box hedges.

Next to the dining room is the kitchen with three fireplaces. The chapel has a lovely late 16th-century altarpiece and an unusual lunette fresco of the *Dormition of the Virgin*. Stairs continue up to the loggia on the top floor. Off the main staircase is the bedroom of Georges de Challant, which has a pretty wood ceiling and a little oratory with a *Crucifixion* and the kneeling figure of Challant. Another room has views of the two castles of Verrès and Arnad. A small room used as a schoolroom has sums scratched on the walls. The Sala baroniale has delightful painted walls depicting the *Judgement of Paris* and lovely landscapes with birds behind painted crystal columns.

Roman road near Montjovet
Several stretches of the ancient road are visible in the municipality of Montjovet (*map E, D2*); two are extraordinarily well preserved.

The first is located **between the towns of Balmes and Toffo**, along an easy path that runs halfway up the hill, above the SS26: here are several stretches of Roman roadway, characterised by a background in chiselled rock, where you can see the furrows left by the carriages, and a retaining wall at the foot of the perfectly chiselled vertical rock. The roadway at this point is more than 4.5m wide, which would have enabled two wagons to pass.

The other preserved area is located at the southern edge of the town, in **Vervaz**, above the SS26, behind a big farm: here is a long stretch of substructures, made of *opus caementicium* (stones and lime mortar) with regularised facing. Ruts can still be seen on the poorly preserved road surface.

PARCO NATURALE DI MONT AVIC

Near Champdepraz is the Parco Naturale di Mont Avic (*map E, C3*), a protected area surrounding the pointed peak of Avic (3006m). The mountain is particularly interesting to geologists: the valley of the Torrente Chalamy, which bounds it on the north, lies within the calcareous schist with green stones complex of Piedmont. The complex, here including ophiolites from the ultrabasic complex of Mont Avic, represents an oceanic fragment of the Piedmont basin that was caught up in the Alpine mountain-building processes that followed the continental collision between Africa and Europe. The 5747ha park embraces the middle and upper valley of the Chalamy; more than a third of the protected area is covered by a large forest of hooked pines (rare in the Italian Alps but particularly well adapted to the poor quality of the soil in this area), Scotch pines, larch and beech, and there is a surprising number of crystalline alpine lakes, streams and marshes. The latter are populated by an extremely interesting relict flora. Among the rarest species are *Carex limosa*, *Carex pauciflora* and *Eriophorum vaginatum*; there are also floating islands of bog moss (*Sphagnum magellanicum*, *S. squarrosum* and *S. angustifolium*). The park is an entomological treasure trove (of over 1,000 macrolepidopters, rare dragon flies, and more than 110 species of forest phytophagous Coleoptera), and there are also mammals and birds typical of the mountain environment of the Valle d'Aosta (ibex, mountain hare, golden eagle, goshawk, rock ptarmigan, black grouse, rock partridge, black woodpecker, rock thrush, chough, and nutcracker). Part of the Natura 2000 system, the ecological network of the European Union aimed at preserving habitats and species, the park is subject to a particularly strict land management plan demanding maximum respect of its geology, hydrology, flora, vegetation, and wildlife, with special attention to its broadleaf and conifer forests, peat bogs, and high-mountain ophiolitic sites. There are visitors' centres at Champorcher and Covarey (*montavic.it*). Spectacular observation points are Pra Oursie (Trail 7), the Barbustel mountain hut (Trail 5c), the Lac de Leser (Trail 5), and Quicord (Trail 3). The Col Medzove (Trail 5c) and the Col de Kiva Chevrère (Trail 6a) offer wide views towards Aosta and the northwestern part of the region. From the summit of Mont Barbeston (Trails 7b–8) you can see much of the park and the middle and lower Aosta Valley all the way to Ivrea.

SAINT-VINCENT

Saint-Vincent (*map E, D2*) is the second most important town in the valley after Aosta. It is famous for its casino and has numerous hotels. The approach road passes the remains of a Roman bridge that collapsed in the 19th century. Archaeological excavations in the parish church in the 1970s unearthed the remains of **Roman thermal baths** dating from the late 2nd or early 3rd century AD. This complex, perhaps belonging to a *mansio* (a resting place along the Roman route), occupied a site inhabited since at least the late Bronze Age. The facilities cover an area larger than that of the church above and continue westward, under the churchyard, and to the north where oldest archaeological remains have been found, dating from the late 1st century BC or early 1st century AD. The first thermal complex was laid out along an east–west axis, with a typical sequence of cold, warm and hot baths. Later, towards the end of the 4th century, the complex was expanded to the north and east, and an apsidal hall with four buttresses was added on the south side. During the 5th century, probably because it fell into disuse as a bath, the eastern area was used as a Christian cemetery. It seems there was also a simple chapel, orientated east–west, which partly reused Roman structures. The archaeological area beneath the present church was opened for guided visits (Sat 2–6) in 2012.

Beside the Art Nouveau Hotel Billia (1910), and a congress hall built in 1983, is the **Casinò** (*casinodelavallee.com*), which was opened in the 1950s and renovated in the 1970s. The Region of Valle d'Aosta has a majority holding in the casino, which is closed to residents of the valley. It is frequented mostly by Italians, and there are direct train and bus services from Turin to St-Vincent in the afternoon. The casino is open 3pm–2am, although chemin-de-fer is usually played throughout the night.

The old **church**, built on a prehistoric and Roman site, has a 14th-century fresco in a niche outside the apse. The interior, with Romanesque columns, has 15th- and 16th-century frescoes and a little museum. The frescoes in the window jambs are attributed to the school of Giacomo Jaquerio.

St-Vincent has been known since 1770 as a health resort, and the **spa** (*termedisaintvincent.com*) is reached by a funicular railway from the centre of the town in 3mins. The Palazzo delle Fonti was built in 1960 above the source of the mineral spring (*fons salutis*).

Of the **Roman bridge** over the Torrente Cillian, which collapsed (perhaps following an earthquake) on 8th June 1839, a section of the road and parts of the piers remain visible. The bridge originally consisted of three parts, for a total length of over 49m. The first was a wide round arch of 9.71m supported by powerful piers in large square blocks, based directly on the rock; the two symmetrical lateral parts were joined to the road surface at an obtuse angle and had a blind arch on the side facing the valley. The central and lesser arches were framed by strong buttresses. The upper walls alternate stone slabs with bands of stone chips, enlivening the front of the monument in a way that is both simple and effective. The core of the walls is made of splinters of stone bound by lime mortar. The roadway, 4.64m wide, was protected by high parapets.

CHÂTILLON

Châtillon (*map E, C2*) is built on the Marmore torrent, with 19th-century foundries, mills and forges on its banks. The **Castello Gamba** at Cret de Breil (*castellogamba.vda.it*), in actuality an early 20th-century villa, is set in a magnificent 7000 square-metre Romantic park that is older than the building: the giant California sequoia (*Sequoiadendron giganteum*) and the bald cypress (*Taxodium distichum*, from the Florida Everglades) were planted in the 1880s. There are also gorgeous large beeches (best in autumn), cedars, Douglas firs, lindens, spruce, oak, ash, chestnut and several varieties of maple. The park opens out into a larger estate comprising 17,000sm square of meadow (alive with tulips and daffodils in spring) and 33,000m square of forest, all with marked walking trails. The 'castle' holds a small (150-piece) collection of modern art, featuring paintings and sculptures by Carlo Carrà, Felice Casorati, Filippo de Pisis, Renato Guttoso, Luigi Mainolfi, Arturo Martini, Giacomo Manzù, Arnaldo Pomodoro and Mario Schifano, among others.

The **Roman bridge of Châtillon** enabled travellers to cross the Torrente Marmore. It consisted of a single substantial round arch of about 15m, supported by sturdy shoulders, which, still used by the modern bridge, rests solidly on the high rocky banks of the stream. The bridge was made of nine arches cemented together: five were made of stone wedges with chips of stone joined by lime mortar. The roadway, now lost, was probably around 4.6m wide.

On high ground across the valley stands the **castle of Ussel**, erected by Ebalo II de Challant around 1350. The first 'monobloc' castle in the Valle d'Aosta, consisting of a single, compact cubic mass, the building is a landmark in the history of feudal military architecture in the region. The main (south) façade has four pairs of mullioned windows and two cylindrical turrets at the top, the only concessions to decoration. The castle is open in summer, for exhibitions (*details on lovevda.it*).

SAINT-DENIS & FÉNIS

Saint-Denis

In the village of Saint-Denis (*map E, C2; approached from Chambave*) is the **castle of Cly** (*open for guided visits in the summer*), perched majestically on a knoll with a backdrop of snowy peaks. Originally a possession of a branch of the Challant family, it presided over a vast territory, before passing to the royal house of Savoy. It was despoiled in the 17th century, for building material that went into the Roncas palace in Chambave. Today the early 11th-century keep is an impressive sight and the Chapel of St Maurice preserves traces of frescoes.

Nearby, in the hamlet of Marseillier (Verrayes), further north, the picturesquely sited **Cappella di San Michele** has precious 15th-century frescoes by Giacomino d'Ivrea, depicting biblical scenes including the *Flight into Egypt* and *Massacre of the Innocents*.

Fénis

Fénis castle (*map E, C2; for info, see lovevda.it*), is the most famous medieval fortress in the Valle d'Aosta and former seat of the Challant family. With numerous towers, it is enclosed by double walls (the outer circuit was reconstructed in 1936). An older fortress, possibly dating from Roman times, was rebuilt c. 1340 by Aimone de Challant and heavily restored at the end of the 19th century. The charming courtyard, with wooden balconies and a lovely semicircular staircase, has remarkable frescoes in a refined International Gothic style by Giacomo Jaquerio and his school (15th century), including *St George and the Dragon* and a frieze of philosophers and prophets holding scrolls with proverbs in Old French. The rooms of the castle have interesting local furniture, although not all of it is authentic. The furnished guardroom contains a model of the castle. The recently restored Crucifix in the chapel is attributed to the workshop of the Master of Oropa, which produced most of the late 13th-century and early 14th-century Crucifixes in valley churches.

Just down the road from Fénis castle, at Chez-Sapin, the **MAV** (Museo dell'Artigianato Valdostano di Tradizione di Fénis; *lartisana.vda.it/mav*) provides a delightful glimpse into local craft traditions. Some 800 items from the 18th century onward document local material culture. There is an especially fine display of wooden toys.

Beyond Fénis is **Nus** (*map E, C2*), where the Maison Rosset, a historic farmhouse, offers rustic dinners by a roaring fire. The vaulted ceilings do little to absorb sound, but the noise and bustle are part of the atmosphere of this very friendly establishment (with rooms), where residents and visitors rub elbows (*maisonrosset.it*).

From the village of Villefranche, further up the valley, you can walk to the **castle of Quart** (*map E, C2*), which is seated in a very picturesque spot on a rocky outcrop along the route of the Via Francigena pilgrim route.

THE VIA FRANCIGENA

The Via Francigena was the medieval pilgrims' way from Canterbury to Rome. Sigeric, Archbishop of Canterbury, travelled along it in the year 990 to receive the pallium, the symbol of his investiture, from Pope John XV. The manuscript description of his return journey is preserved in the British Library in London.

The name Francigena dates from the 9th century because the main course of the route originated in Frankish territory. It was one of three pilgrimage routes in medieval Europe; the other two led to Santiago and Jerusalem. The journey from England to Rome took about two and a half months, and most pilgrims probably made the entire trip on foot (carrying a characteristic staff), although prelates such as Sigeric may have travelled on horseback.

The road was rough and only paved in places, therefore unsuitable for wheeled vehicles. Numerous *ospedali* or stopping places grew up along the way (Sigeric mentions 80), offering help and accommodation to travellers.

The importance of the Via Francigena diminished in the 13th century, when other routes were opened over the Alps. Today, however, sections of it have been cleared and restored and it is growing in popularity with walkers.

THE VALLEY WEST OF AOSTA

Just outside **Gressan** (*map E, B2*) to the south, La Tour de Villa (*tourdevilla.it*) is a splendid castle-hotel overlooking the plain. Founded in the late 12th century, it consists of two buildings: the 20m high keep, with walls more than 2m thick at the base; and the residence, both enclosed by a tall enceinte. It maintains much of its medieval atmosphere thanks to the owners' dislike of decorative frills. The dining hall has frescoes with the coats of arms of noble families of the Valle d'Aosta and other places with whom the De la Tour were allied.

Sarre
The castle of Sarre (*map E, B2; see lovevda.it for details*) was built in the early 18th century by Giovanni Francesco Ferrod di Arvier over the remains of a 13th-century fortress and acquired in 1869 by King Vittorio Emanuele II. This was the sovereign's base camp during his hunting expeditions in the Gran Paradiso reserve. It is notable for its hall decorated with thousands of hunting trophies, including numerous ibex, and its portraits (in the Cabinet des Gravures) of queens Margherita, Elena and Maria José of Savoy.

Aymavilles
At the entrance to the Val di Cogne the road from Aosta passes the unusual castle of Aymavilles (*map E, B2; castelloaymavilles.it*), altered in the 14th century when the turrets were added by Aimone of Challant, and again in the 18th century when Giuseppe Felice of Challant built the arcades between the towers, eliminated many defensive features, gave the interior a Baroque overhaul and the exterior a park.

Pondel
Just off the main road, a by-road (*signposted*) descends to the tiny isolated hamlet of Pondel (Pont d'Aël; *map E, B2*), with a remarkable **Roman bridge** that once also served as an aqueduct. As the inscription states, two Paduans built it privately in the 3rd century BC; 50m long and 56m high, it crosses the ravine made by the Grand'Eyvia torrent. A splendid covered passageway runs beneath the aqueduct channel; it is still usable, but open only for special events. The bridge is extremely well preserved and is considered by scholars to be among the greatest Roman constructions in the Alps. It is not known just why the aqueduct-bridge was built: some hypothesise a link between the bridge and mining activities in the Cogne Valley; others relate the aqueduct to the irrigation of the rain-shadowed mountainsides between Aymavilles and Villeneuve.

Saint-Pierre
At Saint-Pierre (*map E, B2*), the castle was first built in the 12th century but transformed in the 19th, when the four cylindrical towers and castellations were added. In a splendid position on an isolated rock, above the church and bell tower of St-Pierre, it has a good view of the snow-capped mountain of La Grivola. It now

houses the **Museo Regionale di Scienze Naturali Efisio Noussan** (*museoscienze. vda.it*) with exhibits illustrating the geology, flora and fauna of the area as well as the history of the castle itself.

In the township of St-Pierre, in the midst of apple orchards down on the river, is the castle of **Sarriod de la Tour** (*see lovevda.it for details*). The oldest part of the edifice, the chapel and the square central tower, adheres to a building type documented in the Valle d'Aosta as early as the 10th century. Jean Sarriod de la Tour built this castle in the 15th century on the site of a 14th-century tower already in the possession of his family; his additions include the spiral staircase in the tower (viret) and the cut-stone cross winders, which are characteristic of 15th-century Valdostan architecture. Towards the end of the century Antoine Sarriod de la Tour renovated the chapel, adding frescoes of the *Crucifix* and *St Christopher*, and the stout bell-tower. The enceinte was given its cylindrical towers at the end of the century; the west wing was added in the 16th century and the north tower in the 17th. Acquired by the Regional Council in the mid-20th century, the castle now hosts a number of paintings from Quart castle (no longer extant), dating from the 13th to the 16th centuries.

Villeneuve

At Villeneuve (*map E, B2*), in a strategic position overlooking the road to the Little Saint Bernard Pass, rises the ruined castle of **Châtel-Argent**, so called because money was minted there in the Middle Ages. The castle, a possession of the Counts of Savoy, was built over a settlement probably reaching back to the Bronze or Iron Age. What you see today probably dates from the late 13th century: the castle was rebuilt around 1275 by military engineers in the service of Count Peter II of Savoy, including the architect Jacques de Saint-Georges, active two years later in Wales in the service of the king of England, Edward I. The walls, built at the edge of a rocky terrace overlooking the valley, surround a tall cylindrical tower, which stands at the highest point of the site. Up against the walls are residential wings and the 11th–12th-century chapel, the oldest part of the complex. The simplicity of the design suggests the fort was used exclusively for practical purposes.

Introd

The castle here (*map E, B2*), surrounded by almost circular battlemented walls, belonged originally to the Sarriod family. A bull of Pope Nicholas V, allowing the marriage of Pierre Sarriod to Catherine de Challant (1543) is part of the display. The Fondation Grand-Paradis maintains the castle: the ground floor and gardens can be visited (*grand-paradis.it*).

Arvier and Avise

There are several bits of Roman road here. At **Arvier** (*map E, B2*) there is a section still clearly visible by the Leverogne tunnel, along the SS26. It is a substantial part of the containment wall, cement work (stones and lime mortar) with external facing articulated in a sequence of high, narrow arches with strong buttresses at the sides. Another stretch lies at the east end of the Mecosse tunnel, along the SS26. Here are about 30m of the retaining walls of the roadway, displaying two small blind arches, made with long, thin stone slabs with a buttress made of cement work. In the best preserved area the masonry is divided into five parallel bands separated by offsets, and the holes for scaffolding can still be seen.

The road at **Avise** (Pierre Taillée; *map E, B2*) is elevated, cut into the rock and grandly supported above the Dora Baltea. The preserved stretch, about 400m long, reveals remarkable technical skill in supporting and raising the road surface at the same time. Long stretches of the road rest on concrete (stone and lime mortar) walls with buttresses and offsets, supported by blind arches resting directly on the rock. The road proceeded for short, straight segments joined at an obtuse angle: the roadway was 3.5 to 3.7m wide, as can be seen in another section of the road, about 40m long, at **Runaz**, above the SS26.

Between Pré-Saint-Didier and La Thuile

The remains of two Roman bridges can be seen in the stretch of road between Pré-Saint-Didier and La Thuile. The first is located in the hamlet of **La Balme**, below the modern bridge: here, on the left bank of the torrent, is a massive pier made of large blocks of stone laid directly on the bedrock. The second, hardly visible because it is hidden by the modern bridge at **Pont Serrand**, preserves portions of the piers and arch, which is thought to have measured 16.7m across and to have carried a road 4.2m wide.

THE SLOPES OF MONT BLANC

Courmayeur (1228m; *map E, A2*) is a famous ski resort in a deep vale at the southern foot of Mont Blanc. It has a much milder climate than Chamonix, on the other side of the mountain in Savoy. A museum illustrates the history of alpinism in the area. La Palud is the starting point of the cable railway to Chamonix, which crosses over Mont Blanc in c. 1hr 30mins. It runs every hour (weather permitting) and provides a magnificent panorama of the Graian Alps and the south side of the Pennine Alps. It crosses the French frontier at an altitude of 3462m.

Mont Blanc (4807m; *map E, A1*) is the highest mountain in western Europe (the summit is in France). It was first climbed from Chamonix in 1786. The Col de la Seigne (2512m), on the French frontier, is the watershed between the basins of the Po and the Rhône. The Mont Blanc Tunnel, built through the mountains in 1958–65, is 11.6km long. The road descends over 100m from the Italian to the French side

> *On Italy's highest mountains*
>
> The great ones, the giants of Alps, stood about us here and there in a cloudless sky, a burning serenity. Their immobility never seems to me static; it has a vitality that seems to us repose, like that of a humming top at rest on its axis, spinning along its orbit in space.
>
> Freya Stark, *Traveller's Prelude*, 1950

Exploring the Side Valleys

The tributaries of the Dora Baltea rush and tumble through steep, wooded alpine valleys that are every bit as interesting as the main Valle d'Aosta and often more dramatic in their natural beauty. There are four main side valleys: the Val di Gressoney, Valtournenche, Great St Bernard Valley and Val di Cogne, renowned for their immaculate farms, stony little villages and majestic alpine vistas.

VAL DI GRESSONEY

The Val di Gressoney, which leads towards Monte Rosa, is ascended by road from Pont-St-Martin (*map E, D3*). It contains the largest and oldest of the German-speaking colonies formed by settlers who crossed over from Valais in the Middle Ages. The people of this valley, known as the Walsers, are mentioned as early as 1218. They were subjects of the Bishop of Sion and have kept their language and customs even more distinct from their Italian neighbours than have the people of Alagna or Macugnaga. The attractive chalets (*rascards*) in the lower valley, the farmhouses (*stadel*) in the upper valley, and the costume of the women (which is brightly coloured in red and black, with a remarkable headdress adorned with hand-made gold lace) all suggest a northern origin.

Fontainemore, Issime and Gaby

There is a lovely medieval single-arched bridge across the Lys at **Fontainemore** (*map E, D3*) and some fine vernacular architecture, including eleven lovingly restored little chapels in its eleven component hamlets. It is the gateway to the **Riserva Naturale Mont Mars**, a textbook example of a glacial landscape, abounding in heaps of stones (angular detritus deposits of various sizes with associated boulders) and rocky walls, lakes and wetlands. The reserve, at the head of the valley of the Torrente Pacoulla, is known particularly for its ice-carved circular glacial basins, which with time have become lakes and peat bogs. Tall forests prevail at lower altitudes, yielding higher up to verdant meadows in those areas where the ice has not abraded the rock and the slope is not too steep. At **Pra dou Sas** is a little eco-museum with working water-mills and a bakery that makes bread from the flour.

Issime (*map E, D2*) has an interesting German Walser dialect, known as *titsch*, and the signs here are written in all three languages. The church, rebuilt after 1567, has a fresco of the *Last Judgement* on the façade, opposite which is a pretty porch with niches, painted in 1752. Inside is a little museum. The elaborate high altar, in gold and turquoise, is decorated with numerous statues (1690–1710). At the west end is an interesting judge's chair, with a chain collar for those found guilty: it was used up to 1770 in the piazza.

Gaby (*map E, D2*), where the poet Giosuè Carducci used to stay at the end of the 19th century, is a French-speaking village.

Gressoney-St-Jean and Gressoney-la-Trinité

The German dialect is used at **Gressoney-St-Jean** (1385m; *map E, D2*), the principal village in the valley and a summer and winter resort. The pretty little village is German in atmosphere. The church has a bust of Queen Margherita on the façade and a Baroque interior with charming wooden altars and a small museum. A statue of King Umberto I (assassinated in 1900; Queen Margherita was his consort) graces the adjoining piazza. You can still see some old houses here, and there is a fine view of snow-covered Monte Rosa (4637m) at the head of the valley. Set high among fir and larch woods is the turreted Gothic-Revival **Castello Savoia** (or Villa Margherita; *see lovevda.it for details*), built in 1899–1904 by Emilio Stramucci for Queen Margherita, who spent every summer and many winters here up to 1925. There are five towers, all different, and carved or painted daisies (*margherite* in Italian) adorn the interior, part of which is laid out as a house-museum (the rest is the Town Hall). The veranda enjoys a splendid view of Monte Rosa. The kitchen was in a separate building, connected to the castle by a miniature underground railway.

The sister village of **Gressoney-la-Trinité** (1628m) is a ski resort for Monte Rosa, with a view of the grand line of snowy peaks from Monte Rosa to the Gran Paradiso.

VAL D'AYAS & VALTOURNENCHE

Val d'Ayas

The scenic Val d'Ayas leaves the main valley at Verrès (*map E, D3*) and follows the River Evançon. **Brusson** has lovely stone-and-wood houses with flower-filled balconies. The ruined 13th-century castle of **Graines** stands on a prehistoric site in an attractive landscape with cherry trees. The valley has pine forests and massive wooden chalets. **Antagnod** (1710m) has a fine church. **Champoluc** (1570m), surrounded by splendid forests, is an important ski resort for Monte Rosa.

Valtournenche

This famous valley, extending from Châtillon to the base of the Matterhorn (Monte Cervino in Italian; 4478m) along the Torrente Marmore, has numerous resorts, including Valtournenche itself (1528m; *map E, C1–D1*). **Breuil-Cervinia** (2004m; *map E, D1*) has become one of the most popular ski resorts in Italy, with numerous cableways ascending the main ridge of the Alps, dominated by the Matterhorn and

Breithorn (4171m) on either side of the Théodule Pass on the Swiss frontier. Most of the early attempts to scale the Matterhorn were started from Breuil, but the summit was not reached from this side by a direct route until 1867. Today the town is distinctly modern in character, and manifestly overdeveloped.

VAL DI COGNE

The whole of the Gran Paradiso Massif (4061m) to the south of Aosta, above the valleys of Cogne, Valnontey, Valsavarenche and Val di Rhêmes, lies within the **Parco Nazionale del Gran Paradiso** (*map E, B3–C3*), an area of some 70,000 hectares and the oldest national park in Italy (established in 1922). Although the integrity of the park has been threatened by attempts to open up part of the Valsavarenche as a resort for skiers, the Gran Paradiso remains one of the largest semi-wild nature reserves in Europe. The park was created as a hunting reserve for Vittorio Emanuele II in 1856 and presented to the state by Vittorio Emanuele III in 1919. Many of the bridle paths made by Vittorio Emanuele II are still in use. This is the only part of the Alps in which the ibex (*stambecco*) has survived in its natural state (some 5,000 live here). The chamois and Alpine marmot are also common. The flowers are at their best May and June. Information on climbs and walks can be obtained from the Comunità Montana Gran Paradiso in Villeneuve and the information office in Cogne. There are three entrances from the Valle d'Aosta: at Valnontey, Valsavarenche and Val di Rhêmes. The rest of the park lies within Piedmont (*see p. 91*).

The most direct road from Aosta follows the delightful Val di Cogne, the upper reaches of which border the national park. The road passes Aymavilles and Pondel (*see p. 211*). The pretty little resort of **Ozein** (1300m; *map E, B2*), with a few hotels and a fine view of the peak of the Grivola, stands above the main road. The valley opens out into a wide basin at **Cogne** (1533m; *map E, B3–C3*), just outside the limits of the National Park. It has a large common (where you can often see ibex in May), across which rises the snow-capped Gran Paradiso. Cogne was developed as a resort after the magnetite mines were closed down in 1974. You can see remains of the mines, at an altitude of some 2000m on the hillside (the miners were transported by lift), and there is a museum (open May–Sept) in the mining district of Boutillères. Next to the church are a small museum illustrating the craft of lace-making, for which Cogne is famous, and the modest hunting lodge of Vittorio Emanuele III.

A by-road ends at **Lillaz** (*map E, C3*; also reached by a path along the river from Cogne), where most of the houses preserve their typical slate roofs. A path leads past a number of waterfalls.

The other road from Cogne enters the park along the Valnontey, which runs due south to the Gran Paradiso and ends at **Valnontey** (*map E, B3*), an attractive group of houses with a few simple hotels, the starting point of numerous nice walks in the park. The Paradisia alpine garden (1700m), founded here in 1955, is open July–September.

WHERE TO STAY & EAT IN THE VALLEYS

COGNE (*map E, B3–C3*)
€€€ **Bellevue**. A lovely building, locally crafted antiques, staff in traditional dress and a small collection of arts and crafts from the valley make this more than just an upscale hotel; add absolutely breathtaking views, a marvellous spa and a restaurant that is not easily forgotten and you have one of the finest establishments in the Alps. *Via Gran Paradiso 22, T: 0165 74825, hotelbellevue.it.*
€€ **Lou Ressignon**. A rustic *osteria* (with rooms) famous for its game and other mountain dishes, Lou Ressignon is always crowded with locals at weekends and can be quite lively at other times, too. Well worth a visit. *Rue des Mines de Cogne 23, T: 0165 74034, louressignon.it.*

€ **Les Pertzes**. This is a wine bar and brasserie offering good, simple fare at reasonable prices. Interiors are warm and welcoming, with lots of wood and exposed stone, and there is outside seating in warm weather. *Via Grappein 93, T: 0165 749227, brasserielespertzes.it.*

VALTOURNENCHE (*map E, C1–D1*)
€ **La Garde**. This delightful, inexpensive B&B is in a magnificent setting just 4km from Valtournenche. The three double rooms are warm and cosy, with fluffy duvets and, in one case, a fireplace. The breakfasts, with their homemade cakes and jams, are equally inviting. *Frazione Pesontze, Valtournenche Cervinia, T: 327 450 8749, bblagarde.com.*

The Passes

North of Aosta the Valle del Gran San Bernardo extends to the Swiss frontier. People have been coming and going this way since prehistoric times. The Roman road to Summus poeninus, as the Great St Bernard Pass was anciently known, left Augusta Praetoria (Aosta) by the city's north gate, the Porta Principalis Sinistra. One of the main routes from Rome to the northwestern provinces of the empire, the road appears on ancient road maps and in ancient guides, such as the *Tabula Peutingeriana* and *Itinerarium Antoninum*.

The route to the pass
On the way to the pass is **Étroubles** (*map E, B2*), whose Latin name was Stipulae, 'straw', indicating the tow straw left on the ground after the wheat harvest. Until the 1960s, undulating expanses of (organically grown) wheat and rye, speckled with red poppies and blue cornflowers, could still be seen amidst the villages of Étroubles. There is no lack of history in this one-time capital of the Valle del Gran San Bernardo. Étroubles has a stone campanile built in 1480 with a carved-wood portal of the 17th century that was the entrance of the old church. The present parish church was built in 1814 and houses the Trésor de la Paroisse with sacred objects ranging in date from the 14th century to the present. The town is known for its narrow cobblestone streets, ice-cold fountains, slate-roofed stone houses and the wood-and-stone barns of its environs. Étroubles is famous also for its DOP fontina cheese, reputedly the best in the Valle d'Aosta. It iss used in the town's signature dish, *zuppa con fontina e pane nero*, featuring a rye bread baked just once a year (in November) and dried on special racks. The hamlet of **Vachéry** preserves its 12th-century tower.

Further north, beyond a section of road that folds back on itself like a large intestine, is **Saint-Rhémy-en-Bosses** (*map E, B1–B2*), one of the prettiest villages in the Valle d'Aosta, where the Hotel Suisse on the charming main street has a restaurant known for its delicious regional cuisine and warm 18th-century ambience (*suissehotel.it*).

THE GREAT ST BERNARD PASS

The climb to the saddle (*map E, B1*) was very steep, and the ancient roadway, originally just a mule track, was made suitable for carriages only in the late 1st century AD, when the emperor Claudius widened and improved it to facilitate the passage of military vehicles bound for the conquest of Britain. If you look closely you can still discern the ancient road, carved in the rock among the last hairpin turns before the pass. Various traces of Roman architecture have been found on the relatively flat basin near the top, where a sanctuary devoted to Jupiter, the god of mountain summits, and associated accommodation for travellers and their animals (*mansiones*) had been built. Archaeologists have brought to light numerous coins and several bronze votive tablets near the cliffs here.

The pass was much used by pilgrims and clerics bound to or from Rome, and between 774 and 1414 it was crossed 20 times by medieval emperors, including Frederick Barbarossa in 1162. Coaches that entered Italy here in the 18th century had to be dismantled and carried piece by piece over the pass on the backs of local mountaineers. Both French and Austrian soldiers crossed the pass in the campaigns of 1798–1800. The most famous passage was made by Napoleon, who on 14th–20th May 1800 led 40,000 troops by this route into Italy and a month later defeated the Austrians at the Battle of Marengo (*see p. 142*). Numerous engravings were made of the pass after this event and throughout the 19th century. A proper road was constructed only in 1905. Today the last stretch has become a motorway (toll).

The busy tunnel was built in 1958–64. It is 5.8km long and rises slightly from the Italian side (1875m) to the Swiss (1918m). The road over the pass (2473m) is usually closed Nov–June and can be wet and misty at other times, but on a fine day with crisp blue skies it is a magnificent way to enter Switzerland.

Just beyond the Swiss frontier is the **Hospice du Grand-St-Bernard** (2469m), a massive stone building on the summit of the pass, exposed to storms from the northeast and southwest. On the northwest it is sheltered by the peak of Chenalette (2889m), on the southeast by Mont Mort (2867m). The hospice was supposedly founded in the 11th century by St Bernard of Menthon, a native of Savoy; by 1215 it was kept by Augustinian canons from Martigny. Since 1925 the hospice has been managed by ten or twelve canons and a number of lay brothers called aumoniers. In their rescue of snow-bound travellers the canons are assisted by the famous St Bernard dogs, a breed said to be a cross between the Pyrenean sheepdog and the Newfoundland.

ST BERNARD OF AOSTA

The St Bernard passes are named after Bernard of Menthon (d. 1081), archdeacon of the diocese of Aosta where he founded schools and churches, and built guest-houses for mountain travellers. The twin perils of snowdrifts and brigands made traversing the Alps extremely hazardous. St Bernard's guest-houses tended victims of exhaustion or assault, and the specially trained dogs which bear his name helped track down wayfarers lost in the snow. The dogs were also put to work in the hospice kitchens, where a specially constructed running wheel also turned the roasting spit. Pope Pius XI, a keen mountain-climber, made Bernard patron saint of mountaineers in 1923.

THE LITTLE ST BERNARD PASS

The Little St Bernard Pass (2188m; *map E, A2*), approached from La Thuile, is just over the French frontier, on the watershed between the Dora Baltea and the Isère. It has been a key point of the trans-Alpine road system since prehistory.

A short distance to the north (back towards Italy) are the remains of the **Roman infrastructure** at the pass: *mansiones*, which here as elsewhere in the Roman road system provided hospitality to travellers and their means of transit. This civil complex was flanked by a place of worship, a small Gallo–Roman temple (*fanum*) with a square cella surrounded by a portico. The latter is thought to have been dedicated to a local deity, perhaps Hercules, depicted on a silver lamina found in the so-called western *mansio* (on the French side of the pass). Recent excavations on this site have brought to light the remains of a rectangular building measuring 18m by 8m and divided in two by a row of five piers that probably supported a loft or low wooden floor. The masonry has survived remarkably well, having been executed with particular skill, and abundant fragments have been found of the terracotta tiles and cups that covered the roof (as well as quite a few carpentry nails).

The high point of the pass itself is marked by a **circle of standing stones**, one of the oldest archaeological monuments in the Alps. Placed exactly on the watershed between Italy and France—and cut in half by the modern road (for the construction of which the stones were removed, and then returned to their original positions)—the Iron Age stone circle is just over 73m in diameter and probably counted 50 stones originally (there are 43 now).

In France are the **Colonne de Joux**, probably a Roman monument of cipollino marble, with a statue of St Bernard added in 1886; a **botanical garden** established in 1897 by Abbot Pierre Chanoux (whose mortuary chapel lies just beyond); and the ruined **Hospice du Petit-St-Bernard** (2152m), founded c. 1000 to offer free hospitality to poor travellers. Other remnants of the past include fortifications of 1630, bunkers and anti-tank blocks from the Second World War, and customs and border checkpoints used before the Schengen Treaty.

Practical Information

GETTING THERE & GETTING AROUND

By air: Turin Airport (TRN, *aeroportoditorino.it*) at Caselle Torinese, 16km north of the city (*map A, C2*), is connected by daily flights to most European capitals. A railway links the airport to Turin (GTT Dora Railway; *www.gtt.to.it*), with departures every 30mins to the airport c. 5am–7pm and to Turin c. 6am–9pm. Journey time is 19mins. There is also an airport bus from the arrivals concourse to Porta Susa (in front of Exit D) and Porta Nuova station (Corso Vittorio Emanuele II 57A). Buses run to the city at 30min intervals c. 6.10am–12am, and from the city to the airport c. 5.15am–11.30pm. Services also run to Milan Malpensa (c. 2hrs) three times daily; for Malpensa airport information, milanomalpensa-airport.com/en. The airports at Genoa (*www.airport.genova.it*) and Nice Côte d'Azur (*nice.aeroport.fr*) are convenient for anyone heading to the Wine Country and the Maritime Alps, respectively.

The international airports nearest the Valle d'Aosta are Turin (117km), Geneva (141km) and Milan (179km). There is no direct public transport between the valley and Geneva airport, and connections with Milan are infrequent; the most convenient airport for visitors not renting a car is therefore Turin. Buses run from the airport to Turin Porta Susa station every 15–30 mins (operated by Autolinee SADEM; *sadem.it*) and from there to Aosta four or five times daily (operated by Arriva; *aosta.arriva.it*).

By road: The quickest way to Piedmont from Milan and Lombardy is by Autostrada A4; from Bologna and Emilia Romagna, by A1/A21; from Genoa and eastern Liguria, A10/A26 and A21; from Savona and western Liguria, A6. From Geneva, use the San Bernardo or Mont Blanc tunnel; from Lyon or Grenoble, the Mont Cenis (Fréjus) tunnel and E70/A32. From Nice, E74 via Breil-sur-Roya and Colle de Tende.

In the Valle d'Aosta the main routes from Pont-St-Martin, at the foot of the valley, to Courmayeur, at its head, are Autostrada A5 and state highway SS26. The 84km take roughly 1hr to drive non-stop.

By rail and bus: The main train station in Turin is Porta Nuova (*map Turin A, 9*), though Milan-bound trains often stop also at Porta Susa (*map Turin A, 1*) and Genoa-bound trains, at Lingotto. Timetables and tickets are available at trenitalia.com and italotreno.it. Serravalle Scrivia, Novi Ligure, Alessandria and Asti are on the main line from Genoa to Turin; Mondovì, Fossano and Savigliano are on the main line from Savona. There is a very beautiful railway line through the mountains between Cuneo and Ventimiglia, traversing nearly 100km of the Italian and French Maritime Alps in just over 2hrs; trains continue to Nice.

There are trains from Torino Porta Nuova to Aosta (2hrs) more or less every hour from 6am to 10pm. A pretty line built between the two World Wars continues from Aosta to Pré-St-Didier, a few kilometres south of Courmayeur, in c. 50mins (information and tickets at trenitalia.com).

Paper (i.e. not electronic) tickets which do not show a date and time (in other words, open-validity tickets) must be validated at the stamping machines on the station platform before you board. The aim of this is to prevent you using the ticket again or to enable you to claim a refund in case the train fails to depart. You can be fined if you forget to validate.

Buses run all year from Aosta (opposite the railway station) to towns and villages in the Valle d'Aosta as well as to Turin and Milan; via the Great St Bernard Tunnel to Martigny, and via Courmayeur and the Mont Blanc Tunnel to Chamonix. For the side valleys a change is usually necessary at the town at the beginning of the valley. The buses are run by Arriva; for details of routes, timetables and journey planners, see their website (*aosta.arriva.it*).

DISABLED TRAVELLERS

All new public buildings in Italy are obliged to provide facilities for the disabled. Historic buildings are more difficult to convert, and access difficulties still exist. Hotels that cater for the disabled are indicated in tourist board lists. Airports and railway stations provide assistance, and certain trains are equipped to transport wheelchairs. Access to town centres is allowed for cars with disabled drivers or passengers, and special parking places are reserved for them.

VISITOR CARDS

The **Torino + Piemonte Card**, valid for different numbers of days, gives free access to all urban public transport and free entrance to museums, monuments and royal residences in Turin and Piedmont. It is also good for free rides on the panoramic lift in the Mole Antonelliana, boats on the Po, or the Sassi-Superga cog railway, as well as reductions of up to 50 percent on theatre and music events. The card is available online (*turismotorino.org/en/your-trip/torinopiemonte-card*) and at Turismo Torino information points, hotels, and participating museums and monuments.

The **Aosta Valley Card** also comes in different packages, with discounts on various sights, activities and attractions (see *aostavalleycard.it/card*).

ACCOMMODATION

A very small selection of hotels, chosen on the basis of character or location, is given in the various chapters of the guide. They are classified as follows: €€€€ (€900 or over), €€€ (€350–900), €€ (€150–300) or € (€150 or under). It is advisable to book well in advance, especially between May and October; if you cancel the booking with at least 72 hours' notice you can claim back part or all of your deposit. Service charges are included in the rates. By law breakfast is an optional extra, although a lot of hotels will include it in the room price. When booking, always specify if you want breakfast or not. If you are staying in a hotel in a town, it is often more fun to go round the corner to the nearest café for breakfast.

FOOD & WINE

Italian food is usually good and inexpensive. Generally speaking, the least pretentious *ristorante* (restaurant), *trattoria* (small restaurant) or *osteria* (inn or tavern) provides the best value. A selection of restaurants is given in the individual chapters of the guide. Prices are categorised as follows: €€€€ (€80 or more per head), €€€ (€60–80), €€ (€40–50) and € (€30 or under). Many places are considerably cheaper at midday. It is always a good idea to reserve.

Prices on the menu do not include a cover charge (shown separately, usually at the bottom of the page), which is added to the bill. The service charge (*servizio*) is now almost always automatically added at the end of the bill; tipping is therefore not strictly necessary, but a few euro are appreciated. Note that many simpler establishments do not offer a written menu.

PIEDMONTESE CUISINE

The cuisine of Piedmont is considered by many to be the best in Italy; indeed, many visitors to the region come here to eat rather than to look at monuments and museums. Piedmont's traditions have been influential, but they also remain local and self-contained. Each valley and village has its own, peculiar culinary repertoire. But Piedmont is also home to many items of food and drink that have become household names. The native arborio rice used for Italian risotto is mainly grown in the wetlands of the Po Valley around Vercelli and Novara. Cinzano, Martini and Campari all have their roots in Piedmont (the first two in Turin, the last in Novara); *grissini* were invented here. Piedmont is a land of butter, not of olive oil; the cooking is not Mediterranean. Pork, veal and game birds, mushrooms and truffles feature prominently. The wines of the region are extremely important: Barolo and Barbaresco, both from the hillsides of the Langhe, are the most aristocratic of all Italian wines.

Outstanding regional dishes include the appetisers *vitello tonnato* (*vitel tonné* in dialect), made with boiled spiced veal sliced thinly and smothered in a sauce of tuna, anchovies and capers), and *cipolle ripiene* (baked onions stuffed with parmesan cheese, egg, butter, spices and, sometimes, braised beef or sausage).

Good first courses are *agnolotti* (ravioli of Provençal origin; *agnolotti grassi* are made with veal and other meats mixed with egg and cheese; *agnolotti magri* with spinach, cream, egg and cheese), and *fonduta* (a hot dip with fontina cheese, milk, and egg yolks sprinkled with truffles and white pepper).

Delicious main courses include *bagna cauda* (a hot spicy sauce with garlic and anchovies used as a dip for raw vegetables), *brasato al barolo* (beef marinated in a Barolo wine sauce with lard, carrots and spices, then slowly braised in the marinade together with meat broth and tomatoes) and *bollito misto con salsa verde* (various types of meat stewed together with a green sauce made with herbs).

A very special Piedmontese dessert is *zabaione* (named after San Giovanni Baylon, the patron saint of pastry chefs: egg yolks, Marsala wine and sugar whipped together in a double boiler and served, usually, with dry biscuits).

Turin was the first city in Europe to process cocoa. The most famous expression of this tradition is the *giandujotto*, the famous chocolate made from cocoa and hazelnuts, named after the Torinese Carnival character Giandjua. In the Langhe, where the preparation of food is considered a fine art on a par with painting, sculpture and architecture, the white truffle of Alba vies with *tajarin*, the only authentically Piedmontese pasta (thin ribbon-like egg noodles, handmade and served with meat drippings, butter and sage), as the most typical item.

THE WINES OF PIEDMONT

Piedmont is one of the finest wine-growing areas in Italy. The region counts 50 DOC and DOCG wines, and one district—Asti—is second only to the Chianti in terms of quantity of wine produced.

Dolcetto. Among Piedmontese reds, Dolcetto is a dry single-varietal red wine that takes its name from the intense sweet flavour of the dolcetto grape. Grown throughout Piedmont, it has a robust structure, intense spicy nose, rich colour and is high in tannins and alcohol. The most famous is Dolcetto d'Alba, from the Langa of Alba.

Freisa. This is a single varietal red available in dry (*secco*) and sweet (*amabile*) versions. Garnet-red to light cherry in colour, it takes on orange nuances with ageing. It has delicate raspberry and rose scents and a fresh flavour. The best comes from Asti and from Chieri; Freisa di Chieri is also vinified *frizzante* and *spumante*.

Grignolino is the signature wine of Asti and the Monferrato. Difficult to make, it has a light, ruby-red colour that develops orange shades with ageing; the flavour is grassy and tart, dry and tannic, with a pleasantly bitter aftertaste.

Nebbiolo. As many as 12 Piedmontese DOC wines, including Barbaresco, Roero and the world-famous Barolo, are made from the Nebbiolo grape (the oldest in the region, documented since the 13th century). Served with robust first courses or with red meat, these wines are an intense ruby-red, tending toward granite-red when aged. They have a light, delicate nose recalling raspberries and violets, which grows and improves with age. Pleasantly tannic when young, they age well to become full-bodied, smooth and harmonic. Barolo, possibly Italy's best red wine, is grown in a small area south of Alba. It is rich, tannic, strong (minimum 13 per cent alcohol), dry but wonderfully deep and fragrant; it can age up to 15 years and is *riserva* after five.

Barbera is a single-varietal wine made from grapes grown on the hills around Alba, Asti and in the Monferrato. It has an intense, delicate nose and a dry, full-bodied and pleasantly bitter flavour that mellows with ageing to become rounder and more harmonious. Barbera's popularity in the past as a low-priced table wine has tarnished its reputation, which is now improved thanks to new growing and vinification techniques. Barbera del Monferrato, made with a small percentage of Freisa, Grignolino and/or Dolcetto grapes, can be lightly sparkling.

Cortese is a single-varietal white wine grown in three areas: Alto Monferrato, Gavi and Colli Tortonesi. Sometimes made with small percentages of other non-aromatic whites, it is perfect with appetisers, delicate pasta and rice dishes, and soups. Light straw-yellow in colour, sometimes with a touch of green, it has a delicate but persistent nose and a dry, pleasantly bitter flavour. It is Piedmont's oldest and most familiar dry white wine.

Gavi, probably the most famous white wine of Piedmont, is grown in a small area between Gavi and Novi Ligure. Made with the Cortese grape, it has a straw-yellow colour and a distinctive dry, fresh, harmonic flavour. Good with fish and seafood, it is also vinified *spumante naturale* or *frizzante naturale*.

VALLE D'AOSTA FOOD AND WINE

Cooking in the Valle d'Aosta is simple but tasty, with a high reliance on meat, eggs, cheese and potatoes. The region is noted for its fontina cheese, some of which is still made in the old slate-roofed farm buildings raised on wooden stilts. Other specialities include *mocetta*, a salami made from goat or chamois meat, and the highly prized *lardo d'Arnad*, made from the fat of pigs fed on chestnuts. Polenta is an important staple here, and veal is also popular.

The indigenous Blanc de Morgex grape is used in the delicious Valle d'Aosta Blanc de Morgex and La Salle white wines; other good whites are Chambave and Nux. Excellent reds are Aymavilles (Torrette) and Donnas.

ADDITIONAL INFORMATION

EMERGENCIES

In general, there is good mobile coverage in the towns of the Valle d'Aosta and its side valleys, though coverage quickly becomes sketchy in the mountains. Don't count on your mobile phone to call the rescue service when hiking or skiing off piste. For life-threatening emergencies in remote places, phone the Alpine Rescue Service, T: 118.

PUBLIC HOLIDAYS

Italian national holidays are as follows:
>   1 January
>   Easter Sunday and Easter Monday
>   25 April (Liberation Day)
>   1 May (Labour Day)
>   2 June (Festa della Repubblica)
>   15 August (Assumption)
>   1 November (All Saints' Day)
>   8 December (Immaculate Conception)

25 December (Christmas Day)
26 December (St Stephen)
Each town keeps its patron saint's day as a holiday.

TIPPING

Service charges are normally included and tipping in Italy is not routinely expected. It is normal to round up the bill and leave a few coins in appreciation.

Index

Acqui Terme 171
Agliè 88
Agnelli, Giovanni 25, 107
Alagna Valsesia 74
Alba 152
Alberini, Giorgio 169
Albertini, Amedeo 24
Albertoni, Giovanni 74
Albugnano 32
Alessandria 139
Alfieri, Benedetto 11, 14, 17, 21, 22, 28, 31, 141, 143, 169, 177, 179
Alfieri, Vittorio 178
Aloisio, Ottorino 179
Alta Langa 161ff
Alta Valle del Po 109
Alto Canavese 87
Andrea del Sarto 146
Angelico, Fra' 15
Angera 55
Anselm, St 195
Antagnod 214
Antonelli, Alessandro 22, 69, 142, 143, 144
Antonello da Messina 10
Antonio da Viterbo 146
Aosta, city of 195ff
Arbasia, Cesare 114, 117
Arienti, Stefano 73
Arnad 205
Arona 44
Arte Povera 29, 76
Arvier 211
Asti 177
Austria, Austrians 6, 55, 142
Avigliana 95
Avise 212
Aymavilles 210
Balla, Giacomo 26, 27, 76, 145

Bambaia 48
Barbarossa, Frederick 139, 145, 218
Bard 203
Bardonecchia 101
Barolo 158
Baroni, Eugenio 9
Bartolomeo da Pisa 61
Bassa Langa 152
Bassano family, painters 16, 49
Basso Canavese 81
Baveno 47
Beaumont, Claudio Francesco 14
Becchi 32
Belgirate 46
Bellino 118
Bellinzago Novarese 144
Belloc, Hilaire 47
Bellosio, Carlo 11
Bellotto, Bernardo 16, 26
Benard, Michel 28
Bene Vagienna 157
Berber, Giovanni Battista 169
Beretta, Carlo 61
Bergognone (Ambrogio da Fossano) 44, 98, 146
Bergolo 162, 163
Bermejo, Bartolomé 172
Bernard of Aosta, St 218
Bertola, Ignazio 98, 100, 106, 141
Biella 75
Biella, Felice 134
Bissoni, Domenico 173
Bistolfi, Leonardo 170, 171
Bo, Ludovico Antonio 90
Bobbio Pellice 109
Boccioni, Umberto 27
Boetto, Giovenale 123, 130, 155, 157
Boldini, Giovanni 76

Index

Bombelli, Augine 175
Bonaparte, Napoleon (*see Napoleon*)
Bonaparte, Pauline 17
Boniface VIII, Pope 72
Bonzanigo, Giuseppe Maria 179
Borgaro, Ignazio Birago 88
Borgese, Giovanni Antonio 161
Borghi, Ambrogio 143
Borgomasino 84
Borgosesia 70
Borra, Giovanni Battista 30
Borromeo family 44, 48ff, 54, 55, 64
Borromeo, St Charles 44, 45; (giant statue of) 45
Borsalino milliners 141
Bortoloni, Mattia 134
Bosco Marengo 176
Bosco, St John (Don Bosco) 31
Botticelli, Sandro 16
Bourbon, Giulio 169
Bra 165
Brandi, Giacinto 143
Breuil-Cervinia 214
Briosco, Benedetto 48, 114
Browne, Sophie 51
Brueghel, Jan the Elder 146
Brusson 214
Buck, Jan de 142
Buren, Daniel 73
Busca 126
Bussola, Dionigio 65
Butler, Samuel 74, 97
Byron, Lord 46
Caccia, Guglielmo (il Moncalvo) 31, 140, 170, 176
Cafassi, Alberto 140
Calandra, Davide 24, 116
Caldè 55
Calderara, Antonio 62
Calderini, Marco 76
Calosso 181
Caluso 83
Cambiaso, Luca 175
Canaletto, Giovanni Antonio 26
Candelo 78
Canelli 181
Cannero Riviera 54
Cannobio 54
Canonica, Pietro 9
Canova, Antonio 26
Caraglio 124
Caravino 84
Carducci, Giosuè 85, 91, 214
Carena, Felice 103
Carignano 31
Carlevalis 49
Carlo Alberto of Savoy 9, 11, 14, 15, 19, 30, 127, 142, 154
Carlo Felice of Savoy 19, 204
Carlone, Carlo 22
Carrà, Carlo 27, 117, 140, 208
Carracci, Annibale 86
Casale Monferrato 168
Cascata del Toce 66
Casorati, Felice 76, 180, 208
Casotto, Castello Reale 135
Cassinari, Bruno 140
Casteldelfino 118
Castellamonte, Amedeo di 26, 30, 118
Castellar 111
Castelli, Filippo 83
Castello Savoia 214
Castelnuovo Don Bosco 31
Castiglione Falletto 160
Castiglione, Giovanni Benedetto 175
Catinat, General Nicolas 96, 106, 110
Cavour (village) 105
Cavour, Camillo 6, 8, 160, 204
Cerano, il (*see Crespi*)
Ceresole Reale 91
Cerrione 78
Cerro 55
Cervelli, Federico 177
Cesana Torinese 107
Cézanne, Paul 107
Chagall, Marc 76
Challant family 195, 205, 208, 210, 211
Chambave 208
Champoluc 214
Chanoux, Emile 195
Châtel-Argent 211
Châtillon 208
Cherasco 155
Chieri 31

Chirico, Giorgio de 27, 76, 86, 117, 180
Chiusa di Pesio 132
Claudius, emperor 217
Clemer, Hans 111, 113
Cly, castle of 208
Cocker, Henry 50, 51
Cogne 215
Cogrossi, Giovanni 86
Cortemilia 162
Costigliole Saluzzo 117
Cottian Alps 95
Courbet, Gustave 27
Courmayeur 212
Cremolino 173
Crespi, Antonio Maria 61
Crespi, Daniele 49
Crespi, Giovanni Battista 45
Crivelli, Angelo 48
Crosato, Giovanni Battista 28
Cumiana 104
Cuneo 122
Cuorgnè 90
Cuzzi, Umberto 26
D'Amato, Federico 172
D'Andrade, Alfredo 24, 88, 89, 97, 155
D'Annunzio, Gabriele 9
D'Errico, Giovanni 73
Dabbene, Simona 165
Dalí, Salvador 76
De Carlo, Adolfo 87
De Nittis, Giuseppe 76
De Pisis, Filippo 117, 208
Delleani, Lorenzo 75, 103, 117
Demonte 127
Dickens, Charles 46
Dogliani 158
Dolce, Pietro 117
Dolcino, Fra' 71
Domodossola 65
Donnas 202
Dormelletto 42
Dronero 125
Duccio di Buoninsegna 16
Dürer, Albrecht 11
Dyck, Sir Antony van 16
Emanuele Filiberto, Duke of Savoy 14, 17, 27, 177; (monument to) 21
Entracque 128
Étroubles 217
Eusebius of Vercelli, St 77
Exilles 100
Eyck, Jan van 10, 15
Fattori, Giovanni 27, 76
Fenestrelle 105
Fénis 209
Ferrari, Defendente 16, 18, 95, 96, 146
Ferrari, Ferruccio 172
Ferrari, Gaudenzio 23, 44, 54, 62, 70, **71**, 73, 74, 142, 143, 146, 169
Ferretti, Dante 20
Fiammenghino 143
Fiasella, Domenico 175
Fiat factory (Turin) 25
Figini & Pollini, architects 87
Filiberti, Francesco 180
Fontainemore 213
Fontana, Lucio 125
Foresto Gorge 98
Fornara, Carlo 145
Fornari, Michele 147
Fossano 115
Fossati, Bernardino 153
Fouquet, Nicolas 102
Frabosa Soprana 133
Francia, Francesco 146
Frankl, Wolfgang 87
Fruttuaria, Abbazia di 82
Funi, Achille 143
Gabetti, Roberto 87, 154
Gaby 214
Gaglianico 78
Galletti, Ignazio 77
Gallo, Francesco 126, 130, 131, 132, 133, 134, 161
Gambogi, Raffaello 145
Gandolfino d'Asti 175
Gandolfino da Roreto 140
Gardella, Arnaldo 141
Gardella, Ignazio 86, 141
Garessio 134
Garibaldi, Giuseppe 142
Garutti, Alberto 73
Gavi 174
Genestredo 64

Gentilleschi, Orazio 16
Ghiffa 52
Giacomino d'Ivrea 208
Gianotti, Giovanbattista 141
Gibbon, Edward 49
Gignese 47
Giordano, Luca 49, 173
Giovanni del Biondo 86
Giovenone, Girolamo 147
Giugiaro, Giorgetto 134
Gonin, Francesco 11
Govone 167
Gozzano, Guido 89
Graglia 77
Graham, Dan 73
Graian Alps 81
Graines 214
Gran Paradiso 91, 215
Gray, Thomas 8
Great St Bernard Pass 217
Gressan 210
Gressoney-la-Trinité 214
Gressoney-St-Jean 214
Grien, Hans Baldung 146
Grinzane Cavour 160
Grissini 38
Grosso, Giacomo 103
Guala, Pietro Francesco 170
Guarene 166
Guarini, Guarino 11, 17, 18, 19, 22, **23**, 30, 165
Guercino 16, 22
Guglielmino, Giuseppe 98
Guttoso, Renato 208
Hardwick, James 27
Hazlitt, William 8
Hemingway, Ernest 46
Honorius IV, Pope 71
Huchtenburg, Jan van 16
Induno, Girolamo 146
Intra 52
Introd 211
Isola Bella 48
Isola Madre 50
Isola San Giulio 62
Isola, Aimaro 15, 87
Isole Borromee 48

Ispra 55
Issime 213
Issogne 205
Ivrea 85
Jacques de Saint-Georges 211
Jaquerio, Giacomo 96, 196, 209
Jewish communities 130, 147, 156, 169, 179
John XV, Pope 209
Julius, St 62
Juvarra, Filippo 9, 10, 14, 21, 22, **23**, 26, 27, 28, 29, 30, 77
Kandinsky, Vassily 180
Kauffmann, Angelica 146
Klee, Paul 76
Kürten, Xavier 31, 88, **89**, 117, 126, 154, 167
La Balme 212
La Morra 159
Lagnasco 116
Lago d'Orta 60
Lago di Candia 83
Lago Maggiore 42
Landriani, Paolo Camillo 143
Langa Astigiana 163
Langhe 152
Lanino, Bernardino 23, 77, 142, 146
Lanino, Gerolamo 52
Laveno 55
Le Nôtre, André 11, 30
Lega, Silvestro 27, 76
Leggiuno 55
Legnani, Stefano Maria (il Leganino) 19, 22
Legros, Pierre 14
Leonardo da Vinci 11
Lepontine Alps 60
Levi, Carlo 17
Levi, Primo 24
Levice 163
LeWitt, Sol 159
Lillaz 215
Lippi, Filippino 15
Lippi, Filippo 23
Little St Bernard Pass 219
Locarni, Giuseppe 147
Loo, Carle van 28

Lorenzi, Francesco 170
Luini, Aurelio 52
Luini, Bernardino 55, 70, 146
Luino 54
Macrino d'Alba 153
Macugnaga 66
Magritte, René 76
Mainolfi, Luigi 208
Maloberti, Marcello 73
Mancini, Antonio 76
Manet, Edouard 26
Mango 161
Manta 115
Manzù, Giacomo 208
Maragliano, Anton Maria 173, 175
Marengo, battlefield 142; (exhibits) 140
Margherita, Queen 17, 214
Marinali, Orazio 51
Maritime Alps 122
Marochetti, Carlo 21
Marseillier 208
Martini, Arturo 51, 172, 208
Marussig, Pietro 143
Masio 182
Master of La Manta 115
Master of Oropa 75, 209
Matisse, René 26
Matterhorn 214
Mazzè 83
McEacharn, Captain Neil 51
Melano, Ernest 154
Mella, Edoardo Arborio 98, 153
Mengs, Anton Raphael 16
Meo del Caprino 18
Merz, Mario 22, 27
Micca, Pietro 26
Migliara, Giovanni 140
Miró, Joan 76, 180
Modigliani, Amedeo 26
Molare 173
Mombaldone 164
Mombasiglio 134
Monastero Bormida 163
Moncalieri, Castello Reale 28
Moncalvo (see Caccia, Guglielmo)
Mondovì 129
Monevi, Giovanni 164

Monferrato region 167ff
Monforte d'Alba 158
Mont Avic 206
Mont Blanc 212
Montalcini, Gino Levi 90
Monterosso 172
Monti, Gaetano Matteo 49
Monticello d'Alba 166
Montjovet 205
Morandi, Giorgio 27
Morazzone, il (Pier Francesco
    Mazzucchelli) 44, 61, 74, 143
Morbelli, Angelo 145, 170
Morello, Carlo 10
Moretto da Brescia 49
Morsasco 173
Mottarone, Mt 46
Napoleon 38, 42, 49, 65, 66, 99, 134, 140,
    142, 155, 179, 218
Neive 161
Nervi, Pier Luigi 24
Newdigate, Sir Roger 199
Nicholas V, Pope 211
Nizza Monferrato 181
Nizzoli, Marcello 87
Nomellini, Plinio 143, 145
Novaglio 53
Novalesa 99
Novara 142
Novi Ligure 176
Nus 209
Nuvolone, Carlo Francesco 61
Nuvolone, Giuseppe 61
Occitan 125, 133
Oddone, Pascale 110
Oggebbio 53
Olgiati, Giovanni Maria 174
Olivero, Matteo 114
Olivetti company 85, 86
Olivieri, Giuseppe Maria 87
Omegna 62
Oropa 77
Orta San Giulio 60
Ostana 111
Ovada 173
Ozein 215
Pagani, Paolo 175

Palagi, Pelagio 11, 22, 30, 154
Palizzi, Filippo 146
Pallanza 50
Palmezzano, Marco 146
Parco Naturale
　delle Alpi Marittime 129
　del Gran Bosco di Salbertrand 101
　del Gran Paradiso 91, 215
　di Mont Avic 206
　del Monte San Giorgio 105
　del Monte Tre Denti–Freidour 104
　dell'Orsiera-Rocciavré 106
　della Val Grande 64
Partisans 125
Passanti, Mario 180
Patois 194
Pavese, Cesare 161
Pavone Canavese 87
Pejrone, Paolo 73, 85
Pella 62
Pellico, Silvio 114, 159
Pellizza da Volpedo, Giuseppe 76, 140, 145, 173
Pennine Alps 69
Penone, Giuseppe 30
Pérez Arroyo, Salvador 52
Petrolino, Francesco Antonio 54
Pettenasco 63
Piacentini, Marcello 18, 51, 172
Piano, Renzo 26
Piasco 118
Piazza, Callisto 142
Pietraporzio 127
Piffetti, Pietro 10, 158
Pinerolo 102
Piossasco 104
Pistoletto, Michelangelo 76
Pitocchetto, il (Giacomo Cerruti) 50
Pius XI, Pope 218
Plana, Antonio 22
Pliny the Elder 193
Pogatschnig, Giuseppe Pagano 90
Pollenzo 154
Pollone 77
Pomodoro, Arnaldo 208
Pondel 210
Pont Serrand 212

Pont-Saint-Martin 202
Porcinai, Pietro 73, 173
Pozzo, Andrea 22, 123, 130
Pra dou Sas 213
Pragelato 107
Prasco 173
Pray 70
Pregliasco, Giacomo 30
Prestinari, Cristoforo 61
Preti, Mattia 175
Previati, Gaetano 145
Procaccini, Giulio Cesare 61
Quadri, Bernardino 22
Quarna Sotto 63
Quaroni, Ludovico 87
Quart, castle 209
Racconigi 30, 117
Radetzky, Field Marshal 142
Rana, Carlo Amedeo 84
Raphael 11
Rapisardi, Ernesto 172
Rembrandt 11, 16
Reni, Guido 16
Renoir, Auguste 26, 27
Revello 110
Reycend, Enrico 103, 117
Ridolfi, Mario 87
Riserva Naturale Mont Mars 213
Rivara 89
Rivoli 29
Rocca de' Baldi 126
Rocca Grimalda 174
Roccaverano 163
Roddi 154
Roero region 164ff
Romagnano Sesia 69
Ronchelli, Giovanni Battista 169
Rosmini, Antonio 46
Rossignolo, Giacomo 117
Rousseau, Jean-Jacques 22
Rubens, Peter Paul 16
Runaz 212
Rusnati, Giuseppe 65
Sacri Monti, general 53
　Crea 170
　Domodossola 65
　Ghiffa 52

Graglia 77
Oropa 77
Orta San Giulio 61
Valperga 90
Varallo 73
Sada, Carlo 135
Saint-Denis 208
Saint-Pierre 210
Saint-Rhémy-en-Bosses 217
Saint-Vincent 207
Salassi, Gallic people 193
Salesians 31
Saluzzo 112
Salvi, Victor 118
San Giorgio Canavese 82
San Giorio 97
San Marzanotto 180
San Michele, Abbazia di 96
San Nazzaro Sesia 144
Sanfront 111
Sanmicheli, Matteo 114, 169
Sansovino, Jacopo 16
Sant'Antonio di Ranverso, Precettoria di 96
Santa Fede, Abbazia di 81
Santo Stefano Belbo 161
Sarre 210
Sarriod de la Tour 211
Sassu, Aligi 140
Sauze d'Oulx 101
Savigliano 116
Savinio, Alberto 27
Savoy royal residences
  Agliè 88
  Govone 167
  La Mandria 30
  Moncalieri 28
  Pollenzo 154
  Racconigi 30
  Rivoli 29
  Stupinigi 28
  Turin 9ff
  Venaria Reale 30
Scamozzi, Ottavio Bertotti 170
Scapitta, Giovanni Battista 170
Schiaffino, Francesco 175
Schiaparelli, Ernesto 199
Schifano, Mario 208
Scorza, Sinibaldo 175
Segantini, Giovanni 145
Sella, Vittorio 76
Serralunga d'Alba 160
Serravalle Scrivia 175
Sesto Calende 56
Sestriere 107
Severini, Gino 26, 27, 117, 141
Sezzadio 176
Sigeric, Archbishop 209
Signer, Roman 73
Signorini, Teleamaco 27, 76
Silvestrin, Claudio 27
Simi, Filadelfo 86
Simplon Pass 66
Simplon Railway Tunnel 66
Sironi, Mario 76, 117, 180
Soave, Felice 55
Solimena, Francesco 16
Sordevolo 78
Sormani, Giovanni Lorenzo 153
Spanzotti, Giovanni Martino 18
Spanzotti, Martino 90
Staffarda, Abbazia di 110
Stark, Freya 212
Stella, Fermo 61
Stendhal 46
Strada della Lana 71
Stramucci, Emilio 214
Stresa 46
Strozzi, Bernardo 175
Stuart, James, Old Pretender 179
Stupinigi 28
Superga, basilica of 27
Susa 98
Sutherland, Graham 125
Tabacchetti, Giovanni 73
Tabacchi, Odoardo 170
Tagliolo Monferrato 174
Tanzio da Varallo 74, 143
Taricco, Sebastiano 156
Tempesta, Antonio 49
Terentius Varro 195
Thorvaldsen, Bertel 142
Tibaldi, Pellegrino 22, 44, 51, 143, 147
Tiepolo, Giovanni Battista 26, 49

Titian 146
Torre Pellice 108
Tortona 144
Tosi, Ignazio 173
Tot, Amerigo 173
Tour de Villa 210
Tozzi, Mario 51
Tramezzini, history of 9
Tremlett, David 159
Trisobbio 173
Trivero 71
Troubetzkoy, Paolo 51
Turin 8ff
Turin Shroud 17
Urbini, Carlo 52
Usseaux 106
Ussel 208
Vacca, Luigi 118
Vacchetta, Giovanni 158
Vacciago 62
Vachéry 217
Val Chisone 105
Val d'Ossola 65
Val d'Ayas 214
Val d'Ossola 66
Val di Cogne 215
Val di Gressoney 213
Val di Susa 95
Val Divedro 66
Val Formazza 66
Val Grande 63
Val Vigezzo 66
Valdieri 127
Valduggia 70
Valizzone, Cristoforo 140
Valle Anzasca 66
Valle d'Antrona 66
Valle d'Aosta 193ff
Valle del Gran San Bernardo 217
Valle Gesso 127
Valle Pellice 108
Valle Sessera 70
Valle Stura 126
Valle Varaita 117
Valle, Gino 87
Valnontey 215
Valperga 90

Valsesia 69
Valtournenche 214
Varallo 73
Varzo 66
Vasari, Giorgio 176
Vedova, Pietro della 74
Vela, Vincenzo 9
Velotti, Nicolao 77
Venaria Reale, Reggia di 30
Verbania 50
Vercelli 146
Veronese, Paolo 16
Verrès 205
Vervaz 206
Vezzolano, Abbazia di 33
Via Francigena 209
Vicoforte 133
Victoria, Eduardo 87
Victoria, Queen 48
Vignale Monferrato 171
Villeneuve 211
Vinadio 127
Viscounts of Aosta 195
Vitozzi, Ascanio 134
Vittone, Bernardo 84, 132, 134, 166
Vittone, Bernardo Antonio 82
Vittorio Amedeo II of Savoy 6, 14, 16, 38, 102, 110, 141, 178
Vittorio Emanuele II, King 6, 10, 15, 19, 28, 103, 128, 135, 142, 210, 215
Vittozzi, Ascanio 18, 21, 26
Vogogna 63
Volpedo 145
Voltaggio 175
Waldensians 105, 107, **108**
Walpole, Horace 8
Walsers 74, 213
Wine 223
Zandomeneghi, Federico 76
Zegna, Ermenegildo, foundation and park 73
Zuccarelli, Francesco 49
Zucchi, Cino 24
Zucchi, Giovanni Matteo 164

234 | BLUE GUIDE PIEDMONT & THE VALLE D'AOSTA

MAPS | 235

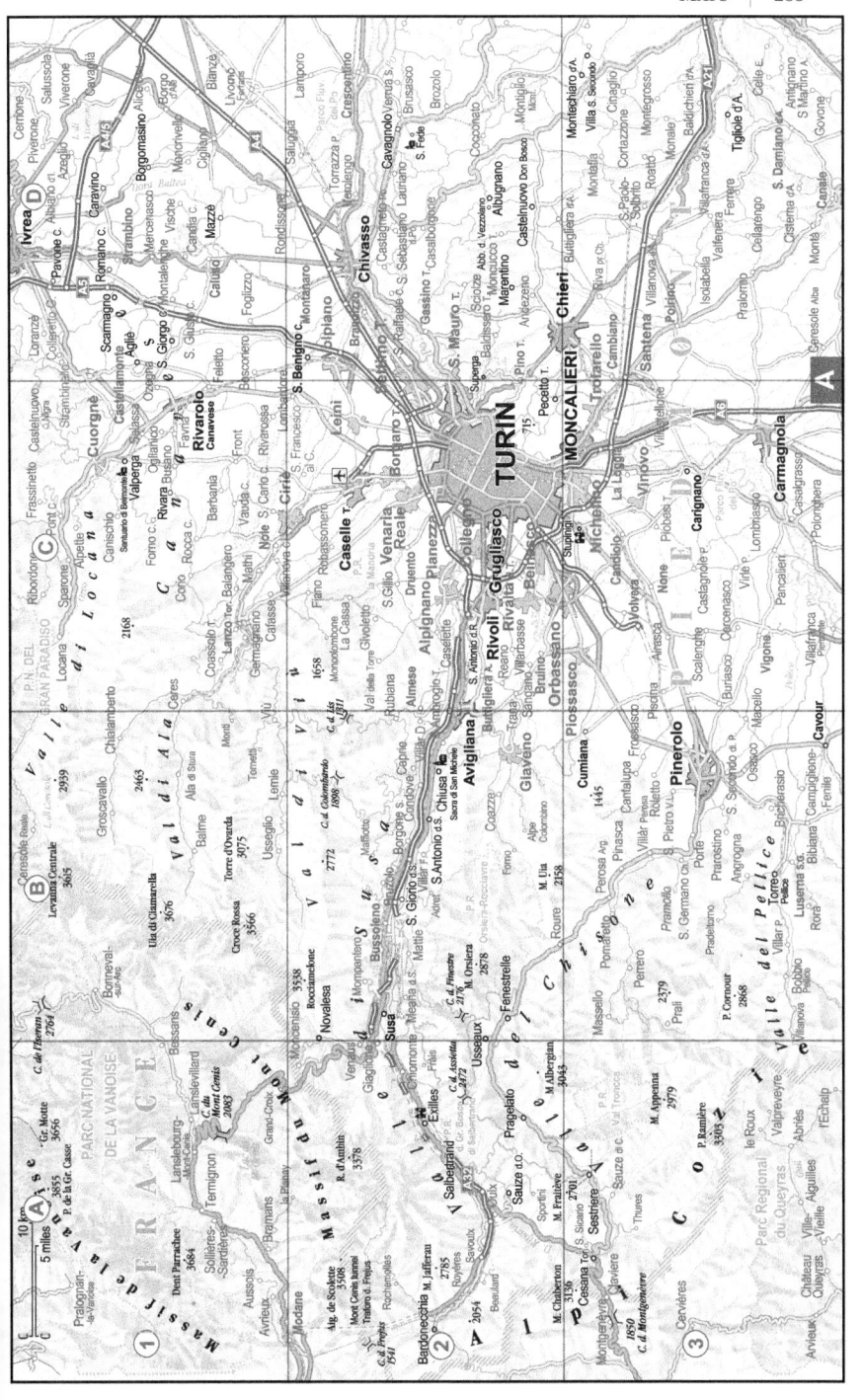

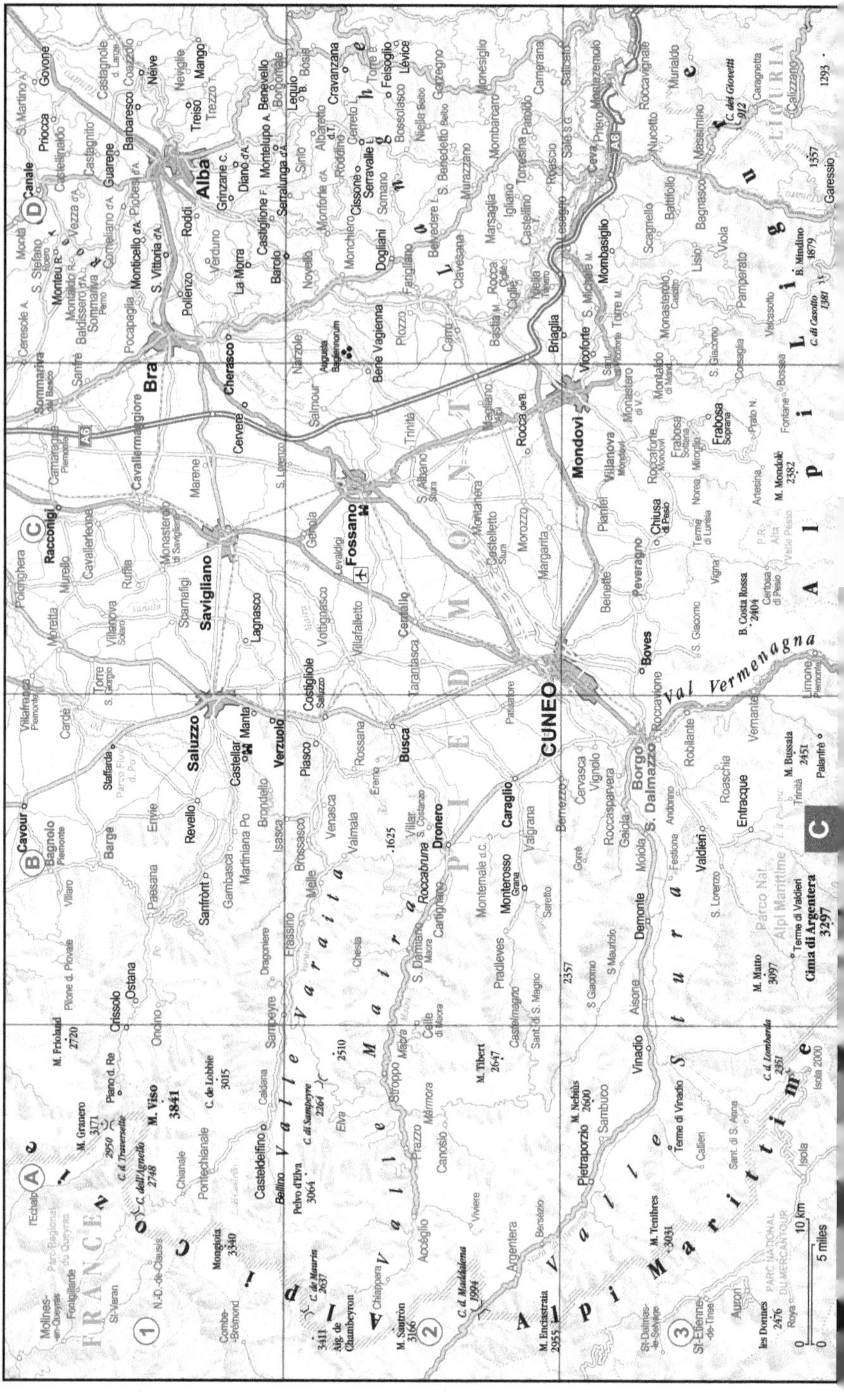
CUNEO
Alba
Bra
Saluzzo
Savigliano
Fossano
Mondovì
Racconigi
Cherasco
Dronero
Busca
Verzuolo
Ceva
Borgo S. Dalmazzo
Caraglio
Boves
Peveragno
Chiusa di Pesio
Canale
Govone
Barolo
La Morra
Dogliani
Carrù
Bene Vagienna
Cavour
Barge
Revello
Paesana
Sanfront
Crissolo
Ostana
M. Viso 3841
Vinadio
Demonte
Valdieri
Entracque
Limone Piemonte
Cima di Argentera 3297
Val Vermenagna
Valle Varaita
Valle Maira
Valle Stura
Alpi Marittime
Alpi Liguri
Langhe
PIEMONTE
FRANCE
LIGURIA
Cozie
A6
10 km
5 miles

MAPS | 237

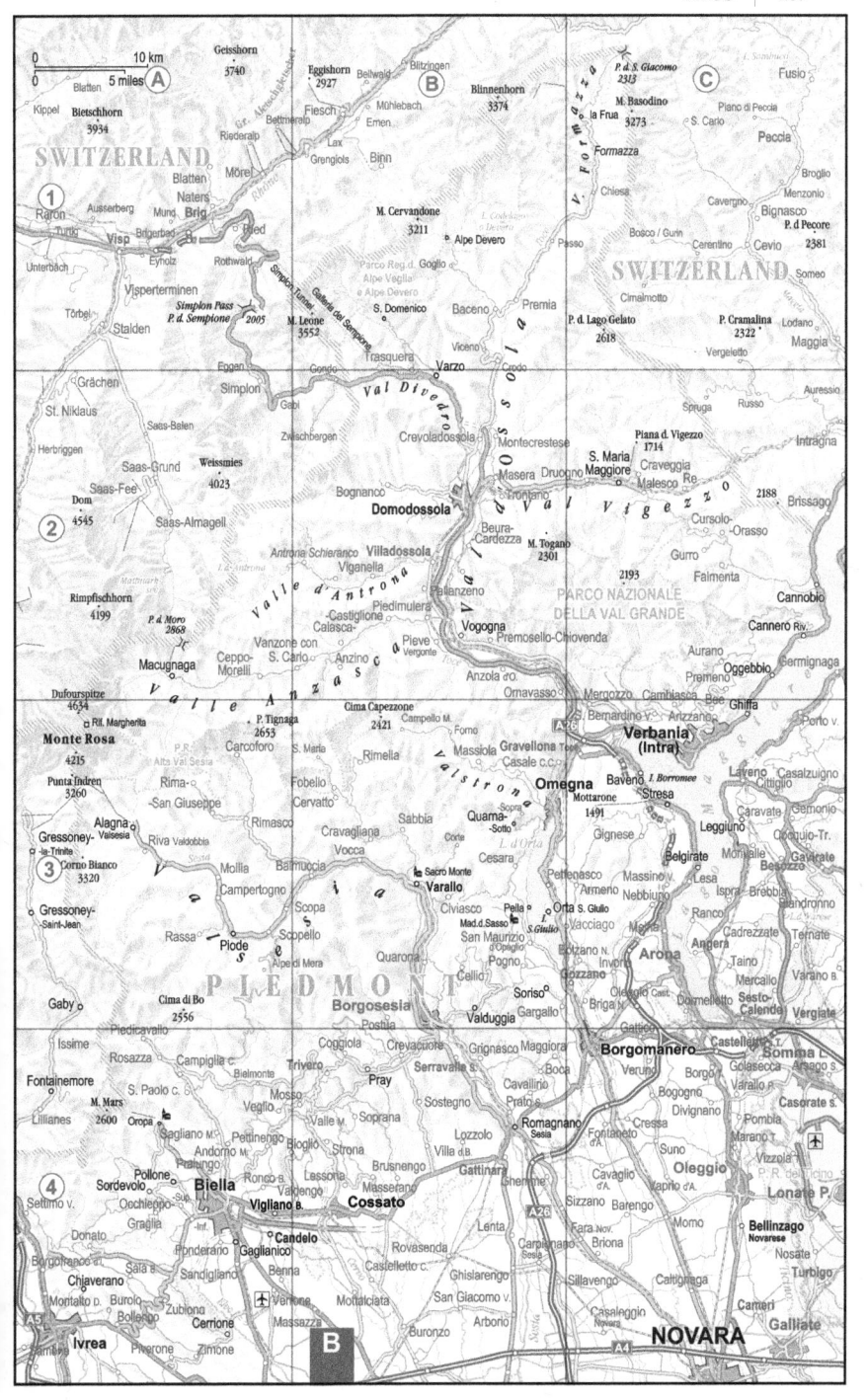

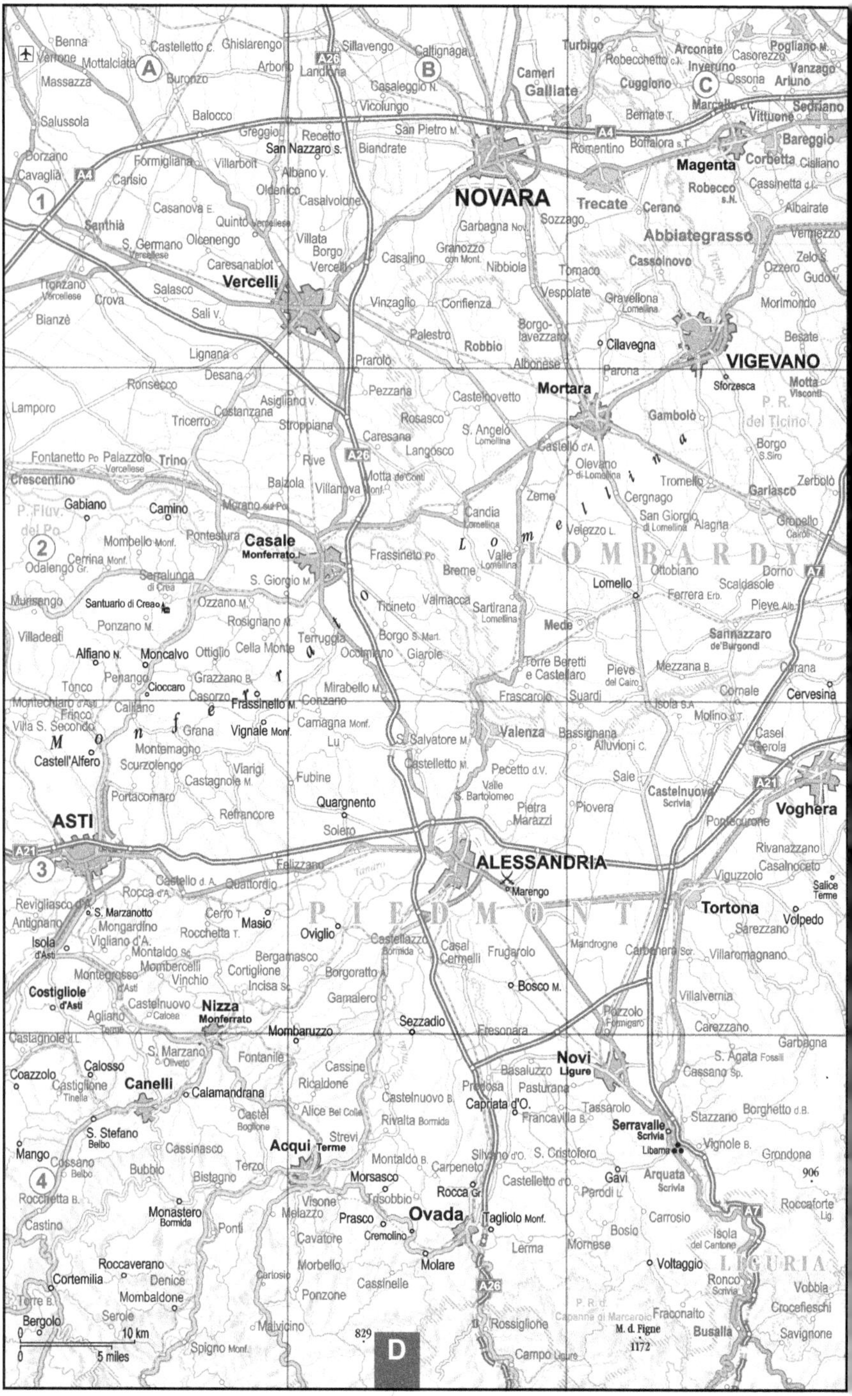
A
B
C
D
1
2
3
4
Benna
Verrone
Mottalciata
Massazza
Castelletto C.
Ghislarengo
Buronzo
Arborio
Sillavengo
Landiona
Caltignaga
Casaleggio N.
Vicolungo
Salussola
Balocco
Greggio
Recetto
San Pietro M.
San Nazzaro S.
Biandrate
Borzano
Cavaglià
Formigliana
Villarboit
Albano V.
Carisio
Oldenico
Casalvolone
Casanova E.
Santhià
Quinto Vercellese
S. Germano Vercellese
Olcenengo
Villata
Borgo Vercelli
Casalino
Caresanablot
Vercelli
Tronzano Vercellese
Crova
Salasco
Sali V.
Bianzè
Vinzaglio
Confienza
Palestro
Robbio
Lignana
Desana
Prarolo
Ronsecco
Lamporo
Asigliano V.
Costanzana
Tricerro
Stroppiana
Pezzana
Rosasco
Caresana
Langosco
Fontanetto Po
Palazzolo Vercellese
Trino
Crescentino
Rive
Balzola
Villanova Monf.
Motta de'Conti
Gabiano
Camino
Morano sul Po
P. Fluv. del Po
Mombello Monf.
Pontestura
Casale Monferrato
Frassineto Po
Cerrina Monf.
Odalengo Gr.
Serralunga di Crea
S. Giorgio M.
Murisengo
Santuario di Crea
Ozzano M.
Rosignano M.
Villadeati
Ponzano M.
Terruggia
Alfiano N.
Moncalvo
Ottiglio
Cella Monte
Occimiano
Penango
Grazzano B.
Tonco
Cioccaro
Mirabello M.
Montechiaro d'Asti
Calliano
Casorzo
Frassinello M.
Conzano
Frinco
Villa S. Secondo
Grana
Vignale Monf.
Camagna Monf.
Lu
Castell'Alfero
Montemagno
Scurzolengo
Viarigi
Castagnole M.
Fubine
Portacomaro
Quargnento
ASTI
Refrancore
Solero
A21
Castello d. A.
Quattordio
Felizzano
Rocca d'A.
Revigliasco d'A.
S. Marzanotto
Cerro T.
Masio
Antignano
Mongardino
Vigliano d'A.
Rocchetta T.
Oviglio
Isola d'Asti
Montaldo Sc.
Mombercelli
Bergamasco
Cortiglione
Montegrosso d'Asti
Vinchio
Incisa Sc.
Costigliole d'Asti
Castelnuovo Calcea
Nizza Monferrato
Agliano Terme
Castagnole d.L.
S. Marzano Oliveto
Mombaruzzo
Fontanile
Calosso
Coazzolo
Castiglione Tinella
Canelli
Calamandrana
Castel Boglione
S. Stefano Belbo
Mango
Cossano Belbo
Cassinasco
Bubbio
Bistagno
Rocchetta B.
Castino
Monastero Bormida
Roccaverano
Cortemilia
Denice
Mombaldone
Torre B.
Serole
Bergolo
Spigno Monf.
0
10 km
5 miles
Malvicino
Ponzone
Cartosio
Morbello
Cavatore
Melazzo
Visone
Acqui Terme
Terzo
Strevi
Alice Bel Colle
Ricaldone
Cassine
Castelnuovo B.
Rivalta Bormida
Montaldo B.
Morsasco
Trisobbio
Prasco
Cremolino
Ovada
Molare
Cassinelle
829
Gamalero
Borgoratto A.
Castellazzo Bormida
Casal Cermelli
Frugarolo
Sezzadio
Bosco M.
Fresonara
Predosa
Capriata d'O.
Basaluzzo
Pasturana
Carpeneto
Silvano d'O.
Rocca Gr.
Tagliolo Monf.
Lerma
Castelletto d'O.
Rossiglione
Campo Ligure
A26
ALESSANDRIA
Marengo
Valenza
Bassignana
Pecetto d.V.
Valle S. Bartolomeo
S. Salvatore M.
Castelletto M.
Pietra Marazzi
Piovera
Alluvioni C.
Sale
NOVARA
Cameri
Galliate
Turbigo
Robecchetto c.I.
Arconate
Inveruno
Cuggiono
Casorezzo
Pogliano M.
Vanzago
Arluno
Ossona
Marcallo c.C.
Sedriano
Vittuone
Bernate T.
Boffalora s.T.
Romentino
A4
Bareggio
Magenta
Corbetta
Cisliano
Robecco s.N.
Cassinetta d.L.
Trecate
Cerano
Albairate
Garbagna Nov.
Sozzago
Abbiategrasso
Vermezzo
Granozzo con Mont.
Nibbiola
Cassolnovo
Zelo S.
Tornaco
Ozzero
Gudo V.
Vespolate
Gravellona Lomellina
Morimondo
Borgo-lavezzaro
Cilavegna
Besate
VIGEVANO
Albonese
Parona
Sforzesca
Motta Visconti
Mortara
Castelnovetto
Gambolò
P. R. del Ticino
S. Angelo Lomellina
Castello d'A.
Borgo S.Siro
Olevano di Lomellina
Tromello
Zerbolò
Garlasco
Zeme
Cergnago
Candia Lomellina
San Giorgio di Lomellina
Alagna
Gropello Cairoli
Velezzo L.
LOMBARDY
Lomellina
Valle Lomellina
Breme
Ottobiano
Dorno
A7
Lomello
Scaldasole
Ferrera Erb.
Ticineto
Valmacca
Sartirana Lomellina
Pieve Alb.
Mede
Sannazzaro de'Burgondi
Borgo S. Mart.
Giarole
Torre Beretti e Castellaro
Pieve del Cairo
Mezzana B.
Corana
Frascarolo
Suardi
Cornale
Cervesina
Isola S.A.
Molino d.T.
Casei Gerola
Castelnuovo Scrivia
Voghera
Pontecurone
Rivanazzano
Viguzzolo
Casalnoceto
Salice Terme
Tortona
Volpedo
Sarezzano
Carbonara Scr.
Villaromagnano
Mandrogne
Villalvernia
Pozzolo Formigaro
Carezzano
Garbagna
Novi Ligure
S. Agata Fossili
Cassano Sp.
Tassarolo
Francavilla B.
Serravalle Scrivia
Stazzano
Borghetto d.B.
Libarna
Vignole B.
S. Cristoforo
Gavi
Arquata Scrivia
Grondona
906
Parodi L.
Roccaforte Lig.
Carrosio
Bosio
Isola del Cantone
Mornese
Voltaggio
LIGURIA
Ronco Scrivia
Vobbia
Crocefieschi
P. R. d. Capanne di Marcarolo
Fraconalto
M. d. Figne
1172
Busalla
Savignone
Monferrato
PIEDMONT

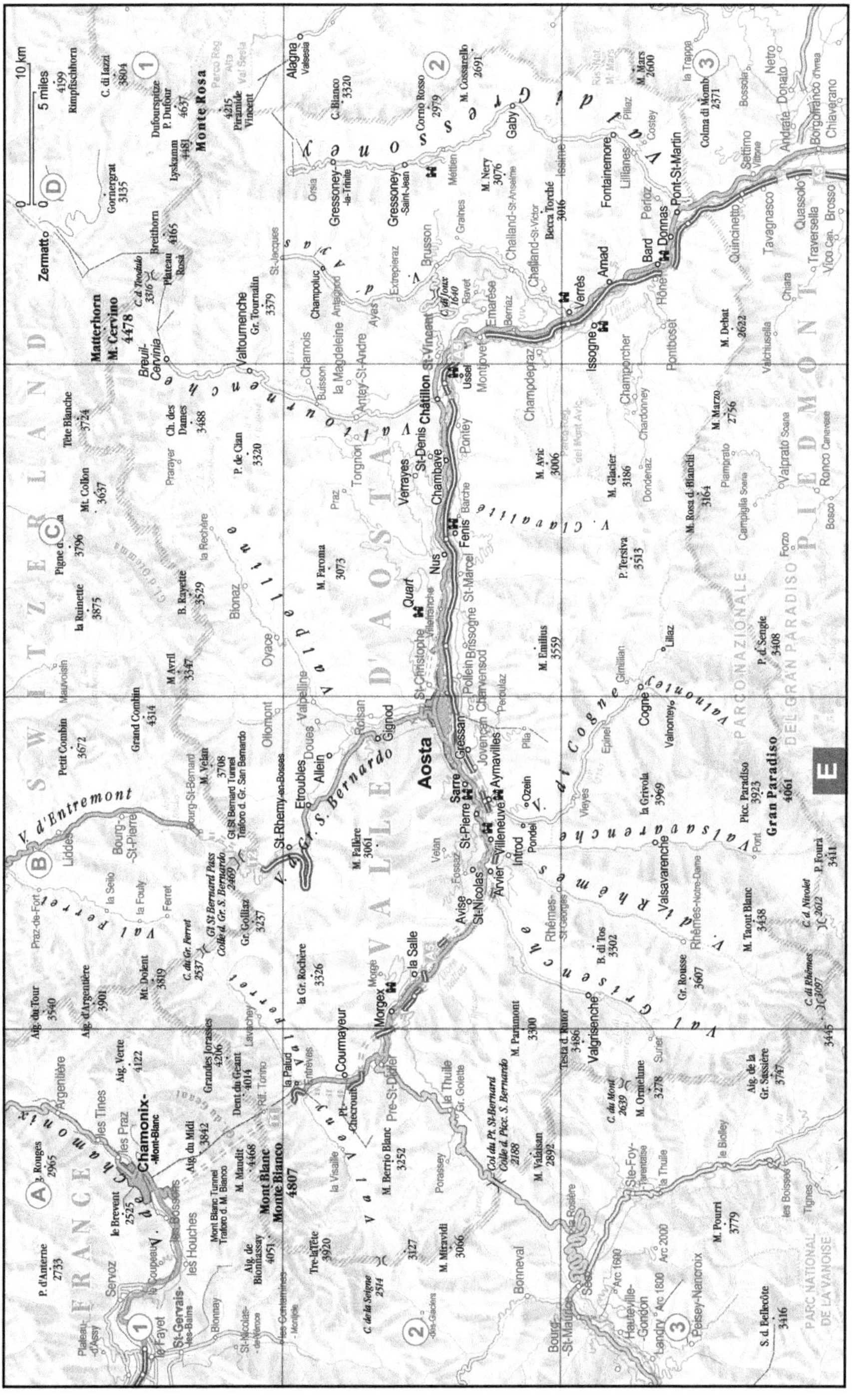
SWITZERLAND
FRANCE
VALLE D'AOSTA
PIEDMONT
PARCO NAZIONALE DEL GRAN PARADISO
PARC NATIONAL DE LA VANOISE
0 5 miles
0 10 km
Aosta
Chamonix-Mont-Blanc
Courmayeur
Zermatt
Breuil-Cervinia
Mont Blanc Monte Bianco 4807
Matterhorn M. Cervino 4478
Monte Rosa
Gran Paradiso 4061
Grand Combin 4314
V. d'Entremont
Val Ferret
Val Veny
Valtournenche
Valpelline
Val d'Ayas
Val di Gressoney
Val di Cogne
Valsavarenche
Val di Rhêmes
Valgrisenche
V. Clavalitè
Valnontey
V. de Chamonix
V. d. Gr. S. Bernardo
Gr. St Bernard Pass Colle d. Gr. S. Bernardo 2469
Col du Pt. St-Bernard Colle d. Picc. S. Bernardo 2188
Mont Blanc Tunnel Traforo d. M. Bianco
Gr. St Bernard Tunnel Traforo d. Gr. San Bernardo
St-Vincent
Châtillon
Verrès
Pont-St-Martin
Bard
Donnas
Issogne
Fénis
Nus
Quart
Sarre
St-Pierre
Villeneuve
Aymavilles
Introd
Arvier
Avise
la Salle
Morgex
Pré-St-Didier
la Thuile
Cogne
Etroubles
St-Rhemy-en-Bosses
Gressoney-la-Trinité
Gressoney-Saint-Jean
Alagna Valsesia
Champoluc
Brusson
Ayas
Bourg-St-Maurice
St-Gervais-les-Bains
les Houches
Ivrea

Milton Keynes UK
Ingram Content Group UK Ltd.
UKHW051432030823
426279UK00016B/118

9 781905 131983